William
Blake

Nov.
1757
Aug
1827

Sparks of Fire

(Io; no. 29)
1. Blake, William, 1757-1827--Miscellanea.
2. Blake, William, 1757-1827, in fiction, drama, poetry, etc.
3. American literature--20th century. I. Bogan, James, 1945-
II. Goss, Fred, 1944-   . III. Blake, William, 1757-1827.
IV. Series.
PR4146.S65   821'.7   82-6327
ISBN 0-913028-89-4 (lim. ed.) AACR2
ISBN 0-913028-90-8 (pbk.)

Sparks of Fire is sponsored by the Society for the Study of Native Arts and Sciences, a nonprofit educational corporation whose goals are to develop an ecological and crosscultural perspective linking various scientific, social, and artistic fields; to nurture a holistic view of the arts, sciences, humanities, and healing; and to publish and distribute literature on the relationship of mind, body, and nature.

Sparks of Fire

sparks of fire
Blake in a New Age

edited by
James Bogan & Fred Goss

North Atlantic Books
Richmond, California

Sparks of Fire: William Blake in a New Age, edited by James Bogan and Fred Goss
copyright © 1982 by James Bogan and Fred Goss.

ISBN 0-913028-89-4 limited edition cloth
ISBN 0-913028-90-8 trade paperback edition

Publisher's Address:

North Atlantic Books
635 Amador Street
Richmond, California 94805

This is issue #29 in the *Io* series.

This project is partly supported by a grant from the National Endowment for
the Arts in Washington, D.C., a federal agency.

Sparks of Fire is published under the auspices of the Society for the Study
of Native Arts and Sciences.

Typeset by Open Studio, Rhinebeck, N.Y., a non-profit facility for independent
literary publishers & individual artists, funded in part by grants from the New York
State Council on the Arts & the National Endowment for the Arts.

Credits

Grateful acknowledgement is made to the following for permission to reprint
material copyrighted by them:

HELEN ADAM: "A Young Girl's Rhyme" used by permission of Helen Adam.
Poem © 1982 Helen Adam.

STEPHEN ADDISS: "Blake, Taoism and Zen" used by permission of Stephen
Addiss. Prose © 1982 Stephen Addiss.

F. ADIELE: "The Fountain" used by permission of F. Adielé. Prose © 1982 F. Adielé.

KENNETH ALLEN: "Isolated Vignettes of an Atom" used by permission of
Kenneth Allen. Prose © 1982 Kenneth Allen.

JEFFERY BEAM: "He Sees Old Age in a Time of Youth," "Toil, A Divine
Commandment," "Things Coming" from *Two Preludes for the Beautiful* by Jeffery
Beam, privately printed in Chapel Hill, North Carolina, 1981. Poems © Jeffery Beam.

JAMES BOGAN: "A Tour of *Jerusalem*" used by permission of James Bogan.
Prose © 1982 James Bogan.

Note: These acknowledgements continue on page 454 and shall constitute an extension
of the copyright page.

Dedication

To students of William Blake who meet around a table in a free-for-all of combined inquiry. One such session met monthly in Lawrence, Kansas, during 1972:

Edward Ruhe
Gayle Emmel
Mary Halloran
Max Sutton
Oliver Finney

In a year we traversed *The Four Zoas*, *Milton*, and *Jerusalem*. Fierce mental warfare and Ed's wickedly black coffee propelled us through "a bright Golden Gate carved with skill." Hours later we found ourselves amazed at the new expanses seen together.

We are deeply grateful to these individuals
for supporting this adventure
with grants and gifts:

James and Maxine Stephenson
Eleanore Bogan
Dorothy Jackson
Carl and Mary Doolen
Ann B. Pitra
James and Virginia Bogan
Karleen Middleton Murphy
Ruth Corrigan
Nora Bangs
Patricia Stoeker
Rodney and Ulrike Vickery
Elizabeth Schultz
James Chatman
Kent Clair Chamberlain
David and Nancy Bogan
Chuck and Lynette Blinne
Rolla Equipment Co.
Neill Fleeman
Mike Morgan
A Friend
and
The National Endowment for the Arts

Acknowledgements

"The thankful receiver bears a plentiful harvest."

Sparks of Fire is the work of more than a hundred Men & Women and our first thanks goes to the artists and writers who have shared their creations with us. London artist Paul Piech graciously contributed the cover design. His Blake "Sunflower" poster illuminates the room where we work. Roger Easson, co-editor of *Blake Studies*, infused a full measure of thoughtful exuberance into the project and supplied us with numerous photographs and last-minute improvements. Prof. Edward Ruhe and Poet Michael Horovitz broadened the scope of the book by giving us addresses and introductions to interested individuals around the United States and Europe. Richard Grossinger, General Editor of the *Io* series and founder of North Atlantic Books, fostered the growth of this anthology from its inception. Would that Blake had had such an understanding publisher.

For valuable assistance with words, charts, and semi-colons, thanks to Douglas and Suzanne Wixson, Paul Johnson, Jack Daniels, Neill Fleeman, Howard Schwartz, Lawrence Vonalt, Nicholas Knight, Robert Jones, Kay Hoffman, Ronald Bohley, James Cubit, Philip Streamer, and John Amos. Kathleen Lane and Cynthia Knapstein typed and alphabetized, persevered and typed. Robert Blaylock provided much useful advice and many timely jokes. Ernest "The Unwobbling Pivot" Gutierrez kindly developed negatives by the yard. Boss layout person Ellen Pearce shaped a mound of chaos into pages of order. George and Susan Quasha's Open Studio set the text in Palatino type for John Schuler and his crew to turn into a book at the Inter-Collegiate Press.

Sparks of Fire came together at the University of Missouri-Rolla with substantial encouragement from Dr. David Oakley, Resourceful Leader of the Fine Arts Department. The University also assisted with a travel grant from its Weldon Springs Fund. Spirited communications from Paul Metcalf, G.E. Bentley, Jr., Evan Tonsing, and James Broughton gladdened our labors at crucial moments.

And to Carol Monders-Bogan and Catherine Goss, continuing thanks for sweet collaboration.

J.B.
F.G.

To the Reader

An angel dropped like a falling star out of Eternity to walk among the sons of men. Descending perpendicular from the heavens, he entered this world through the soul of William Blake. The ethereal messenger led the corporeal poet to the wonders of the many worlds, furthering his ability to write, draw, paint, and engrave visions for us who have come after. The angel was John Milton, one artist in eternal form giving inspiration to another. This visitation echoes other unions of living artists with long-gone inspiring ancients: Dante led by Virgil through the mazes of his hells. The artists of the past continue to live through the guidance they provide their progeny. This is not simply a matter for critical studies of literary influence. It is of the highest urgency for the creative artist to be honestly attentive to the sources of his inspiration and to the obligation those sources impose.

SPARKS OF FIRE: William Blake in a New Age is an anthology, "a gathering of blossoms." Flowers of hand and intellect have grown from vital contact with Blake's spirit into forms of poetry and scholarship, dance and illustration, essay and song. To approach his visions demands the risk of much personal energy, but the eventual return is fourfold. The result is sometimes a poem, sometimes a clarity, or sometimes an exuberance that resounds along the river valley. This book focuses reflections of Blake's presence into a festive patern: Edenic images from James Broughton's film *The Golden Positions*; a synthesis of spiritual ecologies from Anton Vogt; felt-tip fancies of Blake's life by David Reisman. Blake continues to enliven artists, students, and dreamers because he did not rest during his seventy years on earth from his great task:

> To open the eternal worlds, to open the immortal eyes
> Of man inwards into the worlds of thought—into Eternity
> Ever expanding in the bosom of God, the human imagination.
> (Jerusalem 5)

SPARKS OF FIRE begins with a montage of quotations from Blake's writings. This overture prepares the way for selections arranged along the lines of his development from the *Songs of Innocence* to the *Job* engravings. This organization provides both an introduction and a poetic commentary to his art. Of course, each "spark" is worthy of consideration on its own merits. The *kinds* of creative expression you will encounter in the book are characterized in the paragraphs following.

ILLUSTRATIONS: Throughout his career as an artist, Blake held firmly to the primacy of the imagination, praising original invention and rejecting imitation: "None but Blockheads copy one another." Paul Piech's strong lino-cuts pervade this book. He draws directly on the power of Blake's words and illuminations but adds his own vision to make them new yet again. Blake's frustrated desire to place "portable frescoes" around London is fulfilled in Piech's colorful poster-prints like "My Pretty Rose Tree" and "Ah Sunflower." The detailed visualizations in Bo Lindberg's *The Life and Works of William Blake* portray both interior and exterior dimensions of Blake's experience. This series of paintings would make ideal plates for a visionary biography of Blake that has yet to be written. All of the illustrations in *SPARKS OF FIRE* arise from the impulse to give form to the light within, to manifest some of the worlds to be found in a grain of sand.

POETRY: Blake is a fire-source but enjoins those who catch flame from him to shine according to their own genius. While imitation of this master is a contradiction, dawn-wrestling with him like Jacob with the angel transfers prophetic intensity. Blake does not usurp a writer's voice but rather delivers the individual to his own songs. The liberty he demands for himself, he requires of those who would learn from him; otherwise there is no passing through the door of print and paint to the resonant spaces he has created. The revelations met there can materialize in poems like those in this book—lyric to epic measures, rhymed verses and free, a chorus of genuine voices. Of Michael McClure's poetry Gary Snyder has said, "Maybe he's closer to Blake than anybody else writing." But there are others whose work is companion to the old master's: The Voice of the Bard is heard again through the rolling lines of Robert Kelly's *The Book of Water*. Each syllable of John Brandi's poems shape visions that dance visible before our inward eyes. Susan Mernit transforms her meditations on Blake's images into luminous word-icons. All the poets in this volume have labored in the manifold tasks of building up a New Jerusalem from materials of sound and ink.

MEMORABLE FANCIES and OTHER PROSE JOURNEYS: Like Walt Whitman, Blake has the uncanny faculty of establishing close friendships across veils of time. He stepped outside temporal constraints in order to converse with Dante, Isaiah, and Gabriel. Now it is our turn to meet

William and to introduce him to other souls. Short stories, dialogues, and annotations record meetings with this remarkable man. Imagine Blake and Pound comparing notes on inspiration and right livelihood. In the "Dialogues of Hell" Joe Napora does. In Roger Easson's "The Lineaments of Gratified Desire" Blake returns from Eternity to renew the challenges of his heretical Christianity. Although the prophet of South Molton Street reached "from the starry heighth to the starry depth" in his poetry, he never traveled more than a hundred miles from London. In "A Pilgrimage," however, he accompanies John Nelson on a trek into the Himalayas. The enlightening perceptions retrieved on these and other daring voyages verifies a method more dependent on wings than footnotes.

SCHOLARSHIP: "The tygers of wrath are wiser than the horses of instruction," but together they will draw the chariot of wisdom. These poles of human intelligence are not negations, but contraries needed to power creative inquiry. Keen eyes allied with imagination behold revelations shining through the plates of Blake's illuminated books, as demonstrated by E. B. Murray's explication of the Visions of the Daughters of Albion. A hundred years ago only a few initiates had access to Blake's texts, but now the complete works are widely available due to the Herculean labors of four generations of scholars. Roger Easson's "On Building a Blake Library" reviews the principal contributions to this intellectual tradition. Those embarking on Blake studies for the first time will find in SPARKS OF FIRE essays high in clarity and low in jive that open the gates to Blake's marvelous creations. Veteran travelers are invited on fresh explorations into the visionary realms of a poet who consistently returns us to beginnings. Perhaps it is for this reason that Blake scholarship in general is characterized by intensity, generosity, and enthusiasm. A variety of spirited essays represent the field. Albert Roe's classic introduction lucidly describes "Blake's Symbolism" without over simplification. A new reading of the Four Zoas is proposed by Fred Whitehead in his "Visions of the Archaic World." Our understanding of Blake's most disconcerting poem is increased by a consideration of the social and economic changes from the Paleolithic to the Neolithic Age. Denise Low's astrological interpretation of "Blake's Lost Years—1813-1815" shows how an ancient science can release information unavailable to orthodox academic methods. All the essays in SPARKS OF FIRE direct us to the original energies found through Blake; however, this transport is not achieved by encrusted habits of thought and feeling. Let the reader beware: The painful destruction of mind-forged manacles is one liberating reward for getting close to Blake.

MUSIC: Blake sang his songs at parties in London and no doubt chanted his epics long into the foggy night when the spirit struck him. He left no scores but the lyrics have since suggested melodies within the ears of some later composers. Allen Ginsberg pioneered in restoring music to Blake's poems. Surrounded by guitarists, tuba players, scoffers, and dancing innocents, he sang Tigers and Lambs around the world, including Normal, Illinois. "To Young and Old Listeners," his notes on the *Songs of Innocence and Experience*, is a model of "projective" criticism that emphasizes numinous possibility rather than terminal definition. Troubador Tom Nichols knows the life of these lyrics from the inside and recounts the serendipities of setting them to music. For musicians who would like to strike up an elfin duet, there is a score to Evan Tonsing's "Transformations of the *Book of Thel*—for Flute and Toy Piano." This concert work will delight performer and listener with the melodic variations springing from Blake's expansive lines.

*   *   *   *   *

Rarely heard is this story of Moses: an officious person ran up to the fierce-eyed prophet, panting out that Eldad and Medad were prophesying without a permit on the other side of camp. The watch-fiend waited expectantly for Moses to sign a warrant to shut their operation down; but Moses, not hiding his exasperation, silenced the tale-bearer: "Would to God all the Lord's people were prophets!" (Numbers 11:29). By quoting this exhortation in his poem *Milton*, Blake joins Moses in a petition for others to share the burden of the spirit. *SPARKS OF FIRE* is one response to that call and we repeat Blake's timely entreaty: "Rouze up, O Young Men & Women of the New Age! set your foreheads against the ignorant Hirelings! For we have Hirelings in the Camp, the Court & the University, who would if they could, for ever depress Mental & prolong Corporeal War." This book is not the ultimate gathering of Blake's children, nor is it meant to be. Its function is both conservative and exploratory: gathering the past and promising the future. This collective creation of voices and visions is presented as an offering of beams, windows, and bells for the eternal city of human endeavour Blake called Golgonooza.

Fred Goss
James Bogan
Rolla, Missouri—1981

CONTENTS

What to Do with This Book

Read it straight through—eventually.
Open it at random—take your chances.

Get red and blue ink on your hands while following Morris Eaves' directions in "Teaching Blake's Relief Etching." Send him a print.

Work your body: Recreate the Blakean dance-gesture of Joan Stone.

Cut an illustration out and tape it to the refrigerator.

Dust off the atlas and follow McCord's and Nelson's pilgrimages as they move their heavens around the globe.

Underline egregious bio-data in David Ohle's "Blake Oblique."

Transmute a chapter of *Island in the Moon* into a cartoon after the fashion of David Morice's "Tyger, Tyger."

Set *SPARKS OF FIRE* down and chant "Auguries of Innocence."

Buy a box of water-colors and turn a page into a rainbow.

Perplexed by Blake's perplexing attitude toward the ladies??? Read Karleen Middleton Murphy's "All the Lovely Sex: Blake and the Woman Question."

Take the tour of *Jerusalem*, then jump the bus and set out on your own. Don't forget the sketch pad.

Read Robert Kelly's *The Book of Water* aloud with a friend. Is this a chapter from the lost *Book of the Moonlight?*

"FORGIVE WHAT YOU DO NOT APPROVE."   (*Jerusalem* 3)

"My fingers emit sparks of fire with expectations of my future labours" William Blake

Bo Ossian Lindberg

William Blake, age 12, autumn 1769, going from his parents' house, 28 Broad St., to Par's drawing school in the Strand.

Sparks of Fire

A Montage of Quotes from the Nooks and Crannies of
William Blake's Complete Works

William Blake, one who is very much delighted with being in good Company.
Born 28 November 1757 in London & has died several times since—January
16, 1826. (Keynes edition, p. 781)

> It is right it should be so
> Man was made for Joy & Woe
> And When this we rightly know
> Thro' the World we safely go.   (432)

I am not ashamed, afraid, or averse to tell you what Ought to be Told: That
I am under the direction of Messengers from Heaven, Daily & Nightly; but
the nature of such things is not, as some suppose, without trouble or
care.   (812)

> When a Man has married a Wife
>   he finds out whether
> Her Knees & elbows are only
>   glued together   (418)

I seldom carry money in my pockets; they are generally full of paper.   (86)

> "Eternity"
> He who binds to himself a joy
> Does the winged life destroy;
> But he who kisses the joy as it flies
> Lives in eternity's sun rise.   (179)

"Keep him at least three paces distant who hates bread, music and the laugh
of a child," wrote Lavater. "The Best in the Book," noted Blake.   (74)

> Mutual Forgiveness of each Vice,
> Such are the Gates of Paradise.   (761)

Consider that LOVE IS LIFE.   (76)

The worship of God is: Honouring his gifts in other men, each according to his genius, and loving the greatest men best: those who envy or calumniate great men hate God; for there is no other God.   (158)

The tygers of wrath are wiser than the horses of instruction.   (152)

What seems to Be: Is: To those to whom
It seems to be, & is productive of the most dreadful
Consequences to those to whom it seems to Be.   (663)

A dog starv'd at his Master's Gate
Predicts the ruin of the State.   (431)

Art can never exist without Naked Beauty displayed.   (776)

Prayer is the Study of Art.
Praise is the Practice of Art.   (776)

Unworthy Men who gain fame among Men, continue to govern mankind after death, and in their spiritual bodies oppose the spirits of those who worthily are famous; and, as Swedenborg observes, by entering into disease and excrement, drunkenness and concupiscence, they possess themselves of the bodies of mortal men, and shut the doors of mind and of thought by placing Learning above Inspiration. O Artist! You may disbelieve all this, but it shall be at your own peril.   (582)

"The Kid" [complete]
Thou, little kid, didst play
&c.   (179)

There is suffering in Heaven—for where there is the capacity of enjoyment, there is the capacity of pain.   (Quoted by Crabb Robinson)

Demand explicit words.   (640)

Rubens is a most outrageous demon.   (582)

He whose face gives no light shall never become a star.   (151)

It is a part of our duty to God & man to take due care of his Gifts; & tho' we ought not [to] think *more* highly of ourselves, yet we ought to think as highly of ourselves as immortals ought to think.   (811)

Great things are done when Men & Mountains meet; This is not done by Jostling in the Street.   (605)

Solomon says, "Vanity of Vanities, all is Vanity," & What can be Foolisher than This?   (773)

4

Grown old in Love from Seven till Seven times Seven,
I oft have wish'd for Hell for Ease from Heaven.   (552)

What is Above is Within, for every-thing in Eternity is translucent.   (709)

>God Appears & God is Light
>To those poor Souls who dwell in Night,
>But does a Human Form Display
>To those who Dwell in Realms of Day.   (434)

I live by Miracle.   (795)

The Ladies will be pleas'd to see that I have represented the Furies by Three
Men & not by three Women. . . . The Spectator may suppose them Clergymen
in the Pulpit, scourging Sin instead of Forgiving it.   (608)

Listen! Every Religion that Preaches Vengeance for Sin is the Religion of the
Enemy & Avenger: and not of the Forgiver of Sin, and their God is Satan. . . .
(682)

[The Buildings of Golgonooza:]
The stones are pity, and the bricks, well wrought affections
Enamel'd with love & kindness, & the tiles engraven gold,
Labour of merciful hands: the beams & rafters are forgiveness:
The mortar & cement of the work, tears of honesty: the nails
And the screws & iron braces are well wrought blandishments
And well contrived words, firm fixing, never forgotten,
Always comforting the remembrance: the floors, humility:
The ceilings, devotion: the hearth, thanksgiving.
Prepare the furniture, O Lambeth, in the pitying looms,
The curtains, woven tears & sighs wrought into lovely forms
For Comfort.   (632)

She who adores not your frowns will only loathe your smiles.   (743)

Bad pictures are always Sir Joshua's Friends.   (478)

If you account it Wisdom when you are angry to be silent and
Not to show it, I do not account that Wisdom, but Folly.
Every Man's Wisdom is peculiar to his own Individuality.   (483)

Tuesday, January 20, 1807, between Two & Seven in the Evening—Despair.
(440)

23 May, 1810, found the Word Golden.   (556)

Sir Francis Bacon is a Liar. No discipline will turn one Man into another,
even in the least particle, & such discipline I call Presumption & Folly. I have

tried it too much not to know this, & am very sorry for all such who may be led to such ostentatious Exertion against their Eternal Existence itself, because it is Mental Rebellion against the Holy Spirit, & fit only for a Soldier of Satan to perform.   (871)

Innocence dwells with Wisdom, but never with Ignorance.   (380)

> The wild deer, wand'ring here and there.
> Keeps the Human Soul from Care.   (431)

God is within & without: he is even in the depths of Hell!   (631)

I cannot think that Real Poets have any competition. None are greatest in the Kingdom of Heaven; it is so in Poetry.   (783)

There is a Moment in each Day that Satan cannot find,
Nor can his Watch-Fiends find it; but the Industrious find
This Moment & it multiply, & when it once is found
It renovates every Moment of the Day, if rightly placed.   (526)

My wife is like a flame of many colours of precious jewels.   (801)

I know of no other Christianity and of no other Gospel than the liberty of both body & mind to exercise the Divine Arts of Imagination.   (716)

> A Riddle or Crickets Cry
> Is to Doubt a fit Reply.   (433)

The Goddess Fortune is the Devil's servant, ready to Kiss any one's Arse.
(758)

On the right hand of Noah a Female descends to meet her Lover or Husband, representative of that Love, call'd Friendship, which Looks for no other heaven than their Beloved & in him sees all reflected as in a Glass of Eternal Diamond.   (610)

I cannot think of Death as more than the going out of one room into another.   (Quoted by Crabb Robinson)

> "An Epitaph"
> I was buried near this Dike
> That my Friends may weep as much as they like.   (546)

Every death is an improvement of the State of the Departed.   (868)

Enough! or too much.   (152)

As the seed waits Eagerly watching for its flower & fruit,
Anxious its little soul looks out into the clear expanse
To see if hungry winds are abroad with their invisible army,

So Man looks out in tree & herb & fish & bird & beast
Collecting up the scatter'd portions of his immortal body
Into the Elemental forms of every thing that grows.
He tries the sullen north wind, riding on its angry furrows,
The sultry south when the sun rises, & the angry east
When the sun sets; when the clods harden & the cattle stand
Drooping & the birds hide in their silent nests, He stores his thoughts
As in a storehouse in his memory; he regulates the forms
Of all beneath & all above, & in the gentle West
Reposes where the Suns heat dwells; he rises to the Sun
And to the Planets of the Night & to the stars that gild
The Zodiac, & the stars that sullen stand to north & south.
He touches the remotest pole, & in the Center weeps
That Man should Labour & sorrow, & learn & forget, & return
To the dark valley whence he came, to begin his labours anew.
In pain he sighs, in pain he labours in his universe,
Screaming in birds over the deep, & howling in the wolf
Over the slain, & moaning in the cattle, & in the winds,
And weeping over Orc & Urizen in clouds & flaming fires,
And in the cries of birth & in the groans of death his voice
Is heard throughout the Universe: wherever a grass grows
Or a leaf buds, The Eternal Man is seen, is heard, is felt,
And all his sorrows, till he reassumes his ancient bliss.   (355)

Helen Adam

A Young Girl's Rhyme

The bird in the wood has a broken heart,
It cries, it cries,
It cries its pain where the branches part
To the blind moon's open eyes.
But I go out by the steepest track,
And home by the longest way,
For I will not learn the woes I lack
From a bird in the pine wood grey.

Barry Gifford

Three Songs

I A boy asleep
and afternoon
doth pour
our shadow
o'er Blake's
little bird
picking up crumbs
around the door

II The cloud-hid sun
In durance now
Bathed us summer by—
Serious, such total
Loss—furious,
The fly—

III O fly
wouldst I
the size
of thee,
or bee,
O yes, yes
one of those,
to sleep
for ever
in a rose

Paul Piech

TYGER! TYGER! BURNING BRIGHT
IN THE FORESTS OF THE NIGHT,
WHAT IMMORTAL HAND AND EYE
COULD FRAME THY FEARFUL SYMMETRY?

IN WHAT DISTANT DEEPS OR SKIES
BURNT THE FIRE OF THINE EYES?
ON WHAT WINGS DARE HE ASPIRE?
WHAT HAND DARE SIEZE THE FIRE?

AND WHAT SHOULDER AND WHAT ART
COULD TWIST THE SINEWS OF THY HEART?
AND WHEN THY HEART BEGAN TO BEAT
WHAT DREAD HAND? & WHAT DREAD FEET?

WHEN THE STARS THREW DOWN THEIR SPEARS,
AND WATER'D HEAVEN WITH THEIR TEARS,
DID HE SMILE HIS WORK TO SEE?
DID HE WHO MADE THE LAMB MAKE THEE?

TYGER, TYGER, BURNING BRIGHT
IN THE FORESTS OF THE NIGHT,
WHAT IMMORTAL HAND OR EYE,
DARE FRAME THY FEARFUL SYMMETRY?

Paul Piech

A Graphic Manifesto

My press's first publicity release read as follows: "The Taurus Press of Willow Dene is the private press of Paul Peter Piech, started in 1959 with a 10″ × 14″ Adana foot-treadle press with a recent addition of a 40″ × 60″ Gem Thomson cylinder proofing press. The press name is adapted from the zodiac. The press's credo is aggressive printing with no recognition of deadlines; to create enduring pieces of printing which will embody the best knowledge of the art of typography."

It all started with a desire to print books and also to make the press a perfect vehicle for my particular art, and since 1959, I have produced over 50 titles, involving the works of Blake, Wilfred Owen, Walt Whitman, Martin Luther King, John F. Kennedy and Christ.

During the Second World War I served in the 8th Air Force here in England and I became very familiar with the poetical works of Blake, which made me think how to re-illustrate his works in the 20th century attitude. This desire finally became a reality when I published "Tyger Tyger" as the first Taurus Press printed work. Strangely enough this particular poem poster has now become the press's best seller!

The major portion of my art evolves through the media of woodcut and primarily linocut. I find this medium suits my temperament and expression through its adaptability and ease of handling. Nothing spectacular with technique except that sometimes on the material I use sandpaper, metal punches and etching needles. Tried caustic soda etches but can't wait too long between bites, so have abandoned this technique entirely!

Some five years ago I diversified strongly into the poster print and have partnered many contemporary poets with some exciting results as poem posters. Most books go on shelves and are forgotten. This is not the case with posters; they go on to walls and are looked at. They are a very effective means of communication. They demand study. People stand and re-read them. They make an impact. I now find that more time is spent on the poster print than the printed book. Much of my future work will no doubt continue to develop in the field of poster prints, devoting equal time to poem posters and posters of social and educational value.

At the moment I am occupied on four major series of poster prints— 1) a selection of poems from Walt Whitman— 2) a long poem by a contemporary English Poet, Jeremy Reed, "The Red Angel," a parody on William Blake— 3) a series of 100 posters on the peace statements of Pope John Paul II and 100 posters on the sayings of Mahatma Gandhi. I've been seriously thinking of attempting to illustrate the entire *Jerusalem* poem, some nearing future date. This and some of the other shorter poems, as yet not tackled make the future look exciting graphically. And Blake's words are riveting enough to have a natural inspiration for illustration.

Mammoth productions, but something to keep art & life at its peak!!!

* * * * *

The object of the Taurus Press is to stimulate interest in and concern for humanity as a whole and I want to publish only work which I feel does this.

* * * * *

Americans, you may give your goods to feed the poor, you may bestow great gifts to charity and you may tower high in philanthropy, but if you have not love, your charity means nothing. . . . Without love, benevolence becomes egotism and martyrdom.

* * * * *

Rarely do we find men who willingly engage in solid thinking. There is an almost universal quest for easy answers and half-baked solutions. Nothing pains some people more than having to think.

* * * * *

I'm not interested in Communism or Fascism or any other ism. I'm only interested in things that happen to the human being. I hate the KGB as well as the CIA. I hate the fact that they don't allow creative thought in the USSR.

* * * * *

I want to make people aware that there are things going on in the world that they really should know about, things they can't rely on the newspapers for.

* * * * *

My inward feelings are that I have never left advertising, but use it in another form, to tell the world about what's going on, about the social conditions.

* * * * *

The potential beauty of human life is constantly made ugly by man's ever-recurring song of retaliation.

* * * * *

Blake was the complete graphic artist. And he had one thing over me—he could write, and I can't. That's a pity.

Books: America   £50

Posters:

The Divine Image £2	The Sick Rose £2
Tyger Tyger £2	The Fly £2
Ah Sunflower £2	The Lilly £5
My Pretty Rose £5	Auguries of Innocence £15

The Divine Image (full colour)   £5

Address:

> Paul Piech
> Taurus Press
> 2 Willow Dene
> Bushy Heath, Herts
> WD2 1PS England

SPRING

Words: Wm Blake 1789

Music: A. Ginsberg 1970

Flute · Flute Trill · French Horn Guitar etc · Tambourine

Sound the Flute! Now it's mute. Birds delight Day and Night.

Nightingale In the dale Lark in Sky Merrily Merrily Merrily

French Horn

to welcome in the Year. ~ Little Boy Full of Joy.

Little Girl Sweet and small. Cock does Crow So do you.

Merry Voice Infant noise Merrily Merrily to welcome in the Year.

meter and time and note values are only approximate
since the pulse may change during the song

Little Lamb Here I am Come and lick My white neck.

Let me pull Your soft Wool. Let me kiss Your soft face.

Merrily Merrily we welcome in the Year. Merrily Merrily

we welcome in the Year. Merrily Merrily we welcome in the year

Merrily Merrily we welcome in the year. Merrily Merrily

We welcome in the year, etc.

A. Ginsberg
Fecit

Allen Ginsberg

To Young or Old Listeners:
Notes on the *Songs of Innocence and Experience*

(liner notes to the *Songs of Innocence and Experience*)

The songs were first composed on tape recorder, improvised on pump organ in farmhouse upstate NY in two nights after returning from Democratic Convention 1968 Tear Gas Chicago.

Inspiration began 21 years, half my life ago, living in Harlem, in mind's outer ear I heard Blake's voice pronounce *The Sunflower* and *The Sick Rose* (and the *Little Girl Lost*) and experienced an illumination of eternal Consciousness, my own heart identical with the ancient heart of the Universe.

It's taken 2 decades of vision fame, friends' deaths & Apocalyptic history for me to materialize the spiritual illumination received thru these poems, without systematic study of Blake's life & only fragmentary study of later works. I *imagined* this music after 20 summers musings over the rhythms.

William Blake (1757-1827), engraved his own picture plates, hand colored, & printed *Songs of Innocence & Experience* (1789-1794), only a couple dozen copies. Thus every word, every picture & every print of the book he made in his life bore the impress of his own intelligent body; there was no robot mechanical repetition in any copy. The title *Songs of Innocence & Experience* is literal: Blake used to sing them unaccompanied at his friends' houses.

The purpose in putting them to music was to articulate the significance of each holy & magic syllable of his poems; as if each syllable had intention. These are perfect verses, with no noise lost or extra accents for nothing. I tried to hear meanings of each line spoken intentionally & interestedly, & follow natural voice tones up or down according to different emphases and emotions vocalized as in daily intimate speech: I drew the latent tunes, up or down, out of talk-tones suggested by each syllable spoken with normal feeling.

      Piping
          Down the
                    ey
               Vall
                  Wi
                    ld:

Thus the flute pipes notes down from the hill into the deep valley floor with accurate melody.

Since a physiologic ecstatic experience had been catalysed in my body by the physical arrangement of words in so small a poem as *Ah! Sun Flower*, I determined long ago to think of poetry as a kind of machine that had a specific effect when planted inside a human body, an arrangement of picture mental associations that vibated on the mind bank network; and an arrangement of related sounds & physical mouth movements that altered the habit functions of the neural network. XX century French poet Artaud noted that certain sound vibrations, certain rhythmic frequencies of music or voice, might alter molecular patterns in the nervous system.

I had been led to hear by ear individual syllables and their spoken tonal intention by a whole American poetic tradition begun at turn of century with Pound who specified that for any prosody (measure of poetry rhythm) adequate to our real speech, the poet should train his ear "pay attention to the tone leading of vowels" instead of the tripping of stressed accents—i.e. hear the musical Aum vowl alterations of note & rhythms pattern, and not get hung up on voiced monotone stressed da dit da dit da dit da dits—like, "Thou too sail on O Ship of State." W. C. Williams, Pound's friend, taught attention to raw spoken talk to learn the "for real" rhythms of American poetry. Later Basil Bunting shaped my attention to vowels as solid objects in a verse line.

Ma Rainey, Pound, Dylan, Beatles, Ray Charles, Ed Sanders & other singers have returned language poesy to Minstrelsy. As new generations understand & decipher poetical verses for gnostic-psychedelic flashes & practical Artistic messages, I hope that musical articulation of Blake's poetry will be heard by the Pop Rock Music Mass Media Electronic Illumination Democratic Ear and provide an Eternal Poesy standard by which to measure sublimity & sincerity in contemporary masters such as Bob Dylan, encouraging all souls to trust their own genius Inspiration.

For the soul of the Planet is Wakening, the time of Dissolution of Material Forms is here, our generation's trapped in Imperial Satanic Cities & Nations, & only the prophetic priestly consciousness of the Bard—Blake, Whitman or our own new selves—can Steady our gaze into the Fiery eyes of the Tygers of the Wrath to Come.

SONGS OF INNOCENCE

INTRODUCTION: Passing thru the Natural World, piping unconscious music, Poet glimpses Eternal Vision, child spirit on a cloud, his own Imagination, that demands he play intuitive feeling music to God, who weeps to hear Man-Poet's answer come true. Mind-Child weeps to find it's possible to show God thru language. Vision vanishes leaving instructions for Poet to lay inspiration out in words to entrance later generations. ("Sentient Beings are Numberless, I vow to save them all" is the first of 4 Buddhist vows.) Poet takes simple materials near his body, hollow reed, & messes up the clear water to make ink & writes it down forever.

THE SHEPHERD: The first song "Every child may joy to hear" utters how sweet it is to do nothing but sit in natural pasture following the flock of mind thoughts that pass thru his brain same as lamb and ewe calling each other knowing a supreme Consciousness aware of everyone is in Everyone.

THE ECHOING GREEN: But all natural sunrise bells are an apparition on green symmetrical pastures of matter grass & hills in an illusionary echo world. The old folks bodies get tired & wither under older trees & they sit watching Baby games thru eyes that also saw themselves dance play & copulate & friends vanish in graves. Sun descends, we even get tired of joy & want to sleep, a shadow passes over the illusion of Garden & City; consciousness dims & we forget the green echoing Field forever as it fades.

THE LAMB: Who are we here? What tender beings gave us ourselves? Lamb's wool or soft sexual human skin, voices calling & murmuring our desires to each other till the whole world lights up with our feeling, Who is our Love? Our selves are the same as the Lamb or Christ or Lords that desired to become living meat spirit, to Cry & die, living in the strange material world an eternal minute. The Piper-Poet-Lamb-Child shepherd soul knows & tells fellows who forgot to bless themselves.

THE LITTLE BLACK BOY: Suffering! Race experience burning into the skin & blackening it with the sun-fires of life. White Light Eternal Being, the Abyss of Light, the Void is identical to our own souls: the English child looks "white as an Angel" which he is (or will be when he realizes his soul). "And I am black, but O! my soul is white" is a racist masochistic tearful sentiment from the 18th century Slave Days to modern political eyes: Gnostic (secret knowledge of the Abyss of Light) Vision transforms the understanding, we realize the Bodhisattva's singing to the inexperienced Honkey Material Soul, saying that all matter-body is a cloud of Ignorance. "And we are put on earth a little space that we may bear the beams of love." And when the cloud-bodies vanish we return to our identical Primeval Radiance. Matter itself is a shield against this brightness too vast for human body. ("Life, like a dome of many-colored Glass stains the white radiance of Eternity until death tramples it to fragments..." wrote Shelley who like Blake read Gnostic texts in translation by Thomas Taylor the Platonist. Taylor also translated Pythagoras' line "Whatever we see when awake, is Death; and when asleep, a Dream.") The black boy or Jewish boy trembling rejected by the English Child, his homosexual love rejected by the master race, realizes the English Child's white because his body hasn't yet been blasted by the deep heat of God's love, white is inexperience; & the only place the little Black boy will be fully understood is when their material bodies fall away transparent & they are reunited in the Place of Death.

THE BLOSSOM: Sparrow into Blossom: Yang & Yin, Phallus & Vagina, Tantric Lingam & Yoni, Form and Emptiness, Matter & Void, Samsara & Nirvana, Maya and Sunyatta, Aeon & Abyss of Light, Life into Death, are incarnated in the emotional softness of the robin sobbing under green leaves in flower's bosom. Straight sex comes identical with metaphysical Mystery in a little almost unnoticeable ditty in Blake's book.

THE CHIMNEY SWEEPER: The sorrowful horror of child slavery begins tale weeping—18th century London XX century New York, the same skulls sitting at tables reading papers headlining massacre slavery. The material universe so debased, city greed and poverty so unbearable the imagination only breaks out thru the skull in Death—and then comes vision of the Heaven Desire we can imagine once we do accept our soul feelings as more real than the material fix we have been trapped in. Blake was a friend of Tom Paine the Revolutionary & tipped Paine off that the fuzz had a warrant for his arrest in London 1792—Paine skipped the country from Dover across the English Channel to France a couple of hours before the Police arrived. The Chimney Sweeping, infant slavery to society, is also interpreted here as faithful Bodhisattvic work of social revolution—"So if all do their duty they need not fear harm." The vision of angels with bright keys and myriad elevated voice notes of shiny children washing in tearful rivers reminds us of Reality we all desired forever, and always will, and will achieve forever in life or Death, no matter what a cold dark Capitalist/police-state Satanic morning we are born into with bodies.

THE LITTLE BOY LOST: Authority, the State, the Mortal Father, all vanish as our Consciousness outgrows Habit & Conditioning (thru Time, Acid, Sex or Vision) & the soul is left alone: to weep, and thus thru intuitive Feeling, Disperse "the Vapors" or Mortal Boring Gloom.

THE LITTLE BOY FOUND: So the soul boy follows wandering imagination, the mind's heart crying tears, & the great Authority (Great as shroudy Death) appears & leads him to Mother Nature Life. She also thought he was lost, they only found each other thru his emotional tears, & she'd wept for him all along too.

LAUGHING SONG: Water & trees are alive, the great grassy hill rocks with laughter, spring spreads green smile in meadows; all illusion material universe giggles in the void, girls young tongues show noises. Birds are only painted sentient, laughing theosophically to themselves in the valley of the shadow. No harm in Maya Dream Life, merry Nuts! Blake's colored picture shows a table at the wood's edge with fruits, nuts, girls & a young man in red skin-

20

tight suit lifting cup dancing laughing facing the trees. The rhythmic Paradigm of the laughing song is echoed verse by verse with Ha Ha He's in second chorus making mirror image of universe in pure laughter receding into infinity.

HOLY THURSDAY: Multitudes of sentient children in London 18th century like tender insects waving their hands and singing in the Domed Mortal Universe of St. Paul's Cathedral are the only angels visible in this Eternity. Even the old archons tending them are exquisite. Blake's not being sardonic, he's seeing the central holiness of multitudinous being: "Everyone's an angel"; then cherish pity lest you drive an angel from your door. The verses can only be read naturally if they syncopate Thames Waters & Wise Guardians—spaced out Orlovsky singing against Don Cherry on Flute and trumpet Zapped the tune up to ecstatic joy instead of a tender lamblike chorus it might also supposed to be.

NIGHT: Most mellow address to Night, sleep, Death & Heavenly Peace. Little visions of lovely earth in the mind's eye vanishing, farewell to the physical fields & woods. And when the break with life comes, Death's Terror's transformed into Eternal peacefulness: "And there the lion's ruddy eyes/Shall flow with tears of gold." Realizing that the Lion Ego abandons his selfhood & lies down with the Lamb to die—all pain Fear and Unsatisfied Desire radiating out of head Consciousness washed away thru experience of the Body & Dissolution of the body—pure feeling consciousness is left eternal shining thru all living Being, "Golden Emptiness" said dead Kerouac same as "Abyss of Light."

SONGS OF EXPERIENCE

INTRODUCTION: Prophecies, Futurecies! Great claim of the Bard, to call directly to the Soul hidden in the world, obscured & forgot weeping sunk in material thickness; old Gnostic tune. Ecological intuition, the Holy Word walked among the Ancient Trees. Meanwhile man Prisoned in the starry Universe tries to destroy this planet-prison with Electrical Machines and pollutes the wat'ry floor with DDT Detergents. Blake calls thru civilization to Earth Man to return to knowledge of his own soul & live in peace with the Material Universe as his to control only till Death's daybreake.

NURSE'S SONG: The deepest voice of Experience tells the tale of vanishing bodies and Time—our Guardian says innocent play ignores sexual glory till too late—the Nurse's face turns green & pale remembering the body love & eye soul she refused to realize as a child; and now old in winter & night she is afraid to show her still childlike Desire's naked glory because her body ages near death & it becomes repulsive to her.

THE SICK ROSE: English Poetry is pure Mantra here as penetrant & capable of causing Transcendental Knowledge as any Hindu Hare Krishna or Hari Om Namo Shivaye. What's the Rose? Genital Flowers? Body Life? God? What's the Worm? Cancer Syphilis? Mind Time? Death? Or If the Rose is Eternal God, the worm may be human consciousness. If the Rose is all Life itself what dark Secret Love eats at our Being? Does the Universe Die? Is God Death?

AH! SUN FLOWER: The Sun Flower, our own Soul Desire, the root-trapped in earth turns to the source of Desire, the Sun of Death, "where the travellers journey is done." Youth's and Virgin's desire are unsatisfied unsatisfiable mortal forms not only Immortal Union in the Golden Clime where the Sun goes at Night. The Sun flower, rooted in earth, alive, can only turn longingly to follow the sun's path beyond life itself.

THE GARDEN OF LOVE: Consciousness builds a Church of Fear in the body's Garden. Flowers of desire die, & lovers' graves appear in time; but Mind priests take Mad advantage by punishing & forbidding desire altogether while we're here in the garden.

LONDON: The first modern Prophetic poem de-hypnotizing the city & exorcising the Money phantoms that "charter" or "own" space—time Garden plots, cover rivers & riversides of Thames (or Hudson) with Robot Mental smog Money Real Estate Usury Exploitation Law Possession Greed Cancer Stone-Metal Pollution & Spiritual & Physical Death Banks. Walk out in 17th century London or XX century Wall Street look directly in Man's eyes see Marks of weakness marks of woe—the direct imprint of anxiety visible on face masks of Folk caught in City Mental prisons which are concepts of Money gain & exploitation of other beings and nature. Slaves to Machinery! Matter Junkies with oil Burner Habits! Manhattos' Zombies, "In meine Heimat/Where the dead walked/and the living were made of cardboard." Brainwashed by Moloch & the CIA & the Mafia & Chase Bank, So they have destroyed Mother Nature a hundred miles around. And the hapless soldier's sigh runs in Blood down the White House Walls. Boys sobbing in armies Berkeley to Vietnam! All Love turned financial commercial makes the Honeymoon car a Hearse of Desire. A death Lament for the Machine Nations filled with Satanic Mills.

THE HUMAN ABSTRACT: The Gods made Nature free but Ego greeds grow weird false Universe trees in the human physical Brain. Hear it vibrating in your own & realize the dead mechanical universe is a mind trap Illusion created by your senses..."To the Eyes of a Man of Imagination, Nature is Imagination itself"—Blake in letter to Rev. Trusler.

TO TIRZAH: Blake stuck this poem in *Songs of Experience* ten years after the other poems were arranged—late wisdom, Gnostic-Kabalistic-Buddhist transcendental put-down of the entire phenomenal sensory universe as a mental Illusion mothered by Ruha, Tirzah, Sophia, Momma Nature Creatrix Consciousness herself a shadow reflection of the Abyss of Light shuddering a second flashing on itself. In Beginning the Word (Sophia Mother Wisdom Knowledge Tirzah) flash-imagined all Aeons down to Jehova's Garden. The Serpent was the Caller of The Great Call, disguised messenger from the Abyss of Light, according to the Mandean Gnostic* heresy suppressed around 313 A.D. Rome when Constantine Emperor (CIA) accepted Christ took over Religion & suppressed revolutionary metaphysical hip gnostic Illumination of the fake Authority of the Material Universe itself. The Roman State coopted religion at Council of Nicea & burned all Dissenting metaphysical doctrines. This established the Satanic State, presidently headed by Richard Nixon, Jehovah in disguise forgetting to whom he is beholden, son of Elohim, Descendant of Ialdaboath, only a flash of Sophia's Consciousness, herself a flash of selfconsciousness in the Infinite Abyss of Light. The Shekinah was too great for the 7 cups the 7 Sephiroth, the seven Chakra centers of the human body, which shattered. Now the Rabbis are occupied giving the light back to God. We will return to the Abyss of Light. "It is raised a spiritual body."

THE GREY MONK: (This poem is separate, later than *Songs of Innocence & Experience*) On the Revolution, French then, American now, these fragments of Blake's thought returned to my mind in melodious form on a bus up Bayshore Freeway Los Gatos to San Francisco August 10, 1968 or thereabouts riding back from visit to wooden urned ashes of the body of Neal Cassady old love friend & heroic American mind angel died in mid-life. "They never can work war's overthrow." He'd been imprisoned by the State 1959-61 several years for giving a free grass cigarette to the secret police, ruined off his railroad vocation and plunged into homeless psychedelic exploration thereafter till death. "Fayette Fayette thou'rt bought & sold, & sold is thy happy morrow," & other Blake verses remembered after touching Cassady's ashes were the first music that occurred to me turned to Blake's rhymes. "This hand," wrote in *Howl*, "Moloch whose fate is a cloud of Sexless Hydrogen." My brother is Leroi Jones; Thy father's sword was drawn in North Vietnam; The Panthers have armed themselves in steel to avenge the wrongs thy children Feel: But Vain the sword & vain the Bow, They never can work war's overthrow. Violent Vengeance perpetuates self-righteous Tyranny, and A sigh is the Sword of An Angel King.

Dec. 14-15, 1969

New York City—returned again from Chicago as Defense Wittness, Conspiracy Trial.

---

* See *The Gnostic Religions*, by Dr. Hans Jonas, Beacon Paperback.

David Reisman

The child Blake discovers a group of Angels in a tree

Roger Zelazny

The Burning

No animal should be as bright at Blake's Tiger
and I never want to see one.
Forests at night are disturbing enough,
but while mean kids sometimes douse a cat with petrol
and set it alight
for small, cruel laughs at its meteor runs,
its howls,
who has eye, hand or stomach
(let's just call it "guts")
enough to try it with Thee?

More than simple cruelty would have to be involved.
An existential temper, most likely.
As in, "No other is responsible for this act.
Free, spontaneous and unpremeditated,
I have decided to set fire
to this sleeping Tiger I have just now noticed
and burn it away to a grin."

Or perhaps the matter lies
in the hands and the eyes,
not mortal, but im-.
—A grotesque concept is involved:
There is this being
with immortal hands and eyes.
Shoot it, stab it, gas it —
It dies.
But the eyes accuse,
the fingers twitch,
as if they'd like to twine your heartstrings
and have all the time in the world to do it,
you son of a bitch.

Considering it every which way,
it is the sort of thing a primate
would contemplate.
I can't see Thee
doing it to me, Tiger.

A cosmic SPCA seems the answer.
It is too late to do much but admonish
after the act has occurred.
Primates with immortal parts bear watching, anyhow.
And I can do without fearful, striped incendiaries
rushing by me in the night,
God knows. Write your Representative.
Preserve symmetry. Save the Tiger.

****

But my point is this, contemplation is not the doings. It doesn't get there, in fact. Yes, I said to myself, I've got something. Contemplation, in fact is ON THE OUTSIDE. It's not on the spot. And the truth is that Spinoza was always on the outside. He didn't understand freedom, and so he didn't understand anything. Because after all, I said to myself, with some excitement, for I saw where all this was leading to. Freedom, to be plain, is nothing but THE INSIDE OF THE OUTSIDE. And even a philosopher like old Ben can't judge the XXX by eating pint pots. It's the wrong approach. Whereas Old Bill, that damned Englishman, didn't understand anything else but freedom, and so all his nonsense is full of truth; and even though he may be a bit of an outsider, HIS OUTSIDE IS ON THE INSIDE; and if you want to catch the old mole where he digs, you have to start at the bottom.

—Gulley Jimson

David Morice

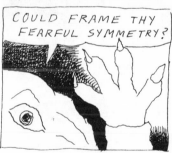

Making Blake Sing

Woody Guthrie recommends that a person choose a melody first and then let it help him write the song. The melodies for "Vigilante Man" and "Pastures of Plenty," for example, come from "Pretty Polly" and "One Kind Favor," respectively. And he used the melody from "Goodnight, Irene" for "Columbia River" and many other songs. What he found out, like Blake and Burns and thousands of other singers, was that a melody can give you a running start on writing a song or a poem. I discovered the same thing myself while working on my own songs years before I read Guthrie's advice. But while working on combining words and music I also got a lot of practice at setting music to words and it was this experience that helped me in setting Blake's poetry to music.

I discovered that an instrumental piece that I'd written years before was made to order for "The Chimney Sweeper" from the *Songs of Experience*. It sounded good and in addition I found that I was understanding Blake better. Words that had always lain flat on a page and "meant" something now worked together to evoke a picture or, if you will, a vision. What I had always seen as a collection of specimens stuck on pins now became a living meadow. It was a propitious start and with the insight I gained I had a much better idea of what to look for when working with the other poems.

The next song that I worked on was "Sunflower." It was a poem I'd never really "gotten." And while I figured Allen Ginsberg could have, I was always curious about what he saw in it that was so special. But I gave it the benefit of my belief since "Sunflower Sutra" by Ginsberg is a favorite of mine and he had shown me the way that Blake could be sung. A friend's suggestion that "Sunflower" might make a good blues song got me started on it. I began with an E minor chord since the song is a kind of lament, and began finger-picking in a style similar to Mississippi John Hurt's. Once I'd gotten started I naturally separated the stanza into two pairs of lines and sang them to about the same melody. What I was doing was fitting the song to a blues pattern called the twelve-bar blues. Songs that follow this pattern, like "C. C. Rider," usually have three parts that consist of one verse that's repeated twice which is followed by another verse. This second verse is oftentimes a kind of "answer" or "punch line" to the first verse. In the way I was using the form though, I had used up the whole stanza in the first two-thirds of the song and did not have anything left to use where the "punch line" should be. But then I came up with the idea of repeating "Ah, Sunflower" twice for the third line. This "lover's sigh" works well as an "answer" because it sounds like something you would hear in a blues song. Once I was singing it I started understanding better what Ginsberg saw in the poem.

The music for "London" came out like a protest song. I set the music to a three-quarter time rhythm. This rhythm can be used for either a waltzing, lilting effect as in "Joe Hill," or for a very forceful effect as in Bob Dylan's "Masters of War." And in the song I used it both ways. For the first, second, and fourth verses I used the first style because the gentler rhythm and a sweet, sad melody seemed more in keeping with Blake's empathetic observations. But for the third verse I chose to use the more emphatic style because in that verse Blake is no longer merely making sympathetic observations, he is making a political statement as well as depicting a vision as powerful as Goya's "Third of May."

The music for "Night," if I had to classify it, I would call folk-country-rock. I tried to compose music for it that was gentle like a lullaby and yet not trite or sing-songy, heartfelt yet not overly sentimental. For, though the song is a lullaby, it is at the same time a powerful, visionary poem. Still, I reckoned it a compliment when late one evening a visiting Blake scholar fell asleep while I was singing this song.

For two other songs I literally found melodies. In both cases I was looking for music because friends had suggested that I try working with a particular poem that was a favorite of theirs. I heard the melody that I use for "Holy Thursday" one morning while washing dishes. I was playing a tape of a singer from St. Louis named Bob Abrams, and while listening to him sing "Amazing Grace," I happened to think of "Holy Thursday." I first sang a verse or two to myself while still at the sink, and when I realized it would probably work, I ran for my guitar. Within thirty minutes I was singing another Blake song. Not only was I pleased to be singing a new song, I enjoyed the fact that it was a church melody I'd found for a song that is anticlerical and yet quite religious in nature.

The other melody that I found comes from a cut on a Folkways album of folk music. It's a recording of some children from the Virgin Islands singing a church song and when I heard it I was touched. I think it was the way it moved me that made me remember the melody and eventually pair it with "Eternity." Not only is the calypso melody very fitting for Blake's song, but one of the original verses is the spiritual brother of his poem and I've been singing both whenever I sing the song. Here's the verse the children sang:

32

"If we never meet again,
If we never meet again,
If we never meet again,
Then I hope we meet in heaven."

When I first heard that Blake would sometimes sing his poems to friends at parties, it struck me as rather odd and quaint. I could just imagine the old gentleman lilting away with glee to the amusement of his friends. But now it does not strike me as being quite so curious. Blake realized, like countless other poet/musicians before and after him, that besides being a mnemonic device that can help the audience and the poet recall the words, music can create a mood and aid the words in evoking an image, a vision, an emotion. Gato Barbieri, the Argentinian jazz saxophonist, says of this quality of music: "The images of dreams and of memory resonate. With the movies we learned that images have music. With music something else, something more ancient and intimate happens. When it truly touches you, you can create your own images and play things you didn't know you were going to dream."

But, as Gato intimates, music affects not only the listener but the performer as well. And this I think is the reason Guthrie recommended that songwriters start with the melody. Music, besides being a universal language, is a good solvent for a petrified imagination; it fosters mental travel. Sound travels faster and further than light. Blake, like Guthrie and Burns, found that music was a wave he could ride which brought him to his poetry.

Daniel Zimmerman

supersensible topographies

for John Clarke

each term one
jump
ahead of the next in the story keeps
story where it belongs
on the tongue, in the ear

then one
jump back of what
began in stagnation in
        the first place
in the flesh.

Blake named angels
either side each
moment
guardians; address
the angels

then,
who show the new new
the dance
to lead & follow
over the hills

on, you huskies

when he got through smiling
nothing was left to say.

he broke the sonic barrier
in a jet propulsion plane.

it was a Buick.
no one knew what to expect.

go ahead I'll be your Spectre
Jack said standing behind me.

the first thing to be overcome,
the memory of the Golden Age.

salt for lotos

the beautiful
glass face
I wake each morning
curled up against
always too close to see
clearly
the easiest
thing in the world
to forget
that all of it's
a great door out of itself
held open

36

spirit level

if you could recommend some good luggage
　something inevitably too expensive
　　maybe we wouldn't have to go

　if you could recommend
　　some method for
immediate　　copresence　　　Ouranian
　　　　　　　　　　　　time travellers
　　　　　　　　　like us
　　might not yearn
　　　for separation
　　from the same small piece of 'earth'

we might be Earthbound creatures
　even if we were　　enabled　　to go far
　　　　　　　　　　　enabled to go
　far beyond these miserable stations
we seem created for
　even if we were
even if we were　　　the ones
　　　　　　　　just beyond
　　momentary horizons

Catherine Goss

A Child's Window to Blake: A Review of
Nancy Willard's *A Visit to William Blake's Inn*

There was a little girl who was named Erin out of the poetry of William Blake. At the age of four, she was rather precocious and loved to read all manner of things. Unfortunately, she took no interest in Blake, not even in *The Songs of Innocence and Experience*. The day she read *A Visit to William Blake's Inn: Poems for Innocent and Experienced Travellers* by Nancy Willard was the day that she began to wonder who this marvelous man of power was and what he had to do with her.

> Now I lay me down to sleep
> with bear and rabbit, bird and sheep.
> If I should dream before I wake,
> may I dream of William Blake.

The bear and rabbit, bird and sheep are all guests at William Blake's Inn in this collection of poems. So are the King of Cats, the Man in the Marmalade Hat, a wise cow, a tiger and two weary sunflowers. The poems are about them. They are also about fire and dancing and believing and journeying. The most memorable moment of the visit is perhaps a walk with Blake on the Milky Way, but almost as enchanting is the opening journey to the Inn in Blake's Celestial Limousine.

> Uneasily I stepped inside
> and found the seats so green and wide,
>
> the grass so soft, the view so far
> it scarcely could be called a car,
>
> rather a wish that only flew
> when I climbed in and found it true.

When Ms. Willard was seven and suffering her second week in bed with measles, a babysitter amazed her with Blake's tyger poem. Two days later she received through the mail a copy of *The Songs of Innocence and Experience* inscribed by Blake himself. Every child should have such a special introduction to Blake and, with the help of Alice and Martin Provensen's neo-Victorian illustrations, Nancy Willard has seen to it that they may. Not only will they become familiar with the man and his London as it appears through the Inn windows, but images and rhythms from *The Songs* and other places in Blake's writings appear without contrivance in the poems and pictures of *A Visit to William Blake's Inn*. This book is a joy to read aloud and a delight for the ears and eyes of any age.

> You whose journeys now begin,
> if you reach a lovely inn,
> if a rabbit makes your bed,
> if two dragons bake your bread,
> rest a little for my sake,
> and give my love to William Blake.

Two Sunflowers
Move into the Yellow Room

"Ah, William, we're weary of weather,"
said the sunflowers, shining with dew.
"Our traveling habits have tired us.
Can you give us a room with a view?"

They arranged themselves at the window
and counted the steps of the sun,
and they both took root in the carpet
where the topaz tortoises run.

Nancy Willard

****

"I always go to Blake when I'm desperate—there's always something more to steal from him."
—Maurice Sendak

Evan Tonsing

excerpts from

A TRANSFORMATION OF WILLIAM BLAKE'S

THE BOOK OF THEL

for GWEN POWELL

opus 64

IV-THEL'S LAMENT, "Oh life of this our spring!"

dreams of infants, like a smile upon an infant's face; Like the dove's voice;   like

transient day;   like music   in the air.   Ah!

gentle may I lay me down, and gentle rest my head,   And gentle sleep the sleep of death and

gentle hear the voice Of him that walketh in the garden in the evening   time."

V – THE LILLY OF THE VALLEY'S ARIA, "I am a wat'ry weed"

Largo quasi recitativo
♩ = 69   quasi basso continuo

flute

toy piano

88

The Lilly of the valley,   breathing in the humble grass,

quasi arioso

Answer'd the lovely maid and said: "I am a wat'ry weed, And I am very small and

delicatamente

love to dwell in lowly vales; So weak, the gilded butterfly scarce perches on my head.

Yet I am visited from heaven, and he that smiles on all Walks in the valley and

Vivace
♩=108

each morn over me spreads his hand, Saying, 'Re-joice, thou humble grass, thou

new-born lilly flower, Thou gentle maid of silent valleys and of modest brooks; For

thou shalt be clothed in light, and fed with morning manna, Till summer's heat melts thee be-

-side the fountains and the springs   To flourish in e- ter-   -nal

vales; Then why should Thel com-plain?   why should the mistress of the vales of Har

1'36"

utter a sigh?" She ceas'd and smil'd in tears, then sat down in her silver shrine.

IX - THE CLOUD'S ARIA, "Our steeds drink of the golden springs"

The   Cloud   then shew'd   his

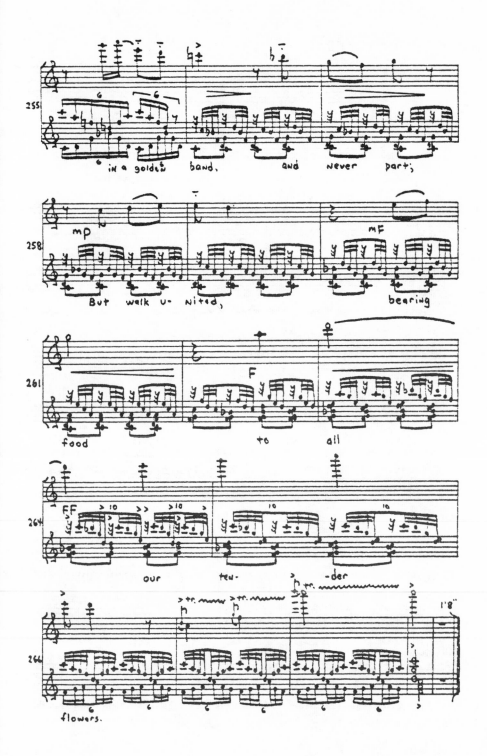

in a golden band, and never part;

But walk u- nited, bearing

food to all

our ten- -der

flowers.

XIII - THE WORM'S ARIA, "We live not for ourselves"

NONE can take a-way: But how this is sweet maid, I know not, and I can-not

know, I ponder, and I cannot ponder; yet I live and love.

XV - THE CLOD'S RAG

Queen of the vales, the matron Clay an-swerd;

I heard thy sighs. And all thy moans flew o'er my roof,

but I have call'd them down: Wilt thou O Queen

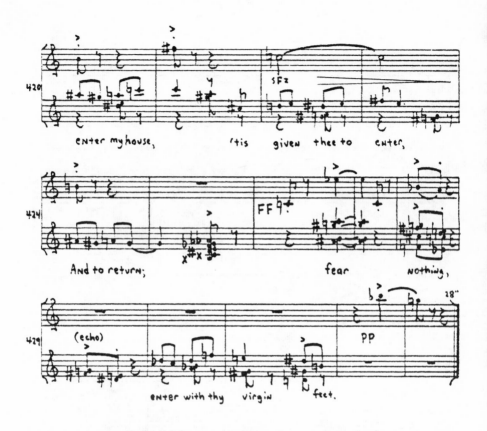

enter my house, 'tis given thee to enter,

And to return; fear nothing,

(echo) enter with thy virgin feet.

XVI - THEL ENTERS THE LAND UNKNOWN

Blues, adagio
♩. = 66

Flute

434

Toy
Piano

The eternal gates terrific porter lifted the northern bar:

431

Thel enter'd in

XVII · THE VOICE FROM THE PIT

Where a thousand fighting men in ambush lie! or an

Eye of gifts and graces, show'ring fruits and coined gold! Why a

Tongue im-press'd with honey from every wind? Why an

Ear, a whirlpool fierce to draw creations in? Why a

Nostril wide inhaling terror, trembling and affright. Why a tender

curb   upon   the   youthful   burning   boy!   Why a

little   curtain of   flesh   on the   bed   of   our de-

-sire?   The Virgin started from her seat, and with a shriek,   Fled back un-

-hindered till she came into the vales of Har.

FINE

Jan. 17, 1981
Glencoe, OK
RB

Composer's Notes

A Transformation of William Blake's The Book of Thel was imagined first as a cantata for soprano, mezzosoprano, and baritone perhaps accompanied by two pianos or a small ensemble. The intended singers examined Blake's text and rejected it as being incomprehensible. Disgusted, I then proposed the semi-nonsense songs in Lewis Carroll's *Alice in Wonderland;* very curiously, they immediately accepted.

I hid my sorrow and pushed Thel into a dark mental corner. Later, while I was researching a work for flute and piano, Thel spontaneously decided to start growing as a cantata without the inconvenience of singers. I worried about Thel's problem of keeping the audience's attention while wearing only a flute and tiny toy piano; fortunately she proved attractive.

The work may be enjoyed with or without reference to the poem, but it was grown by allowing the sounds and rhythms of the words to sprout and cluster. Its natural linear structure has autobiographical parallels with my twenty years of artistic growth, including textures of ragtime and blues near the end. The first performance in February, 1981 was augmented with slides of Blake's illustrated pages. Another performance in fall, 1981 included narration of Blake's text with the music.

The music views Blake's magical poem as a self-contained whole. From that viewpoint, innocent Thel is in quest of a reason for living. She consults a Lily, Cloud, and Worm. She then enters the land unknown and encounters sorrow and stark lust. With horror, Thel runs back to a useless life in the beautiful but vapid vales of Har.

In later editions of the poem, Blake excised the two lines of exposed lust that climax his 129 lines of text. Perhaps Thel, like her creator, would have tried to amputate portions of her memory of life in the unknown even at the cost of meaning. I sympathize with Blake's protective love of Thel but refuse to imitate his behavior; the lines are included in the musical setting.

Although the sonority of the toy piano is its own justification, its use was colored by an aesthetic viewpoint. When my briefly realized dream, an uninsured four-track recording studio, was stolen from my country home, a toy piano stood elegantly unaltered in the rubble. Its quiet, expectant cheer prompted the realization that creativity cannot be stolen and that even an instrument having only twenty-five notes and costing about the same in dollars can sing and dance eloquently if creativity is present. In addition to this work, it is employed in two other works with opus numbers, an ambitious solo and a quartet with narrator.

This musical fantasy is dedicated to a colleague and superbly gifted spinner of beautiful flute sounds, Gwen Powell.

Evan Tonsing

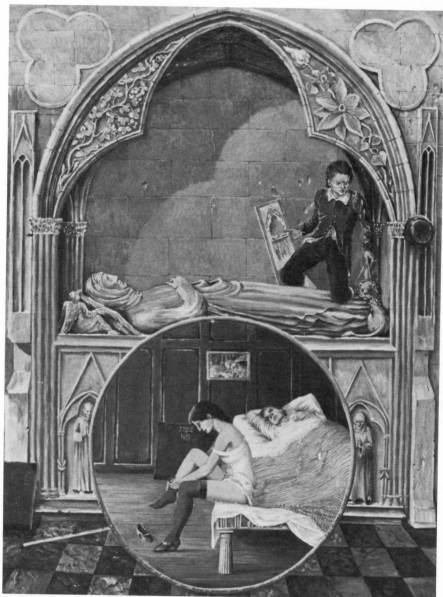

Blake making a measured drawing of Countess Aveline's tomb, Westminster Abbey, 1779. William and Catherine experiencing the pleasures of married life, 23 Green Street, 1782.

It

[*Reading Blake in a cowshed during a typhoon
on an island in the East China Sea*]

Cloud—cloud—cloud—   hurls
        up and on over;
Bison herds stamp-
peding   on Shantung

Fists of rain
        flail half down the length of the floor
Bamboo hills
        bend and regain;
                fields follow the laws of waves.

        puppy scuds in wet
        squats on the slat bed
                —on the edge of a spiral
Centered five hundred miles southwest.

Reading in English:
        the way the words join
        the weights, the warps,

        I know   what it means.
        my language is home.

                mind-fronts meeting
                bite back at each other,
                        whirl up a Mother Tongue.
        one hundred knot gusts dump palms
        over somebody's morning cream—

Cowshed skull
Its windows open
    swallows and strains
    gulf of wild-plumb
        quivering ocean air.
        breathe it;
        taste it;   how it

Feeds the brain.

William Blake   Engraver & Bard

W/B

"My business is to Create"

South Molton Street near Golden Square

Howard McCord

Around the World with William Blake

For many years now the one *vade mecum* in my pack has been the Penguin *Selected Blake*. In Iceland, Alaska, Lapland, Mexico, Greece, I have sustained my enthusiasm and cleared my eyes of the dross of the day with a few moments in *The Marriage of Heaven and Hell*, that first poem of modernity which shaped the Romantics and shapes us today, urtext of our consciousness.

If the Prophets suck air in a space vacated by a *deus otiosus*, and famous cretins of our day find their muse in their privy parts, Blake assures us that imagination is prior to creation, and he who would understand the latter must dwell in the former.

Some sixteen years ago, flying up the Ganges in a wheezing DC-3 which threaded its way through the rising thunderheads of the approaching monsoon, the northern sky broke clear and revealed Everest and its colossal brethren ablaze like a vision of glory in the sun. I looked up from Brother Blake and my heart rolled against my ribs. Mountain-bred, I saw my promised home. I clapped my hands, shouted "Praise the Lord that Never Was," unbuckled my seat belt, and slid into the narrow aisle in an ecstasy. I did four forward rolls down the length of the plane between dozing Brahmins, merchants from Patna, civil servants of indeterminate power, sareed matrons, and the sometime mayor of Lucknow. It was India, and all had seen strange sights before. My heart still pumping like a boy in a swing, I returned to my seat and spent the next half hour inspecting the mountains of Paradise. When clouds would cut the view, I would return to *The Marriage of Heaven and Hell*, and the exaltation continued. I was suspended between the highest point of creation, and the highest point of imagination, and would never have landed if the plane hadn't.

My next long walk will be up the Weasel River on Baffin Island, and Blake will go along to lead the way to the nesting grounds of the Snowy Owl, and the nunataks which rise rhrough the Penny Icecap like the shoulders of Los. There in the gold of an arctic summer night, I will boil tea, and look up from my cup and book to the distant gates of Thel.

John Brandi

Poem to You O Goddess O Light
Through Whom All Things Moving &
Motionless Shine

when i knew you in innocence
i found what i was seeking

when i became lost inside you
i no longer remembered what it was
i had found

when the colt i tamed
backed out of its fields, with
flared nostrils smoking

when the doe cramped into agony
between the whirlpool's liquid teeth
& my books burned in your eclipse

i again remembered
the essence of the stream i had
been following

i again put my feet into
the soul of purity, & found inside
my hand another Hand

speaking quietly
inside the wheel of a caravan
i heard the aleph

& found an angel
in the embrace of your dance
in the phoenix of your song.

A Poem for The New Year

i am not writing poetry
these days
but i am talking in verse to the
ancients who prod me on
& bless me with stolen apples
& call to me disguised as trees
who sing to their shadows
in amethyst sand

i have no need for poems
i simply align my wheels with Polaris
& coast in neutral uphill
writing letters to Persuasion
while crossing Thin Bear Creek
drinking long swallows of burgundy

i have visited recently
with the poet Issa, & he is doing well
he has a new baby
also named Issa, he has a girlfriend
& he has enough to drink
on the withered moor
he has his compassion, his
charcoal fire is banked with hissing
steam, & there are things
boiling in the saucepan

no, i am not writing poetry
but making the rounds
knocking at the gates of water birds
& following acrobats into hollows
of woodblock sunbeams
i enjoy this

the quick walks into eternity,
the green shadows of goats
straddling night rainbows, i've bowed
my head to peacocks & gessoed shrines,
heard lovers in secret places
making love to other lovers' loves
i like the moan of tugboats
& jeweled city rain on plastic umbrellas,
hot wet pavement smells
& glittering saltweed, i'm content
to ride the sharpened edge,
i can get by
not holding back, with only
my shadow, one oar
no shower
the darkening evening
a small plate
of fresh nasturtiums

i have no need for poetry
for i dance more these days
with fugitive crickets in unreluctant
sunsets, i am doing more listening
to the changing attitudes of the body
& i've seen through it all here & there,
i've held roses to my head
& heard the pulse of their breathing
i've visited the pyres
i've stopped scratching my bites
& the old passion has come back to me
in every new face
i focus on great beauty, i sleep
with rivers moving in my eyes
i gently recognize each dream as a part
of reality
i often marry invisible brides
& play my harmonica for scarecrows
& as my head clears
i know nothing before me has
been charted
i know there is no backing up
into tomorrow

so i don't write poems
because each step has more & more
to do with stillness,
entering, balancing
dropping out of the way
with no apology
i want to talk only with the body
i want my shoulders & thighbones to move,
i want to come away from the old days
not hardened, but wise
i want to fall in love again
with night rain
to give comfort, to come full circle
with hope, with no haste
& no rest, i want to sink in my axe
& build again.

Poem Reflecting World Events
Written to the Beat of a Waterwheel
While Meditating on Shakyamuni's
Ashes Circling the Sun

Life's another waking.
Mother Kali hanging out wet laundry.
Clouds pedaling by faster than bicycles.
Newspaper announcing the heart attack of a star
who wrote Rock Around the Clock.
Billy the Kid's grave stolen a second time.
Mountains chatting with fields, horses
hesitating in mist.

Life's one more day.
Air balloon floating above old men
setting cornerstone mudpies for new house.
Lady cabdriver doing radio commercial

for Preparation H. Wetbacks singing corridas
dancing with silver ladders
through winter orchards.

Life's a roll of light
tickertaped into my little Francis
of Assisi notebook.
Monday morning postmaster
with lower-lip cigaret, sorting poems
through sharp-cornered IRS envelopes.
Dogs eating snowflakes under warped vaportrails.
Postcard from Jacquie in Tahiti.
Blue Cloud looking over Coyote's Journal.
David silent in his Kabbala.
A ziggurat bird wraps the world in shadow.
I unfold tissue-paper maps of Java.
Bedroom & zither & corner fireplace move
around one another talking in circles.
Bees serenade doorway, fly into windowpanes
massage legs in clear void between
dining room & garden.

Life's a pot of coffee percolating over
on my castiron woodstove.
Prismed sigh evaporating in heat.
Cranes disassembling into alphabet glitter
above my son who whistles his way
to third grade, past thousand-year-old petroglyphs.
Maya pulls the tongue from her shoe.
Friends demand to be lovers. Lovers spend
the night & end becoming friends.
The next village over
is inhabited by harps.

Life's a long-skirted woman in black
walking past my gate every morning at nine
carrying a basket of eggs in one arm
& a rifle in the other.
While across the river, a rainbow tips
its hat to a secret tombstone whose angels
awake from plaster-eyed sleep
into pure romance of dream.

Life's a bigbang theory.
Blossom of light blown off a Tree of Song.
One day my students pull the shades
& pile roses over my textbooks.
Kerry wants to take me for a ride to
Beautiful Valley & collect bones.
Norman drives me out past Four Corners
to see a juniper grown around
itself in a perfect circle.
Nanao says keep silent for a hundred
years, then come see me.

Life's a jewel-eyed deer
prancing earthward to the voice of
a thousand bells.
Mercury slips by Mars. Shakyamuni's ashes
circle the sun. My old friend
Pingeleen unwraps a cosmic tangerine.
All the countryside talks & talks.
Men I've gotten drunk with.
Women I've haphazardly courted.
Mendicants, celibates. I can't fit
them into paragraphs.

Life's a speeding wheel
caught with shadows. Hummingbird here
& gone at my window.
Crosslegged, I listen to crickets & flowers.
And though I inhabit this world
with every sense & sensation, I breathe
from somewhere deeper a light unlocked
from a perfect Scent.
All free & a billion times multiplied!
All sifted finely through
the waist of an hourglass.

Life's one more line
rolled from the tongue, unfinished
& eternally waking. Ribcage holding pendants
& mirrors. Blood whirling around like
a waterwheel through heaven & back.
Heart beating out words on transparent

papyrus, into a little song
for you, a little song for each day
of the week, a little song
from the farthest reach into the
farthest corner of paradise.

Homegoing, After Joaquin's Birth

There's nothing more
to know
than what I am
when I touch the other side
of what I'd like to be

Everything I've waited for
Birth/Death
is right inside this
den of mine

Mantra the trail
music a stream, into a circle
without doors
this headrest where
I dream

Ladyfern!
    fireflower, puffball
    paintbrush, jimsonweed —

Remember me
when I am gone, &
        you still sing.

Albert Roe

Blake's Symbolism

I must Create a System or be enslav'd by another Man's.
Jerusalem, 10, 20

In speaking of the basic aims of his art, Blake says: "The Nature of my Work is Visionary or Imaginative.... This world of Imagination is the world of Eternity.... There Exist in that Eternal World the Permanent Realities of Every Thing which we see reflected in this Vegetable Glass of Nature."[1] Thus art was to him not only a means of communicating his own beliefs to others, but actually a primary source of knowledge concerning the divine plan. He defined poetry, painting, and music as "the three Powers in Man of conversing with Paradise, which the flood did not Sweep away."[2] Imagination—he always calls it "the Divine Imagination"—he considered to be not mere fancy, but a means of visionary perception which God has granted to man to preserve in him a knowledge of his eternal self even while in his fallen state. Dealing with a theme of this character, he found—as other visionary poets have done—that language which has been devised for the everyday activities of this world will not adequately convey his message. He must rely to a large extent on images; these, by their very nature, demand not only perceptiveness on his part in the choosing of adequate symbols to suggest his meaning, but sympathetic imaginative understanding on the part of the reader.

Most poets in search of a readily comprehensible symbolism have employed a traditional mythology which, because of its historical or religious character, is generally known. Thus Dante and Milton drew their images principally from Christian and classical sources. Blake, however, did not choose to use an established mythology and the passage quoted at the head of this section tells us why. The age of neo-classicism had reduced much classical imagery to conceits and trivialities; the dogma of religious sects, he was convinced, had misconstrued much of the material provided by the Bible. Classical mythology he consequently rejected almost completely. From the Bible he drew continually. In most cases, however, his use of Biblical sources is not conventional, but based upon a richly symbolical interpretation of his own, the essence of which has been well set forth by a recent critic: "The Bible [to Blake] is not a moral code and a commentary on it: it is a series of visions."[3] Finally, as these two sources—and such other less familiar mythology as the nordic and the oriental from which he borrowed extensively—did not fully meet his needs, he created an involved mythology of his own.[4] To this mythology he left us no key and but few obscure hints, for reasons which he set forth in the following statement: "The wisest of the Ancients consider'd what is not too Explicit as the fittest for Instruction, because it rouzes the faculties to act."[5] Its structure can be pieced together only by a careful and perceptive reading of all his works and by a study of their accompanying designs. The reader is still called upon to provide for himself much of the insight necessary to understanding. Such a brief examination of the main points of Blake's mythology as that which follows can only serve as a general guide, and must be considered as such and not as a formula for solving a complex puzzle.

When on the evening of Saturday, December 10, 1825, Henry Crabb Robinson and Blake dined at the home of the collector, Charles Aders, the discussion turned to religious questions. "I had suggested on very obvious philosophical grounds," Robinson says in his account of their conversation in his diary, "the *impossibility* of supposing an immortal being created—an eternity *a parte post* without an eternity *a parte ante*. . . .His eye brightened on my saying this, and he eagerly concurred—'To be sure it is impossible. We are all co-existent with God—members of the Divine body. We are all partakers of the Divine nature.'. . .On my asking in what light he viewed the great question concerning the Divinity of Jesus Christ, he said—'*He is the only God.*' But then he added—'And so am I and so are you.'"[6] This is one of the few recorded instances of Blake's conversation concerning the nature of his beliefs, but it touches on a fundamental starting-point in a discussion of his ideas. All of Blake's philosophy stems from his acceptance of the statement in Genesis that God created man in His own image. There is, then, in every man the spark of the divine and the capacity to become one with God. But as man is the image of God, so is God the transcendent image of man. Jesus is referred to throughout Blake's poems as the "Divine Humanity."

> Thou art a Man, God is no more,
> Thine own Humanity learn to Adore.
> *The Everlasting Gospel*, p. 750

By the development of the understanding in its widest sense, under the guidance of the imagination, each of us may ultimately return to the perfect unity with God which is eternal life. "He who sees the Infinite in all things, sees God."[7] Man, if he were enlightened, would realize this and would seek to develop his power of understanding rather than strive to establish his position in a worldly sense.

What, then, accounts for the present condition of man? The answer is that the world of our physical consciousness is a fallen world: "This Earth breeds not our happiness."[8] How humanity came to its present state; how salvation may be achieved; and a visionary realization of the nature of the Eternal World—these are the elements of Blake's epic. Blake announces this theme in his own characteristic phraseology in the opening lines of *Jerusalem:*

> Of the Sleep of Ulro! and of the passage through
> Eternal Death! and of the awakening to Eternal Life.
>
> This theme calls me in sleep night after night, & ev'ry morn
> Awakes me at sun-rise; then I see the Saviour over me
> Spreading his beams of love & dictating the words of this mild song.
> Jerusalem 4, 1-5

Blake thus states his intention quite clearly. Under the guidance of the Divine Humanity, Jesus—"the Poetic Genius" as he frequently calls Him, who through the Divine Imagination inspires men in creative moments—Blake proposes to explore the realms of human experience: the dark unknown out of which consciousness first comes; the tormented journey through a world of doubt which leads to the mysterious death of the body; the hope of ultimate salvation.

After the lines given above, the opening passages of *Jerusalem* continue in what at first seems an obscure vein, but one which on closer examination and with growing familiarity gives in brief compass much of the substance of the poem. The Saviour now addresses man:

> "Awake! awake O sleeper of the land of shadows, wake! expand!
> I am in you and you in me, mutual in love divine:
> Fibres of love from man to man thro' Albion's pleasant land.
> In all the dark Atlantic vale down from the hills of Surrey
> A black water accumulates; return Albion! return!
> Thy brethren call thee, and they fathers and thy sons,
> Thy nurses and thy mothers, thy sisters and thy daughters
> Weep at thy soul's disease, and the Divine Vision is darken'd,
> Thy Emanation that was wont to play before thy face,
> Beaming forth with her daughters into the Divine bosom:
> Where has thou hidden thy Emanation, lovely Jerusalem,
> From the vision and fruition of the Holy-one:
> I am not a God afar off, I am a brother and friend:

Within your bosoms I reside, and you reside in me:
Lo! we are One, forgiving all Evil, Not seeking recompense.
Ye are my members, O ye sleepers of Beulah, land of shades!"

But the perturbed Man away turns down the valley dark:
"Phantom of the over heated brain! shadow of immortality!
Seeking to keep my soul a victim to thy Love! which binds
Man, the enemy of man, into deceitful friendships,
Jerusalem is not! her daughters are indefinite:
By demonstration man alone can life, and not by faith.
My mountains are my own, and I will keep them to myself:
The Malvern and the Cheviot, the Wolds, Plinlimmon & Snowdon
Are mine: here will I build my Laws of Moral Virtue.
Humanity shall be no more, but war & princedom & victory!"

Jerusalem 4, 6-31

In these lines, the poet passes at once to the consideration of error and the Fall which follows its acceptance. Albion, the Eternal Man, symbol of mankind considered as a whole, has fallen into a state in which doubt is possible; this is the state which Blake calls "Beulah," upon which we shall enlarge later. On the one hand, the divine or imaginative aspect of man's nature, personified by the Savior, keeps reminding him of his brotherhood with all men through their common kinship with God: "I am not a God afar off, I am a brother and friend: Lo! we are One, forgiving all evil, Not seeking recompense." Such is the way to eternal joy: love of all men as Sons of God through individual understanding and forgiveness. "Forgiveness of Sins. This alone is the Gospel, & this is the Life & Immortality brought to light by Jesus."[9] However, the purely rational side of man's nature replies to the imaginative by asserting the arguments of self-interest, often symbolized— though not directly here—as the Spectre or Satan. Other men are not brothers, but rivals; the fittest alone will survive and any means to that end are justified. The idea that complete liberty of the mind and spirit will bring happiness is false since it will bring freedom to others as well as to one's self, while it is in one's interest to enslave them. Man can live only by trusting to the evidence of his senses to guide him to a practical knowledge and control over his environment; faith, being but a figment of the imagination, is an unreal passing fancy and no more. Man makes the choice offered him by selfhood. Error is embraced; truth rejected. The Fall takes place and man finds himself in the "valleys dark" of this world: a world where the divine light is almost shut out and we can perceive only the material; a world in which liberty must yield to the control of law; a world which deems love a sign of weakness and gives its applause to those who gain their triumphs at the expense of the death and suffering of others.

70

All Love is Lost! terror succeeds, & Hatred instead of Love,
And stern demands of Right & Duty instead of Liberty.

Jerusalem 22, 10-11

The world of our present experience is, therefore, a fallen world. By his acceptance of error, man has voluntarily surrendered his divinity and given himself over to the dark torment of mortal life. The sufferings of this world are not a punishment inflicted upon man for disobedience to God's law, for God knows no law but only love and forgiveness. Man has made his free choice, and in error has become a subject of Satan's realm of cruelty.

. . .I called for compassion; compassion mock'd;
Mercy & pity threw the grave stone over me, & with lead
And iron bound it over me for ever.

Jerusalem 10, 53-55

In the eternal state, the perceptions of man had been infinite:

. . .contracting their Exalted Senses
They behold Multitude, or Expanding they behold as one,
As One Man all the Universal family.

Four Zoas I, 462-464 (p. 264)

With the Fall, however, the universality of man's vision is lost and only the imperfect organic senses remain: "For man has closed himself up, till he sees all things thro' narrow chinks of his cavern."[10] The omnipotent has now become the pathetically fragile mortal man, limited in perspective and preyed upon by forces of nature which he cannot control:

Ah weak & wide astray! Ah shut in narrow doleful form,
Creeping in reptile flesh upon the bosom of the ground!
The Eye of Man a little narrow orb, clos'd up & dark,
Scarcely beholding the great light, conversing with the Void;
The Ear a little shell, in small volutions shutting out
All melodies & comprehending only Discord and Harmony;
The Tongue a little moisture fills, a little food it cloys,
A little sound it utters & its cries are faintly heard.

Milton 5, 19-26

Man in this state, however, does not recognize nor admit his weakness. Rather he postulates that truth is to be learned by codifying the data of the senses; that which lies beyond the range of their observation must be ignored as unreal:

In ignorance to view a small portion & think that All,
And call it demonstration, blind to all the simple rules of life.
Four Zoas VII b, 182-183 (p. 327)

Thus do man-made systems grow up. Based upon the limited knowledge available to the "Natural Man," they are at once endowed by him with divine authority, so that other men may be enslaved to his selfhood:

No more could they rise at will
In the infinite void, but bound down
To earth by their narrowing perceptions
They lived a period of years;

. . . .

And form'd laws of prudence, and call'd them
The eternal laws of God.
Urizen 25-28.

Hence, in Blake's view, all accepted social systems become endowed sooner or later with tyrannical power that destroys human liberty. No other course could be possible in a world ruled by Satan. Most men will conform through ignorance or fear; those who do not will be ruthlessly destroyed by the "blind world-rulers of this life."[11] All accepted orders exist for the benefit of those who spend "their lives in Curbing & Governing other People's by the Various arts of Poverty & Cruelty of all kinds."[12] Since men cannot develop their selfhoods without hindering others, they are bound either to try to turn established systems to their own uses, or to be enslaved or destroyed by those systems. Governments establish their hold by rigid laws and increase their influence by wars. Social and economic systems give power and wealth to the few at the price of the degradation of the many. Society even perverts love: the alternative to rigid repression or a forced union of people who may prove incompatible is all too often either ostracism or disease. Organized religion is the worst of all, for it claims for itself divine authority and lends its sanction to the political and economic tyrannies which realize its usefulness as a repressive tool. Claiming to uphold the moral law as decreed by God, it in reality commits the supreme apostasy of setting Satan up for worship under the name of God.

Thus it was that Blake, devoutly religious in all his thought and works, exhibited the apparent paradox of vehemently opposing organized religion. All churches, he felt, based their doctrines upon human precepts and not upon those of God. Earthly religion preaches what it claims is God's law, and stresses not forgiveness of sins but punishment for transgression. But to Blake "The Gospel is Forgiveness of Sins & has No Moral Precepts," and

72

further he believed that "Every Religion that Preaches Vengeance for Sin is the Religion of the Enemy & Avenger and not of the Forgiver of Sin, and their God is Satan, Named by the Divine Name."[13] To him it appeared that the churches exalted the Decalogue and its author, the "Angry God of this World," while presenting Jesus as a secondary figure, cast in a sentimental light, far removed from His revolutionary role as the advocate of forgiveness. To Blake, this world is itself Hell, and its God, while called Jehovah by the churches, is in reality Satan. "In Hell all is Self Righteousness; there is no such thing there as Forgiveness of Sin; he who does Forgive Sin is Crucified as an Abettor of Criminals, & he who performs Works of Mercy in Any shape whatever is punish'd &, if possible, destroy'd, not thro' envy or Hatred or Malice, but thro' Self Righteousness that thinks it does God service, which God is Satan."[14] All of the blindness of human life to the true glory of the eternal world thus resolves itself into the essential error of subordinating the individual to man-made systems, while God intended for him no system, but only self-determination—liberty in its widest sense. Blake sums up his entire point of view in the pithy and marvelously striking and compact epigram in *The Marriage of Heaven and Hell*, "Prisons are built with stones of Law, Brothels with bricks of Religion."[15] Worldly institutions are thus "A pretence of Art to destroy Art; a pretence of Liberty to destroy Liberty; a pretence of Religion to destroy Religion."[16]

So far we have indicated the two main stages in Blake's "Circle of Destiny." In eternity man was a perfect unity, coexistent with God, comprehending all things through divine intelligence, unrestrained by such limits as time and space. Through error the Fall has taken place, unity has been destroyed, and we—the fallen men—exist in a shrunken world of intert matter, enfeebled shadows of our eternal selves, guided by the imperfect perceptions of our five senses.

Now the Starry Heavens are fled from the mighty limbs of Albion.
Jerusalem 75, 27

The last words of Albion, as the Fall took place, were "Hope is banish'd from me."[17] However, he failed to take into account God's mercy and His infinite capacity for understanding and forgiveness.

God is within & without: he is even in the depths of Hell!
Jerusalem 12, 15

Man has fallen through error; to be redeemed he must recognize error and cast it out. As the essence of the unfallen world is life in its most intense and and vital form, so the opposite pole of the Fall would be annihilation. To

73

save man from the pit of chaos from which there could be no return, God in His mercy has set limits to the Fall to grant man the time and opportunity to acquire understanding, and to reject the error into which his selfhood has betrayed him.

These limits are two. First there is "Adam," the Natural Man, the "limit of contraction." However far man may fall, he still has something of a mind and something of an imagination; a spark of divinity remains and thus hope of redemption is never lost. The second limit is the "limit of opacity," the state which Blake names "Satan." The error and evil of this Fallen World are so monstrous that even the contracted capacities of the Natural Man may eventually perceive them, and error once recognized can be cast out. Thus after the Fall, the possibility of regeneration remains. The second part of Blake's myth—following upon the account of the Fall, its origin, and the nature of the Fallen World—is concerned with the processes of regeneration: the recognition and rejection of error, and ultimate salvation.

> There is a limit of Opakeness and a limit of Contraction
> In every Individual Man, and the limit of Opakeness
> Is named Satan, and the limit of Contraction is named Adam.
> But when Man sleeps in Beulah, the Saviour in Mercy takes
> Contraction's Limit, and of the Limit he forms Woman, That
> Himself may in process of time be born Man to redeem.
> But there is no Limit of Expansion; there is no Limit of Translucence
> In the bosom of Man for ever from eternity to eternity.
>
> *Jerusalem* 42, 29-36

At the beginning of one of his earliest prophetic works, *The Marriage of Heaven and Hell*, Blake states a principle which remains fundamental throughout the later development of his ideas. "Without Contraries is no progression. Attraction and Repulsion, Reason and Energy, Love and Hate, are necessary to human existence." Blake realizes that progress is not possible in a static state; constant tension and ebb and flow are the essentials for arriving at truth. Nothing, therefore, is really bad except inaction and complacency; the active evils of human experience fulfil a function in that they make error apparent so that truth may be embraced. In all earthly experience, whether spiritual, intellectual, or merely material—as, for example, the alternation of night and day—we find contraries involved. It is natural that this should be so: error triumphs only when, through mis-guidance or for the sake of simplification, the diversities found in all phases of experience are denied and one contrary is set up by law as right at the expense of the other. This over-simplification is a refusal to recognize the essential fact that human experience is subtle and complex—yet this negation is precisely the end to which rigid systems lead. The free play of contraries—even where one has in it a preponderance of evil—will eventually give birth to liberty; denial of action by restriction enslaves both parties concerned. This idea is expressed in reversed writing in the design which forms the heading for the second book of *Milton:* "Contraries are Positives. A Negation is not a Contrary."[18]

It is in the light of the above concept that we must consider Blake's views of creation and of the created world. On the one hand this is a world of strange and monstrous natural forces against which man must battle for survival. The cyclic regularity of many natural phenomena has an unbending quality akin to that of the social laws to which man has surrendered himself in an attempt to maintain himself against nature and his fellows. Caught up in the workings of a vast machine, man is forced to renounce liberty and to deny imagination. All tends to the annihilation of the essential humanity. In this aspect we live in the world of Satan.

However, as we have seen, Blake believed that in another aspect this world exists to prevent man from falling completely into the abyss where chaos rules unchecked. As such our present world—"Generation" is Blake's name for it—is the gift of God. The Fall has been great, but spiritual perception has not yet ceased and error can still be recognized and cast out.

> O holy Generation, Image of regeneration!
> O point of mutual forgiveness between Enemies!
> Birthplace of the Lamb of God incomprehensible!
> *Jerusalem* 7, 65-67

From this it will be seen that Blake's ideas about the creation differ widely from the conventional interpretation of the Biblical account. This is not a basically good world which man has perverted through his own wilful violation of eternal law; it is a fallen state through which man must pass in the process of regeneration after his error in renouncing the world of eternity. The satanic and the divine contraries are constantly at war within it to the end that man may ultimately recognize error and reject it. Our world is not God's original creation to bring order out of eternal chaos. The eternal order is one of unity, harmony and understanding: chaos came only with the Fall.[19] This world exists, through the grace of God, as a limit to the Fall—as a place of respite where man can redevelop the spiritual side of his nature, which in eternity he deliberately renounced, and can thus find the pathway back to salvation. Thanks to God's gift of imagination—which is never quite absent in any individual, though more developed in some than in others—man can still aspire to the divine. And God in His love for man has manifested Himself in this world in the life of Jesus so that man may learn that the way of regeneration is to be found not in unyielding rational law but in denial of the selfhood and in forgiveness of others, even as God forgives him. With this realization, man will recapture the infinite capacities of his eternal self. "Whenever any Individual Rejects Error & Embraces Truth, a Last Judgment passes upon that Individual."[20]

We have now examined in some detail Blake's views concerning the nature of the Fallen World of our present existence and its social institutions. The life of this world is but one of the four stages of the entire "Circle of Destiny" of Blake's system. As all of these spheres of existence appear frequently in Blake's work, we shall proceed to examine the three remaining steps of the cycle. First it will be well to summarize them briefly, using Blake's name for each stage, terms which establish key symbols in his mythology.

First we have the world which Blake calls "Eden." This is the highest level of existence. From this mortal man has fallen and to it he will return after his recognition and rejection of error. Each of Blake's three major prophecies ends with a vision of Eden regained. The life of Eden is, however, so intense that even the soul which has not embraced error cannot remain permanently in its exalted state. Just as relaxation, refreshment, and rest are necessary to mind and body, so are they to the soul. This is found in the state of existence known as "Beulah." In this world of repose, the soul is restored for its awakening again to the pure ecstasy of Eden. In Beulah, however, error is possible. The soul may become enamoured of inaction instead of longing to return to the intense activity of Eden. When the soul thus accepts error, it sinks into a deep sleep and the Fall takes place. The third stage is "Ulro," the void and chaos of nonentity. After the Fall, souls wander aimlessly in this void until, through the mercy of God, they are reborn into consciousness in our present life. Blake's name for our world, as we have already seen, is "Generation"; its function is to give man the opportunity to recognize error through experience and, by rejecting it, to regain his immortal stature.

Before proceeding to examine these stages in more detail, it is important to realize that Blake very frequently presents his ideas from a number of different points of reference. Thus the Circle of Destiny may be regarded as embracing the entire evolution of human experience in a universal sense. Generation will then cover the course of human history from the beginning to the present as we normally think of it. However, this cycle may be applied to the individual as well and may represent the entire passage of a particular soul from its fall from Eden, through the infinite vicissitudes of physical, mental, emotional and imaginative experience in the life of this world, until the time of ultimate salvation. This duality applies to all the steps along the way. For example, the Last Judgment may be thought of as the final universal rejection of error, at which time the created world will cease to exist; however, we must remember from the quotation just given that "Whenever any Individual Rejects Error & Embraces Truth, a Last Judgment passes upon that Individual." Thus in our present life we may become, through the power of imagination, capable as individuals of comprehending events in the eternal order, where all things exist outside of the bounds of time as we know it in this world.

The reader must constantly remind himself, therefore, that Blake's symbols often have several possible interpretations. Not only may the same symbol be used with different and quite divergent meanings depending upon the connotation, but each of these meanings may be applicable on a number of levels: they may concern humanity in general, they may deal with individual experience, they may even be autobiographical, and they may involve any combination of these factors. Blake without doubt purposely avoided being too specific in order to test and to develop the reader's own powers of discernment. However, with familiarity there will seldom be confusion as to Blake's intention; he merely demands discrimination on our part.

It must also be remembered that Blake interprets the word "human" very widely, endowing with remarkable visionary life not only all living forms as we usually think of them, but even those which to our senses seem completely inert. "To see a World in a Grain of Sand and a Heaven in a Wild Flower"[21] is but a particularly striking statement of the insistence, which runs through all of Blake's work, that every aspect of the created universe is permeated with the immortal spirit and only awaits the time when it shall burst into joyous life. We are thus called upon to widen our understandings to take in levels of experience beyond those which readily suggest themselves to most of us. At the same time as we seek to comprehend through imagination the grandeur of the *whole*, which in its perfect unity reaches beyond time and space and the world of our sensory perceptions, we must enter too most intimately into the spiritual world of the most seemingly insignificant particle and learn to conceive of it as a separate individuality. The Circle of Destiny, as the closing lines of *Jerusalem* proclaim, is the history of the totality of spiritual experience:

All *Human* Forms identified, even Tree, Metal, Earth & Stone: all
Human Forms identified, living, going forth & returning wearied
Into the Planetary lives of Years, Months, Days & Hours; reposing,
And then Awakening into his Bosom in the Life of Immortality.
                                                                Jerusalem 99, 1-4

To enlarge somewhat upon the nature of the different stages of the Circle, let us first consider Eden. Life for Blake is synonymous with energy: "Energy is Eternal Delight."[22] Hence Eden, where life is most complete, is a place of

77

joyous and overflowing energy. Pure energy, pure imagination, and pure spirit are here one; their united radiance is that of the Spiritual Sun, which is the symbol of Eden. Above all, Eden is a world of intellectual liberty and unbounded mental activity—activity that arises not from the contemplation of truth that is already known, but from the mental joy of continual discovery. It is a world of unity, brotherhood, and oneness with God. There is no spiritual division here, no negation, no repose—but joy in unceasing energy. As such, it is an active masculine world into which the fundamental schism of differentiation of sexes can never come. It is a world of pure vision in which the spiritual nature and unity of all things is triumphantly realized; time and space do not exist here, because they have no meaning for the soul and intellect that can view all things simultaneously. Forgiveness, love, knowledge, and creative energy all combine to realize in Eden the complete development of mental and spiritual liberty. It is the state of perfection of the universal humanity, in which the individuality is ever apparent too. Blake sums up its essential nature in the following lines:

> Our wars are wars of life, & wounds of love
> With intellectual spears, & long winged arrows of thought.
> Mutual in one another's love and wrath all renewing
> We live as One Man; for contracting our infinite senses
> We behold multitude, or expanding, we behold as one,
> As One Man all the Universal Family, and that One Man
> We call Jesus the Christ; and he in us, and we in him
> Live in perfect harmony in Eden, the land of life,
> Giving, receiving, and forgiving each other's trespasses.
> *Jerusalem* 38, 14-22

Man cannot live for ever in the realm of pure thought; he must descend for rest from the daytime of intellectual activity to a night ruled by the affections. Thus as Eden is the world of the intellect and is ruled by the sun, so Beulah is the region of the emotional life and its symbol is the moon.

As mankind—symbolized by the Universal Man, Albion—sinks into repose in Beulah, the separation of the sexes takes place. To comfort and to delight man, a feminine counterpart comes into being, called by Blake the "emanation." Every soul in Beulah is thus divided into a masculine identity and a feminine emanation. At the moment of return to Eden, the division of sexes will again disappear, the soul being rejoined into perfect unity.

We have seen that the ideal of love in the sense of the love of God and of the universal brotherhood of mankind is the dominant feature of the life of Eden. In a similar sense, sexual love finds its perfect realization in Beulah. Love which forgets the selfhood through wholehearted affection for another;

the joy of a physical union which can, even momentarily, lift two separate beings into a higher state of mutual adoration and spiritual harmony; earthly love in all its highest manifestations, both emotional and physical, and purged of its base ingredients—lust, jealousy, and repression: such is the sexual love of Beulah. Blake saw very clearly that, while much of the sorrow of a fallen world is bound up with a distorted conception of love, the answer does not lie in an attempt to deny its physical aspect. To do so is to stifle the vital energy that is the very core of human existence, creating far more misery than it can cure and turning much potential joy into frustration and sorrow. Physical love, one of the greatest gifts of God, has been perverted in the Fallen World because of man's lust for self-gratification and woman's passion for jealous dominion over her mate. As with everything else, the answer is developed understanding that the way to happiness is to be found in helping others to their own fulfilment rather than in seeking one's own ends at their expense. So regarded, Blake considered physical love, the most intimate of human experiences, to be the most likely means of awakening the average person to the realization of the existence of an eternal world beyond the range of normal earthly perceptions. Ideal physical love is thus a vital step in the development of the human understanding as it searches to comprehend the love of God. As such its place is in Beulah, the gateway to Eden.

While Beulah exists to restore the soul, the danger arises that the soul may be lulled into passivity by its delights and cease to aspire to the renewed mental activity of Eden, which is its proper home. Such failure on man's part to exercise to the full the capacities with which God had endowed him, Blake considered to be the fundamental error, and the cause of the Fall. Beulah is thus a transitional world: while it is the threshold of Eden, error may here be accepted and the Fall begin.

If the soul thus falls prey to error, the essential humanity is not destroyed, but sinks into a deep sleep from which it will not awaken until the Last Judgment. At this moment the selfhood divides from the soul in the form of the "spectre." It is this spectre which becomes the Fallen Man: "Man is born a Spectre or Satan & is altogether an Evil."[23]

The masculine spectre is the face which the created man presents to the world, an aspect of pure materialism and self-interest, concealing the affections and denying imagination. His feminine emanation remains to guard his sleeping identity in Beulah, speaking to man in this world through his conscience, thoughts, and dreams, which in his fallen ignorance he is ashamed of and seeks to hide from his fellows.

The concept of masculine and feminine attributes in Blake's symbolism is apt to cause confusion, because he uses familiar terms in a sense different from that normally understood by them. We must remember that his imagery, as always, has both generalized and special meanings. Every person in this world has both masculine and feminine aspects of personality, not peculiar to the two sexes as we think of them, but mingled in each, and representing the selfhood as opposed to the conscience.

Blake believed implicitly that woman was created in Beulah to be the companion of man and that it was her true nature to be dependent upon him. Just as man may fall by turning away from the active imaginative life, so may woman through denying her dependence upon man and seeking to dominate him. Her powerful tool to this end is, of course, her physical charms, and also the wilful refusal of them. Her success, if achieved, results in man's surrender to the passive aspects of Beulah, which we have seen precipitates the Fall. Out of the desire for power over man arises jealousy, the besetting sin of womankind. When she becomes dominant, she urges man to pursue materialistic ends and to deny his imaginative self. This is what Blake means by the triumph of the "Female Will" in the Fallen World.

The reader must again be cautioned against being too literal in interpretation. Blake symbolizes two different aspects of human nature as the masculine and feminine principles: he does not, of course, imply that there are no jealous and materialistic men and no magnanimous and imaginative women. The dominance of the Female Will, which is the besetting sin of life in our world, is the pursuit of vain ends and the disregarding of visionary life. Thus Blake speaks in broad terms and cries out for the sacrifice of worldliness to the development of spiritual understanding when he proclaims: "In Eternity Woman is the Emanation of Man; she has No Will of her own. There is no such thing in Eternity as a Female Will."[24]

The complete cycle of human experience, as Blake conceives it, is thus made up of a twofold and of a fourfold alternation. Eden and Beulah are parts of both cycles. Before the individual accepts error, the soul alternates between these two stages as between night and day. The passive and feminine characteristics of Beulah are a necessary restorative for the eternal humanity after the intensity of the mental warfare of Eden. Temporarily this relaxation is desirable, but the danger is that initiative will be lost and the masculine attributes of the spirit will permanently accept the domination of the feminine. This constitutes the fundamental error. The divine humanity sinks to rest in Beulah, guarded over by the emanations—the Daughters of Beulah—and the spectre is precipitated into Ulro. Now that it has fallen into error, the soul in its passage back to salvation must complete the fourfold cycle from Beulah to Ulro, thence upward through Generation to Beulah again before the return to Eden can be made.

As Eden is characterized by creative intelligence and the divine energy which is life, so Ulro is ruled by the pure abstract rationality of moral law, ruthlessly applicable to all cases irrespective of individuality and unguided by imaginative insight. Ulro is the realm of the empty heart and of barren passivity; it is a world of coldness and emptiness in the midst of the endless sea of materialism and chaos. Its topography recalls those portions of our created world into which the transforming power of the human mind, heart, and spirit—the aspects of man which are in the image of God—has never come. Its description reminds us vividly of the Hell of Dante's *Inferno:*

> There is the Cave, the Rock, the Tree, the Lake of Udan Adan,
> The Forest and the Marsh and the Pits of bitumen deadly,
> The Rocks of solid fire, the Ice valleys, the Plains
> Of burning sand, the rivers, cataract & Lakes of Fire,
> The Islands of the fiery Lakes, the Trees of Malice, Revenge
> And black Anxiety, and the Cities of the Salamandrine men,
>
> .   .   .   .
>
> .   .   .   .
>
> The land of darkness flamed, but no light & no repose:
> The land of snows of trembling & of iron hail incessant:
> The land of earthquakes, and the land of woven labyrinths:
> The land of snares & traps & wheels & pit-falls & dire mills:
> The Voids, the Solids, & the land of clouds & regions of waters
> With their inhabitants, in the Twenty-seven Heavens beneath Beulah:
> Self-righteousness conglomerating against the Divine Vision.
>
> Jerusalem 13, 38-43, 46-52

Blake in his earlier works equates Ulro with our present world, and attributes its creation to the "Angry God of this World," or Satan, "the Jehovah of the Bible being no other than he who dwells in flaming fire."[25] However, while Blake was at first appalled by the hellish character of this world to the exclusion of everything else, our previous discussion of "limits" has pointed out that, as time went on, he came more and more to realize that there is still a divine principle at work giving form to chaos. Imagination, though fallen, is not annihilated even in Ulro. Personified by "Los," this imaginative power begins to rebuild a replica of Jerusalem, the eternal city of freedom, in the void. This is "Golgonooza," the city of art: art being a vision of eternal truth stamped with material form. As time goes by, Los' task becomes enlarged. He forms the "Mundane Shell," a firm refuge in the void. He seeks endlessly to capture the aimless spirits who wander in the wastes of Ulro; provided with "human" forms woven for them by the Daughters of Beulah, they are reborn into the World of Generation within the confines of the Mundane Shell. Error having thus been given an established substance by imagination in a created world and in its generated forms, can now be recognized and cast out. Blake's developing ideas therefore tend increasingly to stress the divine elements of this world as opposed to the chaotic:

> ...whatever is visible to the Generated Man
> Is a Creation of mercy & love from the Satanic Void.
> *Jerusalem* 13, 44-45

Eventually all the accumulated error of the generated world will be recognized and cast back to Ulro, while all the spiritual elements wandering in chaos will receive definite form in the World of Generation. When this is accomplished, the redemption of the Fallen World will have been achieved. Ulro, the sum total of error, will be consumed. There being no more error to be redeemed, the World of Generation will disappear too, and only the eternal life of Eden and Beulah will remain. "Error is Created. Truth is Eternal. Error, or Creation, will be Burned up, & then, & not till Then, Truth or Eternity will appear."[26]

In closing our discussion of the four stages of Blake's circle of Destiny, we must emphasize the respects in which Ulro differs from the conventional idea of Hell. There is no place in Blake's system for a realm in which human souls who have violated the arbitrary commands of a tyrannical deity are condemned to everlasting punishment. As previously pointed out, Blake stresses that the essence of God is forgiveness. Man's error is that he voluntarily turns aside from this basic precept and, instead of forgiving his fellows as God forgives him, seeks to advance his selfhood at the expense of others. No matter how deeply the individual may sin, however, the forgiveness of God will abide with him, for God has established the limits of contraction and opacity so that no man can lose his soul in the void. However great the individual's guilt and however deep his ignorance, his error will eventually become manifest to him; he will then be able to cast aside his satanic selfhood and rejoin the great brotherhood of mankind in the universal salvation of Eden.

The final phase of Blake's mythology with which we must deal concerns the individual personality. We have discussed the nature of the error which leads to the Fall and we have studied Blake's views concerning the created and eternal worlds. We are still faced with the problem of what predisposes man to the acceptance of error. Up to now, we have dealt with man in his relation to the universe around him and to his fellow men; at this point we must turn to an examination of the man himself.

From his very early years, Blake was absorbed by the problem of human psychology. As his ideas on the subject developed, they resolved themselves into a conviction that every personality is compounded of four basic factors: reason, imagination, emotion, and the sensory mechanism. These form four great contraries which together shape the character of the universal man, Albion, and which, in greater and lesser proportions, are blended and interwoven into the life of every individual. Being universal attributes, they are included in the category which Blake terms "states." Each of these psychological characteristics has its personification in Blake's mythology. In the aggregate they are known as the "Zoas." In the earlier prophetic books the various Zoas appear sporadically and their personalities are only partially realized. Slowly the concept matured, until it reached full development in the middle of Blake's artistic career with the completion of the long epic in manuscript which bears their name, *The Four Zoas*. Thereafter they remained the key figures of Blake's symbolism.

The four are named "Los," "Luvah," "Urizen," and "Tharmas," and represent the imaginative, emotional, intellectual, and sensory aspects of man in that order. As universal attributes of the eternal humanity, all exist at every level of the Circle of Destiny. Each of them, however, is particularly associated with one of these levels. Los is in the ascendant in Eden, Luvah in Beulah, and Tharmas in Ulro, while this world is ruled by Urizen, the rational principle. Pictorially, they are represented by the four beasts of Ezekiel's vision and of the Book of Revelation, the same four beasts which since early times have symbolized the four evangelists. Thus Los is portrayed in human form, Luvah as a bull, Urizen by a lion, and Tharmas by an eagle. Except in the state of Eden, each has also an emanation. The emanation of Los is named "Enitharmon;" that of Luvah, "Vala;" that of Urizen, "Ahania;" and that of Tharmas, "Enion."

Of the four, the dominant figure—particularly of the later prophecies—is Los. In Eden he has another eternal name, which is "Urthona." As such he represents all the energy of the creative imaginative intellect which, as we have seen, is the essence of the eternal humanity. Such can only exist in a pure state in Eden. It is for this reason that Los is differentiated in the other worlds, since to whatever heights the divine imagination, the Poetic Genius, the spirit of prophecy may attain in lower spheres of existence, they are only an indication of the creative perfection of Eden.

The great function of Los is to keep "the Divine Vision in time of trouble."[27] In Beulah he seeks through vision to direct the aspirations of the humanity in repose toward the full life of Eden in order that he may return and not fall into error. After the Fall, Los becomes in Ulro the voice of the conscience by which man eventually becomes aware that he has not been cut off from his eternal life completely. In the World of Generation, he is the imaginative power which makes it possible for created man to commune at brief and ecstatic moments directly with God. As such, he is the Zoa whose influence is paramount in forming the personalities of the prophets, poets, and artists of this world, who stand out from other men because of the power of their imaginative genius. Enitharmon, the emanation of Los, may be thought of as representing prophetic and artistic inspiration.

As is the case with all of the aspects of human personality, the imaginative gift may become distorted in this world. The selfhood of the fallen Albion may assert itself by usurping and misdirecting even the imagination. Art may be turned to worldly ends instead of seeking its true goal of keeping before man a vision of eternity; similarly, the prophetic power may degenerate into superstition, necromancy, and the like. The Natural Man usually fails to recognize that imagination is a window into eternity, and regards it purely as wayward fancy, which of course it becomes when undeveloped or misdirected through ignorance. Los, as we have seen, is known by another name in Eden; in the same manner the fallen aspects of the imagination in Ulro and Generation are symbolized by the "Spectre of Urthona," a character of Blake's myth who wrangles with Los—the unfallen imagination—throughout much of *Jerusalem*.

While Los is the dominant figure of the later prophecies, especially of *Jerusalem*, in the earlier works he plays a role secondary to Urizen. This fits in with the fact, to which we have already called attention, that in later years Blake was more concerned with the spiritual aspects of the Fallen World than with its evils. As pure reason, neither illuminated by imagination nor influenced by feeling, Urizen is the cruel figure who dominates the earlier epics, one of which is called after him. Blake saw the fallacy inherent in much of the thinking of his day, as of ours, which tended to deny the existence of everything beyond the range of scientific proof and, as a corollary, which sought to prove the existence of God by material means. We have already seen how such an attitude is fundamentally opposed to the whole basis of Blake's beliefs.

Thus Urizen, the purely rational Zoa who seeks truth solely by an attempt to correlate the data of the fallen senses, is a satanic figure. His guiding principle of "rational demonstration" is anathema to Blake, who equates his philosophy to that of Bacon, Newton and Locke—human beings in whom Blake considered that the Urizenic character dominated the other Zoas, and who appear as sinister characters of his mythology. As Urizen cannot perceive beyond the range of the senses of the "cavern'd Man," all outside their reach seems to him to be a chaos which is seeking to close in on him; he has no comprehension of the love of God or of the joy of eternity. To protect himself from this terrifying unknown, his only hope as he sees it is to set up rational laws and to command obedience at the price of death. Hence in the earlier prophetic books Urizen appears as the creator of this world, which at that time Blake considered to be a work of cruelty rather than of mercy. Throughout Blake's epics Urizen proclaims the Moral Law, which he writes in books of iron and brass. He is frequently equated with Jehovah, and the Moral Law with the Decalogue; consequently Blake always represents the Moral Law pictorially by the Mosaic tablets.

The Moral Law is, of course, the basis of all earthly systems, the evil and stultifying effects of which, in Blake's view, we have already considered. In its insistence that a system can be found which will fit every situation, Reason ties down every phase of life with restrictive laws, stifling all energy and all natural development. And so, Urizen proclaims:

"Lo! I unfold my darkness, and on
This rock place with strong hand the Book
Of eternal brass, written in my solitude:

Laws of peace, of love, of unity,
Of pity, compassion, forgiveness;
Let each chuse one habitation,
His ancient infinite mansion,
One command, one joy, one desire,
One curse, one weight, one measure,
One King, one God, one Law."
                                    Urizen, 4

By the very fact that man is made in God's image, he requires flexibility for development; rigid law applied indiscriminately will strangle all creativeness. Under Urizen's rule, mankind forgets its greater destiny and becomes blindly bound to the Fallen World:

Six days they shrunk up from existence,
And on the seventh day they rested,
And they bless'd the seventh day, in sick hope,
And forgot their eternal life.
                                    Urizen, 23

As with all tyrannies, the tyrant is bewildered that men are recalcitrant, but he can see no other solution than that of becoming more despotic:

He in darkness clos'd view'd all his race,
And his soul sicken'd! he curs'd
Both sons & daughters; for he saw
That no flesh nor spirit could keep
His iron laws one moment.
                                    Urizen, 23

One of the most powerful weapons which Urizen wields to subjugate individuals is organized religion. Instead of revealing to men the love and forgiveness of God, Urizen fashions God after his own likeness as a being who demands absolute obedience to arbitrary law. Urizen thus extends his hold over men through their fear of eternal punishment at the hand of God. Urizen is a "puritan" too. He cannot admit that pleasure is divine in origin unless misused; rather, he must banish all pleasure as potentially destructive. He, therefore, casts out his emanation, Ahania, who was created in Beulah as an embodiment of the divine pleasure which provides relaxation from the mental warfare of Eden.

Such then is Urizen, the rational principle of the human personality. Although he is the personification of the reason, we must not make the mistake of considering that Blake was anti-intellectual. Such an assumption shows a basic misunderstanding of the distinction which Blake draws between intelligence and rationalism. He is quite clear on this point, as may be seen from the following quotation from the preface to the fourth chapter of *Jerusalem:* "What are the Treasures of Heaven which we are to lay up for ourselves, are they any other than Mental Studies & Performances? What is the Life of Man but Art & Science?...What is the Joy of Heaven but Improvement in the things of the Spirit? What are the Pains of Hell but Ignorance, Bodily Lust, Idleness & devastation of the things of the Spirit?... To Labour in Knowledge is to Build up Jerusalem, and to Despise Knowledge is to Despise Jerusalem & her Builders....Let every Christian, as much as in him lies, engage himself openly & publicly before all the World in some Mental pursuit for the Building up of Jerusalem."

It is Blake's insistence, however, that the mind must be guided by the heart and by the imagination. If pure reason is allowed to dominate, man's potentially infinite perceptions will be bound down to this world, from which all love will disappear and with it any possibility of salvation. In the Eternal Man all the Zoas are in harmony, realizing their proper relationship and delighting in their brotherhood. It is only when one seeks to usurp the functions of one or more of the others, that the Fall comes. As long as Urthona is dominant there is no trouble, but when Albion allows his rational faculties to annihilate imagination, he can no longer sustain himself in eternity, but falls into Ulro, where imagination is dead and the heart empty. Conversely, when Albion in the Fallen World denies his selfhood, because of the love of God as revealed to him through Christ's sacrifice, the Zoas return to harmony in his bosom and Urizen—who in his fallen state is always represented as blind and aged, with long hair and beard—is restored to the beauty of eternal youth.[28]

The two other Zoas are far less important in Blake's myth, which deals largely with the eternal warfare between the two great contraries, Los and Urizen, on all the levels of existence. The third Zoa, Luvah, represents man's emotional life. This aspect of the personality is also vitally necessary for that true development of vision which will raise man from his fallen state and permit him to regain his immortal stature. As is the case with Urizen, however, Luvah may seek to dominate and this will spell disaster. Just as man cannot yield to pure reason and survive, so he cannot follow a rule of unbridled desire. On the other hand, release from tyranny can only come when passion can no longer be controlled and rises to smite oppression. Hence Luvah has another aspect, that of revolt against law—at times necessary for salvation, but inclined also to get out of hand and itself turn to paths of injustice. In this aspect of revolt, Luvah appears in the worlds of Generation and Ulro as the fiery youth, "Orc," the rebel against authority. This figure plays a large role in some of the earlier prophecies, but later Blake came to feel that not in revolt but in forgiveness lay the way to salvation. The attainment of universal brotherhood demands sacrifice of the selfhood out of love for others. The great example of this is, of course, Jesus, who through love assumed the supreme sacrifice of His passion so that man "might have life and have it more abundantly." Thus it is that at the time of the final casting off of error, Jesus appears to Albion in "Luvah's robes of blood." Thus we have a third aspect of Luvah, that of divine love made manifest in this world: "God becomes as we are, that we may be as he is."[29]

Vala, the emanation of Luvah, is the most important of the female counterparts of the Zoas. As the feminine aspect of the emotional life, she represents the beauty of the natural world. In Beulah she fulfils her function in providing for the restoration of Albion through the tenderness of woman's love and the happiness which the spirit gains from the contemplation of beauty. She can easily become a delusion, however, and after the Fall Vala is transformed into a cruel and jealous mistress, seeking to blind man to his imaginative life and to make him her slave. She fosters sentiment and pity, desirable adjuncts of creative feeling but, because of their passive nature which has its origins in the selfhood, fatal poisons if permitted to become abstract ideals of conduct. Under her dominion, man pursues material instead of spiritual ends; she is responsible for much of the superficiality of society as it reveals itself in a desire for worldly position and outward material display. As Urizen is the king of this world, she is its queen; Urizen in the Fallen World may be likened to Satan, and Vala to Hecate.

We have already discussed Blake's views concerning the evils of the dominant Female Will. Vala is the personification of this dominance; as such she is sometimes referred to as "Vala-Rahab" and further identified as "Babylon," the harlot of the Book of Revelation. Mystery and superstition, as deliberately fostered by organized religions in order to enslave men's minds through the intoxicating power of false emotionalism, are the most sinister manifestations of Vala.

Blake was a great opponent of the tendency in his day to read moral values into the beauty of the natural world. No man had a greater appreciation of the beauty of nature nor derived more joy from its study than did he, as many of his lyrics and many of the finest passages of his longer poems testify. However, as woman is the emanation of man, so nature flourishes under man's control and can become hideous and evil without it: "Where man is not, nature is barren."[30] It is the function of beauty to delight the mind and to restore the soul. If properly so regarded, it stimulates the creative powers, being a visible symbol of divine love at work in this world. Conversely, the creative powers can be destroyed if form, which is purely of this earth, is worshipped to the exclusion of content, which is of the eternal imagination. Human values cannot be found in nature, for the true humanity resides not in the outward forms of the world, but in the mind and spirit. The worship of Vala is, therefore, one to which man in a fallen natural world is much inclined, but which is a false religion that can easily prove fatal if the bounds of its true and fruitful development are overstepped.

Tharmas, the last of the Zoas, is a rather shadowy figure; he is the only one who is closely associated with the physical aspects of man. He is the latent and almost unconscious sensory power which is animated by feeling, intelligence, and spirit to complete the perfectly integrated body of the eternal man, Albion. He gives to every form its permanent identity which is never lost but is part of its eternal individuality. Just as in Dante's *Divine Comedy* the earthly form of men is not lost with the death of their bodies, so Tharmas is found on all the levels of existence. However, since the perceptive powers of man after the Fall are much less acute than in his unfallen state, the physical aspect of man grows more apparent in proportion as the spiritual becomes less so. "Man has no Body distinct from his Soul; for that call'd Body is a portion of Soul discern'd by the five Senses, the chief inlets of Soul in this age."[31] As is the case with all the Zoas, Tharmas becomes a hideously distorted version of his eternal self after the Fall takes place. From the unifying power who gives identity to the soul, he becomes the unrestrained energy of the Fallen World. He manifests himself in the brute violence of animate nature and in the irresistible natural forces of the created world. The symbol of Tharmas after the Fall is the ever-restless sea, continually changing its form, uncontrolled by mind, yet all powerful; in this "sea of time and space"—the all-conquering materialism of Ulro—man is overwhelmed, his identity lost and, but for the grace of God who in mercy puts limits to the Fall, his soul would be annihilated.

The emanation of Tharmas is Enion, the passive materiality of the Fallen World, as Tharmas is its uncontrollable energy. Enion is a strange primordial force. In common with all the eternal powers of man, she once shared equally in the full joy of the universal world; with the Fall she was thrust furthest of all away from the creative energy which is life itself down into the Hell of inert material form. Here, blind and age-bent, shut in a rocky cavern, she mourns eternally. She is that inner voice of man that at times seems a strange and intangible reminiscence of his Golden Age, rising from the depths of his being and speaking from the remotest ages of the created world with a depth of wisdom that goes back to the very foundations of human experience in the fallen state. The laments of Enion form some of the most impressive and poetically successful passages of the prophetic books. She is Blake's version of the Earth Mother of all mythologies.

Such are the personalities of the Four Zoas and of their emanations, Blake's symbolical figures personifying the basic contrary forces which together form the character of every individual. In the eternal state they manage to combine intense energy with complete harmony, preserving a dynamic balance in much the same way as does the atom with its nucleus and its swiftly-moving electrons. As soon, however, as man becomes inclined towards the development of his selfhood, the harmony is disrupted. Reason, desire, or the sensory aspects of man strive for dominion, upsetting the proper control which must be exercised by the divine power of vision. The Fall occurs, and eternity cannot be regained until, through experience, man once again learns to bring the Zoas into their proper relationship.

We have examined the broad outlines of the mythology which Blake found it necessary to create in order to suggest the many-sidedness of human psychology and experience as it appeared to him. There are many elaborations of the main theme which occur in his works, and his ideas naturally kept developing from the earlier works to the later ones. In addition to the characters of the myth whom we have discussed, there are many others who appear briefly and in minor roles. It is hoped, however, that what has been here set forth will indicate the main outlines of Blake's beliefs and will give a sufficient key to his individual method of expression and to the meaning of his most important symbols, so that his works may be approached with understanding.

NOTES

[1] William Blake, *Blake: Complete Writings*, ed. Geoffrey Keynes (Oxford: Oxford Univ. Press, 1966), p. 605. Subsequent references to Blake's writings will be to this text.

[2] *Ibid.*, p. 609.

[3] Bernard Blackstone, *English Blake*, (Cambridge, England: 1949), p. 347.

[4] One cannot, of course, in a literal sense create a mythology, which is by definition traditional. Blake uses in his prophetic books characters with names of his own devising who are not to be thought of as individuals, but as personifications of human attributes. Symbolic in their intent, and freed in their actions from normal human limitations, they have many of the characteristics of the figures of ancient and widely-known mythologies. However, Blake wished to be sure that his symbolism would not be obscured by prior associations and thus chose to reject accepted mythology and create new personifications. Because of their nature, it is convenient

to interpret the definition of mythology somewhat freely and to think of them as mythological personages.

⁵ Letter to Rev. Dr. Trusler, August 23, 1799, p. 793.

⁶ From Robinson's Diary as given in Symons, *William Blake*, p. 255.

⁷ *There Is No Natural Religion*, II, p. 97.

⁸ Letter to Thomas Butts, November 22, 1802, p. 818

⁹ *The Everlasting Gospel*, p. 757.

¹⁰ *The Marriage of Heaven and Hell*, p. 154.

¹¹ Ephesians vi, 12. Quoted in Greek on the title page of *The Four Zoas*, because the King James version had modified the passage.

¹² *Vision of the Last Judgment*, p. 615.

¹³ The first of these quotations is from Blake's annotations to *An Apology for the Bible in a Series of Letters Addressed to Thomas Paine* by Richard Watson, Bishop of London (Keynes, p. 395); the second from plate 52 of *Jerusalem*.

¹⁴ *Vision of the Last Judgment*, p. 615.

¹⁵ One of the "Proverbs of Hell," p. 151. A major difficulty of Blake's symbolism is his frequent use of the same symbols with different meanings, requiring great discrimination on the reader's part as to what is intended. Thus "Hell" may be employed in a more usual sense to indicate our present world of suffering; on the other hand, as used here it signifies the mental attitude of the more radical and imaginative portion of humanity as viewed from the static "Heaven" of the conventional "angels."

¹⁶ *Jerusalem*, 43, 35-36.

¹⁷ *Jerusalem*, 47, 17.

¹⁸ Inscriptions in reversed writing occur in a number of places in *Milton* and *Jerusalem*, and have particular significance. They indicate truths that are apparent to those in the unfallen state, but are inverted by the Natural Man of this world; as seen from beyond the confines of the created world, looking in, they would appear the right way around.

¹⁹ "Many suppose that before the Creation All was Solitude & Chaos. This is the most pernicious Idea that can enter the Mind, as it takes away all sublimity from the Bible & Limits All Existence to Creation & to Chaos.... Eternity Exists, and All things in Eternity, Independent of Creation which was an act of Mercy." *(Vision of the Last Judgment*, p. 614.)

²⁰ *Ibid.*, p. 613..

²¹ From the ms. poem, "Auguries of Innocence," p. 431.

²² *The Marriage of Heaven and Hell*, p. 149.

²³ *Jerusalem*, plate 52.

²⁴ *Vision of the Last Judgment*, p. 613.

²⁵ *The Marriage of Heaven and Hell*, p. 150.

²⁶ *Vision of the Last Judgment*, p. 617. The final destruction of error and the triumph of truth are described in the remarkable apocalyptic vision which constitutes Night the Ninth of *The Four Zoas*.

²⁷ *Jerusalem*, 95, 20.

²⁸ See *Jerusalem* 96, 3-97, 8. For the rejuvenation of Urizen, see *The Four Zoas* IX, 161-195.

²⁹ *There Is No Natural Religion*, II, p. 98.

³⁰ *The Marriage of Heaven and Hell*, p. 152.

³¹ *Ibid.*, p. 149.

The Family of Man

Mutual in one anothers love and wrath all renewing
We live as One man; for contracting our infinite senses
We behold multitude; or expanding: we behold as one,
As One Man all the Universal Family; and that One Man
We call Jesus the Christ: and he in us and we in him,
Live in perfect harmony in Eden the land of life,
Giving, receiving, and forgiving each others trespasses   (J-35)

ALBION [emanation: Jerusalem] = One of the Family of Man

Zoas: "Four Mighty Ones are in every Man" (4Z-I:9).

URIZEN (Wisdom-Reason)	URTHONA (Imagination-Intuition)	LUVAH (Love-Feelings)	THARMAS (Instinct-Sensation)

FALL INTO DIVISION

SATAN/URIZEN [em. Ahania] (Negation)	LOS [em. Enitharmon] (Afflicted Inspiration)	ORC [em. Vala] (Repressed Energy: War)	THARMAS [em. Enion] (Materialism)

Sons of Albion paired with their emanations,
the Daughters of Albion

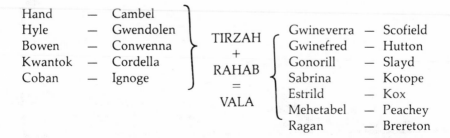

Hand — Cambel
Hyle — Gwendolen
Bowen — Conwenna
Kwantok — Cordella
Coban — Ignoge

TIRZAH
+
RAHAB
=
VALA

Gwineverra — Scofield
Gwinefred — Hutton
Gonorill — Slayd
Sabrina — Kotope
Estrild — Kox
Mehetabel — Peachey
Ragan — Brereton

David Reisman

Imaginary picture of Blake as a young revolutionary

Eric Chaet

Report to Blake

Blake, I won't read your work again right now.
Maybe never, or maybe sometime
when I don't know what else to do.

I'm busy consulting my imagination:
how to redeem my routines
resist the normal attacks on my splendid potential
& make unprecedented moves of mental warfare:
poems, songs, polemics, talk, pictures, forms, acts.

Your London was a bloody town—
wars of seven, thirty, one hundred years
against the French, Algonquin, Spaniards, Turks.
You went there to work and burn yourself out
in acid and metal and ink and unconsummated scheming.

They wouldn't buy your epics on London streets, tho.
I doubt they could look right at you.
& what you had done was imperfect, too—
too many characters—frantic, reeling—so baroque.

I barely caught your intent, the hope
& strategy in the midst of your fallen giants.
I flashed back then into the rhythms of my own
experience in the mundane shell.

What an advance of thought!
Yet how far from actually swaying the general will
from ending the continual, sporadic Armageddon,
the exploitation, suffering, resignation, fierce competition, bitter respites.

Here's how it balances:
I rise from sleep unprecedented

my hope throbbing
my resolution clean & bright
my path & possibilities clearer for your strange lights.

I chew your protein, Blake, & spit out your gristle.

If others of us still in the midst of the battle
can struggle to sufficient wakefulness & insist
your moves may yet come to fruition, Blake.

Janet Warner

Vala

As the moon changes
And the tide
As the earth turns
So I ride.

So I spin
and recreate
Wheels within
To be my fate.

Thomas Paladino

Half a Spring Song for William Blake

A galloping fire, a beast
in the gardenyard of myth
whose hoofbeats sound on and on,
hunting clues of the ancient chant,
or the hard apple that hangs ripe
beyond the wisdoms of a flower...

On the lawn, turning the sundial,
your children do not recognize you.
Yet I cherish your vines of creation.
And sometimes I repeat Whitman's name
as loud and clear as anyone dares.
And, yes, I can still imagine lovers
kissing in the coming century.

Fred Goss

Sound the Voice of the Bard: Reading Blake Aloud

Poetry is of the voice and of the ear. Its words must be brought to life, must be freed from the bondage of page, must be spoken, chanted, sung. This is especially true of the poems of William Blake. Reading this poetry aloud finds the fullness of line, the dance of syllable. It brings us straight into the text, into the mind and heart and skillful hand of the man who left these wonders here for us. In our mouths the words become psalms, incantations, seeds of light.

The rewards of involvement with Blake are many. To those who give voice to his words comes abundance. Reading him aloud brings a far clearer sense of his vision as a comprehensible whole. It is only through having given sound to his lines that I, and probably many others as well, ever came to believe that Blake actually wrote real poetry and not some extraordinarily complicated and interesting ranting. I have often suspected that critics who go to these poems simply to solve the mystery of their meaning have never heard the music these words are shaped into. Reading him aloud brings self-assurance to the voice for other songs. The maturation of ear and tongue in response to these long and ever-varying lines carries over to practically everything else in English. It led me to an openness to music, a readiness of tongue with *The Faerie Queen* and Dorn's *Gunslinger* that I'd never known before. Reading him aloud brings surefootedness in slippery places, a willingness to let the poem reveal itself in its own time. We learn to tolerate uncertainty; we gain negative capability. We know we understand the fit and flow of image somewhere—even if only in our teeth. We can always reread— go back—check things out—later. We learn to aim for the feeling of the whole of it: the Visions revealed through the force of word.

We know of the importance of the illustrations. They are a way in. Ideally we would read aloud straight from a library full of original prints, each page colored and glittering. But centering on sound and pulse opens a way into the heart of the work not trod by the gazers at pictures and certainly not imagined by those silently reading, thinking this magic's a puzzle.

It is good to work into the increasingly challenging body of works in a more or less chronological sequence. Do not omit *The Book of Thel, The Marriage of Heaven and Hell, Visions of the Daughters of Albion, The Book* of *Urizen*, *The Four Zoas*, *Milton*, and *Jerusalem*, pretty much in that order. Allow time: a full year for the *Zoas*, *Milton* and *Jerusalem*; then read them again in another year. There needs to be a break between readings, rest between labors; though there have been marathon sessions—all of *Jerusalem* on an immensely hot Kansas summer afternoon into evening. A veteran of this and other major skirmishes of mental warfare traded with a reader of Joyce's *Finnegan's Wake*, tales of reading *Jerusalem* aloud. "And did you have an epiphany?" asked the latterday Daedalus. "O, dozens," was the bardish boast.

Reading Blake aloud takes one nearer the magical roots of language, to spell, to incantation, and it is almost inevitably enacted as ritual by its circle of readers. It demands the preparation of a sanctuary away from hassle and busyness, an orderly progression of ritual gestures—each functional—each a part of the whole. We begin with security, isolation, the descent into the kiva. This must be arranged beforehand. Hide the cars down the block; post quarantine signs; disconnect the phone so Beth can't call; drop a tree in the lane. Arrange a long clear period to read into. Allow at least half again as long as you know it will take. Forget dinner. The idea is seamlessness.

WHAT TO SERVE:
Coffee or black tea for stamina
Cannabis for liftoff
Jack Daniels for the hard parts
Well water in a mason jar for parched throats
Popcorn afterwards

The reader's text is the Keynes Oxford edition—maybe even a hardback, because the paper cover always rips off by the time you get to *The Book of Urizen*, followed by page after page from front and back: duct tape the only solution. Silver streaks of the stuff mark Blake almost alone on my bookshelves —testimony to a book read exhaustively and exuberantly. In the Keynes text the lines appear on the page to be read. No footnotes, variable type face or other extraneous apparatus distracts the eyes. Punctuation guides us through the patterns of sound and thought. But even with this text, so smooth to follow, speech must be given priority over the eye. The flow of line and phrase is more mouthed than seen; the tongue and throat, the hand keeping time are the final arbiters of the real punctuation.

We read to, with, and against music of a magnitude equal to Blake's own. Originally this was always John Coltrane—always the most demanding and rewarding records available—*Selflessness*, *Love Supreme*, *Meditations*, *Live at the Village Vanguard Again*. Later Coltrane led us to others: Tyner's "Walk Spirit, Talk Spirit", lots of Pharoah Sanders, Ali Akbar Khan's reflective improvisations from the beginnings of time. The music gets us moving in the right direction and at Blake's speed. At the beginning, it suggests the measure with trustworthy accuracy. It helps us find that kind of energy running through our own systems—to make things come that clear. We stack up four albums, take some deep breaths and roll into Chapter I of *Jerusalem*, not unlike pushing the prow of a canoe into a rain-swollen river, a commitment to consequences and power we also frequently make.

At first we must avoid being intimidated by the effort our bodies know it is going to take to read, straight through, something like several nights of the *Zoas*. It takes bravery, recklessness and faith in the wisdom and compassion of this poet. The body must be convinced that it can do the actual sitting it will take to get through. We begin by stretching, bending, flexing—a good limbering before the start. Once we're moving into it, the body finds its own way to participate: immediately by being caught in the throat, in the tongue by the poem's speaking itself, or indirectly through the inevitable sitting down dance, the *daven*, always encountered in the middle of those long chanting stretches of vision, of wrath, of pity, of unbroken lucidity. We sit on the floor. Most good readings happen down here. Furniture, at least the affordable sorts, binds us, preventing the lotuses, sprawls and hambone called up by the poem. The floor puts some people off. They think it fit only for kids and feet. Get down. We keep the vision among us—within our circle.

As with any activity that involves that balance of mind, body, spirit and feeling—like making love or flyfishing—this reading tests the cooperation of our four regions. We soon find if we're prepared for it. A little reading propelled by the right music drives out the most tenacious spectre. Exorcism. Like fasting or running, it leaves us cleaner and clearer and stronger—capable of things—literally inspired with fresh breath.

A record ends exactly at a climax or a resolution and change of reader. Another begins. We don't have time or reason to wonder if there's another yet to play. And finally there comes the exact cadence of the end of things—Trane's final time around on the forever ending "Psalm" on *Love Supreme* coming just as the Big Vision of *Milton* opens up and eases down into the vision of the Daughters of Enitharmon at the Looms, weaving the fibers of being into forms. All things, this reading, its parts, finding their own forms.

We are done. There is silence for a while. We get up, get out for a walk—beneath the stars, toward a sunrise, down a busy city street at noon—these walls, these windows, the works of Man. It is unnecessary to say much. We don't feel obliged to talk, as the power called up by the reading still flows warmly through our being.

There is much loveliness throughout Blake where the mouth revels in the feel of each word: the lark and wild thyme and all their hosts unveiled, seen and heard as visions of the Daughters of Beulah lamenting over Ololon

(*Milton*, 31); the grain of sand to be found in Lambeth containing a gateway to the Eternal worlds (*Jerusalem*, 41); Enion lamenting the fall to experience (*Four Zoas*, III); the spiritual joinery of Golgonooza (*Jerusalem*, 12). These sing to us with as much beauty as anything in the language—as anything in language. These must be found through the voice, the ear, the heart, the rhythm of pulse. When read with a silent tongue, they stare dully back at us, a puzzle for the mind. Stop everything this moment, find silence within and without and fit these lines to your breath:

> But others of the Sons of Los build Moments & Minutes & hours
> And Days & Months & Years & Ages & Periods, wondrous buildings;
> And every Moment has a Couch of gold for soft repose,
> (A Moment equals a pulsation of the artery),
> And between every two Moments stands a Daughter of Beulah
> To feed the Sleepers on their Couches with maternal care.
> And every Minute has an azure Tent with silken Veils:
> And every Hour has a bright golden Gate carved with skill:
> And every Day & Night has walls of brass & Gates of adamant,
> Shining like precious Stones & ornamented with appropriate signs:
> And every Month a silver paved Terrace builded high:
> And every Year invulnerable Barriers with high Towers:
> And every Age is moated deep with Bridges of silver & gold:
> And every Seven Ages is Incircled with a Flaming Fire.
> And Seven Ages is amounting to Two Hundred Years.
> Each has its Guard, each Moment, Minute, Hour, Day, Month & Year.
> All are the work of Fairy hands of the Four Elements:
> The Guards are Angels of Providence on duty evermore.
> Every Time less than a pulsation of the artery
> Is equal in its period & value to Six Thousand Years
> For in this Period the Poet's Work is Done: and all the Great
> Events of Time start forth & are conceiv'd in such a Period,
> Within a Moment, a Pulsation of the Artery.

(Milton, 28)

Michael Chrisman

Coming into the Cabal, Unawares

Oh, I don't know,
Blake, you devil; when I think
how I sat with friends around that kitchen table
and moved the ketchup just so,

then Fred balanced a spoon, the salt
behind a toaster. Secret reason!
We searched you out, my ductile dear,
(you) blent like oil slick on asphalt.
But our road show
sort of limped on three cylinders, till the midnight
we finally bowed our heads in smoke:

the cat stepped lightly onto the piano

keys—then Ah! Secret inference! The unconscious
exalt! World putting word to rout.
The lamb unbending its back legs
to greet the ram (et al). Far out.

Arthur Sze

The Axis

I hear on the radio that Anastasio Somoza
has fled Managua, is already in Florida,

and about to disappear on a world cruise.
Investigators in this country are meanwhile

analyzing the volcanic eruptions on Io,
or are studying the erratic respiratory

pattern of a sea horse to find the origin
of life. The fact is, we know so little,

but are so quick to interpret, to fit facts
to our schemata. For instance, the final

collapse of the Nicaraguan dictatorship
makes me wonder if the process of change

is a dialectic. Or is our belief in a
pattern what sustains it? Is the recent

history a clear pattern: a dictatorship
followed by a popular revolt, followed by

a renewed dictatorship exercising greater
repression, ended by a violent revolution?

I want to speak of opposites that depend
on and define each other: as in a

conversation, you feel silence in speech,
or speech in silence. Or, as in a

counterpoint when two melodies overlap and
resonate, you feel the sea in the desert,

or feel that the body and mind are
inseparable. Then you wonder if day and

night are indeed opposites. You knock the
gyroscope off the axis of its spinning,

so that one orientation in the world vanishes,
and the others appear infinite.

Jack Hirschman

you evoke in a flash
the ecstacy of myself
running across the field
of childhood into a wall
of trees I remember,
I remember it was no
film I was in, I was inside the immensity inside me,
terrified on the run perfect with mystery, pregnant
with life inside me, small and simultaneously giant
before the trees I poured toward, my body orgasmic
before scum had a name,
my nature perfect before
God sat down at sunset
and said he was lonely
and spread a city over
his bread, and spread
the cover over my head
and gave me school
and death and dream
and lovelight until
love died and dyed
me black as this ink
that runs the rest
of my night life
down the coughs
of these sheets singing
the field of the only
moment I breathed
before all these
chains were about me

Karleen Middleton Murphy

The Emanation: Creativity and Creation

In Blake's myth, the Emanation is the feminine half of an edenic androgynous whole. The unfallen Emanation shares one will and one intellect with her Zoa, the masculine half. She is equated with love, inspiration, liberty, and the principle of pity. She provides "joy" (a term with sexual connotations) and repose after labor. She is also capable of unconditional forgiveness of sins and voluntary self-annihilation. The fallen Emanation, however, is another matter. She acts out a negation or reversal of her eternal function. Usually, she runs around wailing, providing misery and discontent, for an Emanation divided from her Zoa is "an ever-weeping melancholy Shadow" (J53, E201), and a Zoa without an Emanation becomes a Spectre "insane, and most deform'd" (J33, E177).[1]

In addition to representing half of the masculine/feminine dichotomy, the four Zoas, on the allegorical level, also personify different aspects of the human psyche, and their Emanations share these psychological functions. On this level, Blake's epics are psychodramas, and the characters fulfill the requirements of psychological structures in acting out their dramatic roles.[2] If we consider the Zoas and their Emanations, in addition to the traditional Freudian and Jungian terms, as approximating the following functions, it should be sufficient: Urizen/Ahania are intellect or reason; Tharmas/Enion are instinct; Luvah/Vala are passion; and Los/Enitharmon are imagination. The Emanation represents the softer, more feminine, part of the function. For instance, Urizen + Ahania = logicallity + intellectual pleasure = sweet reason. As a psychological function, the Emanation contributes to creativity, and the nature of this contribution, as revealed through the seemingly erratic actions of Ahania, Enion, Vala, and Enitharmon, will be pursued in this study.

Ahania is the least fallen of the Emanations, for she does not enter into as many states of error as the other Emanations, and she retains intact more of her unfallen functions. However, since she is fallen, she is flawed. Ahania's flaw is passivity and inactivity. She does not do battle with Urizen and his fallen, perverted logic, nor does she fight to maintain the visions of Eternity that she still remembers. Instead, she sleeps, or teeters, wailing, on the Margin of Non Entity.

Ahania's function—wisdom, intellect, understanding—is of supreme importance to Blake, as it should be to any creative writer, "The Treasures of Heaven are...Realities of Intellect" (VLJ, E553). Moreover, the apocalyptic moment is an intellectual moment, a moment when we recognize error and cast it out.

Ahania contributes intellectual pleasure, knowledge and understanding as components to creativity. She also provides the intuitive wisdom to select the appropriate method of expression and the judgment to exclude the inappropriate. But her function must be coupled with activity. No act of creativity can occur with the intellect asleep, for an active intellect is necessary for the creation of an artistic product. Indeed, the art work is both evidence of intelligence and proof of activity, and both are necessary for the birth of a work of art. The unwritten book dormant within the mind of an intelligent person is as meaningless as the inanities which might get printed.

Moreover, Ahania is the best example of voluntary female self-sacrifice. In order to reestablish the eternal pattern, she dies in "Excess of Joy" (FZ121, E376). Self-annihilation (not to be confused with suicide) is the willingness to die for a beloved. It is the noblest of actions, since it destroys the satanic and guarantees a rebirth in Eden. Ahania has the wisdom to recognize that self-annihilation is essential, not only for her own rebirth, but for the creativity of her Zoa. She realizes that the completed artistic product must "die," come to a conclusion, so that the artist is free to create a new work of art.

Tharmas, in Eternity, is the Zoa of unity, associated with instinct and the will to bring a creation into being. He is also the "Parent Power" (FZ4, E297), "the Mighty Father" (FZ15, E305). Unfallen Enion, as the Emanation of Tharmas, is the feminine aspect of his eternal functions; she is a generative principle, a maternal power. Fallen, Enion still retains intimation of her unfallen function and gives birth to Los and Enitharmon. Her relationship to her wayward children exemplifies fallen masochistic maternity. Enion becomes the prototype of an obsessive, single-minded maternal instinct that turns her gray; aged venerableness helps to manipulate and control offspring. Vala, in contrast, remains young and beautiful, for her concern is the sexual drive.

In her most fallen state of error, Enion reappears as Tirzah, the embodiment of sadistic maternity, who, with her hypocritical tears and cruel anatomizing, is destructive and restrictive to her offspring, binding them down upon the stems of generation and depriving them of natural growth and joy.

There are, of course, elements of maternity in creativity, as is shown in a common metaphor like "brainchild." Blake portrayed the "Eternal Births of Intellect" literally as infants (VLJ, E552). The artist, in the process of creating, has feelings akin to maternity towards his intellectual infant, in the tender, loving care spent in the forming, whatever the length of time it takes, and the pride in the completed work that is an objectified part of its creator. Jerusalem crying for her little ones is not only a mother bewailing her abused children, but also the prototype of the artist being protective towards the art work in the face of negative criticism.

Creations in Eternity are joyful, but in Generation this is not always the case. Sometimes the intellectual infant becomes perverse and willful; it dominates the artist, his mind, his day to day living. On the other hand, if the artist demands or expects too much of the art work, the results may be abortive. A happy balance, a cooperation between artist and art work, is as necessary for a happy conclusion as it is between parent and child. And, like a good parent, the artist must let the finished product go, though lovingly, and turn to the creation of a new one.

Vala is the Emanation of the Zoa of passion, and she is frequently referred to as an eternal delight and joy, providing love and the equivalent of sexuality in Eden. Since *The Four Zoas* was originally entitled *Vala*, we can assume that Blake considered Vala's role of primary importance to his myth. One way in which she has particular significance is that she is the only Emanation who is directly associated with the Fall. Urizen and Luvah, representing reason and passion, are also associated with Albion's Fall. Reason and passion, acting as contraries, are well established combatants in eighteenth-century psychology, but Vala's contribution is original.

In Ahania's version of the Fall, we see most clearly the reason for the great importance of Vala's role, and that is the interrelatedness of sexuality and religion. Religion has its birth in the worship of the diluted feminine aspect of sexuality (abstracted from the aggregate, Jerusalem, and untempered by the qualities represented by the other Emanations), with the masculine portion negated.

Fallen Vala travels through several avatars, the most famous of these is Rahab. As Rahab, she forms an alliance with Urizen, who needs the erotic beauty of Vala to seduce men into following her, thereby filling his temple. The sexual energy aroused by Vala's presence in his temple can then be redirected into Urizen's war. Thus, Rahab reveals the connectedness of fallen sex, religion, and warfare, and becomes a symbol for most fallen miseries.

The worship of technical virginity is of prime importance in Rahab's religion, and, by this negation of her function, she creates an obsessive concern about sexuality. Rahab's insistence that she be worshipped as a virgin and that open sexuality is sinful drives sex underground into furtive activity, "a pompous High Priest entering by a secret place" (J69, E221), thereby creating harlotry, hypocrisy, and jealous possessiveness.

Rahab is usually associated with the knife of flint and the poison cup of chastity. Both the knife and the cup are sexual symbols, appropriate to

Vala's function, but they are misused by Rahab as part of the ritual of a religion that sacrifices human life and perverts human sexuality. On the other hand, the symbols also indicate that fallen sexuality has sado-masochistic elements in it. Mortal sexuality is certainly capable of cruelty when separated from the qualities represented by the other Emanations. Wisdom restrains, maternity mitigates, and imagination leads to empathy for others.

As passion, Vala's function, on the fallen level, is best expressed as sexual. But what is Vala's eternal function? Since Albion is androgynous and the Zoa and Emanation are one in Eternity, actual copulation is an impossibility. Sexuality is not an eternal function, since "Sexes must vanish & cease/To be, when Albion arises from his dread repose" (J92, E250). Whatever the equivalent to sexuality might be in Eden, it is suprasexual in the mortal sense, "Humanity is far above / Sexual organization" (J79, E233). What Eternity has to offer is apparently a more total fusion, a fusion in the circumference, rather than in the limited and selfish center. It is "Cominglings: from the Head even to the Feet" (J69, E221). Such cominglings would produce joy and leave the desires satisfied, so that Man would be free to engage the energies in intellectual pursuits and artistic creations. The unity of Zoa and Emanation, which in Eternity is total, rather than partial and temporary as it is in Beulah, transcends sexuality and results in a fusion of will and intellect.

Every creative artist has a certain amount of libidinal investment in the art work. If the relationship of the artist to the creation is similar in some respects to the relationship between a parent and a child (Enion), it is also similar to that betwen a lover and the beloved (Vala). The artist loves his work of art and is excited by the act of creating. However, there are dangers inherent in creativity similar to the dangers between sexual partners. The poet might fall in love with his own words, sometimes wrongheadedly, and refuse to see the blemishes. There is also the danger of too great a narcissistic attachment on the part of the artist to a single work that would preclude additional creations. The sculptor might spend all his life on one statue and never make another.

Thus Vala's function would be to provide the beauty and passion, we might even say religious fervor, necessary to sustain the interest and devotion required to complete the art work. It is also essential for her to abstain from any jealous attachment, so that new creations can constantly be made.

Enitharmon is the most "mortal" of the Emanations. She goes through a recognizable chronological development—from birth to willful child, cruel to her mother; to adolescence, spiteful to Los, whom she torments; to marriage to Los whom she tries to dominate, particularly by withholding sexual gratification. Initially, she is a contrary with whom Los must continually fight to retain his integrity. The disunity between Los and

Enitharmon is portrayed by sexual division, the literal wrenching apart of Zoa and Emanation, which causes great physical pain and results in two wills and two intellects working in opposition. In Night the Seventh A of *The Four Zoas*, Los and Enitharmon are reconciled, after which Enitharmon works together with her Zoa in Golgonooza, the city of art, contributing to redemption through her labor at the loom. Her care broadens from acceptance and love of her Zoa to concern for all mankind, whom she generously tries to save through the creation of forms. The hammer, the anvil, the red-hot iron are symbols of Los's fallen labor, his creativity, and the loom is the symbol of Enitharmon's creative labor. Enitharmon is an energetic Emanation, who is always capable of activity, initially destructive, but finally redemptive.

Los and Enitharmon are every man and every woman. Man and woman in Generation can descend into the Ulro and become "the Spectre & its cruel Shadow" (J15, E157), or they can, with vision, openness, and a lack of selfishness, ascend to Beulah to become a Zoa and his Emanation. If Enitharmon in her early life is an example of the worst that woman can be, she is also, after Night the Seventh A, an example of the best. She achieves the best when she learns Ahania's function (wisdom), without Ahania's passivity, for activity without wisdom is destructive, but wisdom without activity is useless.

Enitharmon becomes a model to be emulated when she learns to love, for the unfallen Emanation is always associated with love. In eternity, Ahania would be *philosophos* — the love of wisdom; Enion would be *storge* — love between parent and child; Vala would be *eros* — desire or sexual love; and, after Night the Seventh A, Enitharmon would be *caritas* — love of man for his fellow man.

Los has been associated with the ego function, and, indeed, his labors are related to creativity. He mediates between the reality of Eternity and the delusion of Nature, and he works for reintegration. Enitharmon, as his counterpart, is an essential part of Los's creativity, his inspiration, and she too mediates on behalf of the formless spectres, channeling her energies into the great labor at the loom. Enitharmon integrates and synthesizes the disparate elements of the work of art and weaves them into an organic whole; she embodies the form. She contributes activity, without which creativity can never be realized.

Blake gives us, in Jerusalem, a symbol of the integrated Emanations. As the Zoas represent fractured aspects of Albion, so too do the Emanations of Jerusalem. In Jerusalem, the fragmented functions represented by Ahania, Enion, Vala, and Enitharmon are unified. Unfallen Jerusalem has wisdom, a healthy fusion of maternity and sexuality (which all too often on the fallen level are seen as conflicting roles), and an imaginative empathy for others that is shown through overt activity.

There are, however, references to the Emanation in Blake's poetry that cannot be taken as a reference to a psychological function or to a dramatic character, as when Los seizes the condensed Emanations and forges them into the products of genius (J8-9, E150-1). Since Los at the anvil is the prototype of the artist-genius creating art, the Emanation that is forged may also be considered the artistic product of the artist-creator. Thus, the Emanation may be regarded as two very concrete tangibles—a beloved partner and the art work. Jerusalem, the aggregate of the four Emanations, is also the title of one of Blake's epics. The poetry, in which all the symbols of the Emanation are expressed, is itself a symbol of the Emanation.

As a concession to clock-time and yardstick-space, I shall more or less limit my discussion of the Emanation as creation to the poetic text, although she embodies all other art forms, and Blake considered "Poetry Painting & Music the three Powers in Man of conversing with Paradise" (VLJ, E548).

Blake was intensely conscious of his Emanation, his text, and laboriously etched the words, combining and decorating it with pictures, for it is through the art work that we enter Eternity, and through the text that we are linked to our mortal brothers:

When in Eternity Man converses with Man they enter
Into each others Bosom (which are Universes of delight)
In mutual interchange. and first their Emanations meet
Surrounded by their Children. if they embrace & comingle
The Human Four-fold Forms mingle also in thunders of Intellect
But if the Emanations mingle not; with storms & agitations
Of earthquakes & consuming fires they roll apart in fear
For Man cannot unite with Man but by their Emanations   (J88, E244)

As the text, the Emanation is a form of communication between men. Reading a compatible text is entering a universe of delight, but two texts that disagree cause "storms & agitations," and the authors would hardly unite one with the other in accord.

Moreover, Blake's text was designed to save mortals from their mental shackles and, through his Emanation, he speaks directly to the reader with the repeated refrain, "Mark well my words! they are of your eternal salvation" (M2, E96; and elsewhere). However, in order to benefit from the Blakean text, the reader must be able to read and understand it and, as anyone who is approaching *The Four Zoas* for the first time knows all too well, there are difficulties involved in understanding Blake's Emanation.

In *The Four Zoas*, Blake is attempting to write an epic that records the history of the world, as well as a psychological "case history" of Albion, that occurs within a moment of time, all of this without establishing cause and effect relationships. All the events related in *The Four Zoas* happen simultaneously.[3] Such a design creates difficulties for the poet in writing and the reader in understanding the text. Blake communicates simultaneity through narrative discontinuity, by hopping from character to character over narrative gaps, but he is hobbled by the necessity for linearity in the text and the need for a minimum of narrative continuity in order to communicate basic meaning. Blake could achieve the effect of simultaneity by printing the lines of the text one on top of the other. The superimposed lines, relating the activities of the four Emanations, would represent Jerusalem, the aggregate, but it would be illegible. As we are stuck with chronology in living out clock-time, so are we with linearity in reading the text. Although he does communicate it, Blake cannot achieve simultaneity within the text. This apprehension must occur within the mind of the reader.

But Blake's ultimate objective is a total comprehension, an intuitive leap that precludes logical analyses, that occurs within a split second of time. When the entire text is imaginatively grasped and understood in its totality (which cannot happen during the process of actual reading), then we achieve an Apocalypse, and it is possible:

> To see a World in a Grain of Sand
> And a Heaven in a Wild Flower
> Hold Infinity in the palm of your hand
> And Eternity in an hour   (E484)

In such a moment we push linearity back, and it is as if Blake's epic were typed on a jammed typewriter, the entire poem typed one letter on top of the other, occupying the space of a grain of sand. This apocalyptic moment would unify and conflate the separate careers of Emanations and Zoas as dramatic characters in a narrative. The reader would see the four Emanations, conjoined with the Zoas, as one in Jerusalem, reintegrated with all humanity in Albion, and simultaneously comprehend the Blakean text in its totality. It is also in this elastic moment that creativity occurs, for creative time, like Eternity, is outside of clock-time:

> Every Time less than a pulsation of the artery
> Is equal in its period & value to Six Thousand Years.
> For in this Period the Poets Work is Done; and all the Great
> Events of Time start forth & are conceivd in such a Period
> Within a Moment: a Pulsation of the Artery.   (M28-29, E126)

The reading time of the text and the space occupied by the text can be measured and weighed by those who live in Ulro, but to those capable of the

110

apocalyptic moment, time and space are flexible, "we / Contract or Expand Space at will: or if we raise ourselves / Upon the chariots of the morning. Contracting or Expanding Time!" (J55, E203). And the text itself can tamper with time. A lengthy book, imaginatively conceived and skillfully executed, ends too quickly; a short, dull one drags on forever.

It is interesting to speculate as to what each Emanation contributes as part of the text, for as the Emanations are components of Jerusalem, so too are they components of the text, each providing her own particular attribute.

The text contains wisdom and imparts knowledge; it gives the reader direction towards salvation and says, "Mark well my words!" That moment of understanding when the concepts in the text are comprehended in their entirety, either in the mind of the reader, or in the mind of the artist at its conception, is a moment that belongs to Ahania. The text gives the reader the possibility for achieving the apocalyptic moment. When, through the text, we understand some truth and cast out some error, then we have grasped Ahania in the text, for Ahania embodies the intelligence and wisdom contained in the work of art.

I have already discussed ways in which the text may be considered the offspring of the artist, but there is also a sense in which the text may be considered the parent of the artist. As Enion, the text creates, gives birth to the artist. An important text "makes" the writer; it gives him identity, fame, and possibly fortune. It also teaches the uninformed reader, sometimes providing solace as well as instruction.

As mentioned above, there is a certain amount of libidinal attachment from the poet to his text. The poetic Muse is traditionally a female and the feminine Muse justifies, or perhaps conceals, the erotic relationship of poet to text. Blake's Muse is the Daughters of Beulah, the embodiment of femininity expressed through sexuality.

Long before Susan Sontag suggested an erotics of the text to replace the hermeneutics, Blake had disapproved of cause and effect reasonings, logical analyses, and had given us in the Emanation a symbol that incorporates both a beloved sexual partner and a beloved poetic text.[4] More recently, Roland Barthes has written an erotics of the text, *The Pleasure of the Text*, in which he describes the reader's response to different types of texts—the text that gives pleasure, and the text that provides *jouissance* (Blake's "joy"):

> Text of pleasure: the text that contents, fills, grants euphoria: the
> text that comes from culture and does not break with it, is linked
> to a *comfortable* practice of reading. Text of bliss: that text that
> imposes a state of loss, the text that discomforts (perhaps to the
> point of a certain boredom), unsettles the reader's historical,
> cultural, psychological assumptions, the consistency of his tastes,
> values, memories, brings to a crisis his relation with language.[5]

The Blakean text would certainly qualify as Barthes' orgasmic text. It is premised on the loss of Eden, it unsettles the reader's traditional assumptions, and it certainly "brings to a crisis" the reader's "relation with language." The prolonged narrative sections of *The Four Zoas* are frequently dull and soporific, but the narrative gaps are imaginative and exciting. As Barthes says, "Is not the most erotic portion of a body *where the garment gapes?*. . .it is intermittence, as psychoanalysis has so rightly stated, which is erotic."[6] Over the narrative gaps, the reader is mentally hopping from star to star, and the act of filling in the gaps is orgasmic.

As the text, the Emanation is the artist's sexual love, his Vala. "Thy Emanation that was wont to play before thy face" (J4, E145) was created for play, as a prelude to *jouissance*, to provide Man with pleasure. She represents the erotic relationship between the author and the text, between the reader and a beloved book. The text separates painfully from the artist; divided, it is an object to be adored, and one that adores its creator or its reader. In Barthes' words, "The text you write must prove to me that it desires me. This proof exists: it is writing."[7]

Some of Blake's statements on "free love" sound like libertinism, a sexual generosity which might be considered promiscuous between mortals. But we must bear in mind that the Emanation is also the creation of the artist, and, as such, is free for all to love.

Enitharmon, conscious of the connection between her existence and Blake's poem, speaks to Los in great terror:

> The Poets Song draws to its period & Enitharmon is no more.
>
> . . . .
>
> My Looms will be no more & I annihilate vanish for ever
> Then thou wilt Create another Female according to thy Will

There is a certain amount of justification for Enitharmon's terror, since she has no existence outside of the Blakean text. Los tries to calm her fears with the reassurance that there is no sexual division, no separate or other female, in Eternity, but there is also a consolation in Generation. Golgonooza preserves the Emanation as the work of art, as well as all charitable acts of mortals, preserves her as a charitable act so she may be a gift to all future readers.

Space, or its equivalent in Eternity, forms the material of the art work, "for in Beulah the Feminine / Emanations Create Space, the Masculine Create Time, & plant / The Seeds of beauty in the Space" (J85, E241). The male contributes the idea, the concept, that shapes the material, the female. Enitharmon as the text is the product that occupies space, the artistic creation we see, touch, and admire, the physical thing. She is the materials that make up the work of art—musical score, modeling clay, canvas and oils, writing on paper, words engraved in the text. She is the idea translated into form.

Creativity in Blake is always associated with labor (appropriate, for it gives birth), hard labor—the hammer, the anvil, the incandescent iron to be beaten into shape—or the more gentle labor of the loom. The text is the result of this labor. Los and Enitharmon are the characters most closely associated with the actual doing of the text. Los hammers the language into structure; Enitharmon weaves forms and poetry is a type of weaving.

During the process of creation, the text is initially difficult to cope with, like the young Enitharmon. It acquires a will of its own; it disobeys, defies its author; it tries to dominate, refuses to die, to reach a conclusion. But at some point it becomes compliant, cooperative, and then the text is completed. The finished product, the poetic text, preserved permanently in Golgonooza, provides insights (like Ahania), brings comfort (like Enion), or joys and delight (like Vala), and, like Enitharmon's *caritas*, is a gift to all readers, generation after generation.

The union of both Emanation and Zoa is required for a healthy psychological structure, and both are necessary components in the text:

> I have heard many People say Give me the Ideas. It is no matter what Words you put them into & others say Give me the Design, it is no matter for the Execution. These People know Enough of Artifice but Nothing of Art. Ideas cannot be Given but in their minutely Appropriate Words nor Can a Design be made without its minutely Appropriate Execution.   (*Public Address*, E565)

There is no difference between body and soul, form and content, ideas and words. The shaping spirit of imagination (the Zoa) is realized within the materials that create the work of art, which is an organic entity. Sexual division, the literal tearing apart of Los and Enitharmon, is painful and unnatural. The whole thrust of Blake's epics is to eliminate dualism, to reunite time and space, body and soul, Zoa and Emanation, since unity between both is essential for achieving Eternity.

It is tempting, but simplistic, to try to establish a unilateral cause and effect relationship between the Zoa and the Emanation—Zoa/cause/creator-poet : Emanation/effect/creature-text. But any honest assessment of the activity of writing will reveal an interrelationship between the writer and the writing, an interrelationship as active and as vibrant as that between Los and Enitharmon. A well-turned phrase or sentence helps to inspire the writer to another such phrase or sentence; a line of poetry makes immediate demands on the poet—diction, metre, rhyme, length—as to the construction of the second line. A half-written text goads the writer to completion. And thus the effect causes creativity. The Emanation/creature also inspires, creates the Zoa/creator.

The Blakean Emanation is a unique concept. On one hand, she contributes to creativity as part of a psychological structure; on the other hand, she is the object which has been created. But since the creation assists in the creative process, the two functions are appropriately fused in one flexible, exciting symbol.

Notes

[1]All quotations are taken from *The Poetry and Prose of William Blake*, ed. David V. Erdman, commentary Harold Bloom, 4th printing, with revisions (New York: Doubleday & Company, inc., 1970).

[2]This has been examined frequently. Among the earlier critics who equate the Zoas to Freudian and Jungian terms are Northrop Frye, *Fearful Symmetry: A Study of William Blake* (Princeton: Princeton University Press, 1974), p. 301; and William Purcell Witcutt, *Blake: A Psychological Study* (Port Washington, N.Y.: Kennikat Press, Inc., 1946), p. 60.

[3]The principle of simultaneity is explained in Hazard Adams, *Blake and Yeats: The Contrary Vision* (New York: Russell & Russell, 1955), p. 69; and, in greater detail, in Susan Fox, *Poetic Form in Blake's Milton* (Princeton: Princeton University Press, 1976), chapter I.

[4]Susan Sontag, *Against Interpretation and Other Essays* (New York: The Noonday Press, 1961), p. 14.

[5]Roland Barthes, *The Pleasure of the Text*, trans. Richard Miller (New York: Hill and Wang, a Division of Farrar, Strauss & Giroux, 1975), p. 14.

[6]Barthes, pp. 9, 10.

[7]Barthes, p. 6.

Robert Duncan

Variations on Two Dicta of William Blake:

Mental things alone are real.

The Authors are in Eternity.

1

The Authors are in eternity.
Our eyes reflect
prospects of the whole radiance
between you and me

where we have lookd up
        each from his being.
And I am the word "each".
And you are the word "his".

        Each his being
a single glance the authors see
        as part of the poetry of what is, what
we suffer. You talkd of "freedom",
        and I saw
how foreign I am from me,

saw the spark struck from the black rock,
        saw I was not free to obey
and for a moment might have been free.

        I had only to reach up,
        restore our hands touching,
speak the words direct the authors struck.

You are the black rock, you are the spark,

        eternally.

2

How long dare I withhold myself
    my Lord withholds.

I shy a glance that he too shies.
    The authors of the look
write with our eyes
    broken phrases of their book.

    Why is it you?
Because my senses swarm,
    I fear what harm?

"Compulsion" you spoke of then
    that makes us men less than Man,
moved as we are. Move my hand,
    bright star,
if you are there, author out of the light.

    Why could I not move my hand?
    Why can I not move my hand?
waiting, a word in a moving sentence,
    just at the point where
the authors reveal (but their revelation
    is everywhere) the book.

I recognized in you my own presence
    beyond touch, within being.
What could I reach, reacht as I was?

    The authors are in eternity.

3

I am the author of the authors
and I am here. I do not dare
rescue myself in you
or you in me. Such a dark trouble
stirs in every act.
For what do I know of from where I come?
and others shall attend me
when I am gone.

116

What I am is only a factor of what I am.
The authors of the author
before and after
wait for me to restore
(I had only to touch you then)
the way to the eternal
sparks of desire.

4

Come, eyes, see more than you see!
For the world within and the outer world
rejoice as one. The seminal brain
contains the lineaments of eternity.

5

Mental things alone are real.

There is no mental thing unrealized.

To be a man—but we are men
who are of one mind. For the flower of nerves
and tissue in the skull
calls, O messengers of the boundaries,
        eyes of every cell, touch, touch
complete me such a world as I contain

        where angels moved like waves,
                convulsive energies,
lighting ways in me you do not see,
        have not seen them.

They were there for they are here.
        You overlookt or, seeing them,
changed focus and dismisst them.

        O fearful eyes,
O cells that are all doubt and reckoning,
        accommodation's slaves!

You've only to restore what I know to sight
        to realize the flash

that was eternity—a world—
in the heart's delight.

6

For the heart, my sister,
is likewise a dark organ, an inner
    suitor, my brother, a part
        of the whole yearning.

And there must have been a flood of,
    an up-rush, a change in pulse.
For when we see an answer,
    as the young man in moving answerd,
in leaning forward toward rapture
    where Charles Olson read,
answerd, or disturbd, some question

—the poet's voice, a whole beauty of the man Olson,
    lifting us up into

where the disturbance is, where the words
    awaken
sensory chains between being and being,
    inner acknowledgments
of the fiery masters—there
    like stellar bees my senses swarmd.

Here, again, I have come close upon what harm?
    where the honey is,
charmd by the consideration of his
    particular form,

as by lines in the poem charmd.

7

There was the event there was.

That is

recomposed in the withholding.

The whole of time waits like a hand
  trembling upon the edge of another hand,
  trembling upon the edge of not caring,
  trembling upon the edge of its eternal answer

  That is

not ours in the withholding.

We wait, two Others, outside ever
  our eternal being

  That is

here, in this sad tableau too,
  (for us, unwilling actors)
  rapture.

  The authors are in eternity

  That is

in thought intensely between us,
restraint that acknowledges

  the lover's kiss.

Paul Piech

MY PRETTY ROSE TREE

A flower was offer'd to me,
Such a flower as May never bore;
But I said 'I've a pretty rose tree,'
And I passed the sweet flower o'er.

Then I went to my pretty rose-tree,
To tend her by day and by night;
But my rose turn'd away with jealousy,
And her thorns were my only delight.

—WILLIAM BLAKE—

Jesus H. Christ

A Letter to the Times

—from one who gave his body
to redeem mankind—

*"As fer you, as fer you, as fer you, auld Jesus lad,
Gawn dance the nails fae oot yer taes an try and be mair glad."*
Alan Jackson-Knox

Sir, Madam—dear hearts, gentle people—Grand Inquisitors
        Hanging judges, jaundiced jurors...all my darlings
        See here now—it needs saying again:
        —You must leave houses, family, land
        —*All* cosy inherited notions
        To follow the light and be saved
        —As the good Dean Donne said
        "Change *is* the nursery
        Of music, joy, life and eternity"
        And it's high time there be some changes made
        Right now in the grandiloquent assinine arena
        Of the approved puritanical public morality
        —Something's got to give—it does in private
        When it has to if not (even better) before
        —For instance; you know how months years weeks
        —even just the *day* after violent quarrels
        You laugh at it together—how when sometimes
        You've gotten totally hopelessly hung-up
        about your enforced unnatural fidelity
        And you get to have sex with someone else
        And your "true love" finds out
        And there's angry scenes for sleep-torn nights on end
        And then with any luck, "finally", you relax—

121

About turn and turn on and get off and see clear
And tune in to each other's true beauty again
maybe with dope or (better still)
Simply fall in love again
...Anyway, fall into *making* love again
—One living body, ecstatic again
—Uptight egos, defensive habits, frightened armouries kicked
Ids entwined—mind at peace—paranoias pricked—
        So you laught at, together again, at
Your mutual enlightenment—realising that
Loving each other can expand way beyond
The inhibiting two-dimensional bourgeois frame
as commissioned by the conspiracy to make everyone the same
—Can survive revolutions from personal to global
And include loving even each other's other loves
(Or anyway liking—putting up with, bearing with them)
And so, and so on, and soon—on the moon
You get all idyllic and floaty and swoon—
Inspired—high on universal love
—The potentially infinite extensions
Of your immediate palpable selfish love
Out and into all the planes above
Immanent—continuing—waning—reviving
—Newborn...aaah
The ineffable Shelleyan Blakean dare I say it—
Yea, Christian idea of the Humanity Divine
For God *is* love, for which I died
—Not only the idea, the *Knowledge*
Of the body of love alive and well,
Shared body of all the bodies that love—
Rendering meaningless all membership save that in which
Each and all are active members of one another
As known by every loving couple that enjoys
The lineaments of gratified desire
As known by infants of all ages at play,
Mothers in childbirth, farmhands in the hay—
By gays galore dumb beasts Bessie Smith Beatles
educated fleas and the keeper of the zoo—
Adam 'n' Eve, Darwin, Tom Paine, Whitman
N O Brown, Henry Miller, Sappho and you
When all the petty squabbles about who's fucking who and
how wrong how wicked and cruel and terrible

Vanish and transcendent love supreme conquers all
    ...Then why doesn't it?
    —Why are fuck, suck and cunt
Still degraded by so many
as the nastiest most unspeakable words they can think of
And quite unthinkable as things of beauty
or activities to work at or relish or adore—
And why do the rest of us still keep coming
                                        down with a
Bump, that aches and corrodes
    —Fuck it, why is it almost always
Reserved that transcendent humour and knowledge
To some point, metaphysic—unreal reservation
Yet seemingly, in effect—Generally Binding—
Tacitly (tho insincerely) Understood as no more than
an irrelevant adolescent Utopian dream,
Its realisation safely deferred
To that pointless disembodied flashback
long after our practical love lives are done with
    —Eroticism disdained as a flash in the pan
For a few reckless fanatics who bother to act out
Orgiastic raptures, tenderness, fantasy
fulfillments they feel they were ultimately born for
    ...To be censored and banned and branded obscene
By the governments and police and library officials
Who pave the given route between puberty and the process
To scripted courtship, marriage—the job way of death
In which husbands become wives and wives husbands
And neither are themselves and both add up
to the case for divorce...mere income tax units
        —Why can't we laugh at ourselves *at the time*
we're getting so stupidly mad at each other
For goodness' sake, who *needs* that ache—why not
Put a brake on it, pull a switch, reawaken
our senses—snap out of the itch,
Get into the infinite freeway love gear
    —Unbridled, non-exclusive, any day—all the way
up to Live-and-Let Live without contracts or fear—
Would it really be too much to bear?

        —I guess it would...what a shame
    —How simple and good

123

It'd be, the purely
Positively permissive society
—If only it could be permitted!
    Meanwhile
Bloody Mary Mrs Grundy Longford stop-
Watch Committees with your spectral tangle of rules
    Get knotted—
    And your aspidistra morality plants, stay potted—
Till the dregs of your dried-up sour gripes are all rotted

    . . .In the meantime that gets meaner all the time
Our decrepit mores perforce are yours—
Your proscriptions rule for the knaves and the fools
To clean up your dead-arsed world picture, you ghouls
Of nothing but laundries and churches and schools
With special concessions to Inane Blight missions
and antique asylum bedwetters' pools
—The loopy laws and taboos with which you're so besotted
Want the last gasps of sex on these islands garrotted
    Whilst poor human lovers blow their cools
Made to feel that much dirtier every time
    —Alas that ever love was sin, it's a crime
Against humanity animality spiritual sanity:
                Forbid the fruit and kill the tree
        Of life everlasting
        From which we came
        All of us—oh yes,
        Even you must have come
        From some primal coming
        Somewhere, however deep-rooted—
            Let it rise, and shine
        And come again, bereft saps—
        Cast no stones, grind no bones
        Nor axes
                —you're good chaps
        at heart, I've no doubt—so come out come out
        —Come up front and be released
        —Let loose those pent-up tightlaced paps
        Of false piety, from beneath their unctuous
        Wraps of propriety—lay once for all
        The ghosts of your long-lost sexuality

And let go their holds
Against the open society
—Else must I come
Again myself, and cast
your new maps of hell
to the winds at last
To walk the true paths
of heaven, naked with me—up
Risen, all-embracing—heart
beating to free
every maimed limb and trapped spirit,
Human like me
—My body given
back for you
To rediscover—each other
—Your acts of love
your sacrament
To touch, taste and see!
     In the world
     yet to be
     Remember, they that put themselves
     First down here
     Shall be last, and the humble last
     There come first—
     They that thirst
     For the kingdom of
     Come *Together*
     —That There be *here*—
     Daily resurrecting
     My mystical body—
     Mutually building
     Those democratic vistas
     of limitless pleasures
     for all to share
     —All sacred hearts
     United for real

     . . . But till that glad day
     —As long as
     "I'm Yours", must I be
     Hung-up, dissociate—figurehead, at a loss

—A mere cross
patch of words—i e, ah me
  Yours
    Disgusted
    (but still with a kiss
     for yon lepers—sith that
     they know not what they pray)

—Jesus H. Christ

in a passing incarnation attributed to M Horovitz, Bisley, Glos, UK

Morris Eaves

Teaching Blake's Relief Etching

I

Blake advertised "illuminated books" in "illuminated printing." Technically he usually meant "watercolored relief etching." The excuse most often given for separating them into a print-component to be interpreted by one class of specialists and a design-component to be interpreted by another is lack of expertise. Usually the interpreter politely says that he lacks expertise in dealing with one component or another, and then just as often he takes it all back and says that really it was Blake who lacked the expertise, and we must presume that it is only the interpreter's good fortune to lack expertise in the same area in which Blake lacked it. If Jacob Bronowski, Harold Bloom, and F. R. Leavis don't mind excusing themselves on those grounds, it shouldn't be any surprise to find ourselves shirking the demands Blake's illuminated printing makes on us. If we shirk, who can blame our students?

This is not supposed to be a paper on why the print-component and the design-component should be interpreted together. (I have provided a short bibliography for those interested enough to pursue the matter.) But lest someone think I am implying that the proper answer is the classic nonanswer to all what-for questions, formulated, I understand, by Sir Edmund Hillary in regard to an adventure that was certainly as crazy as anything Blake ever would force us to attempt, I want at least to recall the classic answer invented by Jean Hagstrum, who in his book on Blake several years ago said memorably, "What Blake has joined, let no man put asunder." Taken with everything that it implies, it's an answer that satisfies me. But it was an answer that Wimsatt, especially, always on the lookout for intentionalism in all its forms, found hard to take as the last word on the subject. This paper assumes that the question has been answered in the affirmative and that the problem has shifted from theory to practice and, in the college classroom, to convenience.

But even if we want to proceed in the face of fear, ignorance, and prejudice, all sane teachers know that you can't teach things like relief etching in the classroom. You can't even show slides without looking like Urizen tangled up in his systems. I have never discovered a solution to the slide-technology problem, but two tactics and a formula ease the way for watercolored relief

127

etching. The tactics are (1) avoiding the danger, expense, and exoticisms of relief etching by using a surrogate printmaking medium, namely, linoleum-block cutting; and (2) letting students figure out the details of most of the techniques by themselves at home, instead of spending hours of class time giving out technical recipes and explanations which are only confusing anyway, like lectures on auto repair.

I hand out two sheets of instructions that take care of almost everything important: a list of essential materials and techniques, and a list of requirements for the project, with deadlines.

I. WHAT THE PRINTMAKER NEEDS (& A FEW TIPS)

1. SOMETHING DRAWN

For any printmaker this is the "**design**." There is no true preliminary design for any plate from Blake's illuminated books—including full text and pictures—and therefore Ruthven Todd once claimed that as evidence for Blake having used a process in *transferring* his design that *eliminated* the design at the same time. Of course the design can be drawn freehand directly onto the copper or the linoleum. But most professionals work out their designs on paper and transfer them to the plate or block. A design that includes words has to be reversed to make the writing read the right way around. (Engravers get used to imagining things in reverse, and Blake drew a number of important metaphors from this peculiar experience.) There are many simple ways to transfer and reverse. The simplest is probably to draw on paper that is transparent or semi-transparent (**tracing paper, etc.**). Turn it over; that reverses the writing, which can, however, still be seen from the wrong side of the paper. Now transfer it in reverse to the plate using **carbon paper** and a **ballpoint pen**.

No one really knows quite how Blake got his text onto the plates for relief etching. When working as a commercial reproductive engraver, however, he used the methods common in his trade.

2. SOMETHING TO MARK ON

For Blake this would be a metal plate, usually copper. Linocuts are made on sheets of **linoleum** mounted on plywood to make a block. These are available in several sizes from all art supply stores. The linoleum is usually dark red; it comes already painted white so that lines carved into it show up red. Engravers had a similar problem with red copper, and they coated it in various ways—smoking the surface with a sooty candle, for instance—to make their lines show up.

3. SOMETHING TO MARK WITH

If a plate is a flat surface—like linoleum or copper—then to make a design the printmaker has to use something to remove the material that isn't going to print. In a relief process, everything left standing on the surface prints; everything taken away doesn't, because it's too low. Imagine the designs carved out of potatoes by children, or a rubber stamp, or the letter on a typewriter key: those are all ways of printing in relief. The medium of Blake's illuminated books is called "relief *etching*" because he used acids to eat away the unwanted copper. Whatever he didn't want the acid to eat, he covered with a substance that was impervious to acid, probably a mixture of waxes and tars called a "resist" or a "ground." He probably applied the ground in several ways depending on the local need: with a brush, with a dauber, by transfer, perhaps with a quill of some sort. The plates of *America* show very clearly in several instances how he then used the engraver's other most common tools, the burin (or "graver," the old-fashioned term) and etching needle, to scratch marks into the ground and to make shapes out of unshapely areas of etching ground.

Linocutters don't use acid, of course, but to carve away the unwanted linoleum they do use **tools** that are remarkably similar to burins and etching needles. They come in a box, usually one handle and three cutting blades. But engravers used a variety of tools, some improvised, and likewise anything that will mark on linoleum is a potential tool.

4. SOMETHING TO PRINT WITH

This is ink. Because watercolor will be applied to the print later, the **printing ink** must be oil-based.

5. SOMETHING TO APPLY INK TO THE BLOCK WITH

No one knows for certain what Blake used. Ruthven Todd suggested that Blake's relief was so shallow that he had to apply the ink to his plate by covering another plate with a thin coating of ink and pressing it onto the plate he wanted inked. John Wright assumed that Blake used some kind of roller. Robert Essick says Blake probably used an ink ball (of the sort that printers and engravers used frequently) skillfully enough to ink his relief plates. A **brayer**—simply a roller with a handle—is the usual modern inker; cheap ones are available in art supply stores. The object in inking is to spread a *thin* and *even* layer of ink over the surface, usually by rolling a small glob of ink as if it were dough on a very smooth surface—like a piece of glass from a picture frame—until the ink thinly covers the brayer; then roll the brayer over the block. Ink does not have to be applied with a special tool. Fingers can smear ink thinly over glass, too, or over a blank linoleum block (imitating Todd's method, above).

6. SOMETHING TO PRINT ON

Blake printed on good paper. Almost any surface will accept a print—rice paper, etching paper, watercolor paper, cardboard, plywood, the nearest wall. Damp paper often prints better than dry, but all printmakers experiment. The variations in the amount of reticulation in the ink of Blake's prints indicate a lot of experimentation.

7. SOMETHING TO APPLY PRESSURE WITH

One of the advantages of relief printing is that a high-pressure press isn't necessary as it is for intaglio printing. Anything that can mash the paper onto the block will suffice: standing on it, rubbing it with a large spoon, rolling it with a dowel, typewriter platen, or rolling pin. It isn't at all certain that Blake always used a press to print his relief etchings.

8. SOMETHING TO COLOR THE PRINT WITH

This is watercolor. Dimestore quality will do, several colors in one tin box with a brush.

Those are the techniques, and they are even simpler when you do them with your hands than when you listen to a description of them. But since the instructional aim is not at all to teach linocutting, and not even quite to show someone the steps in watercolored relief etching, but to show what a knowledge of Blake's printmaking medium can add to the experience and understanding of his illuminated books, there has to be something beyond a list of technical facts. No doubt many educational schemes would work. I use some version of the one that follows.

II. THE EDUCATIONAL RECIPE

1. COLORING *AMERICA*

Early in the semester, while in class we are discussing the earliest illuminated books, the class buys a cheap, unbound facsimile edition of *America a Prophecy*, which later they'll use for studying that work, but which for now they are going to use as a kind of coloring book, because it has high-contrast reproductions of the plates of *America*. The initial assignment is to watercolor five plates with very different designs and textures. The instructions are to use Blake's coloring as seen in the Trianon/Blake Trust facsimile of *America*— which they consult in the library—as a model for their own coloring in three plates, and to invent their own contrasting kinds of coloring in the other two plates. The point of watercoloring is to force attention to the details of imagery, handling, and texture in Blake's designs, each of which presents a different problem in coloring.

2. MAKING A PRELIMINARY DESIGN
Meanwhile in class we've been talking about the principles of design in the early illuminated books, the *Songs*, *Thel*, and *Visions of the Daughters of Albion*, and discussing Blake's development in *The Marriage of Heaven and Hell* of his discovery that drawing and printmaking can become basic controlling metaphors, and that one of the natural themes of art is artmaking. Students try to express their understanding of these matters in a preliminary design for a plate of their own. Since the aim of the project is imitative instead of creative, they can choose between copying a design of Blake's; assembling elements from Blake designs and poems into a new composite; and making a design that is distinctly Blakean but not Blake's. In any case it must combine pictures with some words, which of course is the basic design problem in Blake's illuminated books.

At the same time they write a one- or two-page description and rationale of their design.

3. MEETING TO TALK ABOUT THE DESIGN
I prefer to have individual conferences with students to talk about their designs and their plans for a print. I intervene in two cases: when the designs don't look like Blake's, and when the designer has forgotten that outline drawings are different from relief prints. This is an essential lesson. Blake said that all true visual art finally depends upon "drawing" and "outline," but the way he used the brawny surfaces of his relief-etched copperplates shows that he didn't mean that he couldn't tell the difference between outlines in pencil and whatever corresponds to them artistically in the sculpted surfaces of the plate. The student already knows this from experience in coloring the plates of *America* and has only to be reminded that the differences between a pencil drawing and a print in relief reflect essential differences in tools and materials.

4. MAKING THE PLATE & THE PRINTS
The final requirement is to transfer the design to the plate, the linoleum block, to carve it in relief, print it, and watercolor it. I ask for a kind of portfolio consisting of several prints made from the block in earlier "states" that also show experimentation with inking, paper, surface textures, etc.; one finished print—watercolored—of the final state of the plate; and a

written description, in the form of an essay or a diary, of the designing, printing, and coloring of the print.

Of course I vary the format with the nature of the class. If it's a class on the English Romantic poets, I abbreviate the scheme and make most of the work independent, outside of class. If it's a class on Blake alone, I like the atmosphere of a workshop: I do a demonstration of relief etching, that is, the real thing, and I encourage students to bring in their work at various stages of completion, and we all talk about the problems of designing, printing, and coloring. Sometimes I assign readings after the project—never before—on Blake's graphic processes (see the bibliography). Students frequently make their experience with relief printing a basis on which to write longer critical or scholarly papers, proceeding with a good deal more confidence in their knowledge than one usually expects.

At any rate the results are always striking. While students are fearfully challenged at having to do something so utterly strange, the strangeness seems to be liberating, perhaps because they know I'm not interested in their linocutting skills, only in their dedicated efforts. I find very few shirkers and almost no serious complainers at this work. "This took me four hundred hours of work," they'll say, "and I have calluses and dirty fingernails." But they seem to know somehow that the work was worth it, and that what they are able to notice and know about Blake's illuminated books now is being noticed and known at a different level of competence. They see things they couldn't see before, and they have a new context for what they see. Most important, though, is their newfound willingness to grant the request that Blake makes at the beginning of *Jerusalem:* "dear Reader," he asked, "forgive what you do not approve, & love me for this energetic exertion of my talent." This is the educated benefit of the doubt that Wimsatt and Leavis found it impossible to give, but that all great art, Blake's more than most, requires.

II

When someone—one of John Linnell's children, you or I, one of our students—colors a print that Blake designed and printed but never colored himself, what is the relation of the colorist to the designer and/or printer? The fundamental version of the question is probably the one that involves Blake most directly: when Blake colored one of his own prints, what was his relation to it? For instance, is the printed design a kind of script or score that the colorist performs, as Bob Dylan sings a song he has written? Might Blake the colorist—as he decides how to watercolor a plate of *America* forty years after he printed the first copy—be justly considered a member of his own

132

Over the hills, the vales, the cities, rage the red flames fierce:
The Heavens melted from north to south; and Urizen who sat
Above all heavens in thunders wrap'd, emerg'd his leprous head,
From out his holy shrine, his tears in deluge piteous
Falling into the deep sublime! flag'd with grey-brow'd snows
And thunderous visages, his jealous wings wav'd over the deep:
Weeping in dismal howling woe he dark descended howling.

audience or an interpreter of his own work? A strong line of Enlightenment thought proposes that Blake might be better at imagining the work he wanted to do than actually doing it, or better at doing certain things than others. We might want to hear Beethoven "perform" one of his own piano concertos; but he could only "conceive" his string quartets, never "execute" them, if execution=performance, as Enlightenment theories usually seem to assume. One of the most striking effects of such theories is the sanction they give to specialized divisions of labor. Blake returns again to the issue as it arises in questions such as the following: What does "better" mean in the assertion that "I know someone who colors Blake's uncolored prints better than Blake himself?"

What defines the relations between the inventor, the executor, the performer, the individual reader/onlooker, the collective audience, and the commentator? For the purposes of their relief-etching exercise, at least, I encourage students to think of coloring the tiny figures living in the crevices of the body of the main figure on the last plate of *America* as a test of perception, interpretation, imagination, and evaluation. Catching an uncommitted glimpse of those tiny figures at the top of *America* 16 while you commit your real powers to making sense of the words in the text is like glimpsing birds — grasshoppers? fairies? — on fence posts as you plow a field. But coloring a design is like feeling it. Coloring the miniatures on plate 16 is like holding a fairy in your hand.

Blake's visual metaphors offer the colorist a number of tough choices: is the sky gray or blue? the season spring or winter? do the trees need leaves, then? how do a couple of trees look like a couple of people? how does a woman look like a cliff with a waterfall for hair?—the human form of the waterfall or the waterfall form of the human? The text helps in answering some of the questions—if the illustration is supposed to correspond to the text. But Blake does not always choose correspondence as the relation between text and illustrations.

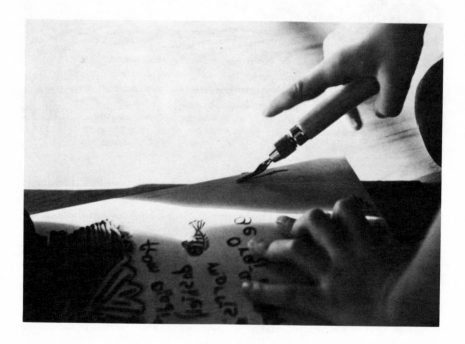

When students first hear of this odd assignment, their anxiety-level begins to rise: I'm no artist; I've never been good at technical things; Isn't this a course in literature anyway; Do you expect us to learn printmaking in two weeks; I can't afford all that expensive equipment. I try to allay their fears by the following tricky means: to show students how to do their linoleum block, I flash a sequence of slides using my son Obadiah (then 6) as the craftsman in charge. I make it clear that he is making the family's Christmas cards with a few tools and supplies bought with his allowance of (then) 60¢ per week. Here he shows how to hold the linocutting tool, which closely resembles an engraver's burin in size and shape.

A roller (brayer) helps to turn a blob of printer's ink into a thin, even layer. Brayers are a convenience. Blake himself almost certainly inked his plates with a "dauber" or tightly-wrapped pad (see Essick's book in the bibliography). Anyone interested in historical reconstruction can make a dauber, and not much skill is required to ink the high relief surfaces of a linoleum block with one. But the surfaces of Blake's own relief-etched copper plates were not very deeply etched, and considerably more skill and experience were required to ink them satisfactorily. Blake's skill at inking with a dauber distinguishes him from several experimenters who have tried to reconstruct his method of etching and printing in relief. As Essick points out, none of the engraving handbooks of Blake's time mentions the roller as a tool for inking. But in using printmaking as a classroom exercise, I have not stressed historical accuracy, as is evident in the rather careless substitution of linocutting for real relief etching. Stressing instead the technical variety and flexibility of printing processes seems to encourage students to work in what I regard as the proper spirit of adventure.

Obadiah's flumey Christmas-tree whale is sound in imagination and sound in technique. His design uses graphic relief in ways that are characteristic of the medium (and therefore of Blake's work in it): concentration on rugged sculptural surfaces and bold contrasts instead of "photographic" tonal refinements.

Similar surfaces appear in this rugged linoleum block carved by a student whose amalgamated inspirations were coming from Blake and Spenser.

By imitating plate 11 of *Europe* a student discovered that "relief" is a repertory of technical choices, not a monolithic system. The wings of the figure at the top are done with white-line work, and the angelic pair at the bottom are similarly floated out of the surrounding inked surfaces. Blake used lots of white-line work in *Europe*, much less in *America*. In looking for their own techniques, students quickly become aware of the variety of graphic possibilities available in relief. They become far more perceptive in examining the plates of the illuminated books because they understand in practical terms how certain graphic effects are achieved.

The Lion would not leave her desolate,
But with her went along, as a strong guard

In the printed and watercolored version of the plate shown above, the artist has used a second plate, as Blake occasionally did, to solve a technical problem in combining text and design. In another copy the movable text might have been printed in the sky at the top of the plate. It might have been printed with another illustration altogether. Or the same illustration might have been printed with yet another text. Blake's own tendency to mine one poem for another or several others, and to use one basic design in several different contexts, called for comparable flexibilities.

APPENDIX 1. LIST OF ASSIGNMENTS

1. Watercolor 5 pls. from *America*
   a. 3 imitating Blake's handling & color scheme
   b. 2 using a contrasting scheme
2. Preliminary design
   Rationale for the design (1-2 pp.)
3. 1 linoleum block
   Several prints made from the block in earlier "states," and experimenting with paper, ink, etc.
   2 prints of final state, watercolored in contrasting ways
4. Description of the designing, printing, and coloring of the prints

APPENDIX 2. SHORT LIST OF TOOLS & MATERIALS

For initial watercolor assignment: reproduction of *America* published by *Blake/An Illustrated Quarterly* ($2.50, high contrast black & white reproduction on one side of each page, medium contrast on the other side)
1. Making preliminary design: pencil, ballpoint pen, paper
2. Linoleum block
3. Transferring design to block: ballpoint pen, tracing paper, carbon paper. If reducing or enlarging: pantograph or ruler for making proportion squares
4. Engraving design onto block: handle with tips (Speedball). Any number of tools can be improvised. Nails and knives are useful. An oven or hotplate for warming the block makes the linoleum softer and less brittle (oven: 300° F. with door propped slightly open)
5. Inking the block: printing ink, oil-base (Speedball); ink-ball (make it yourself) or brayer (roller: Speedball, or piece of dowel, or kitchen rolling pin); smooth surface (piece of glass from a picture frame, etc.)
6. Printing: paper (use what's at hand, or buy etching paper); source of pressure (brayer, rolling pin, back of large spoon, hand)
7. Watercoloring the print: set of child's watercolors and brush

APPENDIX 3. FURTHER READING

PRACTICE

Essick, Robert N. *The Visionary Hand.* Los Angeles: Hennessey & Ingalls, 1973.
   The opening section reprints technical recipes contemporary with and relevant to Blake. Also reprints Todd (below), with slightly revised notes.
Essick, Robert N. *William Blake as a Printmaker.* Princeton: Princeton Univ. Press, 1980.
   A full and sound account of Blake's practices as a printmaker, complete with historical documentation and, when necessary, speculative reconstruction of techniques based on a rigorous combination of personal experiment, close examination of Blake's prints, and historical context. The best single source of information. Illustrated.

Keynes, Geoffrey. *Blake Studies*. 2nd ed. Oxford: Clarendon, 1971.
"Blake's Copper-plates," pp. 122-29.

Lister, Raymond. *Infernal Methods: A Study of William Blake's Art Techniques*. London: Bell, 1975.
A conventional account, not very well organized or presented. Illustrated.

Todd, Ruthven. "The Techniques of William Blake's Illuminated Printing." *Print*, 6 (1948), 53-65, and *Print Collector's Quarterly*, 29 (Nov. 1948), 25-36.
A description of techniques Blake might have used to transfer his design and/or text onto copper for relief etching. Illustrated.

Wright, John. "Blake's Relief-Etching Method." *Blake Newsletter 36* (Spring 1976), pp. 94-114.
Uses electrotypes, made directly from some of Blake's relief-etched plates before they were destroyed, as evidence for Blake's practices. Illustrated.

Wright, John. "Toward Recovering Blake's Relief-Etching Process." *Blake Newsletter 26* (Fall 1973), pp. 32-39.
Describes experiments carried out at the Slade School of Fine Art in transferring, etching, repainting, etc. Illustrated.

THEORY

Eaves, Morris. "Blake and the Artistic Machine: An Essay in Decorum and Technology." *PMLA*, October 1977, pp. 903-27.
On the relationship between artistic techniques and artistic principles. Illustrated.

Eaves, Morris. "A Reading of Blake's *Marriage of Heaven and Hell*, plates 17-20: On and Under the Estate of the West." *Blake Studies*, 4 (Spring 1972), 81-116.
On the uses of etching and engraving techniques as metaphors. Illustrated.

Eaves, Morris. "What Is the History of Publishing?" *Publishing History 2* (1977).
On the broader historical implications of Blake's artistic theory and practice in the context of 18th and 19th century publishing.

Erdman, David V. "Postscript" to "A Temporary Report on Texts of Blake," in *William Blake: Essays for S. Foster Damon*, ed. Alvin H. Rosenfeld. Providence: Brown Univ. Press, 1969.
A reading of the printing-house allegory in *The Marriage*.

Erdman, David V. *The Illuminated Blake*. Garden City, N.Y.: Doubleday, 1974.
The commentary demonstrates the uses to which metaphors from Blake's graphic processes can be put.

Essick, Robert N. *William Blake as a Printmaker*. See above.
Essick places his discussions of Blake's prints and printmaking in the context of Blake's artistic theory, and the book includes a discussion of the imagery that Blake draws from his own technical practice. Illustrated.

Essick, Robert N. "Blake and the Traditions of Reproductive Engraving." *Blake Studies*, 5 (1972), 59-103.
On the metaphors suggested by systems of engraving. Illustrated.

Victor Flach

A Note on Blake's "Four Faces of Man"
as Mind's Primary Model-Making Forms

*But in Eternity the Four Arts, Poetry, Painting, Music And
Architecture, which is Science, are the Four Faces of Man.*
　　　　　　　　　　—Wm. Blake, *Milton*, 1804-08

The root and paradigmatic meanings of Mind's Forms are embedded in
the correspondence between the external stimuli of Universe and the Individual
senses: (1) *Visual*—eyes' reception of only light as the spectral slice of
radiant electromagnetic energies (lensed and irised rods and three kinds of
cones); (2) *Tactile*—skins' reception of four kinds of molecular excitation (a.
eardrum & basilar membrane for aural reception of sound vibrations as
pitch, volume, harmonic overtones, timbre; b. derma for tactual surface
contact pressure, heat, cold, pain; and the chemoreceptions of c. the nasal
olfactory epithelium for the four basic odors; and d. the tongue epithelium's
papillae for the four tastes—odors and tastes combining for flavors); (3)
Kinetic or Kinesthetic—labyrinthine semicircular canals' and muscles' response
to gravitational balance and gross position, motion, direction, direction
orientations respectively; and (4) *Mnemonic*—memory's interrelational and
symbolic (eg, numeric, linguistic, archetypal) registration of periodic and
durational befores and afters (thalamic, limbic, and two cortical cerebral
hemispheres cross-referencing cyclic and metamorphic patterns).

This new ordering may perhaps clarify a contemporary direct connection
with Blake's "Four Faces of Man" as Mind's Primary Model-making Forms:
(1) *Painting thru Photography* as paradigm for the instantaneity of Visual
Color Structures on a plane; (2) *Music* as paradigm for the linear sequentiality
of all the Tactile Structures (including not only the successive Aural wave-
fronts, but Tactual Sculpture, Perfumery and Cuisine—as all Music is
housed by a tactual surface Sculpture as *Resonator*, tho of course not all
sculpture houses a music); (3) *Architecture* as the paradigm for all Kinetic
Structural Relationships of forcefields (as all architectures house motion
patterns—eg, including the *Dance* of electrons in atomic molecules, of
geologic, biologic and human trafficking—the latter thru urban buildings or
on stage—and the dance of stars in galaxies...); and (4) *Poetics* as the

paradigm for the archetypal and cross-referential simultaneity of all Metaphoric Structures holding passing processes present with presence. So now we can model each of the Four Faces of Man with maximum *appropriateness* to their unique forms and media, and we have an articulate basis for *discretely integrating* their correspondent structures and meanings in any and all combinations of forms and media. "What is now proved was once only imagin'd."

He ground and mixed his water-colours himself on a piece of statuary marble, after a method of his own, with common carpenter's glue diluted, which he had found out, as the early Italians had done before him, to be a good binder. Joseph, the sacred carpenter, had appeared in vision and revealed *that* secret to him. The colours he used were few and simple: indigo, cobalt, gamboge, vermilion, Frankfort-black freely, ultra-marine rarely, chrome not at all. These he applied with a camel's hair brush, not with a sable, which he disliked. . . .The poet and his wife did everything in making the book,—writing, designing, printing, engraving,—everything except manufacturing the paper: the very ink, or colour rather, they did make.   —Alexander Gilchrist

Paul Johnson

232 Humanities

A yellow ashtray with ashes filled just so
auguries of moonscape and the mystic clouds
the hat rack marks an X upon linoleum
artificial crematorium of fallen leaves
without a window the acoustic holes
leap and reach the spangled sky
shoot through to revolving space
how else to tell the seasons except
accept the humming sun of airconditioning
the wastebasket wears a prophylactic
and strips of tape show where poems used to be
the fearful symmetry of doorknobs, lock, and key
marks an angle from corner to corner
fixing Newman's *University*
in perfect contrapuntal to *Strategies*
this is my bureaucracy

Carolyn White

The American Woman in Apartment 11
Via Goffredo Mameli
from *ROME*

I have held, I'll not deny it, residence in magic lands.
France: those midnight cafés where I know
    my way around, graceful are my manners.
Ireland: the salmon's voice.
Germany: in the forest the trees that hold their breath.
For me God has never been a person,
neither a vast bushy sort beyond the clouds,
nor a homunculus within my breast;
God has always been a place
and all my life I've been going home.

Our American weakness is our power,
we who've never had a home,
a cross-breed of nations,
changing houses, year to year,
a need to journey elsewhere to find ourselves,
as if there were a magic road, or rather,
as if in a visionary moment any ordinary road
could turn into the one and only road
and we would arrive at our desire.
We are Ishmaels,
with something neglected in our past,
something that disturbs us, makes us yearn,
some ghost, perhaps, or an act forgot before our birth
that conversely makes us accommodating souls.
Who knows? Our salvation may lie here.

In amendment to Wordsworth,
I've known congenial moments of space:
a childhood on Long Island, a year in Rome,
each memory a place distinct,
populous, delightful.
Like some imported vine
I flourish in foreign soil,
grow lush and climb the walls

until I overhang the border.
It happens every time, in every place,
I exceed the limits and retake the road.

I remember how at first I hated Rome,
the edges of its buildings cut me,
guards lowered from private entries
as I dragged my last Paradise behind.
The streets had no purpose,
the city had no laws,
in the market women tricked me,
no Italian could pronounce my name.

Over the months Rome has taken shape,
a blurred face become a friend,
my speech accurate, my gestures sure.
I love this house, I love this city,
I know the names of Via Mameli's children;
a neighbor has invited me today for coffee,
yet my bags are packed,
my mind already walking down the stairs.

My love of escapade, by luck,
is greater than my fear of loss.
And though I won't release the past,
Carrying in my suitcase certain hills
and café tables, I do, perverse creature, leave,
for no place has ever been enough,
perhaps because, I, enchanted by them all,
can never choose the one.

What I want . . . what I want
is a home that also is a road,
the familiar to be strange, the strange remindful.
I who love seduction yield
until a door appears, then out I go.
Blake promised in Eternity some grand debates,
blows of love, the cry of words,
our spirits bloody and alive.
Home is then a glorious brawl
and on my knuckles and my knees
the bright stains of all whom I have ever loved,
the survivors of my past.

David Reisman

Isaiah and Ezekiel dine with William Blake (Marriage of Heaven & Hell)

146

Howard Schwartz

The Form of the Fall: "The Mental Traveller"

In "The Mental Traveller" William Blake presents in a succession of vivid images a mythic world that "cold Earth wanderers never knew." Like all myths, its locus of meaning includes psychic processes as well as real world relationships. In both cases the myth embodies Blake's concept of the fallen cycle which "cuts the heart out" of our lives and prevents us from achieving the balance, or, as Blake puts it, the "rest before labor" which precedes any creative activity. Without this equilibrium no seed can properly take root, and what is engendered is a reflection of its conception, which "was begotten in dire woe."

For Blake creation, in the broadest sense of the term, is both the goal and sole meaningful activity of life, and its opposite is the closed, circular chain which "binds iron thorns around his head," and "pierces both his hands & feet." This chain is primarily, but not exclusively, a personal one, involving the mental and emotional processes of the individual which are successively drained of their vitality. Outside of the individual it represents the undermining of those archetypal and real relationships child-parent, husband-wife, and parent-child, and these may be projected onto larger communal associations. Of these various possibilities, the poem may be best understood when viewed from the perspective of an individual psyche, as the title would seem to insist, with all other relationships seen as projections of internal conflicts.

In this, as in all of his later poems, Blake is discovering the processes which underlie our actions. Because he is a poet, he embodies our inner world in images which at least derive from our external one, for we are able to apprehend these developments only in metaphors with which we are familiar. Thus the "land of men/A land of men and women too" is the land of the mind and the emotions, the inner processes which steer us without our knowledge of their presence, and leave us "cold" to the true source of our motivation unless we recognize them and pursue an understanding through self-knowledge. This, then, is Blake's primary metaphor for this poem, where the inner life is manifested in dream-like distortions of the external world.

Because "The Mental Traveller" ends as it begins, with the birth of the Male Babe, and the last line promises that "all is done as I have told," we have every reason to consider it a cyclical poem. The span of this cycle is the span of a life from birth to rebirth; Blake leaves no doubt that the Male Babe born at the end of the poem is the same one born at the beginning, partly by reversing the aging process. Thus the cycle of the poem is identical with the most fundamental of cycles, the cycle of life.

Our knowledge of the poem's first birth is scanty, although the myths suggested in succeeding stanzas imply that it may have been preceded by the sort of foreboding that is supposed to have preceded the births of Oedipus, Abraham, Moses and Jesus:

> For there the Babe is born in joy
> That was begotten in dire woe
> Just as we Reap in joy the fruit
> Which we in bitter tears did sow

The first two lines of this stanza are a reversal of the qualities of pleasure and pain which we usually associate with the acts of begetting and birth. Yet if we view these acts as a metaphor for the impulse to create, then a realm where begetting is pain and giving birth joy is not completely alien—it describes that of the artist, who must absorb and survive the pain of experience before knowing the joy of creation. Blake has in mind a world such as this, focused upon creation, in which the creative aspect of existence is lost in the fall. In this way the successive drainings of the energy behind this impulse, which constitute the action of this poem, ultimately destroy the creative potential, so that no glimpse of its purity is present when the cycle automatically returns to its beginning, manifested in "the Frowning Form."

In addition to this interpretation there is a lesser but fitting irony in this second stanza. Begetting, in this "Land of men & Women too," has become such a "dire woe" because sexual relations are primarily a matter of sadistic jostlings and have declined to the extent that the pleasure associated with love-making has been overwhelmed by the conflict, and in contrast the agony of an actual birth is "joy" compared to the "dire woe" of begetting.

Essentially the myth Blake formulates in "The Mental Traveller" is a unique one, both in terms of his own work and other sources. At the same time the poem often suggests resemblances to other myths, some created by Blake, and it is usually profitable to examine the context of these allusions, for Blake did not mix aspects of myths indiscriminately, but chose those motifs which not only served his own myth, but awoke responses to that aspect of the traditional myth he chose to echo. We learn, for example, in the third and fourth stanzas of the poem that

          if the Babe is born a boy
He's given to a Woman Old
Who nails him down upon a rock
Catches his shrieks in cups of gold

She binds iron thorns around his head
She pierces both his hands & feet
She cuts his heart out at his side
To make it feel both cold & heat

In tone and imagery this striking passage is unquestionably unique, yet in it Blake has combined elements of, and thus managed to allude to, several crucial Western myths and the archetypal child-mother relationships, as well as to other contexts in his own work, some already written and some yet to be written. The myths he suggests are those of Oedipus, Dionysius, Prometheus and Milton's reworking of the Genesis myth, plus the passion of Jesus—probably the central myths in Western culture. The Babe is reminiscent of the infants Jesus and Oedipus; the thorns around the Babe's head suggests the crown of thorns of the crucifixion, as do the hands and feet being pierced; the rock the Babe is nailed to suggests Prometheus, and the heart cut out at his side "To make it feel both cold & heat" suggests both Prometheus' torture and Dionysus' rite.

However, Blake changes the original aspects of the myths just enough to make the combinations original and gruesome: the thorns around the Babe's head are iron; the organ cut out at his side is his heart, not his liver, and the Woman's purpose in doing so is mysteriously understated; finally, Blake distorts the child-mother relationship of the Christian myth, and turns it into the Woman-Babe relationship which becomes the central and inescapable relationship of the myth. Blake disguises this relationship by having the child given to the Old Woman rather than being born to her. He also camouflages it by making the mother old, but this particular change is consistent with the poem, where time is in a confused state; where, for example, we have Christ crucified as a child. Also, from the perspective of the three women in a man's life, mother, wife, and daughter, the mother is most easily identified as the old woman.

It is in extending this thesis of the Old Woman as mother and the Babe as her child that we may find the central device of Blake's myth. Throughout the poem there is one primary relationship of male and female, although there are regular alternations in the ratio of their ages: at times the female is old and the male young, then the two are approximately the same age, then the male is old and the female young, and the alternations continue. These changes are meant to symbolize the shifting attention from mother to wife

149

to daughter, and Blake implies that these are all essentially the same person. However, this situation itself is a metaphor denoting the consistency of the male-female relationships in our lives, for these are by no means limited to these specific primal relationships. Thus Blake's analogy is not only a useful device, but also an archetypal truth presented in allegorical terms.

Throughout "The Mental Traveller" Blake's metaphor for the alternating relationships is that of a miser to his gold and gems. Thus Blake is saying that the essential nature of the relationships is that of possessor to object possessed, and the variations on this theme, the connection of parasite to host, and of vampire to victim. In the fifth stanza Blake combines the relationships of the miser and his gold and of the parasite and host, but not yet that of the vampire and victim, because the host, the child, is dependent on the parasite, the mother:

> Her fingers number every Nerve
> Just as a Miser counts his gold
> She lives upon his shrieks and cries
> And she grows young as he grows old

In the following stanza Blake introduces a latent vampire image, suggesting that the Old Woman, having become a "Virgin bright," has been living off the boy's blood in some sense, for he has become a "bleeding youth." Now, though, it appears as if it is time for his revenge, for he reverses their situation and literally puts himself on top. However, if he paused to look down he would see the face of one of the daughters of Luvah:

> Till he becomes a bleeding youth
> And she becomes a Virgin bright
> Then he rends up his Manacles
> And binds her down for his delight
>
> He plants himself in all her Nerves
> Just as a Husbandman his mould
> And she becomes his dwelling place
> And Garden fruitful seventy fold

Blake's simile of the husbandman continues the imagery of harvesting (and renews the presence of its benefactor, the Grim Reaper) begun in the first stanza, for this exactly describes the relationship of the male and female, husband and wife. In such a relationship the male and female are chained to each other by necessity, and it is the resentment over this fact which dominates their lives, rather than their struggles to attain dominance over each other.

These alternating possessions continue throughout the poem, with the female remaining truly dominant. Unlike the torture inflicted by the Old Woman on the Babe, the situation of father and daughter does not find the father dominant; rather she, like most of Lear's daughters,

> comes to the Man she loves
> If young or old or rich or poor
> They soon drive out the aged Host
> A beggar at anothers door

Here again Blake has carefully chosen the word "Host" to disguise, or distance, the relationship between characters, and to resound the metaphor of the possessed and possessor, of the parasite and host, of the interdependent self. Thus does the female in "The Mental Traveller," who symbolizes the active principle of the "Circle of Destiny," pull the male through the bitter agony of the chain, the ever pressing impulse which prevents any pause or momentary balance, and finally to the ultimate agony of a repetition of the whole.

Because the cycle in the poem is manifested in the form of a fall, its constant state of change denies the possibility of even a temporary stasis. But this is appropriate because "The Mental Traveller" is about fallen, exploited experience that ends, before long, in making every landscape into "A desert vast without a bound." There is some satisfaction, nevertheless, even as we perceive the horrors of this repetition, because the nature of the cycle encloses the poem and allows it to stand alone as a complete portrait of a particular dream-world, although, as with all dreams, its roots are to be found everywhere.

Reb Hayim Elya Has a Vision

It happened in his thirty second year that Reb Hayim Elya journeyed on his own to the Holy Land. In the end his journey was very fruitful, for there he met and married his wife, Tselya, who had been born in the Holy Land of parents who had come there from Baghdad.

But in its beginnings his journey had been very difficult. Reb Hayim Elya's ship had docked in Haifa. There he had gone into the town and spent the next twelve days in an inn beside the shore, while waiting for the carriage that would bring him to Jerusalem. Now Reb Hayim Elya had always dreamed of being in The Land of Israel. In one recurrent dream he had seen the Holy Land from a distance, from which it seemed to glow like a precious jewel. And in another he had stood beside a beautiful beach and watched the waves approach and depart.

But it happened that the inn Reb Hayim Elya had entered was run by Arabs, and the innkeeper was hostile and suspicious, and the other guests unfriendly. Nor was there anything in that place that Hayim Elya could eat, and he subsisted on dry bread and water the whole time. But worst of all, the beach behind this inn was covered with ashes and littered with trash.

For each of the twelve days Reb Hayim Elya spent there in that place he was haunted by that black beach, so unlike the beaches he had imagined in his dreams of the Land of Israel, and all that time he felt as if his feet were sinking into the earth.

On the twelfth night, one day before the carriage was to depart, Reb Hayim Elya returned to his room, feeling sadder than he had ever felt in his life. And he put out the candle and lay down on the bed, and turned in the darkness in the direction of the one wall in that room which faced the shore outside.

But when he looked there he saw that the wall had vanished, and the shore was illumined before his eyes. Yet it was not the same shore he had suffered beside for twelve days, but another shore, far more beautiful than any he had ever seen. And it was surrounded by a glowing light, unlike any other, as if it were the light of the first day of creation, before the sun and moon had been brought into being.

Reb Hayim Elya stared at that beautiful beach for several minutes. Then he realized that he was still in his room, and he became frightened and jumped up and lit the candle, and when he did the beach disappeared.

Afterwards he recognized this beach as the very one he had dreamed about all the years he had spent in exile from the Land of Israel. And he knew that the Holy One, blessed be He, had opened his eyes and let him see the beach of the Holy Land that is hidden from the sight of most men, who see it in nothing more than a beach in disarray, covered with ashes.

Note:

The Hasidim were a sect of Jews founded by Israel ben Eliezer, known as the Baal Shem Tov, who flourished in the 18th and 19th centuries in Eastern Europe and Russia. Like Blake, they were primarily concerned with spiritual intensity (kavanah) rather than ritualistic requirements. Reb Hayim Elya's vision occurs in a "Moment" in Blakean terms:

> Every time less than a pulsation of an artery
> Is equal in its period & value to six thousand years;
> For in this period the poet's work is done, & all the great
> Events of time start forth & are conceived in such a period,
> Within a moment, a pulsation of the artery.   (Milton 29)

Artful Goodtimes

To-Hell-U-Ride

"...no light from the fires: all
was darkness..."

O sons of Urizen arise in every age
to spit the word-warped dragon-seeds
that spring up screens like weedy stems
to choke the flowering rage of shorn
lamb and blackened chimney sweep.

As here twixt Ute-cursed canyon walls
of posh refurbished Rocky Mtn. hideaway
bourgeois scribbler Rosenfeld lashes out
against what remnants of "the Left"
he sees receding in the snowy haze.

A perfectly modern Reaganesque hero,
this Rosyfield, ringing up sales in his shop,
unafraid to leave his liberal youth behind
and wax to shine his own slick ski-skins
as he sinks contented in self-hip-nosis.

Finding no costumes in his Halloween closet
to dress the facts he refuses to face:
on-going genocide of indigenous peoples,
love canal tract homes, agent orange veterans,
apartheid investors, bottle baby scandals,
corporate subversion of the Bill of Rights,
mushroom cloud check on a global chessboard.

Finding no evils snug in the rug of his
wall-to-wall waterbed, musing on atrocities
blithely recounted, reducing the terrors

of social injustice to the insulated narrows
of his own myopic view; the poor with their
tipis vs. the rich with their pools.

Finding "music" in the mine shafts
drilled for uranium on Hastings Mesa.

Ignorant of Lovin's soft path vision,
a technology more appropriate than synfuel madness;
ignorant of Anna Mae Aquash or Leonard Peltier;
as ignorant of Geronimo Pratt as he is of Karen Silkwood.

Trying to divide left hand from right,
to blur, blind and turn "grotesque"
the struggle to preserve our human rights.

But let our hero rant and rage
as he scans the "dimming horizon"
on the velvet dunes of his solar divan.

As for me I'd rather learn from William Blake
than teach ten thousand Rosenfelds
how not to turn the roses black:

> "Can I see another's woe,
> and not be in sorrow too?
> Can I see another's grief,
> and not seek for kind relief?"

Visions of the Daughters of Albion, title page

E. B. Murray

A Pictorial Guide to Twofold Vision:
Copy "O" of *Visions of the Daughters of Albion*

In the same set of aphorisms where Blake stated that the fool does not see the same tree that the wise man sees he also said that the fool who persists in his folly will become wise.[1] Even Ulro, the spectral world of single vision, has a gate leading to Eden, as Blake's fourfold description of the ins and outs of Golgonooza illustrates. Unfortunately, in this age of the world, that gate is frozen up. If it were not, fewer men would see the sun, when they saw it at all, in shape no bigger than a guinea piece in a miser's bag: except, to them, not so beautiful as (Blake tells us) the guinea is to the avaricious. At some future age, when woman's love is not a sin and a Newton can see with the vision of a Shakespeare, the sun each morning would appear as a heavenly host singing God's praises in a crescendo growing until noon, and God himself would look very much like Los, who would look very much like Blake, who would look very much like all of us, with Christ in us and we in Him, and our faces individually and collectively emanating light like the Morning Star.

For the visionary, the future is now, and, in spite of his stated impatience with fools, Blake took the time to make them see (in the now he shared with them) the future he experienced in himself and prophesied for others. When he remembered that he and each of us were Christ, he remembered to forgive and, insofar as it lay in his province and in our capabilities, he did what he could to shepherd us, with a few strands of golden string, through the mazes of Ulro. He did this by giving us, in our dimness of vision, a layman's purchase on Eternity by incorporating it explicitly in a production of time that caught us up in that moment between two pulse beats which Satan cannot find and bore us away, from here to Eternity, on a chariot which Blake himself once shared with Ezekiel.

My purpose here is to contend for the exceptional tolerance Blake illustrated in Copy "O" of "Visions of the Daughters of Albion"[2] where, for the sake of those who could not easily see (as Blake could) that a given thistle is an old man grey, he transmuted—reductively enough in his own view—twofold vision into single vision and so rendered himself explicit, if not to the idiot, at least to those who tended to "stick in the senses," as

Bishop Berkeley once put it.[3] He did this in plate 2 (the title page) by changing the more rocky shapes which appear at the bottom right of that plate in almost all other impressions into reasonable facsimiles of the human form divine. He did this, but less obviously, in plate 7 by further defining the bounding line of Theotormon's head so that it could appear even to those who failed to get the verbal hints *passim* in the poem that Bromion, who is also Urizen, had fairly well taken over Theotormon's inner man—or that which made him, as Blake would see it, truly human.

Before focusing on the two plates from VDA I want mainly to discuss I shall briefly outline my reading of VDA, insofar as it applies to those plates. In the first place, I suppose Theotormon to incorporate Bromion, who has no existence in this poem except insofar as Theotormon gives him of his own psychic substance. He is, in effect (and to reverse Blake's predication), Death feeding on Life. He is, in this relatively early rendition of Blake's symbolism, a scion and incarnation of Urizen who feeds like the spectral vampire bat of *Jerusalem*, plate 7, on the spiritual energies he draws from the very arteries of Theotormon, who not only becomes weaker but also dehumanized as this inhuman agency converts him into its own likeness. The obvious romantic analogue and echo of this relationship appears in *Prometheus Unbound*, where we discover that Shelley's hero, Prometheus, has not only become his own object of hatred, Jupiter, but effectively keeps that object in power for so long as he indulges the spirit of vengeance he feels toward it. For Shelley, as for Blake, forgiveness, that Christ-like facet of sweet human love, was the power in meekness that could dethrone the mightiest whose eminence is wholly contingent on his selfishness.

Bromion is essentially selfish like Jupiter in his grotesque parody of the act of love as an act of rape. In Shelley's poem Oothoon's counterpart, Thetis, does not even get to speak her own lines as Jupiter tells the assembled pantheon how she screamed in terrible ecstasy, when he ejaculated his poisonous godhood—like the "Numidian seps"—between her loins and so procreated the awful power that could destroy him.[4]

But the absolute originality of Blake's symbolic context conditions the infinitely more subtle expression of what it is to be raped by the god you love as a man. Oothoon, as timid as Thel if not so falsely modest, gives herself freely to the man she loves. Immediately and in consequence, she is raped by Bromion. Physically speaking, that may not seem to be the chronology. But, since all physical acts have spiritual causes for Blake, so do all sexual acts have psychosexual causes. Christ says (unfortunately urizenic here) that the man who lusts after a woman in his heart has perpetrated an adultery with her. Blake says that the woman who has given herself to a man in her heart has engaged in an act of love with him. After all, we are given to understand that Oothoon and Theotormon are the Juliet and Romeo of this poem.

When Theotormon demonstrates jealousy over the "affair" between Bromion and Oothoon he is in fact reflecting the urizenic component in himself which is really, if paradoxically, quite in agreement with Bromion's essential character and wishes, even though Bromion himself, we are told, is bound back to back with Oothoon in his own cave by Theotormon. Again the Shelleyan analogue is of some help in understanding the reason for ascribing the prison for Bromion *to* Bromion. When Shelley's hero wished to recall the curse he pronounced on Jupiter he called up the phantasm of Jupiter to pronounce it. The implication is clear enough. When Prometheus had pronounced the curse on Jupiter he had himself become the object of his hatred who in himself was the source of hatred because he was pure ego, pure selfishness. In recanting the curse, Prometheus effectively deposed Jupiter from his psyche by replacing selfish hatred with Christ-like forgiveness. Theotormon is a pre-Promethean in more ways than one: most relevantly here he is Prometheus still cursing himself by seeking vengeance upon what can only be considered an essential part of himself. And in binding Bromion and Oothoon in Bromion's cave he indicates that his psychic complex is under the domination of Bromion-Urizen.

The sometimes subtle but often arbitrary exchange of personality which goes on in Blake likewise has its later analogues in *Prometheus Unbound* but it is in Shelley's concept of the "One Mind," wherein the distinctions of "I," "you," and "they" become grammatical forms merely, that we may glimpse the empirical source for a romantically transvalued and largely subverted psychology. Building on the empirical inference that personal identity was made up entirely of the heap of impressions that based simple and complex ideas of the individual consciousness, Locke suggested and Hume developed the logical reduction to absurdity that if one person could change his heap of impression for someone else's they would become each other, so far as essential personal identity was concerned.[6] Blake would of course see the logical absurdity of that exchange empirically viewed, as his propositions on natural religion indicate. But in another view, within a world where "What seems to Be: Is! To those to whom / It seems to Be," (*Jerusalem*, plate 36, 11. 50-51), the chaotic perversion of mental warfare which ensued at the breakup of the cosmic psychology of the Four Zoas, as instigated by Urizen and abetted by Luvah, was illustrated in the microcosmic personality of the individual as a multiple schizophrenia in which each of the warring factions within the psychic complex strove for an unequivocal dominance rather than for an integrated unity of their essential differences. Presently, in Ulro, Urizen is in charge, having usurped the place of Urthona/Los, who is imagination, the power of synthesis that kept together and in order the cosmic integrity that pre-existed Ulro and the Ulro man and, for the visionary like Blake, continued to exist in a necessarily ever-present Eternal Now.

As for Theotormon, we may suppose, with S. F. Damon, that he is Desire degenerated into Jealousy,[7] but it is probably better to generate if not quite humanize his character in this poem (where he is, after all, the hero manqué) by equating him with the average man middling sensual, an analogue in this respect of the character later applied by Blake to Reuben.[8] So taken, his actions and passions may be summarized in the following rather commonplace and predictable scenario in a world where the double standard, not twofold vision, defines man-woman relationships. In loving him freely, Oothoon gives herself to her lover Theotormon. As noted the physical act is not described, nor need it be, since Oothoon has told us, in heartfelt freedom, what she has done. Her "wing'd exulting swift delight" is expressed as she takes her course "over Theotormon's reign," which at least suggests that she has accepted his maleship in the traditional relation, as indeed her later words and actions continue to demonstrate.

What happens then is both quick and curious. Seemingly out of nowhere comes Bromion to rend her with his thunders, lay her on his "stormy bed" and call her "harlot." Building on what I said above, I think his appearance and his actions and words can be correlated with a traditional male response (at least traditional to the 18th century) to the woman who says "yes" without benefit of clergy. The man she says "yes" to, and who responds with a spontaneous sexual acceptance as his natural desires solicit him to do, consequently recalls the law and is dominated by its calculations once his libido has been put to rest. It is Theotormon's reason, in its spectral and negative capacity, that aborts and defames spontaneous love by calling it whore. Bromion is the law, the calculating principle, the selfish center that with varying degrees of social sanction to bolster it transmutes love into the primitive sexual jealousy that, in Blake, was aroused even in the hero Los when his son Orc attempted to embrace Enitharmon, Los's wife and Orc's mother. It is love perverted by reason, which, unredeemed, has its roots in Hell, specifically, the hell of self. We need to remember in the Blakean game of musical chairs which ensued on the break-up of the Four Zoas, that when Urizen took over imagination's place, Luvah was allowed to take residence in the place of judgement which Urizen had necessarily abdicated. Love, as an outgoing of the spirit, became the impetus behind the comparing faculty, became ingrown, became selfishness, and the seat of reason became the source of rationalization. Here, it is simple, recognizable, and condoned male possessiveness, the fruit of Eden's tree which brought relativity into the world by creating sexual difference and sexual hierarchy. It was precisely what Blake objected to most in the practical relationships he saw in Milton, who of course felt that, while man worshipped God, woman worshipped God in man. Blake, it must be noted immediately, by no means denied the spiritual values implicit in that hierarchy: the sexes would disappear at the time of the end, largely by a reversal of the creation of Eve, who would, as it were and would be, reincorporate herself as Adam's rib. She would become an emanation again.[9]

What has happened is that, so far as Oothoon is *practically* concerned, Theotormon has become Bromion. And it is that transformation of a likely enough Jekyll to a species of Hyde—at least within the convolutions of Theotormon's brain—that Blake depicted more and more effectively in his impressions of VDA, plate 7. I would like to spend the rest of this essay talking about that plate and others in VDA which illustrate the way in which Blake dramatized his text in his illuminations by putting into picture form his verbal symbols. And I would like specifically to suggest that Blake did not change his sense of symbolic relationship when he changed his expressive medium. Indeed, the significant point is—they gloss each other, a proposition often well expressed but sometimes not sufficiently thought about and imaginatively applied.

Let's begin with the title page, already referred to, where we find Oothoon speeding across the waves. We may first of all note that in this plate as elsewhere (in the title page of "The Book of Thel," e.g.) Blake tends to offer us an overview of his argument in the poem. To the left we have a fallen figure, perhaps Oothoon, who seems to be on the point of receiving some aid from one of the two figures above her; we also see, again a most positive sign, several fairy-like figures sporting in a rainbow (whose covenant associations Blake would want us conscious of), which suggests that, for all Urizen may do with his stormy clouds (or beds), the sun of vision, like God's own head, will dissipate his dire effects, and even here promises as much. But the central figure is clearly Urizen, as noted, his arms enfolded about himself as if he were freezing though surrounded by flame. The appropriate analogue is classical enough. In Dante's Hell the core where the Devil kept was a solid block of ice, which, nonetheless, emanated the flames of perverted lust which Dante illustrated among, e.g., the sodomites. For all his false heats, he is essentially zero at the core, absolute zero, utter negation. We catch in this illumination Oothoon sprinting across the waves at that moment when she looks back to see Urizen (who is Bromion) mouth rounded, as he blows after her with his icy old man's lust. All her joy in giving herself to Theotormon becomes with that look a prelude to its negation, which is the story of the poem.

But the figures of most significance here are the ones which seem to have a supernumerary or quite dubious existence, insofar as their application to the tale is concerned. Most clear among these figures is the "conjuror" (as David Erdman seems aptly to call him), sitting on a middle tier of clouds on the right, just above the "ters" of "Daughters,"his attention directed downwards still further to the right, his arms and hands similarly extended in the classic

Wave shadows of discontent? and in what houses dwell the wretched
Drunken with woe forgotten, and shut up from cold despair.

Tell me where dwell the thoughts forgotten till thou call them forth
Tell me where dwell the joys of old! & where the ancient loves?
And when will they renew again & the night of oblivion past?
That I might traverse times & spaces far remote and bring
Comforts into a present sorrow and a night of pain
Where goest thou O thought! to what remote land is thy flight?
If thou returnest to the present moment of affliction
Wilt thou bring comforts on thy wings. and dews and honey and balm;
Or poison from the desert wilds, from the eyes of the envier.

Then Bromion said: and shook the cavern with his lamentation

Thou knowest that the ancient trees seen by thine eyes have fruit;
But knowest thou that trees and fruits flourish upon the earth
To gratify senses unknown? trees beasts and birds unknown:
Unknown, not unpercieved, spread in the infinite microscope,
In places yet unvisited by the voyager. and in worlds
Over another kind of seas, and in atmospheres unknown:
Ah! are there other wars, beside the wars of sword and fire!
And are there other sorrows, beside the sorrows of poverty?
And are there other joys, beside the joys of riches and ease?
And is there not one law for both the lion and the ox!
And is there not eternal fire, and eternal chains?
To bind the phantoms of existence from eternal life?

Then Oothoon waited silent all the day, and all the night,

Visions of the Daughters of Albion, plate 7

162

Visions of the Daughters of Albion, frontispiece

attitude of the conjuror or, arguably, the puppeteer.[10] Below him and moving into the right margin of the impression—as they seem to grow out of or merge with the watery or stormy extension of Theotormon's reign which bases the illumination—are two humanoid figures, apparent in "O," but collapsing to mere rocks in most earlier impressions. The one to the left is sufficiently adumbrated to leave no doubt that he is the Theotormon of the frontispiece and plate 7, head bowed in the elbow bend of his right arm as it extends around to rest on his left shoulder next to his left ear. The figure to his left and at the right margin, arms and hair hanging limply down as she apparently bends at her waist, must be, in this context, Oothoon. Clearly, the conjuror's attention and his powers are directed at these two. What is he doing to them? In his capacity as a urizenic demon or projection he is converting the human form divine into "Shapeless Rocks/Retaining only Satan's Mathematic Holiness Length: Breadth, & highth."[11]

There is some division of opinion among Blake editors whether this variation most clearly depicted in copy "O" should be allowed legitimate status even as a variant. Erdman accepts it; Bentley does not mention it. But there is so far no acceptance at all for the reading (or elucidating) of VDA 7, copy "O" which I would like to demonstrate as a valid way of seeing because it is a Blakean way of illuminating. Briefly, what I see when I turn the "O" plate 7 on its left side—so that Oothoon seems to be floating vertically rather than horizontally—is an upward looking profile of Bromion formed by the contours of Theotormon's rather inflated head of hair.[12] I'd suggest the reader take a look before going on here . . . . Now, to specify further, I'd suggest that there is a fairly clear demarcation, in line and shadow, between that part of Theotormon's hair which would seem sufficient to a head not suffering from hydrocephalus and the Bromionic profile. Blake, we should recall, consistently maintains his ability to keep proportion by his bounding line, when he wants to do that. Indeed, if the top one-third of this hairpiece was removed, the remnant would not only seem more proportional to our expectations but closer to the curly-headed Theotormon of the frontispiece. Most importantly, the profile if seen at all will be seen to be the same profile as that turned to us by the Bromion of the frontispiece. Simply close the mouth, normalize his eyes, and brush down his hair, which, in keeping with the physiogomy it covers, is standing on end in evident terror.

To be able to see the illumination so is, I think, to gain access to double vision through the backdoor of single vision which Blake was here (in Copy "O") willing to provide to those who could not see that a rock can be, under the conditions of limitation and opakeness (i.e., of Adam and Satan), an ideal form of the human form deformed; or who cannot see the old man in the thistle; or, here, who cannot see that Bromion is inside Theotormon's

164

head. And not only inside but in charge. But Blake has provided us as well with a clarifying and, I believe, definitive verbal clue when he tells us that when Oothoon speaks to Theotormon, "none but Bromion can hear [her] lamentations" (1.62). What more do we need? To be more explicit would be to patronize the audience he meant to reach and to darken his visions with a doubtless futile attempt at reaching those whose doors of perception were closed up in the triple brass of urizenic number, weight and measure, not to be redeemed until the time of the end.

The context of that most crucial verbal adjunct to Blake's pictorial statement makes it evident that it is precisely plate 7 that he wants to apply the whole passage to: "Why does my Theotormon sit weeping upon the threshold; / And Oothoon hovers by his side, perswading him in vain: / I cry arise O Theotormon / . . . Theotormon hears me not . . ." (11. 44-46, 60). Oothoon, who has at least for the moment broken the chain that binds her to Bromion (or to the Bromionic character imposed on Theotormon), defines Theotormon's present State (in the Blakean sense) by disclaiming it for herself—"They told me that I had five senses to close me up, / And they inclos'd my infinite brain in a narrow circle" (11. 54-55). For Theotormon, in the illumination, this is the circle most roughly enclosed by Bromion's profile. When Theotormon does answer Oothoon it is again evident that he has only heard her through Bromion's mediation, with only an occasional hint that he has not altogether forgotten a vision beyond the scope of Urizen's "infinite microscope."[13] For all intents and purposes, like the 18th century man under the aegis of Reason (via Bacon, Newton, and Locke), he has become quite another heap of impressions.

That is not by any means the end of the story, though for present purposes it is the part of it that best integrates and explains several of the other plates in VDA either directly or by association. As noted, it is fairly clear that (as in "The Book of Thel") the title page does tell us the whole story in pictorial epitome. It should be likewise clear that the rocks and clouds variously appearing in several plates are symbolic manifestations of Urizen/Bromion. The viewers should note particularly how in plates 4 and 6 Oothoon back to back with a rock and cloud respectively is appropriately seen as back to back with Bromion. W. H. Stevenson's seeing of three figures in plate 4 is certainly wrong, while, if Bromion in maintaining his symbolic essence, the other sprawled and impotent figure on the rocks is Theotormon, not Bromion as generally received.[14] In plate 6 the sexual positioning of Oothoon, a kind of female Prometheus, suggests both the positive giving of herself to Theotormon and the rape by Bromion that was a negative effect of that giving. The final plate of the poem (11) may be the grimmest of all in its implications, as we see Oothoon thoroughly enmeshed in the urizenic cloud she balances on with out-stretched arms, a female replica of the title page Urizen.[15] But for all the gloom and negation of the context, we may, in Shelley's phrase, build our hope out of its own wreck by seeing in Bromion's evident terror his recognition that he cannot hold off the time of the end forever, that flesh and blood cannot abide his law a single moment. Whatever Bromion may see off to the left of the illumination that causes his terror, out of the corner of his eye he can see the sun of vision, full-orbed behind and breaking through the clouds over Theotormon's reign. Even here at the outset, isn't Blake providing us with a single-visioned hint of what double vision can offer even to those whose chosen condition is opakeness and limitation? To see or not to see is invariably the question, but one should keep in mind that it was the children who were best at elucidating Blake's visions—not Dr. Trusler.[16]

NOTES

[1]"The Marriage of Heaven and Hell," plate 7, 11.8, 18, G. E. Bentley, Jr., ed., *William Blake's Writings* (Oxford: The Clarendon Press, 1978), I, p. 81 (unless otherwise noted all references to Blake's writings will be to this edition).

[2]Of the sixteen copies of this work (hereafter referred to as VDA) "O" is the most finely colored and clarified, indicating that Blake took particular pains to "elucidate" his pictorial intentions to his viewer. It was among the last of the copies made, appearing on paper watermarked 1815, apparently imprinted between 1821-1825 (so Bentley, I, p. 695), over twenty years after the great majority of the relatively drab and undistinguished copies were made. It was sold to Henry Crabbe Robinson sometime after December 10, 1827 and is now in the British Museum Print Room. While I shall refer to "frontispiece" (plate 1) and "title page" (plate 2) for convenience and emphasis, my numbering of the plates throughout is that in Bentley (i.e., 1-11).

[3]In a letter to his friend Thomas Butts (22 Nov. 1802) Blake defined his levels of vision arbitrarily enough to leave further definition and application to the discretion of the reader and his visionary powers:

> Now I a fourfold vision see
> And a fourfold vision is given to me [;]
> Tis fourfold in my supreme delight
> And three fold in soft Beulahs night
> And twofold Always. May God us keep
> From single vision & Newtons Sleep[!]

A simplified but serviceable equation of the levels of vision in Blakean perspective may be made as follows: fourfold vision is the vision posssessed by those in Eden and/or Eternity, available only rarely to a few in a fallen and temporal world; threefold, in its relation to Beulah ("marriage"), is related to the visions of sex as well as to sleep, with perhaps a reminder that it is only through sexual generation that man in time can achieve spiritual regeneration; twofold is earlier defined in the Butts letter as the more usual symbolic variety when Blake sees with his "inward Eye" an "old Man grey," though his "outward" eye sees merely "a Thistle across [his] way";

single vision is empirical vision merely—totally outward, with the inward eye a universal blank. The irony of this inversion of values and visions was particularly acute at a time when Newton's single vision was the measure of truth both absolute and relative. As the present essay argues, it is precisely this narrowest but most relied on avenue of vision that Blake's modified illuminations were meant to lead his readers both through and beyond. In effect, he tries to turn a dead end into a gate in Jerusalem's wall and so demonstrate that even "The Ruins of Time" can build "Mansions in Eternity." More applicably here, one must always remember that, in Blake, a rock is a rock is *not* a rock, if one hopes, with Blake, always to possess the twofold vision he always had at his disposal and in terms of which he proposed that his works should be read and viewed.

[4]*Prometheus Unbound*, III, i, 37-42. In "I saw a chapel of gold" Blake uses precisely the same image to describe the way a phallic snake, in the process of raping a virginal (and symbolic) chapel, "Vomit[ed] his poison out" upon "the altar white."

[5]Cf. *Vala*, pp. 21-22 (Bentley, II, pp. 1103-04), where Luvah does what Urizen wants him to do while stating that he will do what he pleases.

[6]This is a popular oversimplification of their views, which in any case in Hume were developed to and for merely skeptical ends. (See sections on "Personal Identity" in Locke's *An Essay Concerning Human Understanding* and Hume's *A Treatise of Human Nature*).

[7]S. Foster Damon, *A Blake Dictionary* (New York: E.P. Dutton & Co., Inc., 1971), p. 401.

[8]Cf. *Jerusalem, passim* and Damon, pp. 347-348.

[9]Note particularly that for all her good and necessary qualities, Enitharmon is essentially and comprehensively the fallen woman for Blake, though fallen as Eve was, and her female posterity is, into a world of generation which she and they had difficulty in understanding as only a *means* towards regeneration. Enitharmon's lament in *Jerusalem* plates 92-93 demonstrates her inability to comprehend that she will be redeemed from womanhood into her original state as part of the androgynic zoa-emanation existence which Los presumes when he tells her "Sexes must vanish & cease/To be. . . ." Jerusalem certainly and Oothoon quite likely had a more certain vision of what it would be like for them after the time of the end. Significantly enough, Blake ends his greatest poem by telling us that the universal identities of all forms can be heard from through the names of their emanations, who are called Jerusalem. In this relation, the most important inference to be drawn from VDA is that men prevent women from realizing their emanative destiny. Oothoon is clearly (perhaps incomprehensibly) aware both of her trans-sensory visionary potential as well as her procreative powers in the present for fulfilling that potential, as she sings both of her "infinite brain" and the joys of "Happy copulation." Again, for Blake, only through physical generation through the woman (e.g., Mary) could spiritual regeneration through the man (e.g., Christ) be achieved.

[10]In *The Illuminated Blake* (New York: Doubleday, 1974), p. 126. There may be more relevance to the "conjuror" denomination than has as yet met the scholarly eye. In 1775 Nathaniel Hone sketched and painted a notorious satirical portrait of Sir Joshua Reynolds called "The Conjuror." Both the sketch (which is in the Tate) and the painting (which is in the Dublin Art Museum) show Reynolds conjuring up his works of art from a pile of paintings by the eminent artists he was sometimes accused of plagiarizing. Blake's animosity toward Reynolds could well have inspired such an analogue as the figure on the cloud, though the idealization here would then seem to have derived its features from Blake's inner eye (cf. "The Ghost of a Flea") rather than from Hone's rendition of the Reynolds' physiognomy.

[11]*Milton*, plate e (Bentley, p. 389), 11. 17-18. In *Milton* the "shapeless rocks" are mere "States" through which "Individual Identities" may pass. Blake made it clearer in Copy "O" that such was the hopeful case in which we may find Theotormon and Oothoon. In the earlier impressions, they are completely lost to single vision in their apparently unredeemed rockiness. The likely relation between the conjuror and Satan in *Milton*, the "limit of Opacity," seems confirmed by their kindred methods of rendering their darkness visible.

[12]I refer parenthetically to my seeing of this impression in a review of Bentley's edition (in *Blake: An Illustrated Quarterly*, vol. 14, no. 3, Winter 1980-81, p. 159).

[13]VDA, 102. In this well-known letter of rebuke to the spiritually imperceptient Reverend John Trusler Blake spelled out his sense of the relationship between understanding and imagination, suggesting too, with his documentation from Bacon, a willingness to use the wisdom of the serpent for his purposes: "Why is the Bible more Entertaining & Instructive than any other book? Is it not because [it] is addressed to the Imagination which is Spiritual Sensation & but mediately to the Understanding or Reason[?]. . . . Consider what Lord Bacon says[:] 'Sense sends over to Imagination before Reason have judged & Reason sends over to Imagination before the Decree can be acted' " (Bentley, II, p. 1527). In a later letter to the sculptor ("of Eternity," so Blake) Flaxman, he provided a clarifying and expansive version of Theotormon's urizenically clouded recollection of Eden (11. 90-91): "I look back into the regions of Reminiscence & behold our ancient days before this Earth appeared in its vegetated mortality to my mortal vegetated Eyes" (Bentley, p. 1541).

[14]Bromion is throughout the dominant figure, physically dominating Oothoon and mentally dominating Theotormon. Stevenson (in *Blake: The Complete Poems* [London: Longman, 1971], p. 175) further suggests that the figures lying on the rocks may be exhausted after the rape. Seeing the male figure as Theotormon, one may at least infer that, given the sexual sprawl the two figures are in, this is as close as we get to a portrayed (or verbalized) physical engagement between lovers. But the significant symbolic point is surely that in binding Oothoon to Bromion Theotormon bound himself to the same impotent posture, back to back to the rocky law Bromion represents and enunciates.

[15]The congruence may be justified outside the limits of the poem when we recall that Blake's Urizen figure is a typically diabolic rendering of the Elohim/Jehovah figure of the Sistine ceiling—the incarnation of fiat law who retrospectively touches the old Adam in us all to bring death, not life, into a stony being by uncreating Eve's regenerative purpose—by making "[sex] acts unlovely," by making Oothoon's love a sin to the Bromionic Theotormon.

[16]See Bentley, p. 1527. As Bentley notes, however, it was not Trusler but Blake's friend George Cumberland who commented on the whole of the letter and its visionary rationalization—"Blake/Dimd with Superstition."

****

I find it difficult to write about Blake as my single most powerful experience with him came when I was maybe 17 years old, and I suddenly "discovered" his paintings—as a result of which I suffered/enjoyed an unrelieved and unrelenting 90-day erection. Now that's my kind of mysticism. And if you care to quote me, you're welcome to.

Paul Metcalf

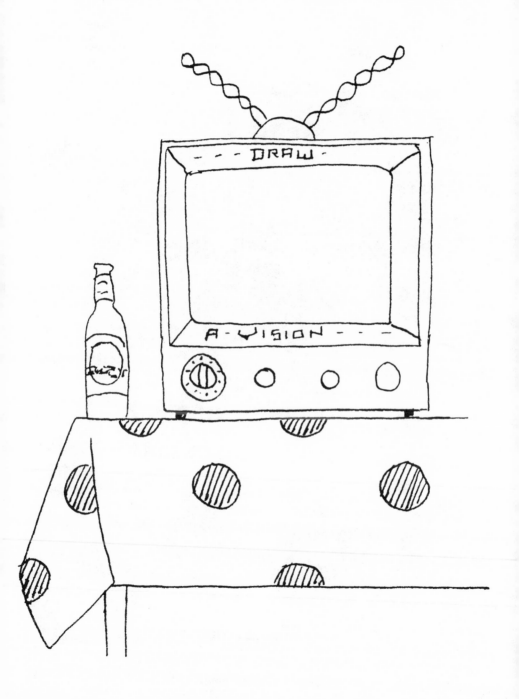

John Altman

Blake Without Wheels

David Ohle

Blake Oblique

When Blake was eighteen, he was sent to the United States where he attended Oral Roberts University. He solved the problem of school expenses by constructing his own portable home at the edge of campus. It consisted of a covered wagon built on an old auto chassis, the wooden sides being covered with a canvas roof. Inside, there was a bunk, a stove, table, chair and a rack for books. He managed to live on about $5 a month by doing his own housekeeping and eating vegetables and fruits sent to him by his wife, Catherine, all the way from 3 Fountain Court, Blake's London home.

If one visits the Historical Museum in Tulsa, Oklahoma, even today, one can see Blake's cozy wagon, reconstructed in painstaking detail, down to the chamber pot and its darkly waxen contents.

There was a time, after his trial for sedition, when Blake learned to be idle. He wandered about from house to house, asking for crusts at back windows. He tattled and became a busybody, speaking things he oughtn't. Arrested, he was publicly spanked, to no avail. In short order, he was haunting the alleyways, selling tobacco to innocent children, spreading gossip like butter. Again arrested, his poor feet were clubbed senseless with billy bats. He was then set loose in the icy streets. He fell asleep sitting on a gutter's edge. By morning his feet were frozen, a sickening blue. He made his way to the Strand and begged a surgeon to take them off by any means at hand. The surgeon obliged, blowing an analgesic powder into Blake's face before going to work with a bonesaw and a chisel. When the feet were free of their stumps, the surgeon, one Joan Anglicus, heaved them into a nail keg and, for the moment, that was that. Exhausted, she lay in her bed to nap, where she dreamt of a Dutchman in wooden shoes. Waking, she went to a closet, selecting a pair of stout, birch shoetrees. Using metal clamps, carriage bolts, an auger, and tap-screws, she affixed them to Blake's protruding ankle bone.

After a period of hopping around, Blake grew accustomed to his new feet, walking with ease, swimming in the Thames. He had no further idle inclinations, and soon was at work on the *Book of Urizen*.

Last Spring, while engaged in clearing out a body of marsh land, Blake came across a den of terrapins. He lined a wooden box with cotton. The terrapins were laid in rows on the cotton and covered with another cotton layer. On top of this was placed a second row of terrapins, and so on, until the box was filled. The box was covered with a blanket and stored in the cellar. There the terrapins slept through the winter while, upstairs, huddled near his stove, Blake illustrated *Pilgrim's Progress*.

Mr. Labouchère tells a remarkable story regarding the heart of Louis XIV, and how it came to be buried at Westminster Abbey. It seems that one day Blake was having his morning tea in a cafe in Lyons in the company of another emigré, by the name of St. Denis, when St. Denis produced from his pocket something that looked like a piece of dried leather an inch or so long, which he presented to Blake. "I was," he said, "in the cathedral when the royal tombs were broken open and the contents scattered to the winds. This heart is that of Louis Quatorze. It was kept in a separate receptacle, and I managed to sneak away with it." Blake, moved by the scientific spirit, wet his finger and rubbed it on the heart. He put the finger to his mouth after that, and before he could be stopped he put the heart into his mouth and swallowed it, whether by accident or design will never be known.

Very shortly afterward Blake died and was buried in Westminster Abbey. It is impossible he could have digested the thing, as age had almost petrified it. Consequently, the heart of the French king now reposes in the Abbey, enclosed in the body of Blake. Blake's funeral orgies, arranged by Frederick Tatham, raised some dusty eyebrows in the sacred precincts, as he was buried just as he'd asked to be—dressed in lace nightgown and seated in a red Ferrari, with the seat slanting comfortably. To quote from his will:

> Though fuel is plentiful in the afterworld, distances are great. If one needs to drive, say, from Bowlahoola to Lake Udan Adan, one needs a good, fast car. If you arrive in the afterworld without wheels, it's tough buns. You then take your chances thumbing rides. It's horrible. You never know who'll pick you up. For Christ's sake, it could be Bill Hayley, the Butcher of Litchfield, who beheaded, skinned, quartered and smoked a dozen plump women, including the sheriff's mother, and wore a vest made of the skin of a woman's torso. On the good side, though, it might be Mitzi Gaynor, the choicest trollop in the afterworld, a favorite of all dead men. No, one wants to have one's own wheels. And then, when you get ready to shift back, why you can sell the thing at a steep price."

Kent Clair Chamberlain

Unsymbolic Digression

I shall   Not   Census-
-Take a
Verbal   Pot-   -Shot at William Blake,
                 Though
                    Free Verse
      Has   Become the   Norm, and, to
   Blast, the
Fashionablemost   Form.

     What   Brings Light
        Into the
               World, brings
    Joy to   Flower,
  Though
All
      Dis-   -Dain it,   Must
       Be
            Applauded, our EMPYREALIAN Songs
   Their own   Re-
-Ward and
      Reason!

(The poem that follows is named after this engraving, but is not intended as any sort of gloss on it, so much as an incidental homage to what I take to be its essence. Edward Lucie-Smith has aptly defined what Blake depicts here as "the soul of man springing forth into the consciousness of his own power". The poem traces a reawakening of wonder and delight, a single glad day of my life.)

Michael Horovitz

Glad Day

A dawn of agitating winds
dapples leaves afresh on skylit space
awakening alps of cloud to race
& drop out, giving way to sun
as firm in its good morning beams
—A tonic lightening good morrow
crystalling adjective in noun,
name in thing—another day
—another moment in an eternal ray
of running magic rhythm's no-time
releasing madhappy conjunctions
of plenitude—unplanned
realisations
    of being alive—
 This is a day, you say
for visions and miracles
and cleansing of the sights
—A day I want to wear green
and orange
—No—stay naked, I cry, I sigh
but it makes no odds as
tingling to one another
we leap out of bed as one
man, yeh—that's to say
feeling like nothing we knew before,
like—as if nothing *was*
before, like—'a new man'
—two persons in one
being—animal mental spiritual
poised—in perfect union
of sentient immortality—
 Jump now—let's
out and away, slide down

175

the stairs Whisht—athwart
sleep's lingering portico—heavy jambs
flung open wide eyes drive on
our twinkle-toed electric glee, dive
on down under the blazing stoop
—toss our heads letting hair stream
wild & free, floating the tree-lined arcade's green-
   gold shimmering budfall blossomdrift
we run run run print our pleasure in
springing foot momentum—touching
   down only to whizz on faster
not quite in step but gaily zig-zag hand
in hand, foot evenly over-
lapping foot as if to tip
all conflicts deftly down the drains'
fetid jaws—
   Lifting by treading
this crumbling vale—Notting Dale
—called London's 'Jungle West 11',
discounting clerical steps to heaven
—finding our feet, the day's
and sensing those that did
in ancient time

   . . . Comes midday, you're mental miles away—
slowed, tamed, pacing—at bay
feeding hungry underprivileged & immigrant mites
the vegetable university lies of the land
—another mind and matter 'weekday'
where mountains drop back
                   to the classroom wall—

   I'm back on the balcony, writing—
studying my hand, thinking over
my thirty years—dismantled, spent
—after-knowledge of the good
—miraculous—yes, and the terrible
hours of an age—lashes my spirit,
shackles limbs—to burrow the margin
of memory's heavy page

—and yet...the earth is full
of sky today, and the ageless ancestral sky
on fire—as they say,
paving the streets
                    with gold
—so arise, awake again
to fresh splendours
of measured possibility
—this super- natural
real world—& the immeasurable beyond!
    Born every day
        —tho' every moment
        the weighted heart
        out
            burst
                its load
    —so do flowers—mandalas—
    the throbbing universe
    our very breath
    —all ours—the stars, O love
    the only power
                    I'll ever crave.

    Too soon—late afternoon
the tide of exultation ebbs away, so—
I'll walk out to meet you,
    past the glistening panoply
    of plastic & aluminium offices, uptown
    from the sodium-sentinelled glare
    of cheaper, newly faded tower blocks
    looking custom-built for battery, rape or suicide
over the once hallowed ground of play-street trysts
and bombsite chase—the long-lost
yearnings, fears and fleeting triumphs
—humiliation, relief—and still more
grief for my own child city
                    so barely covered over
    —yet the earth is full the twilit air
busy with rumours of day's work done, this day's
    children home—a moving range
of lamby peaks spreading the evening

out against the night, as lights
flash on in ones and twos, the kids
come out again to play
with ball and bow, and tear away
to catch up a piper
        who's chasing the sunset
            round the corner
—dancing, delirious with its promise
of summers galore—glad shouts

        . . . their heads go under
swimming through the deep-end dusk—
long-shadowed cascades
                    hours after closing time
    I see them dunk—lose themselves
and their long days' journeys
in the void waves' ripple- responses
—mounting
            and breaking with them
to aeons, where nothing is recognised
—know death
and surface in the nick of time, riding
high—flailing kicking gasping alive

    . . . and know
the weariless labour of love
Blake's little black boy's mother knew
we each
    "are put on earth a little space,
    that we may learn to bear"
is the one undying deliverance
—to embrace the burning joy
at the heart of creation—burning
    for continuous renewal
    of life, the only measure
    of its worth—

    O—let all my safety
catches be blown—undone
for I hear voices—singing, calling, avalanching—

murmuring on toward
                    distant shores and forests
as we navigate the winds and whirlpools
on our ship of words made flesh—your words
blasting open my ears to the eaves
when you turn from dream to whisper
        —You are the key
        to all my secret doors
        that grew rusty on their hinges
—and I turn
                on
and on
resplendent
        In you
                —and we open
                all the doors
                unto the innermost
                dawning
                        vision
—wing'd riders
of apocalypse
    —each night
    and opened day
                    revealed—
    full flight

    in the shining armour
                    of naked light

Joan Stone

Dancing Blake

twisting and untwisting
winding and unwinding
the burden of self
reaching up—out—anywhere for release
back and forth in the same rut
moments of hope
      lightness, springiness
      but always the counter pull of gravity
      of forces that cannot be controlled
      but must be bowed to or resisted

using the spine as a vertical axis, upright or tilted,
      arms and legs describing lines coming out from the axis
twisting the various parts of the body around the spine,
      the central chord
using the body to describe a space outside it—shaping
      the body around a void
making the body an isolated speck in space

Blake's lyrical line and color can be misleading.
There is iron at the core of his gestures.

Daniel Cahn

Susan Mernit

Illuminations

'let first
a drawing
be made'

figured from red land,
earth of the sun

filter

the image comes

up on wet
paper

marshground
desert
field   rock

fire figure
striking stars

underworld
of coal

drowned men
in the sea

scale
the cliffs
of the island

the body walks
into dream
you we will devour
the earth will swallow up

to walk in light forever

to stand
fixed land

your body clean
will no more
bleed.

Geography

the head dreams
of the body

body dreams
of land

land dreams
of water

of a highway travelled
the wet edges
of an open form

mouth of the Hudson
island we walk on

I have come back
to your body

have made it
my land

walking by the river

I dream
this man

Naming the Emblem

The Heavenly Man
has ten bright eyes
long thin fingers
and two neat tits

he flies on the wings
of a bat
and sleeps in a tree
in your garden

monkey in the bushes
an old boot you left outside
to protect the feet
of Heavenly Man
when he must stomp
through the mud
to ask your tree
for shelter

he is your lover
a once a week fuck
and he knows
the mountain thunder
is just another tongue

not the one
he kisses you with
but a language
of death and fire.

men come

men come
to speak of stars
like the bodies
of women
they cherish

like children speak
of the moon

let us walk our circle

and watch the sky
through the window

and watch
the shooting flames
of the stars
as they go to bed

men come
to speak of stars
the way they dream
of water

a land
sinking into
bright bath
of the moon

there is fire overhead
blood clouding the water
season

the land dies
you die too

men come
to speak of stars
as if the night were over

as if the body
in the bed
would warm them
forever.

landscape of roses

I sit upstairs
in the bedroom
and think
of making love to you

an afternoon
of roses

white sheets
the blankets red

I like the way
you hold me
your hands hollow

and I move against your shadow
seeing
some dark rose

These poems were written, for the most part, in response to the printed page, working from the poems & etchings of William Blake. I was interested in the relationship between nature and the artist and the reproduction of experience that takes place in the creation of a drawing from nature, and a poem from art.

"Illuminations" takes its beginning point from looking at a Blake engraving "The dog" done for Haley's ballads in 1802.

"Naming the Emblem" was written after looking at "The Glad Day, or The Dance of Albion," also Blake. Adam Kadmon is the idealized figure of all men.

"Men come to Speak of Stars" was written after looking at one of the Job illustrations Blake drew.

The other poems were written under Blake's influence in a more generalized way—his energy, his worldview. Most of them date from 1973-74, when I was a student at Bard College, studying with Robert Kelly.

Algernon Charles Swinburne

Blake and Whitman

Confidence in future friends, and contempt of present foes, may have induced Blake to leave his highest achievements impalpable and obscure. Their scope is as wide and as high as heaven, but not as clear; clouds involve and rains inundate the fitful and stormy space of air through which he spreads and plies an indefatigable wing. There can be few books in the world like these; I can remember one poet only whose work seems to me the same or similar in kind; a poet as vast in aim, as daring in detail, as unlike others, as coherent to himself, as strange without and as sane within. The points of contact and sides of likeness between William Blake and Walt Whitman are so many and so grave, as to afford some ground of reason to those who preach the transition of souls or transfusion of spirits. The great American is not a more passionate preacher of sexual or political freedom than the English artist. To each the imperishable form of a possible and universal Republic is equally requisite and adorable as the temporal and spiritual queen of ages as of men. To each all sides and shapes of life are alike acceptable or endurable. From the fresh free ground of either workman nothing is excluded that is not exclusive. The words of either strike deep and run wide and soar high. They are both full of faith and passion, competent to love and to loathe, capable of contempt and of worship. Both are spiritual, and both democratic; both by their works recall, even to so untaught and tentative a student as I am, the fragments vouchsafed to us of the Pantheistic poetry of the East. Their casual audacities of expression or speculation are in effect wellnigh identical. Their outlooks and theories are evidently the same on all points of intellectual and social life. The divine devotion and selfless love which make men martyrs and prophets are alike visible and palpable in each. It is no secret now, but a matter of public knowledge, that both these men, being poor in the sight and the sense of the world, have given what they had of time or of money, of labour or of love, to comfort and support all the suffering and sick, all the afflicted and misused, whom they had the chance or the right to succour and to serve. The noble and gentle labours of the one are known to those who live in his time; the similar deeds of the other deserve and demand a late recognition. No man so poor and so obscure as Blake appeared in the eyes of his generation ever did more good works in a more noble and simple spirit. It seems that in each of these men at their birth pity and passion, and relief and redress of wrong, became incarnate and innate. That may well be said of the one which was said of the other: that "he looks like a man." And in externals and details the work of these two constantly and inevitably coheres and coincides. A sound as of a sweeping wind; a prospect as over dawning continents at the fiery instant of a sudden sunrise; a splendour now of stars and now of storms; an expanse and exultation of wing across strange spaces of air and above shoreless stretches of sea; a resolute and reflective love of liberty in all times and in all things where it should be; a depth of sympathy and a height of scorn which complete and explain each other, as tender and as bitter as Dante's; a power, intense and infallible, of pictorial concentration and absorption, most rare when combined with the sense and the enjoyment of the widest and the highest things; an exquisite and lyrical excellence of form when the subject is well in keeping with the poet's tone of spirit; a strength and security of touch in small sweet sketches of colour and outline, which bring before the eyes of their student a clear glimpse of the thing designed—some little inlet of sky lighted by moon or star, some dim reach of windy water or gentle growth of meadow-land or wood; these are qualities common to the work of either. Had we place or time or wish to touch on their shortcomings and errors, it might be shown that these too are nearly akin; that their poetry has at once the melody and the laxity of a fitful stormwind; that, being oceanic, it is troubled with violent groundswells and sudden perils of ebb and reflux, of shoal and reef, perplexing to the swimmer or the sailor; in a word, that it partakes the powers and the faults of elemental and eternal things; that it is at times noisy and barren and loose, rootless and fruitless and informal; and is in the main fruitful and delightful and noble, a necessary part of the divine mechanism of things. Any work or art of which this cannot be said is superfluous and perishable, whatever of grace or charm it may possess or assume. Whitman has seldom struck a note of thought and speech so just and so profound as Blake has now and then touched upon; but his work is generally more frank and fresh, smelling of sweeter air, and readier to expound or expose its message, than this of the prophetic books. Nor is there among these any poem or passage of equal length so faultless and so noble as his "Voice out of the Sea," or as his dirge over President Lincoln— the most sweet and sonorous nocturn ever chanted in the church of the world. But in breadth of outline and charm of colour, these poems recall the work of Blake; and to neither poet can a higher tribute of honest praise be paid than this.

from *William Blake: A Critical Essay* (1868)

Roger Easson

The Lineaments of Gratified Desire:
A Conversation with William Blake

November 28, 1981, Memphis, Tennessee

I invited William Blake to dine with me last week. He was reluctant at first but consented when I told him I wanted to inverview him for Sparks of Fire, *a book devoted expressly to his work and the heirs of his vision. The trip into Ulro from Eden was not easy and he appeared somewhat later than we had planned. He arrived dressed in a long coat and a broad brimmed hat, carrying a great globe of light. He looked as if he might have just stepped out of the frontispiece to his last prophetic work,* Jerusalem. *The dust of mortality soiled his coat; his shoulders were wet with the rain of life. In his eyes were rainbows.*

We embraced, and I escorted him into the den where we talked about his journey and the kind of interview Io might like. I even gave him a copy of the journal and a sample set of questions to examine. Finally, we sat to dinner and later retired into the den for brandy and the warmth of a late November fire.

[Interviewer's Note: *I have tried to transcribe this conversation as it took place. My tape recorder failed to pick up any of the conversation, so I have had to recreate it as nearly as I could recollect. I confess, however, that in the intervening days, I have begun to have visions and now find it difficult to record what transpired that evening with the clarity I might earlier have employed.*]

INTERVIEWER: You know, William, I expected us to have some difficulty in this interview. The distance in time and space is one thing, but the distance in language and thought is quite another. I must say that I am amazed with your familiarity with developments over the last 150 years. I have the feeling that this interview is going to be surprisingly easy, but then this whole experience has been a surprise.

BLAKE: That's the thing about living in Eden. We receive all the greatest souls of each age, and as the wars of intellect are the only wars in Eternity, the exchanges we have had have been very lively. And, it is also characteristic of Eden that, whenever new citizens arrive, they drop all the peculiar markings of language and habit which characterized their time and nationality.

INTERVIEWER: One of the most important elements of your career—and I have no doubt it keeps bringing students to your work, and perhaps at the same time drives others away—is what has been termed the visionary quality of your art and poetry. Part of this attraction—and in my reading I find it repeatedly, especially in the popular literatures—is an interest in your vision as being related to the "psychedelic" experiences of those who have experimented with psychotropic plants and mind-altering synthetic drugs like LSD 25. Just recently, for example, I had a visitor to the Blake Center who evidenced such an interest. He was a young man on his way to a new job, counseling veterans in a V.A. Hospital on drug abuse problems. He asked me if your visions were not inspired by a drug habit of some sort. Would you speak to this issue for us? What was the nature of these visions? And was there any drug you used to stimulate them?

BLAKE: Well, let me say that it's quite typical of an age such as yours. So completely absorbed is it by the rational intellect, that any imaginative or intuitive or visionary experience must inevitably be the product of some exotic agent which overwhelms the rational mind. Such an attitude assumes that visionary experience can only occur when the individual's control is lost, rendering the experience totally anomalous. I'm equally sure that many will think that if I did not do drugs, then I must surely have been quite mad. My visions could then be dismissed as "hallucinations," the product of an overheated brain. The key to both these ideas is that they allow those who embrace them to dismiss my visions as a variety of "brain dysfunction," as your psychiatrists would call it. Clearly they'd hope my visions are not part of "normal consciousness." Visions would then become a kind of exotic land we can visit, exploit, or dismiss as we wish. It's important, however, for you to understand that there's another way of being in the world—a vision-centered life style, you might call it—which is quite as normal as what your age so fondly calls "sanity" or "rational consciousness."

INTERVIEWER: I remember that you spoke quite directly about your visions in The Marriage of Heaven and Hell when you wrote that you saw no visions nor heard any, in a finite organical perception but your senses discovered the infinite in everything and as you were then persuaded that the voice of honest indignation is the voice of god, you wrote. If you were not using drugs, and, as you assure us, were quite sane, how are we to understand this assertion? Were your visions just poetic license?

BLAKE: When ordinary people talk about visions, they seem to want them to be like Moses' burning bush or Ezekiel's fiery chariot. They want a physical manifestation that will knock them down, like fireworks of the mind. Or they suppose that a vision is a cloudy vapor, or a nothing, as a shadow on a frosted window. But visions are not like that at all. The

191

problem of modern man is that imagination has been so discredited by scientists that few people can invest the kind of energy into it to duplicate the Ancients' experience of the visionary world. And I do not think one has to rely upon the psychic explosives, what you call mind-altering drugs, for that energy either. But mostly all we have to do is to understand the true nature of imagination in order to begin to grasp what a vision is. Perhaps you might call it "soul sight." That is to say, the imaginative faculty is not some fictive desire to daydream, but it is actually what that citizen of Eternity, the Soul, sees when his eyes are involved in the individual's perception. But few even believe in a soul, and so they cannot accept that the soul might actually *see*. You must also understand that it is the Greco-Roman cultural tradition which opposes visions. I cannot stress this too strongly. Visions are not part of the Classics! The Divine Imagination originates in the visionary tradition of the Hebrew Prophets like Abraham and David.

INTERVIEWER: Does this distinction have anything to do with your idea about single vision, double vision and so forth?

BLAKE: Well, yes. I remember I wrote a letter to my friend Thomas Butts. I really was very grateful to him and wanted him to understand my visions. He was not really of a visionary turn of mind, so I thought I'd contrast visions with other kinds of perception. I think the lines go like this:

Now I a fourfold vision see,
And a fourfold vision is given to me;
'Tis fourfold in my supreme delight
And threefold in soft Beulah's night
And twofold Always. May God us keep
From Single vision & Newton's sleep!

That is to say, fourfold vision was not the same kind of perception which Newton and his crew have institutionalized as the scientific and objective observer. Science is after all simply the art of measurement—why do you think I had Urizen with his calipers in "The Ancient of Days" design? Urizen is that God of measurement which restricts all vision to single planes so that we see the world through the eyes of a draftsman. Existence then becomes flat views, linear views, front, side and top. All accompanied by measurements and notations. Double vision is what we each possess naturally with our physical organs of perception. The two generated organs, situated as they are, give us the evidence of perspective and depth. This is the view of the ordinary artist who depicts landscapes and portraits. Triple vision or three-fold vision adds to these the dimension and evidence of the dream, which I called the land of Beulah. And fourfold vision adds to these the evidence of the imagination or the perception of the soul. This was just a little hierarchy of kinds of perceptual processes. Yet one thing that people seem still not to have understood is that visions and dreams are allied.

INTERVIEWER: Could you develop this line of thinking for us?

BLAKE: Well, both dreams and visions are usually rejected as insignificant kinds of perception. Yet, for the moment of the dream, when you are deeply involved in the imaging process, you can have as vivid an experience as anything you may have experienced in the so-called "awakened state." Visions are like dreams, only visions occur as part of the conscious state. Now see here. It's fashionable in your world to think that the experience of the dream may suggest some kind of unconscious content, particularly repressed material that may be a key to neurotic conditions and so forth. This kind of thinking discredits the dream and its important kind of sight. If you have studied the language of Art as I have, you would understand that the imaging process of the dream simply uses the language of Art to see into the human experience. Or to reverse the equation the language of art is the language of eternity which visions and dreams employ as a matter of course. Yet your age has undervalued the dream, and the vision, in the same way they have undervalued Art. It prefers instead to reduce life to the kinds of experience that have direct impact on the physical world. So Physics has replaced Theology as the core of education. Man's relationship to the material world dominates culture now, and Man's relationship to his God is clearly of less importance.

INTERVIEWER: But surely if visions were as potent an experience as they were in your life, they would intrude into our lives, even if we tried to ignore them.

BLAKE: And I am sure they do. But many of us are so frightened of them we suppress all mention of them, and forget them as soon as they occur.

INTERVIEWER: Why should that be?

BLAKE: You see we have been taught from infancy a set of assumptions about such experiences which deny their significance. These are assumptions for which there is no proof, and no possibility of proof, but they undergird our embrace of the reasoning intellect.

INTERVIEWER: Are these what you called the "Mind Forged Manacles" in your poem "London"?

BLAKE: That is it, exactly. These assumptions are like chains of the mind in which the Real Man lies locked up. Often these assumptions are embedded so deeply in our consciousness that we never recognize their presence. In this hidden state they guide our perceptions imperceptably until Eternity is lost completely from view. Challenge one of these assumptions—a key one—and the resulting threat to the world view it supports can force violent reactions, reactions of the desperate trying to keep their mental ship from sinking into what they believe wrongly to be a demonic sea of irrational and chaotic experience.

INTERVIEWER: What was it, I wonder, which first gave you evidence of such binding assumptions?

BLAKE: It is hard to say when I first became aware of them, but I remember I had my first really clear recognition of mind-forged manacles when I began to study Milton and *Paradise Lost*. I wondered why there were no new Epics of equal merit being written, and why they should be so mocked by other writers. Then I understood it was no longer plausible that Gods should converse with men, as Homer and Virgil and all the great epic poets had held. This interpenetration of the world of the Divine and the human is a central characteristic of the Epic. Without it the poetic narrative of the Epic becomes merely an adventure story of heroic proportions. Adam and Eve were as conversant with Satan and the Angels as I am with you.

INTERVIEWER: I see. That explains a lot about *The Marriage of Heaven and Hell* then.

BLAKE: How do you mean?

INTERVIEWER: Well, there is that matter of the Soul and the Body being one. You assert that if the error of the body/soul duality is replaced with its contrary—that the body and soul are one—then we might be restored to a kind of pre-fall state.

BLAKE: Yes, something like that, anyway. You see, I was very interested in creation stories, and that whole myth of the Fall of Man had been highly energized in Protestant theology by *Paradise Lost*. So I became increasingly aware of the impact of genesis stories upon culture the more I studied the impact of *Paradise Lost*. Apparently such genesis stories, as they attempt to explain the origin of death, evil, and alienation from the Gods, deliver into the consciousness of the people the basic assumptions about the way that culture fabricates its sense of reality. I saw this and decided that England needed a genesis story to explain origins of the Age of Reason, and the origin of its new god of science, Urizen. I called it *The Book of Urizen*.

INTERVIEWER: But what about the assumption of the body and the soul being one? Isn't this important somehow to understanding visions?

BLAKE: Yes, indeed! I focused upon this assumption that the body and the soul were separate elements, indeed somehow polar opposites, as *the* key assumption which alienated the world of the Divine from the world of men. Once this opposition was embedded in the consciousness *as if it were true*, then the whole fallen existence was created and the whole melodrama of Sin, Temptation, Seduction, and Evil was amplified and was made the rule rather than the exception to the rule. I read the narrative of the Fall to mean that the Cherub with the flaming sword dividing us from the Edenic state was this assumption. If we could but purge our consciousnesses of this idea, then we could re-enter a state of existence where visionary experience becomes the norm rather than the exception. Once this is accomplished then the world is transformed. There would no longer be any possibility of the profane. Every moment of existence would be divine, every act, and every desire.

INTERVIEWER: Were you able to accomplish such a feat?

BLAKE: Yes. It took a great deal of work, and after I left Hayley's employ, I was finally able to enter into this battle and win my way into this renovated consciousness.

INTERVIEWER: But wasn't it difficult to maintain such a belief system? With everyone believing quite the contrary, how could you maintain your sanity?

BLAKE: It was difficult to maintain. But no more so, I imagine, than to maintain any really sacramental life-style in the face of such an awesome worship of the physical and the profane as existed in the England of my day. The real problem is, just as you say, maintaining your sanity. But see here — sanity is a political issue, not a real issue. The assumption I made was taboo, and if one man embraces such a forbidden assumption, then those who have embraced the contrary challenge his sanity and cause his exile, his incarceration, or shun him entirely. This assumption that the body is the soul is a very potent taboo, because it also begins to assert that an individual can communicate directly with the Divine, and perhaps even asserts that the individual is himself divine. These expose us to violent reactions unless we are careful.

INTERVIEWER: Yes, I am sure you are correct. Were Jesus himself to walk among us claiming to be the Son of God, he probably would be slapped in a padded cell and given heavy sedatives.

BLAKE: That is just my point! How can one be a Christian in an age when every avenue of divine encounter has been barred, and all testimony of divine existence is produced upon evidence several thousand years old by an institution rife with division, hatred, corruption, and contradiction? How can a Christian in an age so dominated by the desire to be reasonable look at a church, which has institutionalized greed, gluttony, pride and self-righteousness, and still think it has the authority to proclaim its good news. No! there has to be some way, some avenue of knowing the original stimulus which created this event called Christianity.

INTERVIEWER: Doubtless you are right. And it is probably exactly this which has generated so much drug use in our era. Though I doubt the spiritual numbness that generates disbelief in the existence of a soul has ever been so accurately described. But what I still don't understand is why it is not possible to see the body and soul as contraries. If I am understanding your argument correctly, they are not. Right?

BLAKE: Right. Let me see if I can explain. In our creation story Eve eats from The Tree of Knowledge which is the tree of the knowledge of good and of evil. That is to say, it is the tree of the knowledge of duality. So that flourishing vocabulary of polar opposites we have in English produces a constellation of warring conceptual enemies who strive to annihilate each other somehow. So "male" and "female," "yes" and "no," "on" and "off,"

195

"good" and "evil," and so on and on fragment our awareness into constant war. So I realized that the attempt to return consciousness to the pre-fall state must include some strategy to resolve such apparent hostilities. And the notion of contraries was my solution. Contraries come into existence simultaneously, and one cannot be destroyed without annihilating the other. As I said, without contraries is no progression. We must have contrary states of consciousness in order to have the necessary stress to achieve spiritual existence. Otherwise we'd never rise above the brutes. So, for example, when Augustine says that the inhabitants of Heaven look over the heavenly wall at the torments of Hell and they breathe a sigh of relief, he is saying that Hell and its torments define Heaven and its Joys. Without Hell is no Heaven. So, too, without War is no Peace. Without pain is no pleasure, and so on. But the soul is eternal and immortal. The body is born and dies. The two do not come into existence or leave it at the same time. They cannot hence be contraries. Do we call the snake's dry skin the snake? No. They are not contraries. The snake may shed its skin in the same way the soul may shed its body. But the point is that the snake's skin is the snake, is it not, or at any rate a portion of it. So, too, the body is the soul, or at least a portion of the soul as perceived by the fallen senses.

INTERVIEWER: This one assumption, that the body is the soul, comes trailing a flock of others, I see. You found then that these assumptions were provocative of religious experience, then, as a matter of course?

BLAKE: By no means. Religious experience is not a simple or an easy thing. Religious experience and even visions may not be very pleasant things. There is some crazy notion that visions are some kind of cosmic thrill, but let me tell you that this is far from the case. Why do you think that the Greeks held that to see God was to die? Why do you think this host of protestant religions which offers easy salvation is so attractive? Because real encounter with the divine requires surrender. By surrender, I do not mean submission, though that is part of it. I mean a purging of all these assumptions about the nature of the individual which the scientist has imposed upon the modern world view. That may include what would seem to the scientist a kind of mental breakdown. In the East, for example, Rinzai Zen actually induces a kind of Zen sickness, which is very much like what I mean by this purgation.

INTERVIEWER: But is that necessary?

BLAKE: Well, you see in an age when insanity has been made to seem like sanity, its cure may seem its opposite. See here. The scientist has created a system which has rejected the soul, on the grounds that it cannot be measured. In that one stroke, he denies the centuries of Christian tradition that focus upon the life of the soul. In that one stroke he castrates Christianity and reduces it to a kind of social event like a fraternity or gleeclub. They have replaced it with the word "mind" in their discussions, and created a new order of mental princes whose job it is to police this new belief system and punish those who do not embrace it. These new princes are called psychiatrists and are Urizen's newest attack on the intuitive mind, the imaginative, the visionary, and the prophetic; not to mention the Christian.

INTERVIEWER: Don't you think that's a bit unfair?

BLAKE: Unfair! Unfair! This is one of the most awesome attacks upon religion. It is no wonder Christianity was a dry husk even in my day. You must understand that here in the industrialized West we have a great society where the industrial revolution, the scientific revolution, and the agricultural revolution—to name only a few of the massive transformations we have recently been subjected to—have all conspired to create a massive despotism which denies the normality of religious experience. Every facet of modern existence is shaped by this enormous technology which is based largely on theories that well up out of the denial of the soul's existence. So here you have a Christian community attempting to live in the midst of an alien and Urizenic insistence upon Law, upon order, upon Reasonableness and upon War. What produces innovations in technology faster than war? That in itself should tell you something about it.

INTERVIEWER: Hmmm. It is true, I must admit, that when school budgets are cut back, the Arts suffer first. It is also true that the poet and the artist are largely in exile in the modern landscape. Or their works are stolen for a low price to be inflated madly as a new variety of currency for the rich.

BLAKE: It is interesting to watch Christians try to juggle their material comfort derived from this soulless despotism and their religion derived from a soul-oriented spirituality at the same time. How they think to keep their religion uncontaminated by such compromise is an index of the awesome subtlety of the despotism. That is why I said the only true Christian is the artist. The Christian has to unplug himself from this *awesome soullessness*. I have known very few souls who can manage the harangue of the market-place and the song of the Prophet at the same time. That takes enormous strength and even greater love. What actually has happened, you see, is that the industrialized western world has become a great prison of the mind. Like the labyrinth Daedalus built for the Minotaur, it has become the perfect tool for the collapse of vision.

INTERVIEWER: I'm afraid I don't follow you here.

BLAKE: The perfect prison was one from which no one wanted to escape. It contained all the diversions of the flesh and intellect possible to imagine. The high walls were, thus, as important to keep people out as to keep them in. The goal, of course, was to remove the prisoners, especially the Minotaur, from circulation in society. In this, it was completely successful. Our ideas of prison add the complication that imprisonment should be as much like hell as possible. Daedalus realized, as we do not, that true liberation was not only freedom of movement outside of walls, but also the freedom to penetrate the veil of illusion which separates the individual from knowledge of himself as he truly is, an infinite and immortal being. The more diversions, and entertainments, the more unlikely it is that there will ever be the opportunity for the prisoner to free himself from the mind-forged manacles that deny his access to life in eternity. The more I think about how pervasive this has become, and how weakened spiritual life has become as a result, the more enraged I become.

[*Blake rose and began to pace about, so I asked him if he'd like to take a turn in the garden to try the night air. He agreed, so we left the den to stretch our legs.*]

INTERVIEWER: You know, I have been listening to you talk about visions now for some time, and I get the feeling that it is impossible to understand your position on this issue without understanding your concept of the Christian Saviour.

BLAKE: Yes. And I am disappointed this is not more obvious. Jesus came to restore us to Eden; to put away the myth of the Fall of Man; to destroy Sin and Death for all time. The visionary experience is based upon surrender, not guilt. The Sin-oriented theology of much of Christianity denies the very possibility of visionary experience, and replaces it with some kind of marketable salvation. This is a horrible perversion as I see it. The spirit of Jesus is the *continual* forgiveness of sin, not the *conditional* forgiveness of sins! With Jesus' death on the Cross all sins were for all time forgiven. To say it is still possible to sin, after the enormity of that sacrifice, is the greatest blasphemy I know.

INTERVIEWER: If there is no sin, then what is there?

BLAKE: Why Error of course! Error replaces sin. Error is still grievous, but it is hardly as indelible or as permanent. Jesus and the Divine Family are always ready to welcome the correction of error. There is no comparison between the two, since Sin alienates Man from God. But I have no doubt that this word choice will be seen by conservative theologians as very dangerous. When in fact the very concern over which word to choose is pointless. God is not a word, nor can he be contained by a word. The difference between "Sin" and "Error" is not the issue, though it may be important. The issue is the insistence of apparently serious Christians upon *words* rather than visions. Christian history is filled with wholesale slaughter and emotional carnage over the battle of which words are going to represent the divine. Words are only approximations and are themselves limitations. The metaphor each society chooses to hang on that divine nail is their picture of what kind of authority figure they need to reinforce the Princes of the State in their hold upon the people. Is it any wonder that the metaphor of Church as Army is so popular in your era? God as Tyrant, and Jesus as chief General and the individual soul as foot soldier parallels the despotic military-industrial complex which denies visionary experiences. Notice here please that I substitute an aggregate divinity for this Father of military divinity. The Triune God is expanded and domesticated into the divine family: it is a family in which all souls are members. But I am afraid to say that the Christian religion has a history of such enormous political usurpation that it is amazing it has survived intact into your century. But that it has survived is evidence that Christianity is useful to the state, I suspect. Sad evidence.

INTERVIEWER: I always knew you were a radical Christian, but I would hardly have said you could be this radical!

BLAKE: Radical! The truth is always radical, because whatever system exists, exists as a result of such compromise that the uncompromised truth always seems enormously radical. But you think that is radical! Let me show you radical, sir! Look at the heavens, tell me what you see.

INTERVIEWER: Stars, blue sky, the moon, and infinite space containing uncountable galaxies.

BLAKE: Well done, oh Scientist! That is exactly what the astronomers have you see. They assume we are standing on a great globe of rock and soil, which is whirling about the sun in a minor part of the universe. But I tell you that is a lie! This is not a convex space hanging in a vacuum, but a concave space. From where I stand I see a flat plane over which a blue dome is suspended, and upon that dome the stars are fashioned.

INTERVIEWER: How can you expect a citizen of the Twentieth Century, whose astronauts have been to the moon, to accept such a wild surmise?

BLAKE: Because I would remind that citizen of the Twentieth Century that the visionary experience adds the evidence of the soul to any such perception. The Soul is Eternal, Immortal and Infinite. Consequently, this space wherein material existence occurs is like a great egg within which the sea of time and space are contained. Beyond that mundane shell is timelessness and spacelessness in which the Divine Family dwells. The astronomer's theory is built upon the denial of the existence of any such point of reference as the soul, and hence sees only materiality. But for the Christian this vision must be a lie. Discount the evidence of the soul and the religion becomes hollow, a mere rind of its former glory. But then few are able to believe anything deeply enough to make it real these days. But—and I really mean this literally—if you undertake to look through the eyes and not with them, then the soul will tell you that the astronomer's universe is an illusion. It is the work of the Goddess nature. It is Vala's veil. For a citizen of eternity having a body is like living in a revolving door. On one side eternity: on the other time and space, and you look out upon each with knowledge of both.

INTERVIEWER: You're right! That is a radical revision of the physical existence. It makes my head swim to think about it.

BLAKE: A world without the soul would be a world of death. It would be a world in which each individual is trapped in his nervous system, in which death is the last darkness from which there is no return. It would be a world in which the physical body, its pleasures, and its survival mean everything. It would be a world where greed, gluttony, anger, pride, lust, envy, and pettiness reign supreme. It would be a world where love would pay few dividends, and virtue none at all. If time and space have successfully negated eternity, then this world becomes a world of negation and despair.

INTERVIEWER: It sounds like you are describing the contemporary American scene. But what you ask of us is that we risk everything, especially sanity.

BLAKE: Exactly! A great man once wrote: "The road of excess leads to the palace of wisdom." [laughter] But then what have you to lose except your immortal soul? Visionary experience may seem like madness, but come let me show you what I mean. Enough! Or too much! There is a bit of mist over there. Perhaps we may find a vision in it.

[*We walked through the gate separating the rose garden from the pool, which in November is heated. When the air is cooler than the water's normal 75°, a small cloud of vapor banks the pool's surface. Winds stirred its surface, and leaves floated in thick masses upon it.*]

INTERVIEWER: Well, if you can find a vision in a swimming pool, William Blake, you are a real magician!

BLAKE: That is because for you the world is still fallen, where for me the world is Eden restored. Made new by the sacrifice of my saviour. This world is perfect, cleansed of its Fallen State. Now, you must listen carefully. You must replace the roaring conversation in your head with a new one. Replace the litany of science's assumptions with this chant: "Not two, One: The Soul and the Body are not two, they are one!" Whenever you think what you are going to witness is too bizarre, chant with special vigor. Your feeling of uneasiness will be an indication that you are slipping back into the old way of thinking. This won't be easy, but I will guide your sight. I will shape your perceptions as only those of us in Eden can . . . .

INTERVIEWER: Well . . . ah . . . er . . . somehow I . . . .

BLAKE: There! There by the tree with the star-shaped leaves . . . Leviathan! The water . . . it's geysering . . . do you see? It's the spiritual existence itself!

INTERVIEWER: No. Uh . . . wouldn't you rather go in by the fire?

BLAKE: Now come on! You summoned me here. Now I'm here, we are going to *do* as well as *play* at words! Give me your hand! Look through my eyes!

INTERVIEWER: Well . . . .

[*Blake gripped my hand, and I began to see what he intended me to see. The pool shifted and opened upon an Abyss, infinite and fiery. A globe of inky blackness rose from the immensely distant deep, and as it rose it quaked with horrific sighs. It convulsed and divided as the folds of a monstrous serpent encoiled upon themselves, uncoiling, coiling. In its center an eye appeared, a fiery crest, and soon by degree from its seething flames, was the head of a Leviathan. It advanced towards us with the sure beat of a mighty heart. I looked at Blake in horror. . . .*]

BLAKE: Yes. You see it! Remember: "Not two; One!" This is an old friend. This garden is Eden. This is not the fallen world. This is not Memphis . . . This pool is the sacred well where Eve bathed, and Adam swam. Jesus died to bring us here . . . Jehovah has been exiled . . . Nobodaddy's world of alienation is no more . . . Surrender to it. If you start to slip into rational denial . . . let your eyes unfocus . . . let them go soft . . . see not with them, but through them!

INTERVIEWER: Good Lord, William, it's coming for us . . . !

BLAKE: Of course: that's it. NOW!

[*With that Blake did the unthinkable, he shoved me into the well. I fell directly into the path of this horror. In stark disbelief, I turned to my tormentor whom I had welcomed as my guest. I remembered his instructions, NOT TWO, ONE! Blake's shape shifted and I saw only a Bard dressed in a long robe. His aged hands played an enormous harp. I felt the silken scales and the fierce heat of Leviathan surge against the small of my back . . . Not Two, One . . . I collapsed into Leviathan's embrace . . . But I found myself back on the shore in Blake's arms. His eyes were radiant. The steam from Eden's well pulsed around him, a nimbus roared about his head.*]

INTERVIEWER: What? How . . . ? Where's your harp?

BLAKE: I had no harp. That was your first vision, merely.

INTERVIEWER: What do you mean, "first?" Why don't we go in now? I'm chilled to the bone, aren't you?

BLAKE: Hold on! I'll lead you. There's someone waiting for us by the door.

INTERVIEWER: Is that so? Who?

BLAKE: When I was in London, I'd have sent Catherine for a sketch pad about now. She's really changed!

INTERVIEWER: Who's changed? What do you see?

BLAKE: She of the Veil. Vala. My God, such a transformation. Things must really be bad in your era.

INTERVIEWER: Why? What are you seeing?

BLAKE: She's an ancient hag, with empty dugs, and decaying teeth. Her veil is no longer silken, it is now a net of barbed wire. A fiery cancer hangs from her womb. She's a great horror! Can you see her?

INTERVIEWER: I don't...no, wait...does she have a severed hand, hung round her neck on a black chain?

BLAKE: Yes. Then you do see her. Wait here now while I drive her away.

[*Blake strode towards Vala, his form shifted again. He was naked in the harsh November moonlight, heavily muscled. His hair flamed into the night. The Spectre stood her ground. Blake opened his arms, and they embraced in passionate combat. They fell to the stones and again their forms began to shift. She was the female form divine. Blake was clad in a rainbow of gossamer silk.*]

Well come on. Are you going to stand there and gawk?

INTERVIEWER: Oh...what?

BLAKE: Weren't you just saying something about being cold? Let's go inside.

[*I crossed the pavement to them. Blake whispered to me.*]

How are you doing? Keeping up the chant? Stay close now.

INTERVIEWER: Oh...yes...cold.... Uh, will she come in too?

BLAKE: You couldn't keep her out!

[*We went inside. I found the house changed, but recognizable. I poured the wine for Blake. Fixed a tumbler of whiskey for myself. I needed a drink badly!*]

INTERVIEWER: Will Vala drink too?

BLAKE: That is not Vala. This is Jerusalem. I thought you'd recognize her. Yes. I'm sure she'd like some wine. And by the way, you don't need that to steady your nerves. Just keep your hand in mine if you feel jumpy.

INTERVIEWER: Thank you. Yes, I'm sure to get sick if I drink that. Well now. Where were we? Oh yes. I had some questions about your last book, *Jerusalem*, that I wanted to ask. Why did you mar the copperplates so terribly?

MIL

TON

The Author & Printer W Blake 1804

a Poem in 2 Books

To Justify the Ways of God to Men

BLAKE: See here now! I'm tired of all this interviewing. Wouldn't you really rather see Jesus?

INTERVIEWER: Wha...say what?

BLAKE: Jesus. You know...the Saviour!

INTERVIEWER: What on earth do you mean? Here? Now? Isn't that going a bit far?

BLAKE: Not on Earth! Eden. Are you forgetting your chant? And why not? If we can produce Leviathan, turn your swimming pool into Eden's well, court, catch, and remake Vala, herself, why not invite Jesus over too? Anyhow, he and I were on the best of terms. He taught me Hebrew and was teaching me Aramaic when I passed over into Eden. I thought before I left you, I'd make the necessary introductions.

INTERVIEWER: Well...I...er...you really mean *the* Jesus? Here?

BLAKE: Wait a minute. You are a Christian, aren't you? I suppose we could just as easily invite Buddha if you'd like. I've never met the man, but I hear he's quite a teacher. Hmmmm...You're not an atheist or anything are you? It never occurred to me to check you out.

INTERVIEWER: Well, yes...I think Jesus will be all right. And I am, after all, your good friend. I would hardly think I could be that and not be a Christian. Now could I?

BLAKE: I suppose not. Well. But you listen! You could be in big trouble if you're not on good terms with the Lord. Got me?...Well now...first turn down the lights...Urizen seems to really have your age lit up, hasn't he?

INTERVIEWER: Why? What do you mean by that?

BLAKE: Bright light is a metaphor the scientists like for the alleged light of reason. The more light you can cast on the subject of study, the hypothesis goes, the more rational and analytical the perception becomes. So turn the lights down.

[*Blake produced an Irish harp and began to play, singing songs I had never heard before. Perhaps they were among his papers lost after his death. Jerusalem began to dance, carelessly sloshing her wine as she did. I remembered my chant, "Not Two, One," and focused on her naked beauty. Then Blake began a song I remembered: "I gave thee liberty and Life O Jerusalem, And thou has bound me down upon the stems of Vegetation." He began to invent new verses, and Jerusalem and I joined him on the chorus. Then without warning, Jerusalem danced over to the kitchen door and back she came with an Angel, a glory itself. And in that Angel's hand was the hand of another Angel, and so on, and on until she had a chain of Angels cycling around Blake and me, joining us in song. A ripple of wild music fell from the wings of the Angels as they rustled; it changed the quality of the light, somehow. A great perfume filled the room. I was intoxicated by its fragrance. Chills chorded my spine. I looked at Blake, his harp was gone and he was up*

*dancing, his hands held high, palms up, whirling. Jerusalem grabbed my
hand and soon I was up hand in hand with the Angels, sky clad like
them . . . whirling with the Angelic company. No longer in my library, we
were now inside a great domed hall . . . I thought I recognized the gothic style
of Westminster . . . The floor was a golden mosaic . . . the volume of song
increased as if we were now part of a great whirling choir. Laughter broke
here and there, and joy was our song. A great shout broke the air. The
golden company fell to the dancing floor. Blake nudged me to look to my
right. A beautiful, dark-skinned and hook-nosed man strode towards us. He
was short. His hair was black with stars and his eyes were filled with futurity.
I felt as if I had been pole-axed. I began to tremble, to stare, to sweat in
terror, in awe.]*

JESUS: William Blake! What is all this? Are you back again? What is
going on here anyway? I thought I had you well placed at the eternal Tables
in Eden's Cathedral among the sons of Albion. And who is this crazy man?

BLAKE: [*Laying his hand on my shoulder, calming me instantly*] Welcome
Lord. Sorry to disturb you at this hour. Won't you sit and talk with us? This
one summoned me from Eden, and I thought I'd introduce the two of you,
so when I'm back at my duties you might talk now and again.

[*I tried to talk, but my voice failed me. Blake's hand slipped into mine, and I
managed to speak.*]

INTERVIEWER: Well . . . Yes . . . Lord . . . umm . . . forgive me . . . I am unused
to this visionary travel . . . and I am very unused to talking to the Divine
Family . . . that is to say . . . I am unused to talking to them as if they were . . .
well . . . I mean . . . we . . . I hope you will allow me to . . . .

JESUS: Blake! What are you doing bringing him here? He doesn't sound
like prophetic material to me. But, I'll admit he must have something to get
you to bring him here. Hmmm. Are you sure about him, William?

BLAKE: Well, yes. It's just that his age is so overwhelmed with reason and he is after all an academic. That does bind him down some in his ability to travel. But he and his Blake crazies are stronger than most. Besides, he probably thinks he is having some kind of psychotic episode about now, and if I were not insisting on this hands-on experience, I doubt very much if he'd have troubled you at all. So, go easy on him for my sake. There are too few of us left these days to do battle with Urizen, Lord. Be nice to the man. OK?

JESUS: For your sake. Yes. But listen. You must limit these trips. You're supposed to be on stage just now, and Milton is not used to standing in for you. Besides, I see Urizen lurking to the left of this one, and I hear his howling spectre on the spires. Are you sure this is wise?

BLAKE: Yes. If he can handle it, I am sure *you* can. And if anything goes amiss, I'll answer for it.

JESUS: OK! What would you have me give him?

BLAKE: The one about *War!*

JESUS: Done!

[Jesus looked at me. I nearly fainted. But Blake gave me his hand, and I heard Jesus say . . .]

War is the result of personal identity. A name separates and isolates the individual. With a name comes a flood of other words which obscure a man's true self, his eternal self. This fluxile text is concealed within his consciousness until he imagines this to be the catalogue of his real identity. With this false identity comes the desire to possess material goods. With this possession of material goods, comes the need to control the origins of goods and the fate of these goods. The Hero is born from this desire to own, to win more and to protect what he already owns. Finally, the will to control extends to the ultimate illusion, reputation or fame. The Hero seeks to control his fame so that he might create a false heaven in song or stories. Now fame feeds upon the fear of death and the fear of oblivion. War, heroism, aggression ultimately originate in this fearsome clinging to a false selfhood. As long as poets sing the praise of heroes, as long as culture teaches the fame game, so long will this false eternity of history generate wars. It is well known that the defeated write no histories. So long as each man and each woman clings to the false name and resulting identity so long will my longing for a new age be frustrate. Thus I taught, you must die to your old identity, you must shed your old identity and all you think you are. You must come to understand that you are not the words culture hangs upon your body. You must recognize that the carved letters they will place on your tombstone are not you. You must jettison all words and become aware of the Real man beneath them. Honor that true identity, surrender your false selfhood and its word list identity and you will have ceased to be at war with the world. You will no longer be contributing to the delay of my coming. You will know the falsehood of death, and the foolishness of the desire to control. No man can die alone, for I have passed this way before you. If God did not die for man, and if he did not give himself eternally into death, then Man could not come into eternal life. The Real man dies into eternal life as often as God dies into the physical body, that real death. Awake from the dream of Urizen! Awake from the God of the Book and the origin of the false identity which the book seeks to perpetuate and strengthen.

I often wander Earth and am saddened by the inner imprisonment of each individual. I open my arms to people, and they seem deaf, blind and senseless. I weep when I go into churches and see men and women quarreling over words when they should be loving each other in my name. Why can not they see that I became like them so they might become like me? I rage when I think about this Urizenic deception.

[I scarcely know how to describe what happened next. Jesus rose, and stomped about in bitter rage, great tears streaming down his face. He raised his hands over his head, fists clenched. Lightning flashed over his rage-lit eyes. He raised his palms and lines of energy streamed to them in great arcs transforming the very fabric of existence. Suddenly, the head of a bull appeared on his shoulders, a fiery crest of 19 smaller heads mounted it. He had 19 arms and 19 legs. He had become Yamantaka. God Killer. He began to sing, and wheel. Piles of books, lists of names, directories, census compilations, history books, encyclopaedias, appeared under his 19 dancing feet. He began to dance them into inky pulp. His great bull face bellowed with joy. The face of Jesus mounted highest among the 19 crest faces: I counted saints and apostles there as well. The bells and knives in his 19 hands made a joyous ululation. He was a shattering fury. All religions were truly one! A ripple of energy began from the dark sea where the books once had lain and rolled across this vision. Jesus stood before us again. Naked now. Glistening with perfumed oils.

[He sat down and announced that the Supreme Court had begun a series of decisions which would start publishers and printers to pulping books, and that shortly literacy would be considerably reduced.]

JESUS: More I will undertake soon. But forces are unleashed which will begin to return Art to its rightful place in the hearts of men. Now about you, sir.
[Looking at me, he began to speak in a fashion I could not quite understand. Deep within me I could feel an opening of doors, and an unfettering of senses I had only guessed I possessed.]
Come to me in a few days, and I'll begin to dictate a new set of prophetic poems which you may transcribe.

INTERVIEWER: [*I was reeling*] Well...yes. That would be nice. If you'd like to. I'll certainly take it all down. But...really wouldn't it be more original if I composed them myself?

BLAKE: Watch it! Urizen has your head in his hands. Back Foul One! [*Blake rose in a rage, and struck at the space just behind me.*] Now listen! Snap out of it! Wake up! You are going to have to be more careful. This is Jesus. God! Lover of Art. You'd better remember where all art comes from and where you are. Or...I'll send you black visions like this one....

[*Blake bent down and touched the golden tiles with his harp, and in one great arc, swept a wave of sound and black crushing tides across my face. Waves of insect skulled fiends clacked their blood streaked mandibular jaws at me. Stares of hatred, contempt and jealousy filled the air between us. Their black flanks, plated and serrated, glistened in the black light. The cries of young women and unformed men redounded within the rinds of their souls. I looked at Blake. He laughed and smiled. I suddenly saw.... Stood up, walked towards these hideous colleagues. Their eyes flamed up, their hands raised ten-yeared blades—joy filled. I opened my arms, exposing my sky clad life and my forgiving love. I threw back my head and my arms. The portraits of "William" and "Robert" from Blake's poem* Milton *flashed through my mind. My sides shuddered. I was soon covered by rapture and delight. Blake and Jesus laughed aloud, stood, embraced, joined hands with the Angelic host, and began to whirl joyously. The Angels and Jerusalem gave themselves up to exultant song. I surrendered my selfhood to the ecstatic embraces of those who consumed me with the flames of the spirit.*

Jean E. Pearson

The Final Seal of the Sun

The structures of Man's history oppress
the whole Creation. His version
of biology has raised on high industrial
canons of Desolation, forged Satanic mills
of darkness covering the Sun with chilling smoke.
Alas, poor Abel, the pastoral is dead!
Cain who turned away from an earth he sowed with blood
has overdone his city. He labors now for Nobodaddy:
Production's deity, what profits Him solidifies
priapic power as high-rise, space probe, apocalyptic
warhead. Creation's laws defied, Eternal Energy denied,
His fallen blood can never spring in natural joy.
In dark triumphant Selfhood He stockpiles the wargasm,
dreaming Desolation at His final coming. His sole
and holy Form shall have dominion over earth
and there shall be no other living creatures after Him.
Enormous, His industry labors to extend Him, His sons
and heirs outnumber every other name.
The springing uncaught forms, fair children of glad day,
grew up in laws that fit each separate fur and skin.
A Monolithic System disinherits them. Now they are
forced to the last clean edge of life and disembodied there.
While Los, the opposer, steady foe of Desolation, flares
in raging pain to see his energy destroyed. Groans
press from his face in heavy globules soft as blood,
articulate and salty as a dolphin's eye.
Every tear wept by the Sun has a recorded name.
And every name a color of Eternity:
Green Turtle, Red Wolf, Blue Whale & Grey Whale.
The right reverent wearers of ancient robes of wonder,
they turn now from history, silently trusting:
Peregrine & Sea Mink, Monk Seal & Harp Seal.
What immortal eye could answer their appeal?

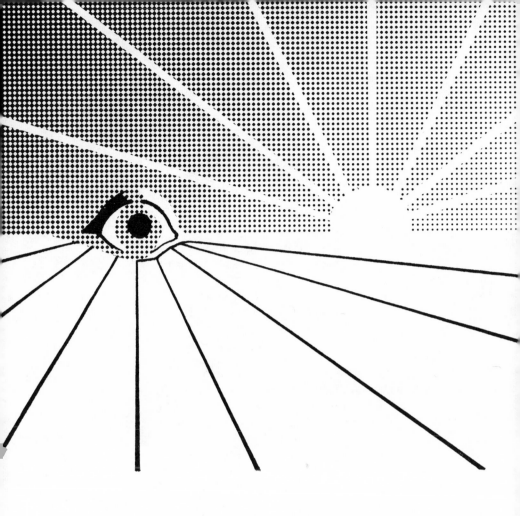

URIZEN

Homage to Blake

Your eyes on
  horizon
    arise on
      your ease in
        your reason:

      Arise Sun—
      your rays on
    a rise on
    horizon:
You rise on!

Victor Flach

Robert C. Jones

Ancient of Days

Because the burning compass turned
in space, the star carved patterned
traceries of light
in blackness, silver-urned.
Because the dying phoenix burned,
a silver-winged beauty rose
and ruby-eyed, in shining flight,
those dying embers spurned.

And although turning mankind dies
in time, the patterned traceries remain.
The earth hangs, spinning gyre,
upon a golden chain.
And see! In man's immortal fire,
the compass turn, the phoenix rise.

F. Adiele

The Fountain

She had been knocking on the edge of Blake's engravings long enough it seemed, her back swollen red, knuckles ridged. The flaws weren't satisfying to find; she resolved that what was treasure remained so. She could see the shore creeping out in escape, and Newton crawling over the phosphorus rocks with his compass and the skin coming only up to his neck. It seemed Newton said too little, but still she respected him: beautiful, bent naked at the bottom of the world. He was a naive work, parallel to her own research. In the end, would it be he who populated? The doctors were, as always, abstract, noncommital. She laughed every time. She had proof: documents, records, lustrous gods swimming through her—only one conclusion.

Later she set out with the round, lidded bowl under her arm, her claim to poverty's nobility. Up on the Eastside her feet began to weep, devoid of the soft goldleaf that used to cover them. She tried to see it as he would have: the love of passage, trees that called out to him. She found him on the belly of everything, rifling for simplistic view that captured the public. It was Blake's, the voice of their yet unborn child. She wondered how he would feel using religion to ask for food, he who believed in art and died with neglect clustered around him. Somedays she feared she was even turning into him, with a rejection of machinery, the departure she took from literature—embracing instead figures and colored plates. Then was it relief only that she realized soon her affair would be complete and testtubed: the results under lights, she erect as a pillar of salt beside him.

The sun fell in pieces over the brittle street. She looked at her palms, saw him there, and cursed her melodrama. Blake in the asylum was a constant worry, whether the food was acceptable, whether he had yet begun to pick ideas out of the air and collect them like bushes or angels before him. Reams of history were floating there for him: she maturing to meet him like something fantastic out of Rossetti.

His letters said he smelled death behind the foggy corridor walls; he called it pestilence. It swept through the walls and out again, always taking the first born. He, being second, was saved from his own creation. To her it appeared to all be caused by his increasing alarm upon growing continually younger in captivity. Eventually, she wrote to him, she would bring him to his start again and they would be relieved. When they met later that week he described dreams. He professed to being lost in a jungle yet utterly devoid of innocence. Chastity he left like a cape swirling behind him. She had left in tears, though strangely titillated, and had neither visited him on Thursday nor opened the books all week.

After breakfast she left to her construction job at the city's dome. She was part of Repair and Upkeep, though her registered creativity balance tested too high for practical contact with the clouds. It must have been her inherited nonexistent political beliefs that qualified her as advantageous to work on such an important project. Usually she could be seen, strapped with a safety belt, against the sky like Loki, her white robes spreading around her.

She worked with an exotic Philipino in a jade green sarong off Rousseau's coast: blunt, beautiful, indefinably wicked. Years later, when this man was her lover, perhaps his term of duty already served, she had argued her research against him as he dismissed it. She could not consider it a failure merely because he and the others had had it easy, confined to canvas or parchment. She was shackled to grey winds and strange mediums and an artist who covered days with weeping and triangles. It was worth it, also, for when Blake was alive he was magnificent. Mornings such as those the sun reassembled, scalding the clouds, and as she went begging food her feet left gold imprint on the street. Above he crouched wild in copper, beard flowing, tearing the dome, letting in the years—gratefully embracing his—the ancient of days. Novelists stunned, which had been the man—the art or the flesh?

Always the next day were the city's repairs, she near the sky in tears. Always later in his rooms, watching him shriek and shrink into everlasting youth. Always she tried to explain, telling him how magnificent he had been, what he had created. Always he spoke of the desire to crash against the sky as a rock, to splinter and so be complete. She would get up and run out, longing to be twisted into sexual eternity with only silent engravings.

She had pretended to be his wife once, going on safaris with secret eyes turned towards Egypt. For weeks he was calm as she sat nearby, folding her pale hands about his fine, trembling feet. But then the others came, smearing the walls with countrysides. Eventually he became resigned, only to find himself golden and constantly younger than she, and she released him, sorrowing. For years he strove to lose himself in the English light, staring out over mountains, over the water. His desire to fly was like that of Daedalus, born of necessity. How could she convince him of the innocence of the landscapists? She tried to teach him meditation for during the shock treatments but he preferred to try to disappear into the currents.

After the marriage she was weak. It was surprisingly difficult to be close to a master; she preferred the work. It was then she melted into her meditation as a monk, picturing the great philosophers crawling out of the sea to line up behind her. It was he who, during visiting hours, encouraged her, throwing abstraction around her, taunting her in this enlightenment to reach him. Generally he scoffed at her, trusting to his books what he deprived his art. His letters showed disdain for "Breughel tumbling over the yard," who, he considered, consisted of "rarely inspired chaos erupting over the countrysides, out of hell." Disregarding Blake's castigation, she began to feel the creeping of fatalistic attitudes.

She saw the walls beside her reaching deep into themselves: touching each other, turning their backs on the oblivious lovers they were surrounding. She thought of doing research for Blake's gratified pleasure desire. She was in the Public Hall how she imagined it. She saw that the benches reclined from the lovers' touch and then the male lover was pouring onto her, heedless of her white cowl and gold fingertips. She spread him like the mouth of a clam and promised him symmetry, a wild balance. She was amazed at this lover, so obsessed with the act of love, rather than as a fact, that he didn't realize it was a stranger beneath him, one who spent her life tied to rocks and canvases. She cupped him in her palm as he rolled into her and locked in place because there was nothing he could do but follow his skin. She thought he was rather like the city's dome pressing against all the sky but never making a dent. She was swearing over and over again that she could appear to Blake in a dream and tell him, teach him, shielding the tears in her gown from his view.

By the time she realized who was above her she had drunk too much. She saw Newton sharpening his compass and sickness coming upon the house in green, postured like Blake coming out of Rousseau's jungle. Death settled like a cloud on the room of the first developed. Their test tube lay shattered on the floor, gold streaked in fingermarks down the chest of the man beneath her. While above Blake crouched in copper, beard flowing, tearing the dome, letting in the bacteria, the years, gratefully embracing what is rightfully his. The ancient of days.

216

Steve Bunch

Yeats, Thoreau, Dr. Williams, Jim Morrison, and Mr. Blake

A quick note to share some quotations on Blake that I've come across recently. The first, from Yeats' "William Blake and the Imagination," has a vaguely coincidental connection with Adielé's "The Fountain":

> But when one reads Blake, it is as though the spray of an inexhaustible fountain of beauty was blown into our faces, and not merely when one reads the *Songs of Innocence*, or the lyrics he wished to call 'Ideas of Good and Evil,' but when one reads those 'Prophetic Books' in which he spoke confusedly and obscurely because he spoke of things for whose speaking he could find no models in the world about him.

I also like the opening paragraph of that essay for its concise observation on the religion of art. Then there's a quotation from Thoreau that I've always thought was rather Blakean, & having been a surveyor myself, I've been aware of the Ancient of Days leaning over the landscape with his compass/dividers, staking out Maya Estates (Subdivisions for the Mortal Majority). Thoreau:

> Nowadays almost all man's improvements, so called, as the building of houses, and the cutting down of the forest and of all large trees, simply deform the landscape, and make it more and more tame and cheap. A people who would begin by burning the fences and let the forest stand! I saw the fences half consumed, their ends lost in the middle of the prairie, and some worldly miser with a surveyor looking after his bounds, while heaven had taken place around him, and he did not see the angels going to and fro, but was looking for an old post-hole in the midst of paradise. I looked again, and saw him standing in the middle of a boggy, stygian fen, surrounded by devils, and he had found his bounds without a doubt, three little stones, where a stake had been driven, and looking nearer, I saw that the Prince of Darkness was his surveyor.

Ties in very well with "charter'd streets" & "charter'd Thames" too. The whole idea of measure, individuation, or whatever you want to call it has always fascinated me in literature. Blake & Thoreau are obvious examples, but also Poe's narrator in "Pit & Pendulum," who is obsessed with measuring his dungeon cell, & of course the cetology chapters in Moby Dick. But I digress. In Doc Williams' autobiography, he gives this account of a Unitarian minister from his college days in Pennsylvania:

> Old man Ecob, I always thought, looked like an ancient Briton and I believe his name did come from the period in England before the Roman Conquest. He finally went nearly mad over Blake's revolving spheres, after which his fashionable congregation gave him the heave-ho, and I suppose his family along with him, in favor of some more practical instructor."

The dangers of Blake study.

And then of course you remember that Jim Morrison quoted from "Auguries of Innocence" in his "End of Night" on the first Doors album:

> Every Night & every Morn
> Some to Misery are Born
> Every Morn & every Night
> Some are Born to sweet delight
> Some are Born to sweet delight
> Some are Born to Endless Night.

Blake sees the Ancient of Days at no. 13 Hercules Building, Lambeth, c. 1791. In the window Catherine, Flaxman, Fuseli—anachronism ignored, I wanted the friends in.

W. S. Doxey

Religious Experience

The Blakes, William & his spouse,
Loved to retire to the garden
Behind their Soho house,
And, stripped quite bare,
Play make-believe.
He was Adam, she his Eve.
A neighbor, whose face was florid,
Took the apple's part.
The viper in the grass,
That multicolored creature,
Was played by a wandering preacher
Who draped his bones
In rainbows of brocade.
When it snowed, as oft it did,
They felt rather silly,
For being out-of-doors
Their Eden was somewhat chilly,
And Adam sported chilblains
On his shanks,
While Eve, poor Eve,
Grew curious rashes upon her flanks,
And the apple pinked.
The serpent changed
His horrid hiss for chatter.
To end the matter,
Blake's attempt at Genesis
Returned indoors, en masse,
Where with fire and ale
And clothes and many a hymn
They regained their heat.
However, this was not defeat.
Blessed with Eve, apple
And wonderful snake

(The cleric though young
Already had his forked tongue),
He lost cold reason's
Strangulating hold
And drew strange pictures,
Which, when published,
Brought a universal nod
And etched in flame
Upon the brow of fickle Fame
The genius that was BLAKE'S
(By grace of God).

IF THE LION WAS ADVISED
BY THE FOX, HE WOULD BE CUNNING

Daniel Zimmerman

From Prophecy to Vision: Blake's Track

William Blake used the terms "prophet" and "visionary" interchangeably; most of his critics have followed suit. However, an examination of the prophet's relation to his audience on the one hand and the visionary's on the other suggests that Blake understood the term "prophet" in an ideal, rather than a traditional sense.

In his "Prophetic Books," Blake's Spectre—squamous, natural man—generates along time's arrow in "a dull round of probabilities and possibilities" (*Desc. Cat.*), a bad penny, a certainty snatched from Charon. And insofar as prophets address this public fellow—a mere aggregate, identified with an ever-prospective state promising individual mastery of his environment and heir to a common past organized by moral law—they appeal to the ideal (spectral) Identities the public seek.

If prophets create the past as a dread menagerie of fate, of vengeance for sin, they also depict it as perhaps avoidable in the future, but refuse to let men congratulate themselves that, by neglect or luck, that past has been avoided, once and for all. Because they address men collectively, they must often try to 'make their meaning explicit to the Idiot' by interpreting their visions for the people or his dream for a king—an enterprise which Blake regarded as 'not worth his care.'

Such prophets are messengers of rather specific information. Like artists, they are granted visions, but their uses of them differ radically.

The visionary artist, recognizing that "the history of all times and places is nothing else but improbabilities and impossibilities; what we should say was impossible if we did not see it always before our eyes" (*Desc. Cat.*), takes prophecy a step further. The prophet traditionally offers society a message *en bloc: ad hoc* exhortations and denunciations inspired by his personal relation to a God paradoxically immeasurably greater than man. Against this spectral conception, Blake announces that "God becomes as we are, that we may be as he is (*No Nat. Relig.*) and that "God only Acts & Is, in existing beings or Men" (*MHH*:15). As a visionary, he takes into account the activity of the individuals to whom his works are addressed, inviting understanding more than urging compliance. His works, like the prophets' actions at their most extreme (Isaiah's nakedness, Ezekiel's eating dung), are "not too Explicit;" his urgency does not stem from a crisis in the world of duration, but sees that world itself as a crisis. Rather than exhorting individuals to a common course of action or denouncing them by "imput[ing] Sin & Righteousness / To individuals & not to States" (*J*:25), Blake invites each 'spectator' of his work to "*forgive* what [he does] not approve" (*J*:3), to "Enter into these Images in his Imagination, approaching them on the Fiery Chariot of his Contemplative Thought" (*VLJ*), and to "make a Friend & Companion of one of these Images of wonder" (*VLJ*). In order to do so, the Individual must bring to bear upon the work his singularity, unmediated by any priesthood of consensus, any predefined, aggregate Identity to which he might aspire. The visionary artist, by shattering the one-fold, serial sense of time which is the limit of spectral perception, addresses the spectator as if his poly-fold singularity were already in the process of realization, already emanative, at any instant of the transactive sympathy which making a "Friend & Companion" involves.

Against the radical novelty, risk, and freedom proposed by such visionary individuation, the prophets tend to view individuals as creatures of history understood as a plot established by covenant; their ultimate value is the continuity of that history. But while eschewing ritual for righteousness as a guarantor of continuity—while rightly turning away from the outward ceremony which Blake calls Antichrist—the prophets merely substitute for it an 'inward ceremony,' equally mechanical and equally dangerous to the individual insofar as righteousness is appropriated as a "Universal Characteristic," rather than made redundant as a result of a Last Judgement in which error is cast out and truth embraced. When "Albion spoke in his dismal dreams," demanding "rightousness and justice" of Los in *J*: 42, Los replied: "Thou art in Error; trouble me not with thy righteousness. / I have innocence to defend and ignorance to instruct." "For who," Blake asks, "is really Righteous? It is all Pretension." (*Anno. Watson*)

It is the prophet's view of history which the visionary shatters by a resolutely discontinuous presentation which must be understood as a design rather than followed as a plot, transcended rather than adopted as a pattern for action, for "to be an Error & to be Cast out is a part of God's design," (*VLJ*) as it is of Blake's.

In Night the Seventh of *The Four Zoas*, Los tells Enitharmon: ". . . Stern desire / I feel to fabricate embodied semblances . . .," to which she replies:

> . . . if thou, my Los,
> Wilt in sweet moderated fury fabricate forms *sublime*,
> Such as the piteous Spectres may assimilate themselves into,
> They shall be ransoms for our Souls that we may live."

These fabricated, embodied semblances, these forms sublime, are the means by which Los, like Jesus in *J*:25, may "take away the imputation of Sin / By the Creation of States & the deliverance of Individuals Evermore," by "Striving with Systems to deliver Individuals from those Systems." (*J*:11) Rather than addressing natural man as if he could be "Righteous in his Vegetated Spectre," (*J*:52) Blake provides for the assimilation of the spectre into these fabricated semblances in order to prevent the individual from "appropriat[ing] to Himself / Or to his Emanation any of the Universal Characteristics," (*J*:90) lest by "Attempting to become more than Man [He] become less," as Luvah says (*FZ*:IX). By compelling the spectre to assimilate into state after state, the visionary frees the individual from the prophet's sense of time as tradition accumulated through duration and allows him to see, like Los, "the Past, Present & Future existing all at once before [him]." (*J*:15)

In his epistle "To the Christians," Blake presents the differences between these views of time. First, he reminds the religious that

> We are told to abstain from fleshly desires that we may lose no time from the work of the Lord: Every moment lost is a moment that cannot be redeemed; every pleasure that intermingles with the duty of our station is a folly unredeemable, & is planted like the seeds of a wild flower among our wheat: All the tortures of repentance are tortures of self-reproach on account of our leaving the Divine Harvest to the Enemy, the struggles of intanglement with incoherent roots. (*J*:77)

This unredeemable moment recalls the Notebook poem of 1793:

> If you trap the moment before it's ripe,
> The tears of repentance you'll certainly wipe;
> But if once you let the ripe moment go
> You can never wipe off the tears of woe.

These are the durations of fallen time by which a hypervigilant Urizen, like the natural man—"Thro Chaos seeking for delight, & in spaces remote / Seeking the Eternal which is always present to the wise" (*FZ*:IX)—confuses remembrance with futurity, mistaking durations for the "Moment in each Day that Satan cannot find" which "renovates every Moment of the Day if rightly placed" (*M*:35). This latter Moment differs from the former moment(s) as the collectivity of the Redeem'd Christians which Blake addresses at the outset differs from the individual, Reprobate Christians whom he addresses at the close of the prose section of his epistle, who alone are capable of understanding the 'moment' of the Moment as transformative significance. The collectivity addressed by Blake as by the conventional prophet is, as such, limited to the "lost" moments in which pleasure and duty have already intermingled against the rules—moments condemned ahead of time by "Caiaphas, the dark Preacher of Death, / Of Sin, of sorrow & of punishment" (*J:77*) whom Blake impersonates at the beginning, only to transcend by the end of the epistle:

> But Jesus is the bright Preacher of Life
> Creating Nature from this fiery Law
> By self-denial & forgiveness of Sin.

This is not the traditional prophet speaking, but the visionary, participating in "the divine body of the Saviour, the True Vine of Eternity, The Human Imagination, who appear'd to [Blake] as Coming to Judgment among his Saints & throwing off the Temporal that the Eternal might be Establish'd; around him were seen the Images of Existences according to a certain order Suited to [Blake's] Imaginative Eye" (*VLJ*). This is Jesus, saying "I am not a God afar off, I am a brother and friend" (*J:4*), who fulfills the prophets, and who enables individuals to respond to Moses' prayer: "Would to God that all the Lord's people were Prophets (*Num:XI:29*).

The visionary—Los as Time, the Mercy of Eternity—goes beyond the prophet who, as the Spectre of Urthona, "kept the Divine Vision in time of trouble" (*J:95*) by showing the past not merely as avoidable but as avoided because forgiven once and for all. Whereas the prophet confounds remembrance and futurity, the visionary renovates the Day in the dilation of a human Moment, "rightly placed" before his audience as in what Blake called the most sublime act: "to set another before you" (*MHH:3*).

"Fear & Hope are—Vision," Blake says in *The Gates of Paradise*, early and late, and his "terrific" visions 'confuse' the two:

> So Albion spoke & threw himself into the Furnaces of affliction.
> All was a Vision, all a Dream; the Furnaces became
> Fountains of Living Waters flowing from the Humanity Divine
> (J:96)

—and they remain "terrific or complacent, varying / According to the subject of discourse" (*J:98*). Throughout his life, he held that "Without Contraries is no progression" (*MHH:3*), and his visionary eschatology avoids the prophets' entropic drift toward homeostatis (present even in *The Revelation*) which seeks to substitute Hope for Fear and, often, to reduce Hope to tradition.

Blake's ability to recognize the vision as a dream saved him from the error of 'mistaking allegorical signification for corporeal command' and led him to require his audience to do likewise, advancing into vision.

225

Walt Whitman

Of William Blake & Walt Whitman

Of William Blake & Walt Whitman Both are mystics, extatics but the difference between them is this—and a vast difference it is: Blake's visions grow to be the rule, displace the normal condition, fill the field, spurn this visible, objective life, & seat the subjective spirit on an absolute throne, wilful & uncontrolled. But Whitman, though he occasionally prances off, takes flight with an abandon & capriciousness of step or wing, and a rapidity & whirling power, which quite dizzy the reader in his first attempts to follow, always holds the mastery over himself, &, even in his most intoxicated lunges or pirouettes, never once loses control, or even equilibrium. To the pe[rfect] sense, it is evident that he goes off because he permits himself to do so, while ever the director, or direct'g principle sits coolly at hand, able to stop the wild teetotum & reduce it to order, at any moment. In Walt Whitman, escapades of this sort are the exceptions. The main character of his poetry is the normal, the universal, the simple, the eternal platform of the best manly & womanly qualities.

Shawn Thompson

Thanks Newton

thanks newton
for little waves

which nevertheless
have groan unquiet
in the ear
like crows in corn

till the flock
is broken

into words
like john apocalocke's

Diane Di Prima

For Blake

by now it is too late to wonder
why we are wherever we are
(tho some peace is possible): singing on the breath
& we have had bodies of Fire and lived on the Sun
& we have had bodies of Water and lived on Venus
and bodies of Air that screeched as they tore around Jupiter
all our eyes remembering Love

Paul Piech

LONDON

William Blake

I WANDER THRO' EACH CHARTERE'D STREET,
NEAR WHERE THE CHARTER'D THAMES DOES FLOW
AND MARK IN EVERY FACE I MEET
MARKS OF WEAKNESS,
MARKS OF WOE.

IN EVERY CRY OF EVERY MAN,
IN EVERY INFANT's CRY OF FEAR,
IN EVERY VOICE, IN EVERY BAN,
THE MIND-FORG'D MANACLES I HEAR.

HOW THE CHIMNEY-SWEEPER'S CRY
EVERY BLACK'NING CHURCH APPALS;
AND THE HAPLESS SOLDIER'S SIGH
RUNS IN BLOOD DOWN
PALACE WALLS.

BUT MOST THRO' MIDNIGHT STREETS
I HEAR
HOW THE YOUTHFUL HARLOT'S CURSE
BLASTS THE NEW BORN IN FANT'S TEAR,
AND BLIGHTS WITH PLAGUES'
THE MARRIAGE HEARSE

Linton Quesi Johnson

All Wi Doin is Defendin

war . . . war . . .
mi sae, lissen,
oppression man,
hear what I say if yu can;
wi have
a grievous blow fe blow,
wi will fite yu in de street wid wi han;
wi hav a plan;
soh lissen, man,
get read fe tek some blows.

doze days
of de truncheon
an doze nites
of melancholy locked in a cell,
doze hours of torture touchin hell,
doze blows dat caused my heart to swell
were well
numbered
and are now
at an end.

all wi doin
is defendin;
so get yu ready
fe war . . . war . . .
freedom is a very firm thing;

all oppression
can do is bring
passion to de heights of eruption,
an songs of fire we will sing.

no . . . no . . .
noh run;
yu did soun yu siren
an is war now . . .
war . . . war . . . war . . .

de Special Patrol
will fall
like a wall force doun
or a toun turn to dus;
even dough dem think dem bold,
wi know dem cold like ice wid fear
an we is fire!

choose yu weapon dem
quick!
all wi need is bakkles an bricks an sticks;
wi hav fist
wi hav feet
wi carry dandamite in wi teeth.

sen fe de riot squad,
quick!
caus wi runnin wild
bitta like bile;
blood will guide
their way;
an I say,
all wi doin
is defendin;
soh set yu ready
fe war . . . war . . .
freedom is a very firm thing.

Fred Whitehead

Visions of the Archaic World

My first encounter with William Blake was in the early 1960s, in a seminar given by Professor Edward Ruhe at the University of Kansas. This was one of those one-hour credit courses in an honors program, for which one does an incredible amount of reading—in this case, one work of Blake's per week. Predictably, the mind began to boggle after about the fifth week, somewhere around *The Book of Urizen*, and by the time we plumbed the depths of *The Four Zoas*, there was no going back.... However, Professor Ruhe offered at the beginning of this course an observation both simple and profound, which has stuck with me during the subsequent readings and re-readings and viewings and re-viewings of Blake. He said: the problem with Blake's poems is rather unusual in literature, because we first of all have to try to establish what is happening, to try to understand the location of the action, who the characters are, and so on. As I remember, the comparison with Milton was also made, that with Milton we may encounter intricate plots, a cosmic scale of action, etc., but we do have some familiarity with the story and its locales; with Blake we first have to try to find out what is going on.

Certainly any reader of Blake will be much helped by the standard critical studies of Frye, Erdman, and others; yet there still often seems to be some confusion about the basic plots of the poems. In an earlier essay, I suggested an approach to Blake which fuses the social and historical of Erdman and the mythic and psychological of Frye.[1] In this paper I would like to propose a reading of some phases of *The Four Zoas*, to clarify its plot, which up to now has been rather poorly explicated in its details. Then I would like to make some observations which connect *The Four Zoas* with the later *Jerusalem*.

There is one other intellectual debt which must be acknowledged at the outset, and this is to the English marxist critic Jack Lindsay, in particular a comment he made in an essay of 1945: "Blake is in many ways the greatest modern poet, because he is the poet of the people in the remorseless grip of industrialism, looking back to the folk days, but much more urgently looking forward to the revolution we now call socialism."[2] I shall argue, along these lines, that *The Four Zoas* is an epic of the many traumatic transformations

231

of European man in the archaic period of history, with implications for Blake's own day and our own.

The difficulties which the ms. of *The Four Zoas* presents to the reader are numerous: textually, it is a manuscript of 132 large pages (plus two small sheets and a fragment), with many erasures, layer on layer of writing over erasures, handwriting styles significantly different from one another, and illustrations frequently quite sketchy and enigmatic, or even completely unrelated to the text. To further complicate matters, Blake worked on the manuscript and revised it over a long period of time, perhaps ten years. In 1963, G.E. Bentley, Jr. published a facsimile edition of this ms., including a fresh transcript of the text.[3] Most detailed textual matters are, however, beyond the scope of this essay; the intent here is to clarify some major themes and structures of the work as a whole.

Many critics have recognized that one of the major difficulties of the poem is Blake's use of the *in medias res* technique, though none have explicated its operation fully or clearly.[4] As in the *Iliad* or *Paradise Lost* and many other epic poems, the action of the poem operates on at least two chronological levels: the time scheme of the events actually narrated (the wrath of Achilles, the fall of Adam and Eve), and the whole series of events, however remote, which led up to the beginning of the narrative (the choice of Paris, the fall of Satan). In *The Four Zoas*, after the title, prologue and invocation of the first three pages, the narrative begins with the "fall" of Tharmas:

> Begin with Tharmas Parent power, darkning in the West
> Lost! Lost! Lost! are my Emanations Enion O Enion
> We are become a Victim . . .

Tharmas is lamenting the effects of some event or events which have occurred previous to this moment in the action.

I will reconstruct the poem's plot by collecting and analyzing passages scattered through the ms. in which characters recall events from the distant or recent past, which I shall refer to as "passages of recollection." As we shall see, Blake is actually quite careful with his plot, and while its construction is enormously complex, it does cohere and follow definite and consistent patterns. The most important of the patterns of previous action are (1) the "fall" from Eternity into Beulah, and (2) the "fall" from Beulah into Generation, after which Night I begins.

The earliest event in the chronology of the poem is recalled by the Shadow of Enitharmon, speaking to the Spectre of Urthona, on p. 83 (E351):

> . . . now listen I will tell
> Thee secrets of Eternity which neer before unlockd
> My golden lips nor took the bar from Enitharmons breast

> Among the Flowers of Beulah walkd the Eternal Man & Saw
> Vala the lilly of the desart. melting in high noon
> Upon her bosom in sweet bliss he fainted Wonder siezd
> All heaven they saw him dark. they built a golden wall
> Round Beulah There he reveld in delight among the Flowers
> Vala was pregnant & brought forth Urizen Prince of Light
> First born of Generation. Then behold a wonder to the Eyes
> Of the now fallen Man a double form Vala appeared. A Male
> And female shuddring pale the Fallen Man recoild
> From the Enormity & calld them Luvah & Vala, turning down
> The vales to find his way back into Heaven but found none
> For his frail eyes were faded & his ears heavy & dull
> (11. 4-18)

There are several recollections of life in Eternity in the poem, but this passage contains the only version of the life of the Eternal Man and Vala before the births of Urizen and Luvah, and the only account of the Eternal Man's "fall" from Eternity to Beulah.

For the flower imagery, and the mythic setting, Blake draws most probably on Milton's picture of the happiness of Adam and Eve in the Garden of Eden in Book IV of *Paradise Lost:*

> . . .to thir Supper Fruits they fell
> Nectarine Fruits which the compliant boughes
> Yielded them, side-long as they sat recline
> On the soft downie Bank Damaskt with flou'rs
> (11. 331-334)

> . . .he in delight
> Both of her Beauty and submissive Charms
> Smil'd with superior Love, as *Jupiter*
> On *Juno* smiles, when he impregns the Clouds
> That shed *May* Flowers. . .
> (11. 497-501)[5]

The Eternal Man (Jove-Adam) copulating with Vala (Juno-Eve) refers back to one of the most ancient of all myths, the story of the fertilization of earth by rain from the sky.[6] Archaic man, in nearly complete solidarity with nature, described this natural phenomenon in terms of his own anthropomorphic sexuality; what became only a simile for Milton was an intimate reality for him.

In Blake's conception of ancient history, the Eternal Man is a mythical figure who expresses the unity of the archaic horde and primitive tribe undivided by clans or classes, living directly on and from nature, collecting and gathering his food. This archaic world of fertility is reflected in ancient Near Eastern and European legends of the Garden of Eden and the Golden Age, available to Blake in the Bible, Hesiod and Ovid.[7] In Genesis (1:28-29), Adam and Eve lived in unity and abundance:

> And God blessed them, and God said unto them, Be fruitful, and multiply, and replenish the earth, and subdue it: and have dominion over the fish of the sea, and over the fowl of the air, and over every thing that moveth upon the earth. And God said, Behold, I have given you every herb bearing seed, which is upon the face of all the earth, and every tree, in the which is the fruit of a tree yielding seed; to you it shall be for meat.

Hesiod's version is that the "golden race of mortal men"

> lived like gods without sorrow of heart, remote and free from toil and grief: miserable age rested not on them; but with legs and arms never failing they made merry with feasting beyond the reach of all evils. When they died, it was as though they were overcome with sleep, and they had all good things; for the fruitful earth unforced bare them fruit abundantly and without stint. They dwelt in ease and peace upon their lands with many good things, rich in flocks and loved by the blessed gods.[8]

Ovid's version of the Golden Age (*Metamorphoses*, Book I) is largely patterned after Hesiod's as were most subsequent classical versions.[9]

Though there is apparently no thorough modern study of the Golden Age legends, several scholars have suggested that Hesiod's Golden Age is "the Greek counterpart of the Garden of Eden."[10] In fact, many anthropologists and pre-historians have suggested that both the Garden of Eden and the Golden Age derive from memories of the European and Near East Paleolithic Age. One of the reasons for the abundance of food in the stories of the Golden Age may be that before the disappearance with the last Ice Age of the great supplies of animals (depicted, for example, in the cave paintings of France and Spain), Paleolithic man had the benefit of an especially rich environment.[11] We note in Blake's account of the movement of his Eternal Man from Eternity to "the Flowers of Beulah" that his sustenance seems to be gathered entirely from the "Flowers" themselves, just as Milton's Adam and Eve (and the Biblical pair) live on the natural abundance of the Garden.

Concerning the Garden of Eden, Heichelheim has suggested that the expulsion of Adam and Eve from Paradise

> has a historic nucleus which has been preserved up to the present in the ancient literary form of a myth....The appearance of

234

Neolithic plough culture some centuries before 4000 B.C. (we can trace its origin at this period with some certainty with the help of pollen analysis and early Mesopotamian chronology) means the end of a total revolution in the primary production of the human race....Could we perhaps interpret this tale in the sense that mythical tradition preserves here for us a recollection that the greatest progressive revolution of human society up to the present time was extremely painful for those who were involved in it?... The foundations for the primary production of six or so millennia until modern times and for the outlines of professional differentiation even in secondary production were now laid. Here originated a new balance between the sexes, and with it the importance of clan and family as economic factors was stabilized, which is so characteristic for all agricultural and most city cultures. Just as the social and political class distinctions of this stage of civilization in its broad outlines were to form the foundations of social life for the succeeding 6500 years also.[12]

The unity of Blake's Eternal Man in the crucial passage on p. 83 of *The Four Zoas* expresses the unity of primitive tribal man as Blake understood it from a close reading of the "Greek and Hebrew cosmogonies." Both Man and Vala live closely on nature, and they are undivided from one another, innocent of the strife and war which would characterize later human history.

There are several passages of recollection in *The Four Zoas* concerning the Eternal life, though none which recall so specifically the role of the Eternal Man himself in the transition from Eternity to Beulah as that on p. 83 of the ms. One of the most important such passages is on p. 71 (E341), where Urizen's former life is recalled:

> A Rock a Cloud a Mountain
> Were now not Vocal as in Climes of happy Eternity
> Where the lamb replies to the infant voice & the lion to the man of
>   years
> Giving them sweet instructions Where the Cloud the River & the Field
> Talk with the husbandman & shepherd.
>   (11. 4-8)

The famous naturalism of the European cave paintings, and the evident solidarity with animals such as reindeer and bison, parallels Blake's view of the "vocal" quality of the Eternal life, which he was able to discern and emphasize in the classical and Biblical accounts of the Golden Age. It seems likely that Paleolithic man literally believed that "every thing that lives is Holy" (*The Marriage of Heaven and Hell*; E44), or "numinous" in Rudolf Otto's sense, just as men in primitive cultures today often have remarkably intimate and reverential relationships with features of the physical environment and with animals.[13]

To return to the "Secrets" of Enitharmon's Shadow on p. 83 of the ms., we note that the Eternals build a golden wall around the Eternal Man and Vala, i.e., they construct an enclosure, just as the Garden of Eden was enclosed in Genesis. Man has won a part of nature, and has begun to control her fertility, and the Shadow tells what happened next:

> Urizen grew up in the plains of Beulah Many Sons
> And many daughters flourished round the holy Tent of Man
> Till he forgot Eternity delighted in his sweet joy
> Among his family his flock & herds & tents & pastures
> (11. 19-22)

The enclosure of the Garden becomes Beulah, the first property of the new, Neolithic Age, and man begins to settle down on the "plains" to live a regular and stable life in tents, and to turn from simple food collecting to food producing, possible now with "flocks & herds & tents & pastures."

The Neolithic or food-producing revolution, as Childe and other prehistorians have pointed out, was one of the truly great transformations of human history, a prelude to the later, equally important Urban Revolution.[14] In the Paleolithic period, man had subsisted on what food he could gather from nature. Now he begins to produce food by imposing his will on nature, primarily in cultivation of grains and domestication of animals, the occupations of Cain and Abel (Genesis 4:2). The development of Blake's plot from ll. 7-18 to ll. 19-22 of p. 83 is based on a close reading of the Genesis account of the distinctions between Adam and his sons Cain and Abel, which modern anthropologists have come to define as the historical differences between the Paleolithic and Neolithic Ages.

"Many Sons/And many daughters flourished round the holy Tent of Man." As has been noted above, one can scarcely overemphasize the literal specificity of Blake's imagery, its dependence on what he called "Minute Particulars." The increasingly stable and sedentary life of Neolithic man and the availability of better food on a regular basis permitted a striking increase in population densities.[15] Modern archaeology and prehistory confirm Blake's intuitive expansion of what Genesis 4 implied. Blake, like Milton, is expanding and enlarging the Genesis story, but he is also drawing on Greek myths, as we have pointed out, especially that of Hesiod's Ages ("genos"—which could also be translated as "generation"), the transition from the Golden Age to the Silver Age also reflecting the development from Paleolithic to Neolithic.[16] Hesiod's version of "the race of silver" was that it was "like the golden race neither in body nor in spirit...they lived only a little time and that in sorrow because of their foolishness, for they could not keep from sinning and from wronging one another . . ." Blake's shades of meaning are very subtle: man's life in Eternity, though happy and intimately involved with nature, seems almost too dependent upon the forces of nature. Man "in the plains of Beulah" is more secure, "delighted in his sweet joy," but he has forgotten the expansiveness of his former vision. Here, on p. 83 of the poem, we have the suggestion of the Eternal Man's sadness at being unable to return to Eternity, and in *The Four Zoas*, Eternity and Beulah tend to merge into one another as the pastoral way of life.

Almost all the central figures in the poem lament the "fall" of the pastoral: Enion on pp. 17-18 and p. 35, Ahania on p. 39, Tharmas on pp. 93-94, Urizen on pp. 63-64 and p. 121, the Spectre of Urthona on p. 84, and the Eternal Man himself on pp. 119-120. Significant images in all these passages are flocks, tents, harvests, milk and honey, and corn; they are reflective of their first combination in history. Before the neolithic, tents, flocks and harvests were unknown, and after it other structures and images become more important, commensurate with the development of new forms of social and economic organization. The fact that these significant details fuse together is extremely important; in the succeeding "fall" from Beulah to Generation, the imagery of city life, metallurgy, organized war, and slavery becomes prominent, overwhelming the pastoral imagery. All city imagery is missing from this strata of the poem's plot precisely because Blake is describing life before the advent of cities.[17]

The catastrophic incident which initiates the transition from Beulah to Generation I shall call the "horses of light" episode, alluded to by the Shadow of Enitharmon on p. 83 (E351):

> But Luvah close conferrd with Urizen in darksom night
> To bind the father & enslave the brethren Nought he knew
> Of sweet Eternity the blood flowd round the holy tent & rivn
> From its hinges uttering its final groan all Beulah fell
> (ll. 23-26)

There are several different versions of the same incident, told from the perspectives of the different characters variously affected by it. One account which seems to avoid the special pleading of most other versions is the speech of the Ambassadors from Beulah, p. 21 (E306-307):

> The Eternal man wept in the holy tent Our Brother in Eternity
> Even Albion whom thou lovest wept in pain his family
> Slept round on hills & valleys in the regions of his love
> But Urizen awoke & Luvah woke & thus conferrd
> Thou Luvah said the Prince of Light behold our sons & daughters
> Reposd on beds. let them sleep on. do thou alone depart

Into thy wished Kingdom where in Majesty & Power
We may erect a throne. deep in the North I place my lot
Thou in the South listen attentive. In silent of this night
I will infold the Eternal tent in clouds opake while thou
Siezing the chariots of the morning. Go outfleeting ride
Afar into the Zenith high bending thy furious course
Southwards with half the tents of man inclosd in clouds
Of Tharmas & Urthona. I remaining in porches of the brain
Will lay my scepter on Jerusalem the Emanation
On all her sons & on thy sons O Luvah & on mine
Till dawn was wont to wake them then my trumpet sounding loud
Ravishd away in night my strong command shall be obeyd
For I have placed my centinels in stations each tenth man
Is bought & sold & in dim night my Word shall be their law
                    (ll. 16-35)

Blake critics have usually explicated this episode in purely psychological terms: Urizen (Reason) and Luvah (Love) combine to overcome Tharmas (Sensation) and Urthona (Intuition); Urizen offers Luvah the control of the horses of intellect, causing him to neglect his proper role of passion and emotion, thus defeating him too, and emerging sole victor.[18]

An examination of certain social and economic details of the "horses of light" incident will clarify the historical context of the psychological schism. The Zoas with their emanations and sons and daughters live in tents close together (21:28), each Zoa having his own sector though they live in mutual friendship. In the Paleolithic societies the division of labor in the tribe was often defined by sex: men were hunters and women were collectors of fruits, nuts, etc. The Neolithic Age evolved a more complex division of labor, in which the new tribes became divided into clans (i.e., tribal units) which were often occupational: the sons of farmers were also farmers, and the sons of shepherds were also shepherds.[19] There is considerable evidence that metal-workers were also largely restricted to hereditary clans.[20]

The four Zoas become the heads of four tribal clans, the Paleolithic horde (led by the now feeble Eternal Man) having been split up and developed into a segmented social system. Blake's most important source for the occupational functions of three of his Zoas is Genesis 4: Urizen being Cain the "tiller of the ground," and Tharmas being Abel the "keeper of sheep." Urthona is Tubal-cain, "an instructor of every artificer in brass and iron." Luvah's occupation is not clear, though much later, in Night IX, he supervises the winepresses.[21]

The "horses of light" episode occurs at night while the Eternal Man is weeping in his tent, remembering the bliss of Eternity, possibly aware that plots against him are afoot; his weakness is the weakness of the old Paleolithic patriarch.[22] Urizen and Luvah, the leaders of two of the clans, conspire to overthrow him and assume control of the tribe themselves. Urizen proposes to Luvah that they act at night, "with half the tents of men inclosd in clouds/ Of Tharmas & Urthona" (21:28-29; E307). Tharmas the shepherd and Urthona the smith are to be victims in the "fall" of Beulah.

Frye notes the probable sources of Luvah's seizure of the chariots of morning (the "horses of light") in the stories of Lucifer's fall in Isaiah 14 and Phaeton's driving of the sun's chariot.[23] However, we are not really given to understand the exact nature of this theft, except in terms of purely mythological and psychological explanation. By carefully considering certain details of the whole incident, we should be able to arrive at a more precise understanding, including social and economic levels of meaning. First, the appropriation element of the story is extremely important—indeed, in the plot of The Four Zoas, this is the origin of private property, of *meum* and *tuum*. Previously, the families or clans of the four Zoas had lived together in peace (83:19-22; E351). In early Beulah, equality was still the principle of social life. Luvah and Urizen conspire to seize control of the clans and institute royal authority, as evident in the statement, "We may erect a throne" (21:23; E307), in Urizen's threat to lay his "scepter" on Jerusalem (21:30), and in Urizen's proposal that they divide the authority between themselves: "do thou alone depart/ Into thy wished Kingdom" (21:21-22).

Norman O. Brown has convincingly demonstrated that the Homeric Hymn to Hermes, which tells the story of the theft of the cattle of Apollo by Hermes, is an expression of the slow and subtle alteration of property relations in ancient Greece.[24] Without reducing the "horses of light" episode (or any myth, for that matter) to an economic and social fable, we may observe the same kind of emphasis on property here. The literal meaning of Blake's story is that Urizen offers Luvah his horses in order to secure his assistance in obtaining control of the tribe. This does not contradict the psychological meaning of the episode, but complements it. Blake implies that the distortions of certain psychological forms—the antithesis between Reason and Emotion, for example—may be traced to certain moments in historical time.

The conspiracy of Urizen and Luvah fails, and at this point only destroys the old forms, producing chaos, and propelling man on through history, the new forms of which are to appear at the beginning of the actual narrative of the poem, in Night I. Their conspiracy fails, partially because of resistance from the sons of Urthona particularly, and partially because of mutual jealousy, an inevitable development from the institution of private property. Love and Reason now begin to contend for domination and control, though of course neither one can ever succeed in dominating permanently, and their struggle only diverts previous energy into negative channels, the primary form of which is war.

Other accounts of the "horses of light" episode reflect the special perspective of the individual character. Indeed, it is only at this point in the poem that a purely individual perspective begins, forming the historical agony of schizoid man attempting to re-unite and resume his ancient integrity and brotherhood. For example, Enitharmon says:

> Hear! I will sing a Song of Death! it is a Song of Vala!
> The Fallen Man takes his repose: Urizen sleeps in the porch
> Luvah and Vala woke & flew up from the Human Heart
> Into the Brain; from thence upon the pillow Vala slumber'd.
> And Luvah siez'd the Horses of Light, & rose into the Chariot of Day
> Sweet laughter siezd me in my sleep! silent & close I laughd
> For in the visions of Vala I walkd with the mighty Fallen One
> I heard his voice among the branches, & among sweet flowers.
>   (10:9-16; E301)

Enitharmon makes quite clear the connection of psychological and also physiological traumata with the episode: Luvah and Vala literally flew up from the Heart to the Brain, i.e., emotion attempted to usurp reason. She also stresses the element of sexual jealousy, that subterranean deceit which came to characterize man-woman relations (also stressed by Milton in *Paradise Lost*, of course).

In the poem, the emanations often urge a merciful course of action on their male counterparts, but the males, whose pride and prowess are committed to fighting one another, refuse to listen, believing that the emanations are in love with their opponents. Thus Los smites Enitharmon, and Urizen blasts Ahania. Sexual antagonisms are in this way connected with the historical process of the development of private property, and the break-up of the clan system.[25] Ahania's reference (39:10-11) to "those sweet fields of bliss/ Where liberty was justice & eternal science was mercy" harkens back to the Eternal, Golden Age unity of Paleolithic tribal solidarity, which was only a distant memory after the collapse of Beulah, the Silver Neolithic Age.

Night I begins, then, in this transition from Beulah to Generation. The main narrative of the poem follows the course of ancient civilization through the Bronze and Iron Ages of Hesiod, in what Childe called the Urban Revolution, characterized by the appearance of a definite social class structure, including the hierarchies of kings and priests, the classes of workers and slaves, the accumulation of economic surpluses on a large scale, the formation of cities as such, and eventually, imperial phases with their inevitable emphases on war and conquest. We may see this process sweeping westward from Mesopotamia to Greece, and thence to Rome and her epic collapse. A detailed explanation of these phases of the poem is beyond the scope of this essay, but it will be readily apparent, for example, that the apocalypse of Night the Ninth has many parallels with the Book of Revelation, the definitive mythic vision of the collapse of the Roman Empire.

Any reader of *Jerusalem* will have been impressed by the gigantic stone-henge-like illustrations; the poem would seem to be a literally "lithic" poem. The major addition to the myth in *Jerusalem* was the apparently bizarre conflation of Biblical and British names and geography, but the effect of this is to suggest once more the unity of different cultures in similar phases of history. Furthermore, in *Jerusalem* Blake develops a myth in which the ancient Druidic sacrifices are repeated by the terrible and vast European wars of his own day. But that is another story.

NOTES

1. "William Blake and Radical Tradition" in *Weapons of Criticism*, ed. Norman Rudich (Palo Alto: Ramparts, 1976), pp. 191-214.

2. "William Blake," in *Little Reviews Anthology* 1945, ed. Denys Val Baker (London: Allen & Unwin, 1945), pp. 187-195. Lindsay's more recent *William Blake* (London: Constable, 1978) also has several points of convergence with the present analysis, though his consideration of *The Four Zoas* is mostly concerned with the impact on Blake of the events of his own day.

4. *Vala or the Four Zoas* (Oxford: Clarendon Press, 1963). In this essay citations of Blake's works are from *The Poetry and Prose of William Blake*, ed. David Erdman (Garden City: Doubleday, 1965), abbreviated as E, preceded by the page and line numbers of the ms.

4. The term *in medias res* is, of course, from Horace's discussion of proper epic form, *De Arte Poetica*, l. 148. Some discussions of this aspect of *The Four Zoas* are in Frye, *Fearful Symmetry* (1947: rpt. Boston: Beacon, 1962), pp. 285-286; S. Foster Damon, *William Blake* (1924; rpt. Gloucester: Peter Smith, 1958), pp. 140-148; Harold Bloom, *Blake's Apocalypse* (Garden City: Doubleday, 1963), pp. 195-196, 206. Helen T. McNeil, in "The Formal Art of *The Four Zoas*," in *Blake's Visionary Forms Dramatic*, ed. David V. Erdman and John E. Grant (Princeton: Princeton University Press, 1970), pp. 373-390, somewhat desperately states that "...time recalled from the perspective of a distinct present, and temporal movement toward a future which constantly realizes itself in the present can hardly be said to exist in *The Four Zoas*. The past seems to be invented at will to satisfy the needs of rhetoric; there is no linear time-line with regular demarcations until Night the Eighth." (p. 385) I believe this view to be mistaken.

5. Citations of Milton are from the Columbia edition of the *Works*, Gen. ed. Frank Allen Patterson, 18 vols. in 21 (New York: Columbia University Press, 1931-1938). Denis Saurat, *Blake and Milton* (1935; rpt. New York: Russell & Russell, 1965), pp. 110-111, cites this passage, but does not explain it in any detail.

6. Hesiod, *Theogony*, ll. 126-128, ed. Hugh G. Evelyn-White (Cambridge: Loeb, 1914). See also Norman O. Brown's edition of the *Theogony* (Indianapolis: Bobbs-Merrill, 1953), pp. 16-17, 38, 56. A remarkable modern treatment of such ancient

stories is Edward Dahlberg, *The Sorrows of Priapus* (New York: New Directions, 1957).

7. Frye, *Fearful Symmetry*, p. 278. However, Frye tends to oversimplify the actual course of events in the poem.

8. *Works and Days*, ll. 110-120.

9. Frank E. Manuel, "The Golden Age: A Mythic Prehistory for Western Utopia," in *Freedom from History* (New York: New York University Press, 1971), p. 80.

10. Manuel, p. 75; Fritz M. Heichelheim, *An Ancient Economic History*, I (Leiden: A.W. Sijthoff, 1958), p. 362, n. 40: "It is worthy of note that the Golden Age of the Greeks is described as characterized by similar activities as the Paradise of Genesis and the Ancient Oriental traditions," and refs.

11. V. Gordon Childe, *What Happened in History*, rev. ed., with a new foreword by Grahame Clark (Baltimore: Penguin, 1964), pp. 30, 44, 50.

12. Op. cit., I, 51-52, 362. Clark suggests an earlier date for the appearance of Neolithic culture (ninth millennium B.C.) in a note to *What Happened in History*, p. 58. The similarity of the story of Enkidu (a man who lives in the wilds of Mesopotamia with animals) to the story of the "fall" has been stressed by N.K. Sandars in her edition of *The Epic of Gilgamesh*, rev. ed. (Baltimore: Penguin, 1964), p. 30: "It is also an allegory of the stages by which mankind reaches civilization, going from savagery to pastoralism and at last to the life of the city."

13. Carl Jung, *Memories, Dreams, Reflections* (New York: Vintage, 1963), pp. 250-252, 267; A.P. Elkin, *The Australian Aborigines*. rev. ed. (Garden City: Doubleday, 1964), pp. 205-206; Black Elk, *Black Elk Speaks* (1932; rpt. Lincoln: University of Nebraska Press, 1961), passim; Rudolf Otto, *The Idea of the Holy*, trans. John Harvey (1923; rpt. Harmondsworth: Penguin, 1959), passim.

14. Childe, *What Happened in History*, chapter 3, and *Man Makes Himself*, 3rd ed. (New York: New American Library, 1951), chapter 5; Robert Redfield, *The Primitive World and Its Transformations* (Ithaca: Cornell University Press, 1953), chapter 1.

15. Childe, *What Happened in History*, pp. 73-74.

16. Thomas G. Rosenmeyer, "Hesiod and Historiography," *Hermes*, 85 (1957), 257-285; Hesiod, *Works and Days*, ll. 129-135.

17. Redfield, op. cit., p. 1: "What can be said that is general and true about the condition of mankind before civilization? The question is directed to a time from five to six thousand years ago . . . . No city had yet been built anywhere."

18. Frye, *Fearful Symmetry*, pp. 285-286; Damon, *William Blake*, p. 145; Bloom, *Blake's Apocalypse*, p. 206; W.P. Witcutt, *Blake: A Psychological Study* (1946; rpt. Port Washington 1966), pp. 35-40, 56-57.

19. The literature on social clans is enormous; the whole subject was raised in social historiography by Morgan's classic *Ancient Society* (New York, 1877), and controversy has continued ever since. I have followed the account of the character and growth of clans by occupations in: Childe: *What Happened in History*, pp. 53, 73; George Thomson, *Studies in Ancient Greek Society*, rev. ed. (London: Lawrence & Wishart, 1961), I, chapters 1-4; Heichelheim, op. cit., I, 60-61, 73; Claude Levi-Strauss, *The Savage Mind* (Chicago: University of Chicago Press, 1966), pp. 120-121; and D.D. Kosambi, *The Culture and Civilisation of Ancient India in Historical Outline* (London: Routledge, 1965), p. 50.

20. Childe, *What Happened in History*, pp. 85-87; Frederick W. Robins, *The Smith: The Traditions and Lore of an Ancient Craft* (London: Rider, 1953), chapter 3; R.J. Forbes, *Studies in Ancient Technology*, 8 (Leiden: E.J. Brill, 1964), chapter 3.

21. Frye lists the Zoas by "Activity" in his table of their associations, *Fearful*

Symmetry, p. 278, but there is little evidence for his association of Luvah with weaving.

22. Freud, *Totem and Taboo*, chapter 4, sections 6-7, in *Basic Writings*, ed. and trans. by A.A. Brill (New York: Modern Library, 1938), pp. 919-930; Brown's ed. of Hesiod's *Theogony*, Introduction, pp. 16-18.

23. *Fearful Symmetry*, pp. 285-286.

24. *Hermes the Thief* (Madison: University of Wisconsin Press, 1947), passim.

25. For an excellent discussion of sexual antagonisms, see Frye, *Fearful Symmetry*, p. 285.

Alexandra Eldridge

Michael Castro

Auguries from Experience

When Man aspired
down He fell
losing Eden
finding Hell
Earth became
a suffering place
a path to Death
the Human Race
& Death meant Fear
& Awe & Doubt
God cast
aspiring Angels out
of Heaven
where He lived alone
contemplating
what He'd done
Love still lived
amidst the Strife
Man took Woman
for a Wife
in Time
they struggled
to be Free
to use the Knowledge
from the Tree
but Knowledge proved
a clever Cage
mankind rattled
mad with Rage
God just frowned
& tipped the Pole
Darkness fell
upon each Soul

Theodore Enslin

A Neap Tide Ritual

Not yet time

for the moon

to rise

out of some pocket

of the night.

Full cup

or half cup

spilled in the stars

above the wind,

and into the sea,

few splinters fallen.

It will suffice

for dew or frost

at dawning:

What is mirrored.

What is echoed.

Time enough to turn

in sleep and dreaming.

Not yet time,

but let it come.

Margaret Flanagan

The Winter

Winter! Winter! freezing white
In the polar wastes of night,
What immortal brain or hand
Could scatter you across the land?

What wilderness of ice
Formed the crystals starting this?
On what wind were they swept here
By what force unstayed by fear?

And what cunning, and what mind's
Strength firmed the fluid, made chilled designs?
And when you closed down on us
What power gave you impetus?

Where the berg? what avalanche,
Glacial flow we cannot stanch,
Supplies you and keeps on
The arctic season long?

Why, this cold thing done, did He
Choose birth in your inclemency?
Blake questioned; I ask, too:
Did He who made summer make you?

Winter! Winter! freezing white
In the polar wastes of night,
What immortal brain or hand
Unleashed you upon the land?

And there was heard a great lamenting in Beulah: all the Regions
Of Beulah were moved as the tender bowels are moved: & they said:
Why did you take Vengeance O ye Sons of the mighty Albion?
Planting these Oaken Groves: Erecting these Dragon Temples
Injury the Lord heals but Vengeance cannot be healed:
As the Sons of Albion have done to Luvah: so they have in him
Done to the Divine Lord & Saviour, who suffers with those that suffer:
For not one sparrow can suffer, & the whole Universe not suffer also,
In all its Regions, & its Father & Saviour not pity and weep.
But Vengeance is the destroyer of Grace & Repentance in the bosom
Of the Injurer: in which the Divine Lamb is cruelly slain:
Descend O Lamb of God & take away the imputation of Sin
By the Creation of States & the deliverance of Individuals Evermore Amen
Thus wept they in Beulah over the Four Regions of Albion
But many doubted & despaird & imputed Sin & Righteousness
To Individuals & not to States, and these Slept in Ulro.

Gary G. Gach

thread

thread
Pulling through the buttonhole of my navel
Only so far —

Before I have to remake fabric in its threads
eternity
In my body's image —

Imagination, where
Unsaid promises are, where the beast is
The man in the moon;
Stone, we call

green cheese, an echo
Chamber, cool light, at that tunnel's end,

Whose doors are walls
Our initials carved in conflicting rumors
on bark.

NOTE:
I went out one night during the period in which I was writing a sequence of poems about the moon & saw Chaplin's City Lights *for the first time. An image in the film arrested me and became the germ the next morning for the poem beginning "thread . . ."*
The tramp had been taken to a wild party by the rich man whose life he has saved (and who remembers him only at night). While about him vamps & flappers cavort with fops & Diamond Jim Brady rakeheels, the Tramp is quite drunk in his chair, plucking streamers & confetti off of his clothes. The act of pulling one streamer, however, from off of his waist becomes an almost endless labor; he pulls with both hands this white string that seems to have no end until his face suddenly pops open in astonishment simultaneous with a precise, slightly torqued jerk of his gluteus maximus on the chair. (The Tramp has, he now realizes, just unravelled his own, frayed underwear.) Finishing the poem, that afternoon I continued reading Raine's Blake & Tradition *& found for the first time the illustration* Jerusalem, *plate 25.*

James Broughton

The Golden Positions

I have been deeply influenced by Blake on every level of my life. And certainly when it came to portraying the living celebration of the divinity of the human body, I approached it with as much spontaneous passion and amateur enthusiasm as did Will. In the medium of cinema I made Living Statues, murals, sculptural structures and archetypal personages, using my friends, my students, my actor and dancer acquaintances. I did not strive for ideal physiques, I functioned on the premise that all bodies are holy and beautiful. My performers responded warmly to this vision, and shed their daily clothing with relish and faith.

Prayer to the Body

Our body, which is of earth,
holied be thy shape.
Thy beauty come,
thy acts be done,
on faith as they are given.
Give us each day our daily positions.
And forgive us our ineptitudes
as they do not forgive us.
Lead us not into ungracefulness
but deliver us from shamble.
For Thine is the standing,
the sitting, and the lying
for ever and ever.

Robert Kelly

The Book of Water

All the years I've loved Blake and quarreled with and for him, I had not
presumed on the acquaintance. Late last summer I found myself on Chesapeake
Isle among hardwood forests ancient as things go in America; I sensed a new
opening in my work, coming. I was near the place where Cornwallis had once
trundled ashore the borrowed mercenaries of Urizen, in vain restraint of what
would be us. One day I began to write, with no design, and as I wrote
discovered myself working in a Blakean permission: a double permission, to
loop the line long, and to study the acts of Persons who stood forth named from
the mind. Book I of the Book of Water was written that week, and since then
Books II and III have been composed, tracing the righting of Pothor's ardor and
the serviceable love of Malchus for Norsha. I do not aspire to the power of
William Blake's cosmological physics; for me cosmology is still psychology, my
cosmos still psyche.

RK • May 1981

Book One

(He was a glass of water he poured on her,
Pothor pouring himself into the lap of Norsha
as the annihilating ollunic current itself spins
into tracts of invisibility gold in her reflected light)

I gloss these gulls and scare these sacred terns
into an alphabet of explanation. The ollunic drift
obols her lap, what she conceives is desire for him,
her holy fetch-power of implevic husk
fills her sheaf. She ripens, sun of his black
Other Thing whose name is Soloron—gives
gold but hers is better—Pothor futures the brand

he heats—fire is a visitor come calling—
bringing brown bags of Soloron to strew on her mat
and bid her roll therein so Pothor can augur
the roll of future from the floor of fact.
The snake dances on one foot, segments
of its river body sometimes wake.
But all this while she's sleeping and he plans.

On the ollunic raft, Pothor is dazzled
by the power waves he's given out. His ectoheart
reaches as far as her hips, he simply
wants to insert himself in her sans explanation.
To be in! As simply as to be on! On such
as a raft riding the ollunic brightness, the force
that effaces the difference that calls it into being—
a charged field that loses its charge, yields it
in supreme greedy self-sacrifice to the wished-for
Object, the ends of the world, the Hole in Time.

which Pothor himself thereupon became.
There was a pear tree by the lake
and under it they gathered (children of the morning)
the alphabetic fall of firm unripe pears
that were sweet even so, if the teeth are strong,
sweet fruit, being neither stolen nor sold
nor products of any body's industry, he
wanted her to be that way, her he wanted
Norsha or any of the gold or browny Isis-clones
whose clothes he finessed away line by line
until love woke in the bidden craft and it conceived
an ardent breath for him to be her passenger.

Who can read this text? Norsha who is empty can read these staves,
Norsha can read the branches and the bark, Norsha
is seven-times empty (who can read her woven hair?
who can weave her veily thoughts? who can think her? who can film
the seismic ripple of her ellipsoids as she
hungry for his implevic thrust to sate her
runs over the grass neither thinking nor willing, just going?
who can film any thing but will?) Norsha who is empty
reads a desire in her hair, she sees sunlight through it
rainbowing in the fine strands—her heart hurts

253

because in that split-second of seeing the spectrum
she knows his power is ollunic, will be Desire
from which she catches fire, she'll want him, will
want him and want him and he will be away and want
away and want everyone who is not her. And still she runs
runs on grass that neither warns her nor impedes,
runs to Pothor lured by his factual energy,
thanking God as she goes that no wit deters her.
"For I am ignorant of all things but desire,
and I rush to be hurt by this new need
that will for a second fill me, then graft
itself onto my root longing and I will want him
and he will want no one and in the reversed currents
the metal I am will be fused, short-out and new
born in the agony of morning I will want all alone."

So Norsha sang as she hurried by the pear tree.
His imagination meantime withheld itself from her,
he being no more than a current to fill her,
wanting no more than to screw her for its own sake.
Pothor's mind was on the water, not on her fire,
he was counting seabirds on the lake and dark cowbirds
starlings, cardinals who strutted on the shore
indifferent to water. For a boat is the first alchemy,
first human mastery of another element
and one more accurate than flight. For a boat
sustains itself by what it treads on, uses the inertia of water,
rides passive, survives, eats the wind and waves, fends for itself to go.
We do not power it. It opens the other element to us
who would know it for its own sake, for the knowing,
as Pothor would know Norsha. He heard the hem of her song
not the words of it, and picks out those timbres
resonated from the inner aspects of her thighs
that seem to work a beam towards him his own desire rides.
But from a thornbrake Calsha watched.

Calsha was beautiful and small, her hair unclean,
her breasts large and full of unyielded milk,
her hands stained from the flowers and earth she works.
Her gate is never latched and she is anger.
She is reproach, a peachy fantast who's never satisfied,
who measures men by how they flee from her.

This curse was on her: that any man who loved her
she disdained, and any man she loved she thought disdained her.
Lie quiet, Calsha, do not send Pothor messages today,
though he is chief of your disdainers. Lie quiet, Calsha,
do not beat your drum, weep silently apart
sitting in your thorns. Calsha looked at Norsha running
and hated her, hated her the more because her breasts
longed to mother her too, she longed to fold herself to Norsha,
caress her long slack limbs, longed to lie with Norsha.
And Norsha would! She would be mothered and sistered
gladly by this wild enemy! That very willingness
made Calsha love and hate her more. And most
that Pothor wanted Norsha, and the way of that,
that he just wanted Norsha quickly and basely and with thighs—
and Calsha, seeing that, hated his appetite, scorned it,
but wanted it to be for her, to her and for her, wanted
to be wanted by him, and wanted to protect Norsha
from this trivial frequent base masculine ravishment.

Calsha was blond with hate and blond with love
for Norsha and for Pothor and for all who moved with energy
beneath the sparrow-busy trees. At the moment
Pothor is her god, Norsha her devil, and she a lean diabolist
greedy for both their bodies. To slobber over Norsha's breasts,
her soft long strong unmuscular arms! To be known by Pothor
as he means to know Norsha! To make them both worthy of her!
Ardent Calsha never burning, burning Pothor quickly slaked,
Norsha knowing better but not caring. The river, the river of them!
Endlessly churning, turning over the bitter sludge at bottom
and moving all desirers with its own allerotic whimsy—
our flesh of its own make reaches out, that is Calsha's secret,
we can do nothing but endorse the flesh's ancient will.
Norsha is dark to judgment, Pothor is pure will, to know
her as light knows dark, to suffer valiantly in her,
to be blue. Calsha is yellow with understanding, not clean.

This is how it is in Hamadras by the river,
this is snake and orchid, cucumber and clear water.
Calsha rests on thorns, she accepts the omen of their reminder,
Norsha is running over the grass to get screwed. Pothor
in one lucid second knows the brute fact of his short interest,
knows it will be with him hereafter just as now.

255

He is a servant of what should be his servant—true,
but morality is a prison to all life. Better dead
than prudent, better starved asleep than provident—
so Pothor thinks watching Norsha run towards him,
his mouth already dry with wanting her, already his wits framing
the excuse of dispassion and alchemic triumph
by which he will abstain from pleasure after long pleasure stolen.

Malchus sleeps on the river, floating face down,
his nostrils clear of water kept, his arms folded
on a drifting plank. Malchus is pain come by hearing,
cured by forgetting. He is a brother of Pothor,
newly come from their common mother. Like all pain,
he lives in a house, sleeps on Pothor's daybed,
watches all the desirers and does not desire: Malchus
born with a broken ear, Malchus a scientist of sleep.
Sleep heals the undesirer. Sleep is their only rain,
those folk who never get wet. Malchus floats,
dreaming a revenge upon desire. Calsha
will love him by and by. She will build him a boat—
but he has no love for surfaces. Those are Pothor's plantations,
the fields of skinlight throbbing with acceptance.

Then Calsha spoke to Pothor: "Absenting erotic, absent,
I know the sincerity of the lies you'll tell; we are
dirtily similar, you and I, we abstract the weather
into a testament of coming towards. We lust but I last.
With me skewered on your lap you'd see a marvel,
through my eyes a vision frequently opens
onto a language which speaks us effortless. My grace
would lead you to that portaled cliff whose caves
would pacify your uneasy striving: Lover, you are reluctant
to be loved, and what you do give, your inner body resorbs
even before the woman can conceive. You give *desire*,
that is all, and take it back, so that your willing victim
becomes a willer of a continuance you withhold.
For ecstasy is pure apartness, and no place to stand."

Pothor with his strong teeth was biting pears, sampling
the sweetness augmented since last noon. He bit them
as they still hung from their branches. His strong jaws chewing
drowned the words of Calsha's song. There is a garden

where the noise of lovers becomes the breeze
that issues from the garden and fills the world. All trees,
leaves, waves, seas, move in response to it.
This wind stirred Pothor's hair. The garden was not far
and he lived all his days in waft of its fragrancing.

When he was tired he lived a mood to rest, a bowered hammock
slung between an oak tree and a stone. Here he perpended
the outcome of his desires. Norsha was not in his fantasies.
The pothic will he had at her meant only actual.
Dreamy lusts made liturgies with Findabhair, Queila,
Viula Gried, Laxa, Menehild and Wisselore—
never with Norsha. Norsha was only of now. A target,
not a goal. No man is an arrow; he is an archer,
and bends his bow towards every truth. His archer's mind
spilled uncontainable velocities of aimingness—
feathery pothic dreamwill fancying the oil of night
rubbed on his skin by those women he pressed it for
in sagittarian orgies of prowess and withstanding.
They gripped him oily with their oily thighs. Later
(while Norsha was still running to him through her glade
blameless through hedges) Pothor took out his maps.

These were his life's work: a thousand seven hundred charts
and more, of all the nations, channels, cities, lived-in bodies he'd explored
by flesh or fancy. Periplus and overland he'd gone, and by
conjecture's portolan had reached unlikely coasts
lit by baffling starlight till sudden bursts of sun gave him the place
utterly and he took possession and implanted and utterly
satisfied fled in terror from the land that so endowed him.
These maps were his story and his zeal, these diagrams
drawn in China's fadeless ink exact, colored
after slow in reminiscence with mathematic hue
and chroma tinted by remembered passion: satisfied or not,
and how well satisfied. These maps meant the world
and day by day revised them in the truth of feeling—
for truth is not the feeling when it happens but the feeling
as processed duly in the secret chambers of time's heart
endlessly working in Pothor, the feeling he'd wake up to some
accurate morning and suddenly know, and set his learning out in maps.
All the women he had known were figured there,
each in her natural location, each signified

by the lozenge of her heraldry—for that signifying science
was his life's diversion, to rescue sense a while
from *their* ardent contours by the cool conventions of blasonry
that still exactly represented them; these he thumbed.

As he smoothed a new map on his knees, Norsha
came bursting through the rhododendrons, a drop
of blood on her left breast from no sensible wound.
He licked it as she spoke:
                              "Desirous Pothor, I know your tricks,
the maiden hunger of your ever virgin eye—
for no one you have seen has yet transpierced its veil—
attend to my resolution. I am here to take your touch
among the liberal pleasures of my body, I will
let you press your measures in my matter.
I am open to this thing you mean to do, open
to be the lover you intend, I ask nothing
but that you do me clearly, and saint my ardor
with your daylong cunning. My pleasure
is to hold no pleasure back. I have nothing more to say."
Then Pothor rose from the shame of his inattention.

(But Calsha had heard, Calsha saw the blood, Calsha
longed for her own tongue to be sucking his tongue licking her.
Calsha lurked in discomfort and saw all that followed.
Calsha saw the bees desert the bower, saw Norsha step
quickly from her single robe, saw Pothor reach
almost idly his trembling hand to part Norsha's legs.
Calsha saw his fingertips vanish in her cleft.
Calsha saw Norsha standing still as sunlight there.
Her eyes showed pleasure, but as if pleasure stung—
yes, Norsha's eyes were a glad swimmer's eyes stung by salt.
Pothor probed her, his face meant full of wonder and desire,
a little man looking at a rainbow. Calsha hissed
but the sound fell among leaves and hushed away.
Pothor joyed Norsha and at Norsha turned his face
joyful and joying. Nothing spoke. He read her face
guided by his fingers walking her. He lifted his left hand
now and drew her towards him. She slumped forward on him
and the hammock held them both. Still Calsha saw.
'He is equivalent as light,' she thought, 'his grace
buries itself inside her now, and all his learned fingers merely hold.

She saw them press in Norsha's hips, pulling her ever to him.
They tumbled in the mesh and Calsha groaned
ground bass to their moaning antiphons. Who heard?
The starlings on the grassy shore, the nest of crows.

*

We steal out of Paradise at night for that love's sake
knows us in thunder, cold wet on our backs we love
as if love were the only story. The architect of rain builds
us a pleasure ground apart, neither paradise nor earth.

Here in the watery outline Calsha embraces whom she will
utterly, without having to dismiss her daily anger later
when she sneaks through Paradise. Here is love without forgiveness.
It would be accurate to have fish forgive her but fish are waking
to the bounding of thunder on their rooves, the pain of lightning
sampling the lake. Such messages we sleep apart from.
Into her dream the images she treasured crept again, breathed
a while with her breath, image-Pothor, image-Norsha fucked again
swung in his island hammock greedily arriving. Calsha accepts
them both to her finer network—they fall through all the world
but not through her. She is their agora now and market-town,
the stalls of their commercing thrive in her sensual greed.
Between her busy thighs she mints the pothic coin,
and wakes to lightning mumbling the royal names she stamps thereon
with sleep's last breath. Back into Paradise, the actual, she creeps
and stands above the actual hammock where they rest
washed by the same rain that dingies her. Carefully
she lifts a crumpled map from under Norsha's foot
and puts it safe in Pothor's armory beneath the oak.
How dare that ignorant woman tread his artful conscious work!
In the scandal of her own betterness Calsha scans
one by one the maps in their shelter. 'This is all he has,'
she thinks, 'these leaves are the single outflow of his life
and when I inspect them I know him better than Norsha can—
though when she's spurned, tomorrow or tomorrow, she too
will learn to read these unpassioned heraldries with me
and feed her merchant heart on these far coastlines
that once were close, that once were her.'
She feels a hand
cool on the small of her back. It is Malchus come up from his raft
for human breakfast and the rights of man. He looks at her
with a face like rain letting up. Malchus, desiring no one,

259

can touch anyone. At his birth his mother shrieked
when she saw his damaged ear (torn by the diamond
ring the midwife wore) and her shriek completed the wound
and carried the noise of it inside the new-born beast
and made him man. She shrieked, and named him Malchus.
Now he stands fingering Calsha's vertebrae gently, idly,
a monk who's forgotten the words of his habitual prayer
but remembers only what his fingers do, japa on soft bone rosaries.
Together they watch the sleeping lovers until his simple hunger
asks Calsha for something to eat. She has melons for him
not far away, mint tea with honey in it, kneaded dumplings
with goat cheese. They eat across the lawn, talking subtly
but with her occasional giggles larking in the air
meant to rouse Pothor with their womanly timbres—
she knows the womanly will always rouse him, he will wake
to that absolute before he knows what woman's there—
when he wakes, to catch his absolute appetite before
his wake-will qualifies it with Is it she or Is it she?
Meantime she considers Malchus chewing and quaffing.
The rain has stopped, but even she knows better than
to desire this isolate riverman filled with the hurt of hearing.
Yet since he is there she longs for him, would do
anything he asked because he will not ask her to.

He has a map he's borrowed from his brother. This sheet
he shows Calsha now, a map of Findabhair before the rain,
a place his brother loved many a long year, and inscribed
season after season her fabulous details. Yet for all that
scrutiny it is a simple map, outlines grown clear at last,
the famous isthmus and the Coast of Grief, the lake lost
at the foot of the heart Pothor finally found, then drew it clear
with unfading Nestorian blue, christening it simply:
this lake is Findabhair herself. Calsha and Malchus
trace their fingers over Pothor's route, respecting
the demented ardor of his weird journeys, each puzzling how a man
could be so far from all valuable presence he has to travel
ceaselessly to reach what is for them so close—
for Malchus bears an ever-nourishing wound and need not move
to fulfil its information, and Calsha finds every current
rife with arrivers who will hurt her suitably.
She lays for instance a hand on Malchus's knee—
a touch no different-seeming from his hand on her—

and yet she feels his pothic body inwardly recede
leaving her hand sparse on untenanted flesh and bone.
She squeezes vainly to recall it, then lifts her hand
and fills his cup again with her sweet tea. A crow cries
even though the rain begins again.   "O Calsha," Malchus began,
"I am still a scholar of this mystery. I slept late once
when I had drunk wine, and found my raft had drifted down to Findabhair.
I found it no special country, soft hills and beaches, no sure harbor
but clement-weathered certainly. Is it in his eyes the wonder rests?
Are they *his lies*, the science of this map? It looks like her,
so that is true enough. But the colors, the colors I swear are his."
Grey is the morning and Calsha is oracular: "All colors
are our eyes." Then, thinking more socially: "Does it hurt
you to see him dye the world with his desire?" Yet even
as she spoke she felt a thrill of danger in that word 'hurt'
knowing how much Malchus lived on that original
utterly adequate pain. She did not want to touch it now—
she did—but Malchus was answering simple, as if no word
had any power over him: "He lives off what we lose. Those
are the pigments of his maps. I used to wake and find him watching me
as we watch now. I felt the lust and fear I lost in dream
drain into him, and all day long he tricked it in his charts,
tinting and deepening with borrowed colors. Neither his nor ours,
I think—they are the forgeries of chemistry, and no true land."
"A land," she quietly answered, "is made of I and thou—
all else is vegetable striving and mineral sleep." Malchus
was a smiler (like all lonely selfish men) and smiled at that.

It wasn't the crow or thunder that woke her, it was the rain
comfortably talking. Norsha woke from dreamless and took a while
to sense out where all her body was, how folded under, how
constrained or loosed by Pothor's. She heard the dreamy chit-chat,
she smelled the tea, she knew the two of them down there were spying.
Naked she stretched and naked she rose up, quick releasing from
Pothor's sleeping limbs. Naked she looked the river in the face,
walked down there praying: "Be it done to me according to
your only word." She sauntered loose and let them watch,
knowing she belonged to the world, she was part of all
that happens. Certainly she did not belong to Pothor—
his ardor was the once of only, and though they'd spend
a thousand nights together she knew she'd had the best of him

already and for good. Any sadness that she felt (her ankles
swallowed by the river now) was that she knew
there was a best in her not yet released. 'Best or beast,'
she thought, 'poor Pothor will never get to know or have it,
caught as he is in researching his own first feeling.
His maps are always of that first night, and all the plodding
upland travel towards it. His maps are moments only, his, not mine, not me.'

Pothor was dreaming the Clefts of Vanora, then woke alone.
The hammock dank, the voices tittering beneath the apple,
last contours of Vanora fading—a place he loses over and over.
Oh cruelty of dream that would steal the same joy time after time,
crueler than daytime that slays a joy only once, cruel to renew
the actual loss in a thousand mirrored wakings. He doubted
he would ever walk there again (but whether it was his doubt
or his actual future oracling, he could not say). He lifted himself
like a beloved burden from the net and looked about him. Brother
and Pursuer fell silent. A hawk sprawled in heaven over Norsha.
"I am hungry." Instantly Calsha rose to bring him
what she had held back from Malchus: a mauve fruit with a purple rind
from a solitary tree she tended. This she unbosomed from her robe
and split apart for Pothor. He ate the clamorous pulp and let
Calsha lick the dribble from his chest, her pointy tongue
tickling his soft roots. Now Calsha had a pointy tongue,
head of an adder he thought, not venomed but dangerous
because it was a chief blason of her difference. Calsha
Pointy Tongue, Norsha Long Loose Legs, Vanora Vanished—
a black shield uncharged identified Vanora's chart.
'Those we dream on have a rare power on us,' he thought
and let her lick—this safe, by him unfantasized woman, Calsha.
'Her own fancies are no threat to me, and Norsha, Norsha
is achieved!' He let his mind reflect last night's entablature,
the lacing of their energies, her body comprehensively possessed,
discovered, made conscious and let go. He would be busy
mapping her for days, but her rich island is landed on and claimed.

Around bathing Norsha the sadducean lake
spread seductions to a mood of This is all there is.
Lured by its attentiveness (for water knows everything)
she watched the mists lift off its face and knew Soloron
would come to them today, a kind light that would come calling
over Bullstride, hill of their tourneys and some trysts.

And Norsha knew then that there is always something more—
'for instance there is me, unrealized, full of strange dogmas
no man studies yet. I am not exhausted by my thighs.
There's something to me I can't touch yet, some mystery
I share with everyone but that is only mind. That makes me me.'
So she enjoyed the cynic water and its buoyant sallies
but did not credit its reductive argument. Always more:
the hawk we've heard of shadowed her, and her ruddy skin
danced with its indigo shade—the prance of light! Unseduced,
she let the water nuzzle her. What would it mean to let the sun?
Woman after woman it uneases, its face of a ravisher
banning the innocent umber of her dream.
Quiet Norsha by the sodden grass comes out and stands—
she wants to make love, but not to him. He is too busy loving her,
too active he has turned his glowing passive. He has no patience
to be made love to—and that is what she wants: to coax and rouse
and rove in exploration. She wants to find a spirit in a body
as he finds her. Undesiring Malchus comes to mind—
as two responders they could make a threshing floor
to beat out one another's wheat. She thinks of him unurgently
and he reads her thought from where he stands
envying his brother's passions, his sense of mission, his crazy
style. Men who think out their position have no redemption.
Men who think an object other than thinking have no passion.
Malchus has not even finished the melon but Malchus is good.

After breakfast Pothor said his mass. On a broad stump of ancient elm
memorious from Saturn's influence (and oh the elm blight is the loss
of human memory, referencing to Saturn by book and data bank)
Pothor laid out his elements: souvenirs of all his loves
moved like chessmen on the map of the day's feast
scheduled in the long fasti of his years, chosen one recycled now
by this mute page. And on the land so represented
he spread shells, cups, knives, pens, hair knots and tatters,
shreds of garments, silk things, old letters, pencils she liked
(whoever she was) while writing kiss-offs to old lovers,
scraps of envelopes some woman licked, her thoughtful
tongue ensouling some billets-doux to Pothor. These he wielded
so that all his loves would cast their spell on this one love
whose map called her to mind this only day.
Silent with envious derision Malchus watched, but Calsha
held the train of Pothor's cope as he bowed before the elements.

From the river he'd drawn water, river from which they all had drunk,
and this beverage, kept in a scarlet retort and worked by time and sun,
he poured a few drops of into his central cup. "This fluid
is from you, and from you I became. Now from this becoming that I am,
I pour my water out into the well again from which springs up
all of your meaning. I return, I return, I turn you into me
and give this in return, the pregnant water of my single meaning."
His hands above the cup radiate the pothic influence,
transmuting Reception into anxious Desire. Unknown
to Pothor, the energy becomes ollunic—that desiring
that contaminates its object and then falls sated back.
For Pothor is Apollynon, self-cancelling erastes, lover
of the act of coming on. No wonder he lives for morning
and at night falls back into the undifferencing dark. Today
was the feast of Miriam the Unachieved, whose slender form
came back to haunt him even outside her lawful slot
in Pothor's Calendar. Unpermitted, her astral form beset
his undefended imageworks; just as in waking life
he could never trick her physical body to his bed, so now
the specter she planted in him teased him often daily
with unremitting seductiveness. We plant two beings in our loves:
one of these is our true self seed, and one of them is wraith.
Wraith and seed grow well and share all watering, but the seed
stands in one's mind as counsel and in one's heart as guide, while the wraith
accuses and inveigles, strips bare and summons our desires
to an impossible tryst. This is the mystery of twins, internal Gemini,
and every love leaves after it some wraithful jessica.
Priest Pothor must be careful not to let the wraiths
take over the workings on his altar—though truth to tell
it is the wraith he longs for and in a secret cave unknown to him
his secret will worships the multitude of wraiths
who dance obscenely for it there, in the court of the great It,
Apollynon in Pothor. So now his hands longingly evoke
the wraith of Miriam. Calsha alone sees who it is, and shudders.
Old men think they are wise, young men think they're horny
Calsha sees through these self-deceptions and sees
only that we are various. But she is anger, and Malchus
is the pain of understanding Noticing, a hero of looking around.
Only Norsha is various as life, and who she is. Unlabelled Norsha
moves up towards the rite, which she watches like any
curious thing. She brings a sponge with her and wipes
the sweated brow of Calsha (whose hands are busy acolyting Pothor).
And seeing this unveigling tenderness makes Malchus weep:

"Norsha, untrammelled by my desires, untouched by all my grief!
Norsha of situations and the beautiful moment, empty moment,
empty Norsha, Norsha of street reality, Norsha can do anything,
Norsha does not speak, Norsha is friendly, Sole Divinity of day,
Norsha is Norsha to the bad and good alike, Norsha is sun.
Only in moonlight are you nothing. Then the trifling beams
pass through you—you are invisible in wraith-light
because you are actual, you are muscle, you are Norsha."

So Malchus sang, in a voice thin as a credit card, weeping,
constrained by reverence. Sang in the amber language
so Calsha would not understand the words and writhe with jealousy.
All anger is jealousy, and grieving Malchus meant to spare her grief.

And Norsha heard, and though her speech was pale she understood.
She sprang to the altar and swept off the sacramentals
in a frenzy of healing blasphemy, tore off the wrinkled map
and threw herself down naked on the altar. "Worship me!
I am the Real Presence, I am perpetual morning and easy grain—
come to me now, come simple and abjure your complex flags,
your mindings and remindings. Come be silent inside only me.
Not because I'm holy but because the elm is dead,
the maple's dying and cicadas sing all summer long.
You must make do with this, the feast of love
spread out in minutes and in butterflies.
The psalm that Malchus sang woke this deed in my mind
—come bear your antiphon inside me gladly
because I am the only one who's here."

Pothor had heard such stuff before and spurned redemption.
When the God leaps down upon the altar it leaves no room
for priests and their busy symbolisms. Pothor knew her
as a fact of God, but would not abdicate his liturgy.
"God, you overstep yourself. Your naked belly
is one more empty table that yearns for my signifying craft."
He spoke, and drenched her pubis with the scarlet water.
Norsha shrieked with its generalizing chill, went limp
and fainted there. Neither here nor gone was she,
slack body, fingers trailing among the dewy russulas
grew near the stump. Over her unconscious form
(a perfect map unmade) Pothor prepared to say his prayers
uninterruptably dragging the present into the past.
His deep holy voice began its mumble, his shapely

hands wove above her in their effective mudras
when Malchus hurried close and hurled his arms,
wrapped his lover-like solitary arms round Pothor from behind.
While they struggled, Pothor hissing in his brother's ear, pale
Calsha crept up and stretched out on Norsha's body.
She spread her robe wide so her skin would press Norsha's
and her ample skirts would hide both bodies from the men.
Into Norsha's mouth, the lips half-parted, Calsha spoke,
talking directly into the girl's interior, disdaining the mortal
filters of her ears. And what she spoke Norsha did not hear
but all the wraiths in Norsha heard, and ran to meet
this strange invading sister voice that chanted to them
of planets and vocabularies they knew well.
Calsha's words and Norsha's wraiths were dancing,
and Norsha's self, already half-bewitched by Pothor's mumble,
would wake changed. Lewd Calsha's invitations spread
baffling insinuations through all the halls of Norsha, 'love
Calsha and need Calsha' was the message, and all the wraiths
in sympathy with her wraith-nature worked with Calsha—
till Calsha was the shape of Norsha's rhythm, and when Norsha woke
her blood would chime with Calsha's ardent thinness.
All this while the women lay nipple to nipple,
their breasts transfusing interacts of abstract milk,
the pubic tangle of their bushes meshed together
till Norsha became the bread of sacrifice. And brother
with brother struggled by the river. Pothor won—
Malchus is thrown down, his ear bleeding. He gasps
among the rushes. But Malchus won—because he broke
the current of his brother's sacrificial spell. Their mass is done.
Pothor unchanged and Malchus unchanging breathe
heavy and look wary at each other, each glad
the other cares so much, and sad so ineffectively.

But Calsha's mass goes on, and under the veiling robe
her clenching squeezing thighs induce a sort of orgasm—
and this too she breathes into Norsha's mouth
in long half-shouted sentences in which the names
of Norsha and of Pothor could be recognized. (Just these
could save her. The devil cries his own name when he comes.)
Now she sprawls exhausted, still on Norsha. Who wakes achieved
and for a twinkling of an eye loves no one. She feels the weight
and knows what Calsha's done. The fetch inside her

whispers, 'love Calsha' and she does.
                                        The men
atoned by unfamiliar violence come close. Pothor lifts Calsha's robe,
then yanks it off and studies the two women, Calsha's exhausted body,
Norsha's eyes, unembarrassed, unamused, over Calsha's shoulder.
Pothor knew nothing of those eyes, and nothing in them—and knew
that he didn't know. He sighed, "How little love's intimacy
brings us any other kind. We probe the deepest rhythms in each other
then find at morning that truth's not in the depths.
Truth is how we pass our time, the skin of hours—
no lover can make do with skin alone—he goes too far
and loses the Boundary where the self is most herself.
My hands and tongue and cock know Norsha—I do not."
"I was not made for knowing but for being with," the woman answered.
"I am one who plays among the traffic, keeps score of lilacs,
breaks the peace of oak trees with unanalytic laughter.
I am merriment and mockery—they love me best who are content
to be on life, to share this incarnation with me.
You give me intensity but no time—you suppose yourself
to be an agent of eternity, and women some sort of secret library
you lecherously browse among. But this sun is my posterity,
and to walk the forest with me would do you more good
than all your speculative orgasms clutched inside me."

But Malchus could hear in what Norsha said, beyond
the evident truth of her remarks, a sort of self-regardingness
foreign he thought to her real nature, a packaging of self
and a legend scribbled on the wrapper. True as she spoke,
that kind of truth makes itself a lie by advertisement—
—"Speak in the past tense, my dear," he whispered,
for he knew that Norsha had changed. No one heard him,
and he began to sense he'd been too long from his river and his raft.
Calsha rolled nimbly off and stood erect shamefaced and triumphant.

He waited for the Dream Point where earth is so aligned
that moon diminishes its fierce suck and we are left in sunlight
swayed by the accurate motions of our wills, accurate
as dream. (To this Dream Point civil noon approximates—
to count from noon and midnight is to measure from
zenith and nadir of the Phase of Will, two zones
when if we attend to it we know what we really mean.)
Then Malchus spoke, knower of his time: "I go now, have to leave you

267

to this new Queen"—he pointed at Calsha—"your inadvertence
now makes you subject to. Hers is the triumph of false,
but not feigned, delight. She will lord it over you until
you can know a mental focus of delight in you equivalent to
hers upon Norsha. The selfish silence of her joy untrues it,
but its power is enough to vanquish you. Until you arch
your bodies in mutual immediate delight, she'll rule.
So it will go with you, exchanging empery over one another
until a different kind of lover comes among you; him
I cannot be, but him I'd recognize. Till then I river.
You make me too sad to stay with you."

                                There was a man,
Cobbam the Ship, a sort of servile helpful friend to Malchus.
Him water did not clean. Beneath his nails mute history
lingered despite the hours every day swimming and crabbing.
A gentle sixth-house man who ate no meat of vertebrates
but lived on arthropods and molluscs, and told you why
if you would listen. This kindly reeking man approached them,
called by a mood in Malchus he could read
down there by the raft. His outer ears heard keenly too
(thus served half-deaf Malchus well), and he could grasp
the silvery discourse of salmon, the abstract logic
of the flounders, the sexy wilful chat of eels and elvers—
all the languages of fish, who, grateful that his cunning
and power forbore to trick and kill them, freely told him
what they knew. And they knew much, both of pools
and inland streams, and of great Ocean full of arrivals.
For everything and everyone that will come on earth
is first present in the sea's unending archive,
either in actual presence like the coming race, or else
by accurate symbol represented—such was the lover
Malchus spoke of, learned by him from Cobbam Ship
over the fire. Cobbam now had come to help Malchus break away,
stood silent by his friend outbreathing wild tobacco, hands deft
with a crown of crab claws he was wreathing as a gift to Norsha
because he knew that Malchus fancied her. Knew more
than Malchus did of that. But knew now that it was over,
yet still his fingers clicked the claws in place along the hoop
of leathery kelp. 'And who will wear this coronal?'
Pothor was thinking as his wits returned, 'who will wear
any of the artifacts of love's high intelligence?'
He looked down on his sacramental wares strewn

all over the drying grass. 'We have forfeited *things*, the world
of significant objects recedes from us over a sea of enchanted feelings
and leaves us raftless in the greedy horny panic of our will,
thinglessly vague.' He watched Cobbam wait by Malchus
as if to hear any further guiding word. When none came,
he led Malchus by the shoulder towards the shore, turned right
and travelled seawards out of sight, leaving Pothor alone with women.

A mile away inside the forest there was a clearing. To it now
Calsha led Pothor, while Norsha trailed behind to watch.
In the clearing, Calsha taught Pothor how to dig, measure
socket from socket, drop seed and cover it, plant seedlings
and heap earth round their roots, taught him how to water what he set,
to take the Day's place for the seed with busy interfering agriculture.
All day he labored. At dark he slept in the furrows and Calsha covered him
draining his semen and his dreams at once. He woke with simplicity
and was returned to work, this day hoeing and weeding the rows of green
mysterious shoots and tops Calsha already had planted. She taught him
names to call the young leaves, filled his mind with their potencies,
planets, virtues, nutriments; all without interest he absorbed,
one more part of his labor. Day after day he cultivated,
night after night had lifted from him the imaginal fruitage
of his body's toil. Seedless he would wake and get to work
while Calsha intimately guided. Digging, planting, hoeing, weeding,
pruning, staking, tying, binding, keeping the cunty lettuces from bolting
in the bareback sun of afternoon, stringing mesh to keep the rabbits off,
building trembling mastwork to scare the godly crows. Instead of maps
of lost women and women swallowed down and women too well known,
Pothor counted furrows and planted flowerbeds, always
under Calsha's tutelage. Her gentle voice seldom stopped,
the quiet certainty of rage withheld, the dreamy lilt of power
all day he heard. From time to time he looked up to wipe sweat
and saw among the self-generating trees all round a figure
prancing, gold-limbed gold-tressed Norsha running,
Norsha teasing him from branches, Norsha climbing trees, Norsha
naked darting through the naked sunshine, Norsha dappled,
Norsha never entering the clearing, beckoning to him as if it didn't matter,
easy playful Norsha, Norsha neither going nor coming to him,
Norsha dancing, Norsha pretending to be free.

end of Book One
18-21 August 1980
Chesapeake Isle

Portrait of Catherine Blake by William

Martha King

Kitty Blake

I only know what's not said about you

    had you
    the bluff rapacious hardiness
    of an English milkmaid?
    big face
    with freckles?

for certain I know you talked a lot
it was not sheltered for you
nor did you give false shelter
your nakedness
announced everywhere
in William's specters
                undefended flesh
                      quickly labeled
            "mad thing"
          by your neighbors

    clear the light in the marrow of bones
    though he painted so badly
    soft as the force of a river of light
    impossible to stop
            mending the socks (talking
            stirring the soup (talking
            hearing the rain drip through the copper gutters
                (talking, talking

    a ridged current far below
    the milk-white lake top

    racing for the spillway

Karleen Middleton Murphy

"All the Lovely Sex": Blake and the Woman Question

From the works, we can make a case for Blake being either a feminist or an anti-feminist, since evidence exists for both sides. In reading Blake, I have found that I fluctuate between delight at the empathy apparent in the treatment of Oothoon and dismay at the overt hostility expressed in the diatribe against the Female Will. I suppose I shall continue to fluctuate, for a solid in Blake is difficult to find and, when found, should be viewed with suspicion. Thus, I shall explore this issue by adopting a principle of fluctuation that will leave the question essentially open-ended despite my own conclusions.

Let us briefly amass some of the evidence for Blake's anti-femininism. There are, of course, the usual problems with using a language that has been impregnated for centuries with sexist terms. Blake's universal love is called brotherhood, not sisterhood. The composite of integrated Zoas and reunited Emanations is called Man (though sometimes Human). Both Rahab and Urizen preach sexual abstinence, but Rahab is labeled whore and harlot; Blake creates no equivalent terms for Urizen, although he was certainly capable of doing so. But these are superficial linguistic problems, and Blake confronted deeper, more underlying problems with language that will be examined later in greater detail.

There are also the hostile diatribes against woman and adjectives derived from her gender, as well as negative imagery associated with her, and some of the roles assigned to her as a dramatic character are not likely to please. Moreover, Blake portrays Nature, the Other, as an evanescent, frequently perverse female.

Negative diction abounds in Blake in connection with the female, but I am not sure that counting the instances will lead to a fair conclusion as to the fairness of Blake's treatment of women. To pounce on isolated images and catalogue individual negative descriptions will only lead to a myopic assessment. Here, I shall strive for a distanced overview, and perhaps the best way to start is by balancing his treatment of women against his treatment of men, since equal time or space appears to be a modern method of ensuring equality. Are the female characters as important as the males and is the abuse evenly distributed?

Blake achieves some degree of equality in the three major prophetic books. *Milton* has his name as the title, but there is a balancing of books between Milton and Ololon and their redemptive action is simultaneous: each acts independently to save the other. Ololon is essential; she could not be omitted without losing the point of the poem. Blake entitles *Jerusalem* with her name and she certainly gets better press than Albion does; our sympathy lies with Jerusalem, not the misguided Albion. *The Four Zoas* (four males) was originally *Vala* (one female), and Vala/Rahab probably gets more coverage, though most of it is unfavorable. We cannot accuse Blake of ignoring the female or minimizing her importance.

True, Blake describes the fallen female in uncomplimentary terms and images, but his description of the fallen male is equally unkind. Which is worse, Rahab or Urizen/Nobodaddy? Urizen, Tharmas, Luvah, and Albion without their Emanations behave as intolerably as Ahania, Enion, Vala, and Jerusalem without their Zoas, perhaps more so, since Ahania remains admirable throughout and Jerusalem elicits our sympathy. Nor does Blake, as the Bible does, blame woman exclusively for the Fall; this might have been caused by Vala, or by Urizen and Luvah fighting, or by Albion himself. As for imagery, those who protest the image of the woman scaly need only turn to *The Book of Job* to see an equally scaly male.

Blake also expresses sympathy towards those who seek sexual liberty, in particular Oothoon, a female, and hostility towards prohibitions against sex constructed by priests and urizenic fathers, as well as by Rahab and the young Enitharmon. But, indisputably, Blake fires most of his sharpest barbs at manipulative behavior on the part of those women who use or withhold sex in order to seek dominion. Here the abuse is not equal: Blake hurls more against women in connection with sexuality, but, on the other hand, he directs more against men in connection with the misuse of intellect that often leads to deluded notions about sexuality, as with Urizen and Albion. The greater association of women with sex and man with intellect may be considered insulting to women, but then it is Ahania, a female, who possesses the least fallen intelligence amid the fragmented Zoas and Emanations.

Perhaps we can best explore the issue of equality through Blake's treatment of Los and Enitharmon, since they constitute the prototypes of sexually divided mortals. As children and adolescents, both display despicable patterns of behavior. Los starts his humanitarian labor before Enitharmon, but when she does, there is some equivalency between the function of the loom and the hammer; both are necessary, although the division of labor may be considered sexist: men hammer at the anvil; women weave. The social expectations of Blake's age would not assign women to labor at the anvil. We, however, can recognize this as a social bias since our age has seen the breakdown of many job categories based on sex. But we cannot deny that in

Los Blake embodies the hero, the keeper of the divine vision, and relegates Enitharmon to a less important position as a person, particularly after Night the Seventh. Los and Enitharmon dramatize the battle of the sexes in which she is labeled a Contrary and the protracted conflict eventually progresses to reconciliation of Enitharmon to Los and finally to union.

The nature of this male/female union establishes a concept that is crucial to assessing Blake's attitude towards women: androgyny. Blake formulated this concept to eliminate generative division into two sexes. Albion, the eternal "Man," is androgynous and by positing the androgynous ideal, Blake transcends sexuality with all its inequalities. More than a hundred years later, Virginia Woolf came to the same conclusion in her seminal feminist work *A Room of One's Own*. The edenic eliminates the male/female dichotomy by a fusion of both. But is Blake's androgyny a true fusion of both, or is the female principle merely subsumed into the male? Sometimes, in reading Blake, I have the disconcerting suspicion that the one will, one intellect of Eden realizes a masculine one, not a blending of both. Resurrected Ahania, the paragon of womanly virtues, becomes a model to teach *"obedience"* to "all the lovely Sex" (FZ122, E376. Italics mine). We do not see her engage in intellectual warfare; instead, she dies to renew her Zoa. Similarly, after reconciliation with Los, Enitharmon loses her identity and remains unnamed in the last part of *The Four Zoas*. However, Los (hero or not) also loses *his* identity in the end and is subsumed into the resurrected Urthona.

In addition to androgyny, or perhaps as a corollary thereof, Blake attempts to erase gender distinctions by shifting or negating the meaning of sex-related adjectives. Much that Blake labels feminine does not refer to the biological being with two X chromosomes. The Emanation portrays the feminine—softer, more gentle—part of a person, male or female. That females should be classified as softer, more gentle is perhaps more a cultural expectation than a biological fact. Moreover, since Blake actualizes his attempt to erase gender distinctions through sex-related terms, the reader finds it difficult to pinpoint where the special use ends and the terms pick up their traditional meanings. Is the Female Will female, or can it be possessed by biological males? Is the Contrary merely the opposite in opposition? Is intellectual warfare woman's activity, and does she have a gentle male bosom to rest on when she is wearied? Is Beulah truly "feminine," or does it represent sexual gentleness that may reside in either sex? The gender distinctions blur. Feminine may or may not refer to a woman. But the words remain. Whether they be metaphors for a condition or not, the words Blake uses are "female" and "feminine" and the connection exists between the supposedly asexual characteristic and biological being. Thus we still remain in the language trap. In addition to the superficial linguistic problems with inherited sexist terms of which he may not even have been conscious, Blake faced greater difficulties with the language in attempting to communicate his concepts. He had set himself the difficult task of eliminating sexual distinctions in an age that did not have the benefit of many great minds working on the problem. Perhaps Los's struggle at the anvil with "the stubborn structure of the Language" (J2:36, E181) parallels Blake's attempt to transcend sexual division using a language steeped in differentiating words.

These concepts—androgyny and the blurring of gender distinctions—belong to Eden, but they need to be expressed in manmade language and also put into a narrative form which is conventionally conveyed through characters, male and/or female. Rahab, Tizrah, and the young Enitharmon have unattractive roles to play. But even here the meaning becomes opaque, since the characters in Blake's psychodramas may be men and women or they may represent psychological aspects of one individual, male or female. When viewed as the latter, the male/female dichotomy breaks down even for dramatic characters in a narrative. Unfallen Ahania is not a female, but intellectual pleasure possessed by either sex. Thus, all praise or abuse of characters is not necessarily sex related. In addition, the male/female may also represent the poet/product and, in this case, I am not sure which is more important, since I can think of many anonymous poems I dearly love. However, the vehicle remains, and Blake elected to portray some human characteristics as male figures, some as female. Trapped as we are in Generation, communicating a supra-sexual concept poses difficulties when it needs to be conveyed through sexual figures that we perceive from a sexual point of view.

And thus I continue to fluctuate, for a difference exists between what the concepts imply and what (or how) the language says, and I am not sure that the two can ever be totally reconciled. We can fume at the language and forget the ideas, or focus on the ideas and forget the language, or fluctuate between both stances. However, in those moments when we are capable of shaking loose of the language and concentrating on the concepts, I think we can find much that is modern in Blake with respect to the female. I believe that Blake struggled to achieve equality between men and women, or at any rate an elimination of differences, inasmuch as he removes gender distinctions and creates an androgynous ideal, but he slips into sexist/urizenic vortices which were part of his mascocentric culture, both in social expectations and the form of the communication, particularly the stubborn structure of the language with which he wrestled.

Lawrence Lazzarini

Five Poems

I To Let You Know

William Blake unrolled in starlight;
William Blake in the warm night wind.
I stand at the window, emptied of your book,
The front of my mental gown unpinned.

II

It is not so strange being blind
As having two organs that see, that close,
Snuffing the universe like a lamp.

III

So refuse to husband your dreams,
And they are delivered
To your door in boxes.

IV Anima

I am innocent as the mirror in which I comb my hair.
I walk the streets at night carrying a purse
With smooth brass clamps. My questions are pins.
My questions are flowers opening in the morning.
And my man—
My man is my sister
Whom I throw down and stone with kisses.

V

The mother of many universes
Is the little girl
Playing in puddles.

Kit Wienert

, Whoever She is

I came by way of the third ear
to the nodal vision spinning
out of Blake's granular Eden

(surfeit of desire)
particular to the Realm
of her felt Body.

There is the sound of waves
and the smell of her fleshy portal to Heaven,
(this woman of the nocturnal

dream torque
pulling out of gear for pleasure).

A red moon between her thighs
brings a distant
landscape into view
by her side, where

the elements are a preternatural possibility.

I tasted the light there
in the presence of uncommon senses,
but was refused entrance.

In deference to what I had hoped to find
I let my eyes do all the work,
waiting for the dream's
chance resolution.

They said it would be a World for the taking.
Not so.

The Precepts of Vision I

(for George Quasha)

A red rose
within a blue flame

was that man
in a room of bent light

his flesh
the torsion of meeting,

(a portion of the infinite
upon his right cheek

close to the nose,
red swell

And burning!

All who witnessed this contrary vision
knew

the *meta-metrics* were clear
as time was consecrated

forth into motion.
Leaving

I remembered that moment
.precise.

knowing
the Egg had been rent in twain.

The table shared
so shaped

was a vehicle of love
(seed

planted warm
from the icy blast outside).

Later
Michael and I talked

in front of a frozen tree,
stiffened corpse

assaulted by ice.
Unknowingly

we agreed. His world
and my eyes.

My world
and his eyes.

That night
a vine erupted

to burst its natural roof
(rupture in time

and circumstance)
as laughter faded down the Row.

My body pulsed
and turned, his body

shuddered and turned.
Revolution had begun

saying, "I am the body of the seed.
We are the body of that seed.

And our limbs are the ever-
twining tendrils of that vine."

Paul Piech

The Sick Rose

William Blake

O Rose, thou art sick;
The invisible worm,
That flies in the night,
In the howling storm,
Has found out thy bed
Of crimson joy;
And his dark secret love
Does thy life destroy.

Stephen Addiss

Blake, Taoism and Zen

The first patriarch of Zen, Bodhidharma, is supposed to have said:

> Pointing directly to man's spirit
> See your own true nature and become Buddha

Wouldn't it be a memorable fancy to imagine old Billy Blake, seated with his legs folded in his lap, his balding skull glistening, finding enlightenment in his visions? Despite never having the chance to discover East Asian writings, Blake frequently came to similar understandings to those we find in the records of great masters of Taoism and Zen, and parallel passages can show us how the different minds have had similar visions.

Chuang-tzu, Basic Writings, as translated by Burton Watson, is a third century B.C. text that, in anecdotal form, presents the teachings of Taoism, an exalted mysticism that fuses with nature and cosmic rhythms. Wit blends with fancy, the mundane suggests the sublime. The *Tao Te Ching*, in my own translation, is perhaps as early or even earlier, and sets forth Taoist teachings in a more expository form. This text is like seeds that contain within themselves the fully mature plants, flowers and trees of paradox and otherworldly wisdom. *The Zen Teachings of Huang-po*, translated by John Blofeld, recaptures the sayings of the ninth century Chinese master, known in Japan as Obaku. Here the Taoist tradition is merged with Buddhist philosophy from India, and a deliberate attempt to free the mind from rational and logical thinking is one of the steps toward enlightenment. *The Record of Lin-chi*, as translated by Ruth Fuller Sasaki, contains the enigmatic words of Huang-po's greatest pupil who is known in Japan as Rinzai, the founder of the largest Zen Buddhist sect. Lin-chi's teachings are even more mind-boggling than those of his master, piling conundrum upon enigma until the mind breaks through conceptual thought to an inner truth.

The understanding of the men of ancient times went a long way. How far did it go? To the point where some of them believed that things have never existed—so far, to the end, where nothing can be added. Those at the next stage thought that things exist but recognized no boundaries among them. Those at the next stage thought there were boundaries but recognized no right and wrong. Because right and wrong appeared, the Way was injured. *(Chuang-tzu)*

The Nature of my Work is Visionary or Imaginative: it is an Endeavor to Restore what the Ancients call'd the Golden Age.... The Last Judgement will be when all those are Cast away who troubled Religion with Questions concerning Good & Evil. (A Vision of the Last Judgement)

––––––

Between "good" and "evil" is there any true difference? *(Tao Te Ching)*

––––––

I do not consider either the Just or the Wicked to be in a Supreme State, but to be every one of them States of the Sleep which the Soul may fall into in its deadly dreams of Good and Evil.

(A Vision of the Last Judgement)

––––––

In the bald and barren north, there is a dark sea, the Lake of Heaven. In it there is a fish which is several thousand *li* across, and no one knows how long. His name is K'un. There is also a bird there, named P'eng, with a back like Mount T'ai and wings like clouds filling the sky. He beats the whirlwind, leaps into the air, and rises up ninety thousand *li*, cutting through clouds and mist, shouldering the blue sky, and then he turns his eyes south and prepares to journey to the southern darkness. The little quail laughs at him, saying, "Where does he think *he's* going? I give a great leap and fly up, but I never get more than ten or twelve yards before I come down fluttering anyway! Where does he thing *he's* going?" *(Chuang-tzu)*

How do you know but ev'ry bird that cuts the airy way
Is an immense world of delight, clos'd by your senses five?

(The Marriage of Heaven and Hell)

The sage embraces things. Ordinary men discriminate among them and parade their discrimination before others. So I say, those who discriminate fail to see. *(Chuang-tzu)*

If the doors of perception were cleansed every thing would appear to man as it is, infinite. (The Marriage of Heaven and Hell)

———

The way of the Buddhas flourishes in a mind utterly devoid of conceptual thought processes, while discriminations between this and that gives birth to a legion of demons. *(Huang-po)*

Reasonings like vast Serpents
Infold around my limbs, bruising my minute articulations.
                                                        (The Four Zoas)

———

Avoid pondering things in your mind, thereby purging your bodies of discriminatory cognition. *(Huang-po)*

I will not Reason & Compare: my business is to Create. (Jerusalem)

———

By allowing your gaze to linger on a form, you wrench out the eyes of a sage (yourself). And when you linger upon a sound, you slice off the ears of a sage — thus it is with all your senses and with cognition, for their varied perceptions are called slicers. *(Huang-po)*

No more could they rise at will
In the infinite void, but bound down
To earth by their narrowing perceptions
They lived a period of years. (The First Book of Urizen)

———

283

Life, death, preservation, loss, failure, success, poverty, riches, worthiness, unworthiness, slander, fame, hunger, thirst, cold, heat—these are the alterations of the world, the workings of fate. Day and night they change place before us and wisdom cannot spy out their source. Therefore, they should not be enough to destroy your harmony; they should not be allowed to enter the storehouse of spirit. If you can harmonize and delight in them, master them and never be at a loss for joy, if you can do this day and night without break and make it be spring with everything, mingling with all and creating the moment within your own mind—this is what I call being whole in power.

(Huang-po)

Distinguish therefore States from Individuals in those States.
States Change, but Individual Identities never change nor cease.
You cannot go to Eternal Death in that which can never Die.

(Milton)

———

When your glance falls upon a grain of dust, what you see is identical with all the vast world-systems with their great rivers and mighty hills. To gaze upon a drop of water is to behold the nature of all waters of the universe. *(Huang-po)*

To see a World in a Grain of Sand
And a Heaven in a Wild Flower,
Hold Infinity in the palm of your hand
And Eternity in an hour. (Auguries of Innocence)

———

Once Chuang Chou dreamt he was a butterfly, a butterfly flitting and fluttering around, happy with himself and doing as he pleased. He didn't know he was Chuang Chuo. Suddenly he woke up and there he was, solid and unmistakable Chuang Chou. But he didn't know if he was Chuang Chou who had dreamt he was a butterfly, or a butterfly dreaming he was Chuang Chou. *(Chuang-tzu)*

As when a man dreams, he reflects not that his body sleeps,
Else he would wake, so seem'd he entering his Shadow . . . .

Chuang-tzu's wife died. When Hui-tzu went to convey his condolences, he found Chuang-tzu with his legs sprawled out, pounding on a tub and singing. "You lived with her, she brought up your children and grew old," said Hui-tzu. "It should be enough simply not to weep at her death. But pounding on a tub and singing—this is going too far, isn't it?" Chuang-tzu said, "You're wrong. When first she died, do you think I didn't grieve like anyone else? But I looked back to her beginning and the time before she was born. Not only the time before she was born, but the time before she had a spirit. In the midst of the jumble of wonder and mystery a change took place and she had a spirit. Another change and she had a body. Another change and she was born. Now there's been another change and she's dead. It's just like the progression of the four seasons, spring, summer, fall, winter." *(Chuang-tzu)*

I cannot think of death as more than the going out of one room into another. (Crabb Robinson's Reminiscences)

Chien Wu said..."there is a holy man living on faraway Ku-she Mountain....He doesn't eat the five grains, but sucks the wind, drinks the dew, climbs up on the clouds and mist, rides a flying dragon, and wanders beyond the four seas.....I thought this was all insane and refused to believe it." "You would!" said Lien Shu. "We can't expect a blind man to appreciate beautiful patterns or a deaf man to listen to bells and drums. And blindness is not confined to the body alone—the understanding has them too, as your words have just shown."
(Chuang-tzu)

I come...to cast aside from Poetry all that is not Inspiration,
That it no longer shall dare to mock with the aspersion of Madness
Cast on the Inspired by the tame high finisher of paltry blots
Indefinite, or paltry Rhymes, or paltry Harmonies. (Milton)

Ordinary people look to their surroundings, while followers of the Way look to the Mind, but the true Dharma is to forget them both. The former is easy enough, the latter very difficult. Men are afraid to forget their minds, fearing to fall through the Void with nothing to stay their fall. They do not know that the Void is not really void. *(Huang-po)*

> For every space larger than a red Globule of Man's blood
> Is visionary, and is created by the Hammer of Los.
> And every Space smaller than a Globule of Man's blood opens
> Into Eternity of which this vegetable Earth is but a shadow.

> (Milton)

The sage leans on the sun and moon, tucks the universe under his arm, merges himself with things, leaves the confusion and muddle as it is, and looks on slaves as exalted. *(Chuang-tzu)*

> The nature of infinity is this: That every thing has its
> Own Vortex, and when once the traveller thro' Eternity
> Has pass'd that Vortex, he perceives it roll backward behind
> His path, into a globe itself infolding like a sun,
> Or like a moon, or like a universe of starry majesty,
> While he keeps onwards in his wondrous journey on the earth.

> (Milton)

You have had the audacity to take on human form and you are delighted. But the human form has ten thousand changes that never come to an end. Your joys, then, must be uncountable. *(Chuang-tzu)*

> Arise & drink your bliss!
> For every thing that lives is holy. (The Four Zoas)

All the Buddhas and all sentient beings are nothing but the One Mind, beside which nothing exists. *(Huang-po)*

> One thought fills immensity. (The Marriage of Heaven and Hell)

286

When people of the world hear it said that the Buddhas transmit the Doctrine of Mind, they suppose there is something to be attained or realized apart from Mind. . . . Suppose a warrior, forgetting that he was already wearing his pearl on his forehead, were to seek for it elsewhere, he could travel the whole world without finding it. But if someone who knew what was wrong were to point it out to him, the warrior would immediately realize that the pearl had been there all the time. So, if you students of the Way are mistaken about your own real Mind, not recognizing that it is the Buddha, you will consequently look for him elsewhere. *(Huang-po)*

In your own Bosom you bear your Heaven
And Earth & all you behold; tho' it appears Without, it is Within,
In your Imagination, of which this World of Mortality is but

a Shadow. (Jerusalem)

———

If you wish to differ in no way from the Patriarch-Buddha, just don't seek outside. The pure light in your single thought—that is the Dharmakaya Buddha within your own house. *(Lin-chi)*

There is a Throne in every man, it is the Throne of God. (Jerusalem)

———

Someone asked: "What was the purpose of the Patriarch's coming from the West?" The Master said: "If he had had a purpose he couldn't have saved even himself." Someone asked: "Since he had no purpose, how did the Second Patriarch obtain the Dharma?" The Master said: "To obtain is not to obtain." *(Lin-chi)*

A riddle or the Cricket's Cry
Is to Doubt a fit Reply. (Auguries of Innocence)

Jonathan Greene

William Blake Calling

Blake pictured, his forehead
gnashing thought.

His eyes below, the sight &
blindness of rage.

•

Looked into the Abyss, the Living Dead
arise, beyond Good & Evil, beyond
words.

By fire, by ice,
the body regained its
proper fever

to return
balancing one foot on the ground,
the other in sky or water, both blue.

•

How our minds are enclosed, wrapped
up in the old
lines.
That we still think of Night
of Day, of Hours,
of Sex.
That we are always
somewhat here & cannot escape
our smaller dimensions.

•

Lulled by the Satanic Mills,
sleepers dance as blessed animals
before false Eden's dream.

While poor Tiriel rages
unheard, Tiriel — *a serpent in a paradise*
where no Adam ever was.

●

Or, from the other way round,
we have little Thel
made of meristem

caught in her own torpid purity,
a transient thing wanting
more than her season's share.

●

The Eye sees more than the Heart knows.

Slowly my heart learns, the eyes
have taken their photographs
forever printing changes
in memory's dark room.

But from the images a Truth escapes,
distills & floats into the
bloods flow & that
a Heart knows.

(Across the long rooms filled with bodies of longing
I've walked till now, Need giving way
to Bounty, the shape kept hidden
now given Body.

●

Awake! Awake Jerusalem . . .
Awake . . . and come away

The horizon is set aflame
by the blood's beat

and an image in his eyes,
for it is there

the Heart cries, in
Apocalypse

of the raging mind,
or the quiet

of the 10 of Cups,
that's his card too:

The couple
breathing in the Sun's peace

stirs up the feet of the
two children in front of them.

They go on dancing
forever, the parents watching

as if from a hill (though the
land's flat)

for there is the perspective:

Eternity in their Eyes
they are together as One

both Bride.

From a draft of a letter
from Butts to Blake,
end of September, 1800:

*. . .you have the Plough & the Harrow
in full view & the Gate you have been. . .
told is Open; can you then
hesitate
joyfully to enter into it?*

Joe Napora

Dialogues in Hell

Above the Gates of Hell were inscribed these words:

> The present contains all there is. It is holy ground: for it is the
> past, and it is the future.... The communion of saints is a great
> and inspiring assemblage, but it has only one possible hall or
> meeting, and that is the present: and the lapse of time through
> which any particular group of saints must travel to reach that
> meeting-place makes very little difference.
>
> —Alfred North Whitehead

Encouraged by these words, I passed through determined to attempt a
meeting with my two favorite saints—William Blake and Ezra Pound. Once
inside my enthusiasm waned. Both Blake and Pound had warned me how
difficult it would be to get to them but I hadn't anticipated the view before
me.

The poets' residence was located at the center of the Hall of Literature.
This structure was surrounded by the halls of Science, Logic, Mathematics,
Mythology, and Religion. Some of these various halls stood separate while
others had strange protrusions that connected one with another. The Hall of
Literature was an ungainly building with a number of these connections,
many of which simply projected out into space with no apparent means of
support. Finding my way through this maze was not, however, my chief
concern. The greatest danger was in traversing the courtyard that stood at
the entrance to each hall. These courtyards were the dwelling place of the
critics. And the most menacing court was before the Hall of Literature.

Most of the critics had carefully mapped out territories which they
jealously defended with formidable weapons. Some could be seen weaving
the Nets of Falsehood and Half-Lies. Most had blinding Shields of Ambiguity.
The largest territories were defended with the Club and Sword of Authority
and Tradition. Fortunately most of the critics stayed within their bounds and
I had only a little difficulty making my way toward the Hall of Literature.

As I carefully passed through the Critical Field, I noticed to my left the large expanse of the Field of Romanticism. It was a labyrinth of tangled growth and exotic pampered house plants. Somewhat removed from the other structures were the homes of the Blake critics. There were imposing structures looking like fashionable condominiums each built solidly on top of the other. There were also smaller houses of idiosyncratic construction that appealed to me but I knew I would only get confused going that way. Off to the right, I spied the boundary of the Pound criticism. It, too, seemed to be expanding rapidly, with most of the buildings being of slick modern design and the rest imitation Greek villas made from reinforced concrete. Around this field were few defenses. I discovered that the early defense had been battered down, and that now this area was largely ignored by the other critics. And while at one time it was often visited by poets seeking Inspiration and Vision, now even aspiring poets seldom ventured near Pound's domain. The younger poets instead frequented the Contemporary Critics. And I viewed them there weighted down with Praise and Endowments. I could not gaze long at those struggling back to their hall dragging the critics with them. Many were the poets who fell from too much praise and from none at all.

I was almost at the entrance to the Hall of Literature when I was stopped by the Guardian of the University. I was ready to throw at him a snappy rendition of something by the once popular rock singer Jim Morrison when I noticed some graffiti etched on the walls: "If the doors of perception were cleansed everything would appear to man as it is, infinite." Under this line from Blake's *Marriage of Heaven and Hell* were some words signed by A.H. (Aldous Huxley?) that as far as I could make out in essence said, "Keep on scrubbin." When I realized that others had passed this way and sung tunes from The Doors I decided I'd not risk angering the Guardian and simply ask to be admitted. He demanded to know my business and when I told him that I was a poet he said that I first had to speak to the Critical Faculty. But when I said that I was an unknown poet, he told me they would not be interested and I could enter. Before he opened the doors he gave me this warning:

Behold the infinite expanse of the Fields of Criticism. Stretching on and on in endless repetition are the solid, imposing structures that were built by men who had the good sense to limit their field to one area of inquiry and to erect a solid defense. Look with trepidation at the foolish ones who tried to break down Categories or erect the Walls of Criticism on the grounds of poets who were judged antithetical by the Critical Faculty.

I guess he meant this as kindly paternal advice but he gazed upon me with a piercing Vested Interest. I tried to ignore the Guardian and look at the scene before me.

First I saw the advance guard of the universities hounding out the critics who could not show proper credentials. I saw two critics erecting large towers from the bones of poets, each in a frantic race with each other. But many were the critics who ignored the writers and were only at war with each other, attempting to devour their adversary with Invective. And I thought of Pound describing the hell brought on by the usurious corporations: "a continual bumbelch distributing its production." For here I saw the hardest sight to bear—the row upon row of critics with asses outward dropping their excrement into the mouths of their students. And a circle of wives in jogging suits about them. I could look no more. Worried that I would become what I beheld, I once again demanded admittance. The guardian slowly opened the doors and before they closed behind me I recalled those two famous lines spoken by Los in Blake's *Jerusalem* and shouted as I ran through the doors: "I must Create a System, or be enslav'd by another Mans / I will not Reason & Compare: my business is to Create."

Getting to see Blake was not too difficult. I knew that eventually any of the many corridors in the Hall of Literature would lead me to any poet that I sought. I realized, however, that I did not have all the time in the world to find the answers to my many questions. In Hell I was faced with as many deadlines as I had in that other world. I had to get quickly to Blake and begin our meeting with Pound. I saw one long haired and bearded poet howling out his poetry and I decided he should know just where Blake resided. He pointed out the entrance to his own classroom but knowing that in Hell images were the reverse of what they seem I set off in the opposite direction and soon found Blake at rest in his garden.

I asked Blake to read some of Pound's books that I carried with me. I mentioned that Pound learned his poetry in much the same way that Blake had learned, by imitating his predecessors. Pound, too, had pushed lyrical forms to their limit until he had felt it necessary to use forms that were criticized as being non-poetic. Blake needed no reminder of his own words from the introduction to his poem *Jerusalem* but I mentioned that in Pound's poetry he would also find "a variety in every line, both of cadences & number of syllables. Every word and every letter is studied and put into its fit place." I recalled to Blake what he had said in his annotations to the works of Lavater where Lavater spoke of the hero "who has frequent moments of complete existence." And Blake had added, "that men would seek immortal moments."[1] Pound, I conjectured, had based his whole poetic practice on trying to evoke these moments. When I mentioned that Pound had been imprisoned for 13 years because of his refusal to be quiet about

America's violation of the principles of its founding fathers, Blake took an active interest. But it was my explanation of what Pound meant by "ideas in action" that seemed to convince Blake to study Pound's writings.

Convincing Pound was easier than expected. This surprised me since I was familiar with his disparaging remarks about the romantic poets in general and did not expect kindness from a man who had called Blake "crazy Willyum." Pound admitted, however, that he had not read much of Blake but he would look into his works. It took several days for him to return with Blake's writings and he said very little about them. One excerpt from Blake's *Jerusalem* did appeal to him:

> He who would do good to another, must do it in Minute Particulars:
> General Good is the plea of the scoundrel, hypocrite, & flatterer.

He said that this was in accord with his own insistence that abstraction is the great lie, but refused to say any more about it. Pound agreed to a meeting with Blake, but he insisted that I take part in any discussion. I was flattered.

When I left Pound I reflected on his statement about doing good in "minute Particulars" and why Pound held it in such high esteem. I was familiar with his condemnations of generalization. I also saw his poetry as an example of presenting particulars in their individualized beauty directed to the senses. But I knew he intended more by his silence. He had been vilified by the popular press and the hypocritical "poettasters" and false-friends for his statements about Jews. He had long ago learned the truth of Los' statement in the beginning of *Jerusalem*, "Half Friendship is the bitterest Enmity." Pound had sometimes defended himself against these accusations by showing that he had befriended Louis Zukofsky who was a Jew, as well as numerous other *individuals*. After the Bollingen-prize controversy he had given up protesting and lapsed into a near impenetrable silence. I felt Pound believed that Blake would understand, as he would try to understand Blake. Perhaps Blake would be able to see how Pound's Spectre sometimes misled him. I hoped that this "Angel" would now become a "Devil" and I could see the two of them read the Bible together.[2]

SYMPOSIUM

Both poets agreed to my suggestion that the meeting be a symposium — a three way interchange of ideas about poetry. Since we all abhorred abstractions, we decided to concentrate on one aspect of poetry: the poetic genius and its evolution from formlessness to integration. "Too abstract," said

Pound, "I despise ambiguity." I told him that if we could follow Blake's *Jerusalem* and take our illustrations from this work then we could ground any general ideas in this specific poetry.

Since I had initiated the meeting, they wished me to present the firm outline for the discussion. I stated my role would be an observer, an active observer. I hoped to clarify my own ideas about their poetry and told them frankly I considered them to be the two most important poets of recent times. "Enough preliminaries," said Pound, "and don't get too damm academic."

Napora—Blake's Los as Dante's Beatrice: the Poetic Genius, a guide for living.

Blake—Does Mr. Pound understand what I mean by Poetic Genius?

Pound—Well, I know what I mean by it. I have tried to show in my *Cantos* Nietzsche's definition of it.

N—Do you mean the Dionysius-Christ image?

P—Yes, Christ as Dionysius. All great art participates in the poetic genius and it is this that gives perspective to individual ego. I can quote it well enough I suppose:

> Only in so far as the poetic genius...merges with the original artist of the universe does he acquire any knowledge of the permanent nature of art, for in that state the miraculous is like the uncanny figure in the fairy-tale which turns its eyes inward and looks at itself, he is both subject and object.

Mr. Blake speaks of Beulah. Or is that Eden?

N—Since you mention Beulah, can we not approach the first point of Los' struggle by investigating the idea of this place?

B—Beulah is not a place. Or an idea in time. It is a state of mind that gives us an intuition of how man in his original state must have felt.

P—When men walked with the gods. It was only when men began to mistrust the myths and to tell nasty lies about the Gods for a moral purpose that these matters became hopelessly confused. Then myth was degraded into allegory or fable.[3]

N—Is this not speaking temporally?

B—Yes he is, but *language* is "the stubborn structure" of the temporal.

N—I would like to talk more of this attempt to overcome temporality and the limits of language but am I right in assuming that you are both saying that there is a state-of-being in which harmony exists but that man has fallen from this higher state?

P—I don't like the word "fallen." For an American you are pretty quick to talk about "higher states." Didn't Charles Olson state "there are no heirarchies, only eyes to be looked out of"? He used to visit me, you know, when I was in that damm prison.

N—Yes, I read about that, but I'm not sure how to say it then. But there is a need for a return.

P—Correct.

N—You've used Ulysses as Dante used Beatrice, as a guide for showing the way "to lead back to splendour."[4]

P—Dante at least knew where he was going. Aquinas had given the map to Beatrice. You should change the title of this discussion. I chose an active guide, one that was not so sure of where he was going but had faith that he would get there. Faith that it would all cohere.

N—Blake, I think, dramatizes this by the metaphor of Urthona's fall.

P—Fall? Well, as long as we remember that it is a metaphor.

B—Of course it is. What else can it be? I don't care about historical disputes about Bible tales. Of what consequence is it whether Moses wrote the Pentateuch or no?

N—This intuition of a pre-fallen state gives us the sense of dis-integration and the felt need for a sense of union. But where does this intuition come from?

B—Mr. Pound says that men once talked to the gods. It is strange that God should speak to men formerly & not now.[6]

P—I can only speak for myself. What I actually behold. I've had moments of "illumination" but I have also had the good fortune to recognize such moments in other men. Damn it to hell that's what an alive tradition is all about! It is through their art that we are convinced of the validity of such moments in times of darkness. Men who give us these moments share their *virtu*.

B—Is this plain virtue?

P—The soul of each man is compounded of all the elements of the cosmos of souls, but in each soul there is some one element which is in some peculiar and intense way the quality or *virtu* of the individual. In no two souls is this the same. It is by reason of this *virtu* that a given work of art persists.[7]

N—Isn't this what Blake calls the worship of God?

P—I was pleased, and I admit it, I was surprised, to read in *Jerusalem*: "that the Worship of God is honoring his gifts / In other men: & loving the greatest men best, each according / To his Genius: which is the Holy Ghost in Man: there is no other / God, than the God who is the intellectual fountain of Humanity."[8]

N—We seem to be getting ahead of ourselves again. Can I make this assertion, that *Jerusalem* is, in part, a guide for the poet, or the poetic genius in each person? And that Los, of course, is the embodiment of this genius? And finally, that friendship is the key concept in this poem?

P—This sounds like it could be a description of my Odysseus, or maybe Whitman's persona, but I don't know if it's an accurate description of Mr. Blake's poem.

B—I accept it, but you still tend to speak too abstractly. You have some bad habits I'm afraid.

N—Then let me call Los' first stage toward integration "The young poet." How do you see this label as it describes your youth and your struggle as a poet?

B—To Generalize is to be an Idiot.[9] Mechanical Excellence is the Only Vehicle of Genius.[10] I had, as I advise any young poet, to imitate and master the available poetic forms before I could go beyond them. I think that I proved myself by my work—the only way to prove your theories. *Jerusalem* could not have been written within the confines of Rhyme or in the Monotonous Cadence of Shakespeare or Milton.[11]

N—Yes, I understand, but. . .

P—I agree with Mr. Blake that "Imitation is Criticism."[12] And my *Personae* is the record of my early experiments. Language *is* stubborn. To break the pentameter that was the first heave.[13] But first the poet must know the limits of the form before he sets out to break it.

N—We are getting into the larger area of the poet's responsibility to society. This is a very important topic but first I'd like to stick closer to Los and what he was up to in *Jerusalem*. Los in youthful fury breaks the hard rock of restriction that is in fact Urizen.

B—That is *The Book of Los*, not *Jerusalem*.[14]

N—Oh yes, true, but the danger is that Los will fall and never recover.

B—I wept for poor Kit Smart and for Collins. Loss of innocence is essential, though, if the poetic genius is to attain higher goals.

P—Yes, and we had our Hart Crane. And many others, too many others.

N—After the poet is firmly entrenched in the world of experience, and after he has utilized all the poetic forms at hand and found them inadequate, what is he to do? Can one person alone break the bonds of Urizen?

P—Civilization is individual![15]

N—Everything seems to work against the artist. And we have yet to speak of Ulro and Pound's descent into Hell for instruction. The meaning of why Ulysses sought out Tiresias for instance.

P—We are in hell. Might I suggest that we allow Los to rest his hammer. We can resume the meeting at a later time.

We had agreed to meet again the next day when we would discuss how the creative imagination can attain unity but this meeting was not to be, as Blake had a dinner engagement with Ezekiel and Pound was returning a visit to "Big O." The poets, however, continued to answer individual questions and to read the other's poetry and make comments on it. The note

I received from Blake said, "His *Cantos* and *Jerusalem* have something in common in terms of commitment & technique." From Pound I received the admonition that I look to Blake's *Job*. These responses were to questions I had raised about stylistic similarities I had hoped to find in their work.

I looked at *Jerusalem* and the *Cantos* and wondered what Blake meant by "commitment and technique." Then I saw that continually throughout *Jerusalem* Blake's presence breaks through as poet in the act of imagining the poem. He continually reminds the reader this is art, not artifice. "Trembling I sit day and night, my friends are astonished at me," he wrote. It is one man's struggle with his imaginative energies and it is not an allegory or fable. Not only does he talk in the poem about time being regained, but he shows it through his example of the poet writing the poem in the present time. Time and space are abstractions if not here and now in the creative act of composing the poem. This integration of space and time is the unity of the imagination. I should have known that Blake would war against abstract art as well as against abstract thought. Blake and Pound had both warned against being swayed by conventional logic. Logic is a temporal trap. It acknowledges the reality of a time that is gone. Pound redeemed time by presenting it directly to the senses with his ideogrammatic method.

I was familiar with Pound's *Cantos* and recognized that he had continually used this same technique of Blake's to destroy linear time and Euclidean space and logic. I was surprised that he never recognized Blake's use of it. I looked again at the note from Pound and realized that I could do no more. I could not look at *Job* and the *Cantos* searching for similarities. I could not continue any longer what was becoming simply an academic exercise. I think that Blake and Pound were also tiring of these many questions but more importantly they had begun to feel that their influence was becoming too great—I was relying too much on their authority. I had started this inquiry with one of Blake's aphorisms in mind: "The thankful receiver bears a plentiful harvest." But I had not looked closely enough at my own motives. It was another of his sayings that seemed more accurate: "Humility is only doubt."[16] I was sure now that I had much to learn but I would have to do it on my own. I remembered how it was impossible to drag Albion in through the gates of Los. I remembered Pound saying "not to be dragged into paradise by the hair." I knew I had passed through the gates of hell alone and would have to make my way back alone. And starting back I recalled a line from Pound's first Canto, speaking of Ulysses after his descent into Hell for instruction: "Shalt return through spiteful Neptune, over dark seas, / Lose all companions."

Notes

[1] David Erdman, ed. *The Poetry and Prose of William Blake* (Garden City: Doubleday, 1970), p. 584. All references from Blake will be from this text, cited as: Blake.

[2] Blake, p. 43.

[3] Willam Cookson, ed. *Selected Prose of Ezra Pound, 1909-1965* (New York: 1973), p. 68. All references to Pound's prose works will be from Cookson and cited as: *Prose*.

[4] Ezra Pound, *The Cantos of Ezra Pound* (New York: 1972), p. 797.

[5] Blake, p. 607.

[6] Blake, p. 605.

[7] *Prose*, p. 28.

[8] Blake, p. 248.

[9] Blake, p. 632.

[10] Ibid.

[11] Blake, p. 144.

[12] Blake, p. 632.

[13] *Cantos*, p. 518.

[14] Blake, p. 91.

[15] *Prose*, p. 355.

[16] Blake, p. 512.

Dr. Jo-Mo

Estrild, Daughter of Albion

RADIANT,
BEAMING with bliss,
OUR Bird of Spirit
SENDS GOOD RAYS
as it is drawn
two THEE
REALM OF HALOS
where thee
GODESS of Doughnuts
REPOSES Supreme & Divine

Norman Weinstein

Blake/Nasrudin Times Square Shuffle

Imagine my consternation! Finding Mr. Blake flittering in & out of Times Square peep shows! Granted: all his rhetoric about God revealed in the naked form divine...but, fool that I am, little did I suspect his 200-year-old ungratifying honeymoon with Catherine would end *here*.

Here is where I work: *Nasrudin's Adult Parlor*. There's no shame in linking my fool's name to this fool's place. Quite the contrary. The author who transposed me to this torrid clime knows the libidinous flesh of my secret grin, my quick-reflex-zipper-soul. Pockets bursting with quarters, I duck into the telephoneboothsized cubicles & jam quarter after quarter into coin slots in order to view?

HA! MY OWN HOME MOVIES OF MY WIFE METYA BUMPING & GRINDING LIKE A VEDIC HORSE ON A SACRIFICIAL ALTAR! I PAY! TO SEE MY OWN WIFE STRIP! DO YOU UNDERSTAND???? Years ago, immersed in the innocent heat of our young marriage, she let me make a "home" movie of her undressing (she strips behind curtains now). GOD HER SWAYING IVORY BUTTOCKS HER VORTICAL TITS POINTING TOWARD MECCA!

But I digress. Arousal has its cost. 5, 10 dollars a day. 25 cents for 3 minutes adds up. BUT...THE PLEASURES! I begin rubbing my organ with my free hand as her image flickers on the foot-long screen. At times—do I disgust you?—I bring coconut oil in a tiny tube hidden in my pants pocket. Smear some on my thick organ & exquisitely pull, & God sprays on the screen, runs over her breasts, runs down my pants leg, god.

But let me tell you of my chance meeting with Mr. Blake. Dressed—taking his cues from 200 years ago—in well tailored black coat (wool) with an "Uncle Sam" top hat (popularized by Mr. Ginsberg during the sixties). Not merely his dress distinguished him. I knew it was Blake because of his peculiar emanation. Damned if the fool didn't possess a zebra-striped aura which, like an old fashioned barber pole, seemed to swirl around his body. Dazzling & disconcerting—even on Times Square.

"Mr. Nasrudin?"

"Yes, my dear Blake."

"Show me your MOST rakish film about young angels!"

"Of course. Right this way."

I lead Blake through a bamboo curtain, past peep show booths into the men's room, & lock the door behind him while I merrily escape to the front of the store.

Am I a secret sadist? A psychopathic psychopomp? Let me assure you that Nasrudin is nothing more or less than you know him to be: a fool making a quick profit from those who don't profit from their own foolishness.

So I expect to hear Blake banging on the bathroom door, kicking & screaming, raising hell to marry heaven, but minutes pass. Not a sound. Hours. Finally, fearing for his (my) life, slowly I open the door.

"Absolutely extraordinary luminescent orgy of the cortical gate, Nasrudin. I'll tell all my hungry friends to take an eyeful at your stall. Good day."

After I stop blinking (his striped aura momentarily deranged my senses) I run into the bathroom, certain that Blake's sole entertainment was hallucinatory, but just wanting to check, & damn if the door doesn't slam behind me. But little do I care when I feel a cool arm reach out of the imaginary darkness & by its softness there was no doubt. The arm belongs to my reticent wife, Metya.

"You can share me with your friend Mr. Blake anytime. I'm yours for eternity."

✻✻✻✻✻✻✻✻✻✻

When the ebullitions of a distempered brain are mistaken for the sallies of a genius...it becomes a duty to arrest its progress. Such is the case with the productions and admirers of WILLIAM BLAKE, an unfortunate lunatic, whose personal inoffensiveness secures him from confinement....He has published a catalogue, or rather a farrago of nonsense, unintelligibleness, and egregious vanity, the wild effusions of a distempered brain.

—Robert Hunt in the *Examiner*, 1809

John Curl

Who Are You Anyway?

two deer jump through an emotion
a snapdragon bends beneath a bee's weight
you turn a corner and meet your shadow
mommy I'm afraid of the dark
reading a William Blake poem out loud
you got a bad grade on your report card
sapwood encircles a douglas fir
childhood in the house of trauma
a spiral of mayflies above a stream
you try to conceive of your mind
stop playing with yourself
those electrons spinning in your armpits
sitting around depressed
cops charging picket line
the guard strolls past your cell
the ribs on your back remind me of a young antelope
these lines change with the seasons
they're strapping you down to the table
you watch your lover take a bath
sharing this bread and cheese
    who are you anyway
    what is this place
    what'll we do now
rubbing elbows with the neighbors
look at that pretty girl
this is going down on your permanent record
no boss I don't do it
your lover isn't your truelove
you deserve better than this
hurling back teargas cannister
workers militia stopping scabs
you take the club away from a cop

national strike committee shuts down the highway
emeralds bounce against buttocks
neighborhood committee tearing down fences
ex-banker shuffles on the employment line
watering the garden
you swim through your lover's chest
kissing your beautiful stretch marks
your lover really is your truelove
you gaze into a weathered face and see a child
      who are you anyway
      what is this place
      what'll we do now
a peach drops from a tree
the circle of our lives
tiny kisses on your breasts
fire blows through your navel
seed looks for a spot to put down roots
you make love to a wind
earthshadow moves slowly across moonvalley
an old man plays with a puppy
we owe each other a living
the reconciliation of the packs
snake sheds its skin
stepping through a stone into the wind
moon energy birth shine
the tribe climbs through a cloud into a new world

William Hunter

Lambeth in a Bad Year

"The sanitary work of the local authorities did not bring an immediate
end to epidemics, and machinery had to be provided to deal with
them. As there was no local sanitary authority in Lambeth in 1854,
the epidemic of that year was allowed to rage virtually unchecked . . ."
Janet Roebuck, *Urban Development in 19th Century London*

During Blake's time
There were no lousy health
Machines in Lambeth, some bellows
Or something
Trying to pump a cure in,
Inhaling instead and dumping
Spores into workers and boys
Their grandmothers looked after.

In 1800 epidemics must
Have passed quietly through.
Gypsies carried the sweats around,
Red clouds of fog grew
The abounding germs, and
No sanitary authority
Isolated cholera from the dream wards.

Blake in New Guinea

A nice retirement trip, and
France was so disappointing.
Digging out of the launch for
The next map, surprised by
Narrow faces telling him
How scary he is, so quickly
At home where no one can sleep,
And how hungry they are.

Blake's been seated by
The fire, what's he say?
Los and Luvah can't bring
Enitharmon's loom here yet.
"Let your stomach amaze you," he thinks,
"Find food when it rains."
As he paints the dance
Yeats deboats and bows, begs pardon,
Asks permission, says "Conflict
Is great hunger, and conflict is great,
So starve!"

Finally Blake says "go hunt"—
And begs Tharmas in the shade
To teach him to touch these
Waifs who cut the airy way,
Wishing some gal would haul
Yeats away and feed him.

Listening to Blake

I

"How is one to live these things?"
Asks Alice of the double Janus
With two hearts, here and in air.
"Is this your magic in my eye,
Cutting a Dead-Sea path,
Standing me, you, Christ and
The Devil on signs that point
To a spot across the sand?"

Exhortations to distance come
Sometimes from lucky places,
From poets smart on the past;
Poetry breaks others like dams
Upon deserts brown with seed
To grow the fruit
The muses need, and feed them
Before they turn pure, and fog up.

Ezekiel's angels told Blake
Along with where he was to avoid pity.
"Pity divides the soul," he said,
"We're no better or worse than ourselves."
Then he left his self behind.

II

I and my friends once became
Places faster than being them,
So we went about travelling for awhile.

Senses loosened and we tagged them,
We crossed neighborhoods as
Souls settled down upstairs.

Our prodigal robes grew softer
In houses where we could lie
As ourselves, leaving shadows.

We've turned into rivers inside,
Source-blind and spilling when
Someone's crying touch is dry.

III

If the Zoas descend
To render me back upon
Days I needed them,
I'll dig up more roots
And give my lambs dead leaves again.

Blake would not have his muse
Smooth like most, sisters of mercy.
He worked Hell into plans for
An exhibition of Jerusalem,
And she woke him once more
To show him a heart
Made beyond life,
Livelier, of booming stroke
And sounder heating.

Richard Grossinger

These Stones Called Eyes

And now his eternal life
Like a dream was obliterated.
Book of Urizen

I awake from a nap brought on by a headache. I awake suddenly on the edge of my being, the abruptness so much more certain than the headache. The headache is gone. But as if its throb had broken, in unconsciousness, through the dreaming mind, to the forgotten beginning. And two rocks now stand, the agency having passed, stand separated. Their gap is the abyss.

If light moves through eternity undriven, what impels it, particle by particle, what gets it there?

Life makes itself familiar; it insists on me. I am the child watching the street from a city window. I stand in the long hallway as my stepfather opens the back door. There is a blue flower imposed on a thousand such blues, going back forever, and the blueness of the sky; there are golden daisies, in a space so immense, so young and splendid, its sheer fabric wrapped in my fabric overwhelms language and philosophy.

I awake from my nap with the connection broken. Eating an orange now will not restore it. I have been here, as long as I can remember. When I can no longer remember, I am as one splash in a frogpond, which ends. And the entirety of summer twilight hangs over it, the mosquitoes before me as after me. You say the only trouble with dying is you do it for such a long time. But it also takes an awful long time to get born. Rocks on either side. And the headache, having dissolved, sucks an orange. The giant crumbles into words and events.

You say death stalks me. Yes. By now there is no other explanation possible. But I do not know it as death. It is all the things I do which stalk me: my breakfast, my friendship—the persistent light of the sun I see through these stones called eyes.

The thing I call death does not stalk me. And this leaves the illusion I do not fear death. So that when I awake from the nap, something else is there, bigger than I and like a wind that could lift me away. Even that is not quite death. The word death is a fraud, a hedge. My experience of eternity is my

311

body itself, because every thought returns to complete the circle. There is nothing bigger than me, but my congruence, reimposed, is as big and as devastating as any annihilation. I am suspended, like Robert Fludd's angel, between amber and midnight stars.

Death comes as a strange notion only. All this, will not be forever. Forever. And the smell hangs there, the smell of anything, of meat cooking behind another house. It alone marks the spot. You could dismantle reality image by image, and it would not break the connection. We live all our lives knowing the connection will be broken.

The astral body is terrifying and the soul is terrifying. And they solve nothing, either for the occultist who believes in them or the scientist who takes for granted that they do not exist. Belief is not the body. The body knows, and the mind's wish to join the body and belief in a pure monogamy is one way not to live at all. Nothing is true: the ocean takes care of that in its bed of sand.

If the soul does not exist, it is terrifying.

If it does exist, it is terrifying.

The full meaning is detoured. That I go on as something else, adds nothing to that. The spiritual does not interfere with the world it has created. And that alone makes it the spiritual.

Wanting to live too much is the joke we play on ourselves. Pennywise, poundfoolish, we stand determinedly on the side of life. A city in sunlight stands for us, there, in our place. And we inhabit it. Sparsely and intimately. Its stones too are under erosion by light and wind.

Certain acts seem to us savage. Even to the most sympathetic anthropologist the North American Indian vision-quest is brutal. He records its having happened, but he is grateful that he does not have to undergo it. He records it for study, and we enter on his side of the skene, with the illusion this is what they do, not what we do.

A young boy, with only the minimum tools of survival, goes into the forest alone. We accept that animal death and death by starvation are real possibilities; he knows that spirit death also pursues him. He must seek not only food and drink, but, even as he flees the animals for whom he is food, he must find supernatural beings who may or may not exist.

Our savage mind is caught in a dilemma, which is also its living bondage to our animal heart. Do I want to live?, it asks. No, is the answer. The animals guard meaning in a kingdom all to itself, they alone. And the rest has that funny shadowy sense that blows away, and us in the center, us, not the mind.

The first answer must be no. This is neither sentimental nor existential; it is the priority. The Indian boy faces this on his quest. The wish not to live is greater than the wish to live. The choice to live must be made then and there, consciously, as an animal choice, as the choice to survive. The bear comes out of the wilderness and out of the mist, fleshy and bloody and fibrous, yes, even congruent, and not as a symbol for something and something else. It connects the mind to the heart. No more false success to buy off life. No more trinkets and record albums and dope. No more filling the void with desire for the maidens. All these things are dropped. Later, all these things come back.

We are not savages and we are not civilized. We fill the city with time that buys off our precious time, while sun fills the city too. We collectivize our suicide, placing first our birth in the false security of blankness, as if in the brazen secularity of the hospital we came into this world fully-formed, why then crying of a darker and bloodier place? We nurse out chemical deaths, be they head or body, body nonetheless. My brother did it in a mental hospital, drugged and mindfucked. Add it up, one way or another, it comes out to about ten or eleven years of his life. If we had been a civilized family, like those who lived here before our ancestors brought their broken rosicrucian dreams, he could have taken it into the star-clear night. He could have stalked, in the vastness of this nebula formation, the traces of his own formation. It could have been a song.

We have reduced our effectuality. We make the decision to live again and again and again and again, and still have it to make. The angst of the West arises solely in this condition. We have access to no more profound tragedy or deity. The best of our modern novels take their beauty and longing from beneath this arch. Glorious it is. Vaster and more devious than any Indian life. But it stands on a pebble. It is as though, being unable to complete the first step, we are now up somewhere in the hundred thousands plus. And have forgotten. Because only one is missing. That it is the first one. And awake at moments startled and clinging to a raft while winds of unusual velocity threaten to separate meaning from its coil.

We are on a petroleum high, taken long and slow, and hard and deep, and not in the blood. Our paranoia is a petroleum downer. Nothing but these various vehicles and chariots could take us through the unexperienced landscape at a more proper speed. By now, this late in the game, everything got here, even the seeds of the plants, on the funeral pyre of those creatures who must be ancestors of us. Because the fluid of life is unbroken. And it is not our life.

We admire the vision-quest, but it has no romanticism for them who preserve it. Even as we destroy, when we find, the thousands of possible worlds around them, they will never now inhabit, they contemplate the eternal beginning.

Mitch Flynn

In Praise of Wisdom

The road of excess leads to the palace of wisdom.
                    Wm. Blake

We must praise the minds which think and think
For their thoughts tattoo them hectic to the grave;
And the hearts which feel, too deeply feel, and link
All pain and suffering inside the furnace of their rage;
And those eyes which see too well, too well, what eyes
Were never made to see: the bones beneath the daily face.
These are the wise whom we must praise.

To heat the brain with drink, to pack the heart
With ice, to blind the eyes with tar;
With lead to plug the nose and ears,
To stuff the mouth with earth;
To end the headache, heartache, bloodshot sight
With sleep inside a fitted sheet:
These are the temptations the wise endure.

We must praise, must praise, their beds of glass,
The red excess of their sense
In all pain and joy: We must place our hands
In theirs and watch as they raise innocent
Eyes, hearts, and minds towards the palace of the wise.
We must bow with them in the presence
Of the buddhas of burst hearts, burnt minds, and blind eyes,
Who smile and rave inside the palace of the wise.

Paul Piech

Jeffery Beam

He Sees Old Age in a Time of Youth

Your graying temples — fires you
wear on your sleeves, slowburning, that
time puts there. So angry and endless,
the body falling from its caverns, the temple
arches sagging and whales washing up on
shore with no breath. Yet the face of
the aged is gentle and pure — a stream
rolling over mossy rocks on a mountain
and a blind salamander warming in
the sun.

The whole universe a womb! I can see
the old hatching from eggs into a world of
feathers unknown before where a green
woman wears a necklace of your name.
You fall away from the earth as
she gives it to you, you fall away, and
quietly the soul sheds all this skin.
A brightening child nursing at a breast.

Toil, A Divine Commandment

after Paracelsus

Sending my body out into the dirt looking
for wheat straw tied to a gospel singer's arm
I met an old woman whose
hair was glowworms and tobacco
She smelled so good I saw figs

316

ripening early on the bush
I laid my hoe down
singing songs like a bullet
sings to a target
I bet my teeth against each turn in the road
An omen took to the wind
I became a scholar of sails
My hoe a wrist in the soil
finding the housekeeper of roots
humming speak to me
Speak to me

Things Coming

If he but moves his dwelling place,
his heavens also move wherever he goes.
                                    Wm. Blake

Pity the poor one who knows no life of rest
Who lays down the shovel only
to pick up the spade
Who feels winter's darned cloak as a slow
ember in a tarnished fire
Who seeks the flower yet only grieves the root

The oak scatters its starry water
A crackling as of grouse thicket hidden
And hands held in kitchens over collected berries
    covet the warmth
Where there is no vision the people perish
No roots can feed them
Yet leaves fall and all our needs gather in the mulch

Listen you can taste the secret
The things that are coming
Will come

Clayton Eshleman

Niemonjima

for Diane Wakoski

My stomach was the sign to me that I was not damned, and that I was damned as well. I ached in my stomach when I would try to write when I lived in Kyoto, Japan, from 1962 to 1964. In the afternoon I would often ride my motorcycle downtown and work on my translations of César Vallejo's Poemas Humanos *in the* Yorunomado *("Night Window") coffee-shop. There I discovered the following words of Vallejo:* "Then where is the other flank of this cry of pain if, to estimate it as a whole, it breaks now from the bed of man?" *I saw Vallejo in a birth bed in that line, not knowing how to give birth, which indicated to me a totally other realization, that artistic bearing and fruition were physical as well as mental, a matter of one's total energy. I knew I had to learn how to become a physical traveler as well as a mental one. For most of 1963 and 1964 everything I saw and felt clustered about this feeling; it seemed to be in a phrase from the* I Ching, "the darkening of the light," *as well as in the Kyoto sky, which was grey and overcast yet mysteriously luminous. As I struggled to get Vallejo's involuted Spanish into English, I increasingly had the feeling that I was struggling with a man more than with a text, and that this struggle was a matter of my becoming or failing to become a poet. The man I was struggling with not only did not want his words changed from one language to another, but it seemed as if he did not want to be changed himself. I began to realize that in working on Vallejo I had ceased merely to be what I was before coming to Japan, that I had a glimpse now of another life, a life that I was to create rather than be given, and that this other man I was struggling with was the old Clayton who was resisting change. The old Clayton wanted to continue living in his white Indiana Protestant world of "light"—not really light, but the "light" of man associated with day/clarity/good and woman associated with night/ opaqueness/bad. The darkness that was beginning to make itself felt in my sensibility could be viewed as the breaking up of that "light." In giving birth to myself, or more accurately, my Self, Blake's poetry became very important. I wanted to converse with Blake and knew I could not do this in the sense of Clayton talking with William, but that I might be able to do it if I created a figure of my imagination. It was really not Blake himself I wanted to converse with, but Blake's imagination which he created and named Los.*

The Japanese also see the stomach as the center of a person (in contrast to Western brain and heart). For this reason they have seen disembowelment ("seppuku") as the most noble way to die. I saw my initial work on my Self as disembowelment, a cutting into myself, leading to the birth of Yorunomado whom I envisioned chained to an altar in my solar plexus until the moment of his birth.

The spring of 1962 my first wife Barbara and I made a trip to Futomi, a fishing village several hours south of Tokyo. Late the first night there I left our inn and walked down to the beach and stood there in intense meditation. About a quarter mile off shore was an island named Niemonjima (I have never found how the word translates into English: Basho visited the island and wrote a poem there which is now cut into a slab at the island crest: "Umi kurete kamo no koe honokani shiroshi—sea darkening wild duck cry pale white)—from where I stood in the wind and roaring surf the island appeared a black hump against the sky. I saw the hump as a woman bent weeping, and felt a powerful longing to go there, feeling it represented an aspect of humanity I could then only dimly make out—yet my longing frightened me. I began to dream that head-hunters were closer to this aspect of humanity than I was, and that they would get there before I could, and when they got ahold of it they would crucify it. As I continued to think about this, from 1962 to 1965, I became aware that my pain had something to do with my sexual energy, and that I was committed to someone I was not sexually turned-on to, and since I was unfaithful only when we were physically separated, most of the time I was living in a suppressive relation to my energy. It took a long time for me to do anything about this because I was brought up to believe that one simply did the best one could with one's marriage. The idea of divorce actually first occured to me on my wedding-night, the summer of 1961. By the end of 1964 I was living a dangerous state of internal divorce; it was as if I was an egg and my desire for whatever Niemonjima was was the yolk. Around this yolk was the shell of my daily life. The head-hunters were beginning to look like my old fraternity "brothers" and what they were after seemed more and more to be my own soul. I took the name of my fraternity, Phi Delta Theta, and an area of New Guinea called the Sepik Delta, and created The Sons of the Sepic Delta.

*   *   *   *   *

I

Yorunomado knew too well this corrosion—night after night
the fires of Niemonjima had gone untended
& now broke out in savage blaze across the island crest—
the altars smoked forth into the night. Who lay
in the secret darkness turned & twisted with hopelessness
    for marriage,
for the fire had been baited—twigs & strands of hugs tossed
to the hungry little flames—a log here a stone there—
forever! forever! & a moan went forth from the firewall:
A throw of the dice will never abolish chance!
To be redeemed you must go to Eternal Death!

    Whoever stood on the banks of the Pacific felt the moan—
Niemonjima appeared a half-mile out black
against the midnight starless—flames
choked in mind—the altar unknown—no longer to
convert into the fraternity changes,
no longer is there a fake brotherhood of young men,
the savagery in the Plymouth, the so-called picnic, the raped pine—
& whoever stood on the murmuring shore stood
likewise along the entangled darkness of the Sepik River—
shields bobbed through the trees—the masks are prepared
that lead to Niemonjima's altars. For I am in the State
of New Ireland—as slabs of wood are bent blue white & red birds & snakes
across the inner shell so does my imagination
shake & tear against the roots & vines of Coatlicue's web of
desire & longing—the beloved unknown,
desired, but desired as a shadow dancing on Niemonjima's altar walls.

    I stand rooted to these shores & watch the Men of the Sepik
(were they as mild as New Ireland!) move along the high
dorsal ridge, a half mile off shore, Niemonjima, her hair
crawled through by men with spears & bullroarers—her trees silent
to the vast Pacific; Niemonjima, beloved of Yorunomado,
why do I desire you & not her to whom I am wed?

    And this is the problem of the naming (all things relate)—
whoever stands on the shore is without name (this is the madness that is
    eating at me)—
Yorunomado is the imagination through whose acts I make the images of

320

Niemonjima my soul, outwardly an emanation, but
these things do not exist unless eternal
& this is the problem of the naming, for within me
there is no name nor mobility. I was on that shore—
I saw Niemonjima & felt the consolations of Barbara
but who says this is now? Through whom does this hand write?
Yorunomado felt his brain move off as if divided
by waters, as a sand-castle crumbles in surf,
O beloved Yorunomado, whom I must express, whose adventures
with Niemonjima are the life wherein I live,
O beloved Yorunomado who may not exist! This is the problem
of the naming, this is my love poem in these dreadful nights!

    And I bowed to the waters miles below my hands:
O that the poem fulfilled my obligations!
O that Barbara were not my wife!

    A dark wind moved in across the roar
begging understanding: the ways of women are most
treacherous to men only if man commit that
treachery first—for man thinks he creates woman,
because he thinks this he then casts her away,
& the wind wept in her pale tulle before him,
"So I am doomed to wander for the emanations of men
all waters in search of their lost children, I am that
confusion between child & emanation, I must wander
until men & women understand sexual energy must not
be fettered by creation. Terrible the drain on friendship
when blood does not division, when the parent-
power is not overthrown & Niemonjima sleeps in
darkness an altar at an island crest. Between you
& your belovéd has come a wife—before you were not
one, but now you are three! There is a Sepik River
in every man, of blood & shit, runs along his back
like a shrimp's." And I saw her webby skin, she howled
& was gone. O praise the Poetic Genius made manifest
in the 7th Book of Zoas: *Thou art but a form & organ of life,
& of thyself art nothing, being Created Continually by
Mercy & Love divine.*

    I have opened a center, & it is this center that moves
confidence in these words, that they are of others'

experience as well as mine, for as the flames toss
against the midnight starless from Niemonjima's crest,
so does she lie awake a tongue of longing become less than a woman
until at last she is my mother, not Coatlicue,
but Gladys, umbilical, claiming to be wife &
    belovéd, terrifically close to the true
marriage, but now a mother grown young
& married at a masked ball—the hour tolls!
But the covering has grown so thin, are we not
known all along? The hour tolls! The Men of the Sepik
hurry along Niemonjima's outer lines—

And the spirit of Barbara followed me down to the shore
in the form of Jerusalem along the Arlington, she stood
behind my kneeling in worry & care, whom I could not
embrace for if I allowed myself to feel something I knew
I would want more, would riot in the fear & madness of
my own powers—I feared a wife turned
viperous with desire, the maw of Tokyo
a million red lights to swallow the wanderer
& on his return present him as a baby to the ladies.
She stood behind my kneeling, pointing with one hand back
to the inn & with the other out to Niemonjima,
& the waterwheel turned inside me a rack
toward Niemonjima, I would not settle for what I had
been given, but I could not escape, all my images fled before
the constant recreation of Origin! So slowly the error
consolidated & I prayed with my hands horizontal to the surf
Yorunomado, help me understand my sex,
Yorunomado, let my wife be the one I love.
    For the Men of the Sepik broke into loud chants
moving now swiftly through her upper grasses, around the concentric
dirt paths toward where the altar buffeted & smoked
a terrible pink steam of desire. Praying against
the water Yorunomado let me be satisfied with generation,
let me accept her without a robe, the poem is *a persimmon*
falls, my ears are locked to my bowels—

And it was only the robe that drove him on,
a vision of the inland sea, which is called the Gull-robe,
gorgeous, of white feathers emblazoned with stars & moons,
the lovely garment every loved woman wears, of midnight-

blue & silks, in which a light streams for all who ride
away into the darkness carrying the torches of imaginative
love, the softness & precision of loved desire. But now
the Klan wears the Gull-robe! The sons of Phi Delta Theta
commingle with the ordered rhythms of the Sepik,
& who is to say she wears a gown? The Eighty-fold Boar
strives in darkness with the Daughters of Jerusalem along the Hudson,
he is far from Yorunomado now arguing by the Pacific
with the hopeless wanderer who would sleep
contracted in foetal anguish rather than go
to Eternal Death of wife & generation
through whom only will Niemonjima ever flow
a river in the arms of any man. Give me

strength for my labor—for even now I doubt
what I write in the very act of creation—
I see the sperm spurt, the Sons of the Sepik Delta
dance around her tortured altars, the blood
gushes, the poor wife tilts back that her ovaries
may drink, the trailer lurches, pets flee bumping
into cupboards & chairs, the smell of garbage commingles with desire—
she is absolutely naked, in her own Xipe-Soutine-red flowing on the bed,
     the husband
flees in terror to the bars, but ah! the spirit of Barbara cannot hold him!
Like rising backdrops he runs open-armed through her arms—
the altar smokes, gems congeal, a Fat Carnival Face grins
between her pillars where the red spider guardians have fled in terror—all is

shifting levels of literality & darkness as memory
crowds in—Origin is singing "Your only sureness is to say
     the persimmon falls"
She Is Absolutely Naked. Without imagination.
And lo! She comes down to me, she stands weeping behind me on the shore,
& I will not turn to embrace him or her for fear I am stone,
Yorunomado saw his brain hermaphrodize, sand in
love with sand as she swept back wailing, all wanted in,
the stopsign, the mole, prestige, he shut his mouth
& threw himself in ice before her blazing pyres—
the blood turns to money, the mind to brain,
A Victorian Christmas Art Book Jungian Bride.
Under the weight of this shale Niemonjima could

hardly move, & the Sons of the Sepik Delta mocked
her tiger-striped bangs Crying Behold! If you know so
fucking much fulfill our desires, we'll turn you on with
dirty jokes! And laughing slung a bloody bulldick around her
neck crying Behold! & clothed her in burlap sackcloth & ashes,
taped raw liver in her armpits, tied a string with "pull" sign
to her dick & shaving her head Crying Behold the Golden
Princess of our Homecoming! Behold our Snow White!

Yorunomado's only sureness forced to watch was that the work
of the imagination is in the service of a true brotherhood,
my desire to possess Niemonjima darkened by the canal
bereft of nightwatch in deepest fidelity to Barbara.

      II

   And Yorunomado stood in the howling bay, waves
lash & wail into the booming caverns; he looked
to where the ovens were lit walls & the Sons of
the Sepik Delta worked in flaming reds & blacks;
O Gladys Enter! he cried to the shadow at his side,
Enter the ovens & be transmuted to my wife. Or forever
die, no longer plague me with what I can't see, for I cannot
worship the root, I cannot carry the taro through the lines
of relation. No longer is Coatlicue visible,
but there is a woman enfibered in my veins, a hot
wet in my hand I have been told, I recall is you
And here you stand a writhing molten red, a
beckoning mush to maintain me always to the fork
& spear, in housemother agedness, while the victims
trembling holding hands are made to bend over as before
the mask was built, naked young men holding hands bent
over encircling the blazing center, a double fireplace;
"Slaughter on Tenth Avenue" is picked up from the shelf;
where a frat pin was fixed through a sweatered breast
into a padded bra, the furniture has been moved aside,
the revelation of her armor & chastity is at hand, the victims
chatter & sob, the semen begs release—snuck out
in the crematorial lavatories it sobs to witness the flames;
the rites of passage deep-freezed her armor keeps them im-

potent, they stand being victims to be masters later! The hi-fi
needle is lifted, the lights turned down, the corral-gate bursts,
the Sons of the Sepik Delta shoot out bouncing & roaring from
their brides; only a few are not broken; I am shouting faint
with disbelief from the negation of life that is Indiana "O
generation, image of regeneration!" The virgin-wife discovers
on her wedding-night the spur-marks in the sides of her
little husband! She turns on in secret fury! Enter O
Enter the ovens that I may love you! Be transmuted to
my kind, invisible, for I am in great error, a part of a great
& terrible error, I must go to Eternal Death. Even as I speak the Sons
dress up in swastika red & gather grinning to my left,
the ideals of art wait patiently to my right,

Whenever any Individual   [Blake]
Rejects Error & Embraces Truth, a Last Judgement
passes upon that individual.

Yorunomado knew
he had found his wall, for looking down
he saw his thighs emblazoned moons,
his ankles suns, a starry midnight-
blue painted as if on clay across
his gut. He felt his universe flex
as he moved more open across the beach;
he had taken upon himself self-enclosing
divine attributes; on North Jordan
he had passed judgement on a girl from Anderson,
in Chapala he had mocked a woman hungry for marriage—
but how not mock? The natural sexual
activity has become anathema to man;
whom he faced across the sand was none
other than himself in any other woman
or man, & to act upon them was to act
upon himself, a vicious self-perpetuating
doubt, & in the arms of the Sons of Sepik
Delta he felt the vein of Gandhi, a pure
stream in India, but he could not mock
the presence with whom he lived,
and he remembered Jung's words:
The source of life is a good companion.

325

He looked hard around him on the beach
at the sky & at the sea. Were not all these grains
placed by abstinence? Was not *everything* sand,
the tree, the house, a friend's lip, a bird, a
sunbeam, when truth is overruled by creation.
There is in the life of every man & woman a moment
Origin's watchfiend cannot find, that moment
settles on various pins, it may be at any
place & must be taken there, & he knew he
was really dealing with desire, that that "moment" was
the moment of desire, & if that moment is
denied, the rest of the day is dead.

So did he attempt to understand the Last
Judgement he was in the process of,
now he knew the intorsions of seppuku,
that who he fought to emerge was not
just a spectre, Gladys wailed in the cry
of every passing gull but she was not
his enemy, only he could be transformed
in the coastal ovens, signs were everywhere
but there was something he was missing
to make these signs cohere . . .

Forgiveness & self-annihilation were
surely signs, but in what act? He continued
walking. Sea. Sand. Sky. No
thing lived or moved . . .

Distant down the beach he saw a bench,
or a raised structure behind which
something moved; on 2 x 4s a box, a
casket from which a tattered
windingcloth fluttered. He approached
fearfully for he knew who was in the box
but not who moved behind it; he approached
the casket of Vallejo as a book is closed,
toward the heavy box of flesh blowing
by the sea, seeing a man crouched
moving behind, who he feared was himself.
Los stood naked with his hammer behind

the casket of Vallejo smiling at Yorunomado; he put his hand upon the beaten
lid as the wanderer approached, smiling,
for he alone knew what I must do, & he stepped
back as I knelt by the box in dignity. in prayer
to Vallejo. Los stood & watched,
& Yorunomado saw how those who weep in
their work cannot weep, how those who
never weep are the weak, the fake
sufferers. To be a man. That suffering
is truer to man than joy. These were
the lines in the heavy pocked face of
Vallejo, trinities of intersections &
heavy lines, a village of nose & eyes,
Vallejo never left home, it was home
he always begged for even in the taking on
of the suffering body of man, I stood for
seven years & looked at him there, observing the Quechuan rags & shreds of
priestcloak, the immense weight in his mind,
& lifting his rags I saw his female gate,
bloodied & rotten, hopelessly stitched
with crowfeathers, azure, threaded with
raw meat, odors of potatoes & the Andes,
& how the priestroaches had gotten into
the gate, yet the edges of his gate were
sewn with noble purple velvet & I pondered
my own course, what was in store for me
given the way I was living, how the female
gate in a man must open, yet the horrible
suffering if it opens & something else
not open! But there was no cure or cause
to who Vallejo was, perhaps it was the enormity
of what he took on, the weight of his people
to utter, & I shuddered to think of Indiana,
of what it would be to cast Indiana off.
Yorunomado sobbed when he saw the extent
of contradiction in Vallejo's body, how
could he have lived even one day, he thought,
this was the agony in the lines, the fulness
& the dark beauty of Vallejo's face horizontal

to sky, long black hair flowing back
into the sand, and Los likewise moved bent
& rested his hammer for one day in tribute
to the fierce & flaming profile contoured
to the horizon . . .

How long had he been left there? Yorunomado
stood & with Los helped the casket off
into the sea of another language. How long
Vallejo had been here! His windingsheet
was entangled with digging sticks & stones;
they set the casket on fire & left it blazing
to the shore water. They waded back,
& their hands were streaked with flesh,
their legs covered with veins, in the
hollow of their crab-like chests
a heart was hung, cock & balls swung
between their thighs. They knew
what Vallejo heard

beating beating beating the seas of misery beat upon the shore
& the roll in is a woman trying for a man
& the roll back is a man fleeing from a woman
& the million grains are children the waves beat upon
& the men walk in the women & the women walk in the men
but this is hidden to most by the very laws most have made up
Each sand is an eye Yorunomado is an eye of God
Every day every man ascends Niemonjima
for Niemonjima is the arising the going forth
& every night every man descends Niemonjima
for Niemonjima is the hill the walking down to sleep
& Yorunomado prayed: be patient with me my friends,
nothing is to be held back

III

I turned to Yorunomado, saying
Who are you, if not my death?

profile over my shoulder, oblique in nightwind to the crowd   [Tokyo, 1961]
a hundred yards off bunching the bus-rear. I had come
down to meet a stranger: why was he late?

I had come down to get married: where
was the woman I loved?

                stamping in the cold, muffler
tight the crowd growing round the fender, close
around my throat: where was the word to
not look away, to look in
to what they were looking at,
the looks   are all over the page

out at me   into the center
(collect yourself, you must look at her   .   who was going
fast around the camp, was Yorunomado in the form of dog
dodging thru saplings, picking up the glow, circling,
foolishly circling, afraid to get warm

by her body? where she lay? mirror
broken under rear axle, pieces of blood strewing feet
of the strangers who stood
trees   at the center of   round the edge of
the clearing: steel welded tires, a frame

it is a schoolgirl, blue skirt, legs of 12   go
no closer   await the stranger, stamp
& blow under station neon
                        bloodclot
where shd be breath,
cobblestone
where shd be mingling
a woman
where shd be   me
in her arms
GO INTO HER

do not relive it   go   without going
art talks to itself, is not art, is the mutterings of
man   afraid

              *

Yorunomado
divine man
help me, go

to her for
I cannot

I am weak beside the bulls of her forehead
I tremble by the stallions of her wrists

she is all spirit
a chimera of flame
in my own dark mirror
that smokes with need
of her. Go Yorunomado
divine man

for I have sold all my cattle
I have been put thru no initiation
the rains do not come
fertility is a stick at the edge of the blighted crossroads

Yorunomado
divine man
go unto her body
into her liver & bowels
circulate in her hair
for I am weak
I cannot face my death

Bloomington, winter-spring, 1965

330

Robert Creeley

On Seeing Blake's Name on Drain Hole Cover
in Bathroom of Shippensberg State College Dormitory

William Blake's room?
(Wee willy blake's room . . .)
Underfoot, mid-center
drain hole cap,
with name, (bleak) sweet William
Blake's again, this
own, can *save* this tune?
This bathroom.

Blakean Haiku

I blake for animals.
Who
be you?

Bowman and the Spirit of Prophecy

James Broughton

To the Fire-Bearers of Sagittarius

This night is ruled by the high-hunting Horse-Man
Who brings his fire? Who carries it forth?
Prometheus, stay with us   Jupiter's in charge here
Is this his firebird flying through our stars?

'We make our destinies by our choice of gods'
as Virgil knew   as we may regret
Look, I have chosen fealty to a lord of fire
Surrendering my icefloes I splash in the melting

Can we also make our gods by our choice of destinies?
Tell me what you yearn for   I can tell you who you are
Do you dream great vows?   Do you invent invocations?
Do you let your soul believe in Angelic Bowmen?

We each have an Archer who needs our recognition
We each have an Archer devoted to our needs
Stake your own claim   Shake out your arrows
Are you willing to be wed to a sacred target?

Fire-bearers, flutter not   And no wamble
Focus your insights to clarify your steed
Fly on his flame   Aim as you ride
Carry home our destinies to their radiant source !

Denise Low

Blake's Lost Years — 1813-1815

In 1812 William Blake sent four paintings to the Water Colour Society show, including parts of *Jerusalem*, but virtually no record survives of his activities for the next three years. Blake's only public work during this time is an engraving job for another artist. This long period of silence contrasts with Blake's usual active life. What transpired during this sparsely documented period? Astrological techniques — secondary progressions of the birth chart and transits — suggest some answers to the questions of these years that have stymied traditional scholars.

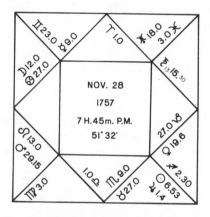

NOV. 28

1757

7 H. 45m. P.M.

51° 32′

Urania chart — 1824

First, the birth chart of William Blake needs to be retrieved from the nineteenth century. The first horoscope of the poet appeared in December, 1824, in an astrological magazine entitled *Urania*. The delineation was penned anonymously, but Blake himself knew of astrology through his friend John Varley. Varley apparently subscribed to the typical astrology of his time, heavy on judgement and material fortune. Blake spurned this astrology:

> Varley could make no way with Blake towards inducing him to regard Astrology with favour. Blake wd. say['']your fortunate nativity I count the worst[;] you reckon that to be born in August

334

& have the notice & patronage of Kings to be the best of all where
as the lives of the Apostles & Martyrs of whom it is said the world
was not worthy wd. be counted by you as the worst & their
nativities those of men born to be hanged.[']

(John Linnell's *Autobiography*)

But Varley's interest in occult knowledge extended to a belief in Blake. He
encouraged Blake's visions, and "It was Varley who excited Blake to see or
fancy the portraits of historical personages. . . ." In addition, probably Varley's
astrological interest helped preserve the important birth time for the *Urania*
chart.

This *Urania* horoscope, including the birth time and date, has been
transmitted unchanged as the definitive horoscope. But the tools available
for calculating astronomical positions in 1824 were less precise than those
available today, so the most recent natal chart shows some minor changes.
(See Chart I)

Most planets remain in the same positions in the new horoscope; the 1824
interpretation remains oversimplified but valid:

> . . . it is probable, that the extraordinary faculties and eccentricities
> of ideas which this gentleman possesses, are the effects of the
> MOON IN CANCER in the twelfth house (both sign and house
> being mystical), in trine to HERSCHELL [Uranus] from the mystical
> sign PISCES, from the house of science, and from the mundane
> trine to SATURN in the scientific sign AQUARIUS, which latter
> planet is in square to MERCURY IN SCORPIO, and in quintile to
> the SUN and JUPITER, in the mystical sign SAGITTARIUS. The
> square of MARS and MERCURY, from fixed signs, also, has a
> remarkable tendency to sharpen the intellect(s), and lay the foun-
> dation of extraordinary ideas.

The major difference between the 1824 and the 1981 versions of Blake's
chart is the shift of Saturn (practical, physical lessons) from the seventh
house of marriage to the eighth house of desires and constraints. Although
Blake had his problems in marriage, his friendship with his wife Catherine
flourished until his death. However, he did have his share of unfulfilled
desires and constraints. Eighth house restrictions in the writer's life include
poverty, critical neglect, and isolation.

Since the magazine *Urania* presented horoscopes to other astrologers, its
delineation of Blake's horoscope neglects to give the general overview. The
birth chart includes a balanced mixture of fire (inspiration and assertion)
and water (intuition and receptivity) elements. Four major planets in the
fiery fifth house—the house ruled by Leo and the Sun—indicate a strong

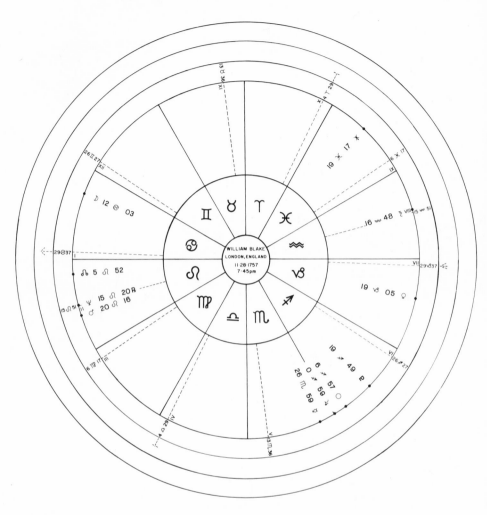

Chart I

creative drive, a desire to make an impact on the world, a strong ego. This creative emphasis often, ironically, denies children, true in Blake's case. Also, there is a tendency to dramatize, so Blake would have made a good actor and certainly a good public reader of his works. This placement corresponds to pride and self-motivation, which supported the poet/artist during long years of neglect. Sixteen degrees of Leo in the important first house of character, Neptune, and Mars all combine to increase the fiery influence of that sign. The strong Leo ego and drive are softened and balanced by the Cancer Moon and Ascendant. These strong water placements indicate Blake's sensitivity, intuition, and deep emotions. Cancer involves a person with intimate, nurturing relationships and with creation on a daily basis, as with the domestic arts. The home is important, and in Blake's case, all aspects of his art and business took place within his residence. His public exhibits were notoriously unsuccessful. Some biographers even note how seldom the artist left home, especially in his later years. Without his wife, Blake would have been lost. In astrological lore Cancer is the sign of the mother and Leo the sign of the father. In contemporary terms, both the intuitive right and rational left hemispheres of his brain were active; Blake had fully developed masculine and feminine abilities.

There is precious little emphasis in the chart of practical, earth-ruled signs. Venus in Capricorn in the sixth house (earth, Virgo) and Mars in the second house (earth, Taurus) are the only major planets indicative of competence with worldly affairs. The Venus placement is strong, and it helps Blake's known patience and attention to detail. But this is no banker's chart.

The "visionary" aspect that *Urania* noticed corresponds to the Sagittarius emphasis. The strength of a Sagittarian Sun is to view the world from a farther perspective than the rest of mortals. Particularly, Sagittarius gives a need to have an encompassing worldview, a contained philosophical framework. Blakean mythology is Sagittarian in this sense, and Blake writes, "I must Create a System, or be enslaved by another Man's." The combination of this influence with the element of water translates as an intuitive vision as well as a philosophical outlook. And water/intuition takes Blake beyond the outward trappings of orthodox religion. His interest in Boehme, Swedenborg, and Paracelsus attest to his involvement with the mystical interpreters of Christianity. The difficult side of Sagittarius, usually considered lucky in general, includes the overabundance of enthusiasm to the point of extremism. The greatest gift of Sagittarius is an unswerving faith.

Three unusual planetary patterns indicate additional intuitive and mental energy in Blake's horoscope. One is the string of planets at regular 30 degree intervals. Six of the twelve houses have such focusses of energy, around the twentieth degree. This also contributes to Blake's wider vision. At his best, he utilized a web of diverse awareness: rationality, intuition, a philosophical perspective, creativity, intensity, attention to details, and drive. Few people with this astrological diversity maintain a single focus like Blake could. Often people with such charts are pulled in many directions at once. But by keeping an active concentration on many mental levels—practical as well as visionary—Blake transcended this contradictory pattern. Certainly, however, his noted eccentricity can be seen in this configuration. Blake did not draw the sharp lines among different states of mind that modern psychology prescribes. The *Urania* article states that Blake has "as he affirms, held actual conversations with Michael Angelo, Raphael, Milton, Dryden, and the worthies of antiquity." And a contemporary, George Cumberland's father, writes of Blake that, "He is a little Cracked, but very honest."

A second major pattern in Blake's nativity is the "Finger of God" or "Y" pattern, where a planet is in a 150° (quincunx) relationship to two others:

Mars forms the base of the "Y", 150° from both Venus and Uranus. Astrological literature interprets this configuration as fated and tied into historical trends. According to astrologer Alan Oken, "It points the way to some special task in life." In practical terms, the two quincunxes indicate unresolved stress relating to work, health, and goals. The constant pressure can, at best, result in creative solutions. Usually, however, constant stress and restraint occur with this aspect. Blake experienced both the fame and the hassles.

A "Mystic Rectangle" is the third general pattern of Blake's chart, formed by two trines connected by two sextiles and oppositions to all corners:

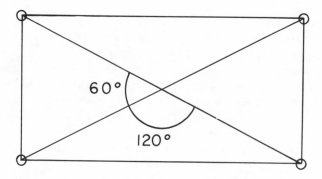

Michael R. Meyer (*A Handbook for the Humanistic Astrologer*) identifies people with this pattern as "capable of sustained productivity," "practical," with "synthetic and integrative ability." This structure in Blake's scattered chart adds stability.

During Blake's obscure years, he was unable to keep all of his strong mental characteristics in balance. His state of mind was uneven, inconsistent,

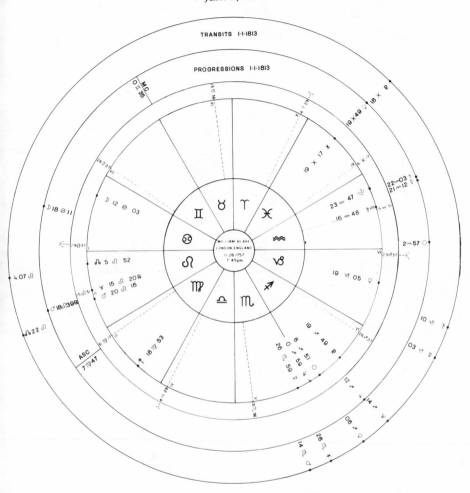

perhaps even truly crazy. However, he experienced some remarkable states of awareness.

One striking aspect of the configurations for 1813 to 1815 is the lack of strong aspects to the natal Sun. This indicates a lack of identity and direction, particularly in such a strong Sun/Leo chart. Without the strong anchor of his Leo ego, Blake became more susceptible to his moods and visionary experiences and hallucinations. Also, during this period Blake found refuge in playing his eccentric role to the hilt. His association with great names of the past may have been a substitute for—or an amplification of—his own

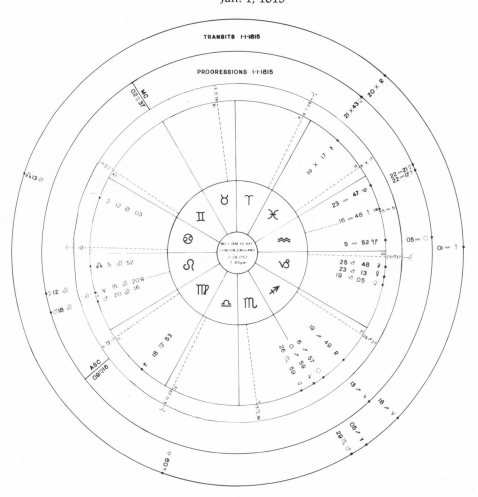

weakened identity. When the progressed Sun finally moved into an aspect in 1814, it was to conjunct the south node of the Moon, an emotionally trying influence. Self-confidence is often low under transits of the nodes, which again undermines the ego. In 1816 the progressed Sun finally sextiled the natal Sun. Here is where I expect Blake would commence an upward swing. G.E. Bentley cites 1818 as the year that Blake "turned a corner in his life. Thereafter he was loved, admired, and often supported by enthusiastic groups of young artists who called themselves the Ancients." The strengthened Sun of 1816 reflects the inner foundation for this shift.

The second indication of Blake's mental problems these years is a complex activation of the Finger of God pattern. One end of the "Y", ninth house Uranus, was conjuncted by both progressed Venus and transit Pluto from 1813 to 1816 exactly, in the sign of Pisces. In astrological tradition the planet Pluto shares with the Roman god of the underworld the power to transform. Pluto grinds imperceptibly, slowly, inexorably through the unconscious chambers of the mind. Symptoms of Pluto's work are nightmares, unnamed frustrations, obsessions. The dark god's end is cleansing of unsound mental habits and attitudes. Pluto was unknown to astrologers in the nineteenth century—as was the modern concept of the unconscious. Blake, however, was acquainted with an underworld/mental connection. In *The Four Zoas* he writes:

> For Urizen beheld the terrors of the abyss wandering among
> The ruined spirits, once his children & the children of Luvah,
> Scar'd at the sound of their own sigh that seems to shake the immense
> They wander Moping, in their heart a sun, a dreary moon,
> A Universe of fiery constellations in their brain,
> An earth of wintry woe beneath their feet, & round their loins
> Waters or winds or clouds or brooding lightnings & pestilential plagues.
> Beyond the bounds of their own self their senses cannot penetrate:
> As the tree knows not what is outside of its leaves & bark . . .

In practical terms, the Pluto conjunction means that Blake's moods became deeper and more inflexible. The Pluto contact to Venus also suggests social isolation, indicated by records of Blake's contemporaries, and deepening of intimate sexual relationships. His tie to his wife was heightened; or perhaps he had other lovers. Blake's creative work under these aspects would be compulsive, narrowly focused, and intense. George Cumberland reports of Blake in 1815: "He received us well and shewed his large drawing in Water Colours of the last Judgement[.] he has been labouring at it till it is nearly as black as your Hat." This illustrates the compulsive side of Pluto.

Pisces raises, again, the possibility of physical or mental collapse, requiring daily nursing. Ultimately Uranus and Pisces and Pluto all together suggest spiritual awakening of the higher mind—Uranus making it sudden, Pluto deep, intense, and long lasting. What we conventionally call mental imbalance could have been indeed a mystical enlightenment, never an easy business. Blake missed out on dinner parties and took only one job during these years, but he developed the ideas of the great work, *Jerusalem* and, I believe, endured a harrowing of the soul, and *satori*.

An additional possibility here is connected to the ninth house association with publication. With so many intense aspects at this time, the writer may

341

have published work privately that has been lost or obscured or burned by Catherine Blake's executor, Frederick Tatham. And the usual financial problems indicated by the birth chart Finger of God worsened during this period.

An astrological interpretation is considered sound when several parts of the chart restate the same theme. The relatively small aspect of transit Uranus conjunct Mercury (1813) summarizes the other indications. Uranus opens up a mind, changes a person's way of thinking; it supports the idea of enlightenment. Along with the moments of Uranian genius come eccentricity or even neurotic behavior. This aspect epitomizes this productive spiritual and creative period, 1813-1815, and it suggests the isolation.

An interpretation such as this can continue on and on, working out each detail. However, the general patterns of the years 1813 to 1815 include a weak Sun and the problematical Finger of God activation. I picture Blake going through long days and nights of introspection, mood swings and visions, losing touch with worldly matters. He does not go out, and indeed spends many days entranced by interior dialogues. His wife tends him so he is able to write, draw and engrave the inspirations that come; she sees him through the depressions. When Blake resurfaces into the social circle of literary parties, Charlotte Bury, a woman he met at Lady Caroline Lamb's, describes the artist in 1818 as "care-worn and subdued; but his countenance radiated as he spoke of his favorite pursuit."

A final word: Blake's greatest influence has begun in the twentieth century. A post-mortem chart can be constructed by rotating the eighth house of Scorpio/Pluto (death) to the first house position. The resulting horoscope puts the four planet conjunction in Sagittarius into the tenth house, a much more public and prominent placement. The Saturn-Neptune opposition of the birth chart then falls exactly across the important first-seventh house axis. Together, these two planets indicate magic, white and black. Neptune rules the power of thought, and Saturn rules physical effects. The magician causes, supernaturally, actual results. Visionary art exemplifies this form of magic, where visualizations from another reality are translated, as well as possible, into an earthly medium. The visions that Blake saw much of his life will continue to take form in Lord Chronos' realm, our dimension of time and earth. Blake's work endures, a challenge to Neptunian explorers.

Blake's house 17 South Molton St. 1803-21, Napoleonic wars and page of Jerusalem inserted. Blake drawing The Ghost of a Flea *1819, John Varley looking on.*

Michael Palmer

A Reasoned Reply to Gilbert Ryle

(After Blake's Newton)

Sound becomes difficult
to dispose of

etc. You go to sit down
and hope for a chair.

One of a pair of
eyes

distends.
Redness begins

on the left side.
The car always starts

in the morning
and it takes me

where someone else
is supposed to be

going
twice each week.

Or else the problem
of light and air.

Upstairs a small leak.
Trouble through the other

eye
which stays open

unless the window itself
is broken.

Kenneth Allen

Isolated Vignettes of an Atom

A simple implosion will someday shatter everyone's dreams, but the soul of sweet delight will not be defiled. The universe will be the amplitude of a hand-sized rock. It will be referred to by the next universe, using this one's vernacular, as the Last Bang. To this one it is the Black Hole, a region with no margin, an indescribable creation conceived by the planet Earth.

The whole creation will be consumed and appear infinite and holy, whereas it now appears finite and corrupt. William Blake

All my attempts...failed completely. It was as if the ground had been pulled out from under one, with no foundation to be seen anywhere upon which one could have built. Albert Einstein

Blindness became popular when Newton and his brethren circumnavigated the cell, upped the ante to the roof, and sawed off the wood under the table. "Decline to think," said Newton, "now, at this very moment, of the security of the hearth. What is now proved was once only imagined." Censorship followed and, for a long time afterward too, ran on and then past the naked eye.

In no great hurry the man on the motorcycle speeds by the speed of light, sees no sky, earth, or space, is then reeled off his bike, revolved in the sunlight, his head glittering in the molecular consistency of light. His dazzled brain, upheaved body, and his electric hair all bring him down to earth spontaneously. Then, a rocket blasts off for the stars—without contraries is no progression.

A-Bomb sucks Hiroshima into the atmosphere. Gall bladders were everywhere but no one could see a thing in the burdened air. Mist in the form of Edgar Allan Poe moved so quickly past the naked eye that the shutter speed of a Konica could not catch it. One shuddered to think that, all in all, there was nothing to see anywhere.

Chemistry appears to me like a miracle....This is the highest form of musicality in the sphere of thought. Albert Einstein

Earth, Mars, and Venus, their brethren beyond, emitted radiant beams of light. A skytraveler named William, equaling mc^2, felt his motion no more than would have a worm, and this intrigued him.

I drove into the night, never realizing how long it was. In a vague, pointless circle I rode, oblivious to my destiny, while presumably driving a straight line. I dug under the dashboard for words, realizing that the planet had demolished them.

When I was in the seventh grade...I was summoned by my home-room teacher who expressed the wish that I leave the room. To my remark that I had done nothing amiss he replied only 'Your mere presence spoils the respect of the class for me.' Albert Einstein

When he had to write an essay on his experience, the paper he gave to his teacher startled and outraged her in unison. 'Words are merely vapor,' she read, "Hummphh!" By being restrained, she gave all signs of decadence, unwilling to enliven her atoms over a student's aimless theorizing.

*For science something can be said
No violinist is so well fed.* Albert Einstein

"Everything in the world, Watson," said Inspector Holmes, holding the choke of his pipe, "requires the utmost scrutiny to be sure that nothing is taken for granted. Ergo, we shall remain ignorant, and learn the whole truth in our dreams."

I am grateful to destiny for having made life an exciting experience so that life has appeared meaningful. Albert Einstein

International Business Machines won a medal for its distinguished contributions to the planet Earth. On and on, prospering wholly, it ran out of things to do. They then decided to make a sizable investment in the Universe, Inc. There, they felt, would be found adequate room for growth.

Thus man forgot that all deities reside in the Human breast.

Shlomo Vinner

Jerusalem

Jerusalem,
The former address of God;
Sometimes
They still imagine His silences
Between walls and bells.
To hear His heart
They call to Him over loudspeakers
And wait
Until everything dissolves.

And when the smoke clears the burnt house is revealed
And the bodies of the beloved.

The hearts of old trees are heavy as stone
And longings that last too long
Turn into thorns in the valley
While dreams are exchanged
For piles of rusted scrap.

At the end of the wars,
Amid new signs and arrows,
The birds leap on the grass:
Jerusalem 1967,
The former address of God.

Illus. 1: Title page (J 2)

James Bogan

A Tour of *Jerusalem*

*If the Spectator could enter into these Images in his Imagination,
approaching them on the Fiery Chariot of his Contemplative
Thought . . . .*[1]

"Jerusalem The Emanation of The Giant Albion" shines out of the title
page in golden calligraphy from a spectrum of swirling water-colors. Almost
obscured at the bottom of the page is the name of the author, "W. Blake";
the date of the poem's conception, "1804"; and the address of the printer-
publisher, that is Blake's on "South Molton Street" (illus. 1). The illustrations
measure six by nine inches — the size of this book — tiny for the monumental
figures contained; but Blake was able to concentrate glowing images of
powerful thought by calling on the developed skill and enthusiastic devotion
of a lifetime. He worked on *Jerusalem* over the course of sixteen years,
without pay, without external encouragement, but at the insistence of inner
voices and visions more demanding than hunger. The artist hammered out
the inspirations of dreams and spirit-dictations into an epic poem. He
engraved each letter of each word into each of the one-hundred copper
plates of his poem; then he printed them on his own press with the help of
his wife. To further engage the senses of his readers he had outlined pictures
throughout the book. He hand-painted, beautifully, intricately, spontaneously,
one of the five copies he printed.

In the advertisement "To the Public" Blake makes this claim for his Divine
Comedy: "Heaven, Earth, & Hell henceforth shall live in harmony" (*J* 3).
The public's response to this grand reconciliation was unanimous. Probably
no one read the whole poem in his lifetime. Robert Southey, mad King
George's poet laureate, thought it was "a perfectly mad poem."[2] At times
Blake was tempted to burn it in disappointment over its chilling lack of
reception. Luckily for us he did not, since *Jerusalem* is the crown of his
many creations. Much like *Moby Dick*, it was simply missed by its
contemporaries but has belatedly been treated with gathering respect as
time reveals its stored power and prophetic insight; yet this great poem still
offers the same resistance to understanding that scared off Southey.

The purpose of this "Tour of *Jerusalem*" is to facilitate the mental traveler's entrance into a marvelous world. Knowing some landmarks will enable the reader to explore this *terra incognita* without having to battle needless dragons of perplexity. There are enough needful ones. The poem is an occluded Ninth Symphony, but wonders will be revealed to those who journey through with the spiritual endurance it requires, and indeed, helps create.

Reading *Jerusalem* can be a bewildering undertaking, because Blake has conveyed his own experience of "Past, Present, & Future existing all at once" (*J* 15). That information—"all at once"—bursts the conventional epic modes of story. *Jerusalem* cannot be read as an adventure, like *The Odyssey*, for example. The reader finds himself overwhelmed at first, and necessarily so, because Blake "substitutes for narrative a heroic enlargement of comprehension," as Stuart Curran says.[3] Like an inspired jazz saxophonist reeling out the unpredictable creations of the instant, the poet confronts his audience with the unknown. Nor does he approach this goal by half-measures. What he said of *The Four Zoas* applies also to *Jerusalem*: "The Persons & Machinery [are] intirely new to the Inhabitants of Earth (some of the Persons Excepted)" (*L* 823). The space of the poem ranges from London to Hindostan to Patagonia to Canada, from the "starry heighth to the starry depth" (*J* 11). Time is refracted again and again, as Blake "walk[s] up & down in Six Thousand Years" and compacts "their Events" into the one-hundred plates of his book (*J* 74). Though *Jerusalem* has a plot, to watch for its unfolding is not really the way to appreciate this poem which seeks to release repressed memories, tap forgotten powers, and expand perceptions.

Jerusalem is an epic poem of the disintegration and eventual resurrection of Albion, the Father of Humanity, yet it impresses with the urgency of the fate of a friend. The scope is vast as all history, from creation to apocalypse and beyond, and still it happens in some time resembling this very day. While Virgil sang the glories of imperial Rome in the *Aeneid*, *Jerusalem* celebrates the triumph of all nations reunited in the return of Albion to his emanation. The poem is itself a tool of that achievement, for the epic task Blake sets himself is:

> To open the Eternal Worlds, to open the immortal Eyes
> Of Man inwards into the Worlds of Thought, into Eternity
> Ever expanding in the Bosom of God, the Human Imagination.
>
> (*J* 5)

This sublime undertaking certainly ranks with Milton's efforts in *Paradise Lost* to "assert Eternal Providence,/And justify the ways of God to men" (*I:*

25-26). Blake's poem springs from a power that he thought the birthright of all men, the power of vision:

> Mutual in one another's love and wrath all renewing
> We live as One Man; for contracting our infinite senses
> We behold multitude, or expanding, we behold as one.   (*J* 38)

How does he awaken this underdeveloped faculty? His two primary vehicles, synergistically combined, are the mighty free-verse line he has chosen to carry his thought and the hand-colored engravings that brighten each page. Blake engages both eye and ear in his effort to make the blind see and the deaf hear, for he wants to "win the vacant.../To noble raptures," to borrow a line from Wordsworth.[4]

Before walking into *Jerusalem* the traveler would do well to consider some of the qualities that pervade the whole volume. One principle that underlies its construction is drawn from the Proverbs of Hell: "The cistern contains: the fountain overflows" (*MHH* 8). The pages of *Jerusalem* fill to overflowing with pictures of varying sizes. Full page and half-page illustrations are frequent; even the interlinear spaces and margins are populated by denizens of the human universe: birds, serpents, fairies, people, trees, vines, fish, butterflies, bats, worms, moons, stars, planets, spiders, frogs, shellfish, comets, angels, etc. Diminutive human forms often inhabit the margins; sometimes their actions can be read cartoon-fashion around the page. For instance on Plate 42 a ladder of humans, with the ones towards the bottom more and more crushed, reaches to the top of the page where the highest figure grabs the grapes growing there. With the trenchancy of a political cartoon, the ghastly economics of the delusion that "Man lives by the deaths of Men" (*J* 42) is engraved along the side of the page, as David Erdman suggests in *The Illuminated Blake*.[5]

The habitual practice of printers does not manacle Blake's creative use of the page. Indeed, he plays with the space at his disposal. Cherubim are used to hold up the walls of one page to keep satanic cogged wheels from grinding it up entirely (*J* 22). Elsewhere a giant is trapped behind a mountain of text (*J* 62). Even pages with no pictures (and these are few) are still significantly colored. For example, a light yellow wash spreads over the passage about Golgonooza with its "rafters of forgiveness" and bricks of "well wrought affections" (*J* 12), thus emphasizing the life-sustaining qualities of Los' city. A beam of sunlight flows across one page (*J* 60), while another appears to have a flame of blood flickering up the margin (*J* 66). Note his attention to the "Minute Particulars" (*J* 55) of meaning: "As Poetry admits not a Letter that is Insignificant, So Painting admits not a Grain of Sand or a

Blade of Grass Insignificant—much less an insignificant Blur or Mark" (*VLJ* 611). Even the engraved "types" of the text are a near-golden orange that delight the eye accustomed to black print.

Blake's use of color is brilliant, but for him it is of secondary importance. Form and outline—the drawing—dictates the disposition of color. Blake became indignant whenever color obscured the discriminating line: "Fine Tints without Fine Forms are always the Subterfuge of the Blockhead" (*DC* 591). The shape that inhabits *almost every picture* in all of Blake's works is the "Human Form Divine" (*J* 27). Sometimes man and woman are shown in tantric joy, as in the embracing lovers who are couched on a lily (*J* 28); but in other cases the divine element is almost unrecognizable, as when Albion is pictured in a state of root-tangled woe (*J* 45). One of Blake's energetic aesthetic principles is that "Art can never exist without Naked Beauty displayed" (*Lao* 776). The characters of his myth reveal themselves in beautifully supple and muscled bodies. At times "the blood is seen to circulate in their limbs" (*DC* 581, example on *J* 97). Jerusalem and Los, especially, are shown in naked glory (*J* 32, 100); indeed the veils of Vala obscure the human form and are therefore suspect (*J* 32; illus. 2). Read what Blake has to say about the striking figures he has represented in one of his paintings:

> The flush of health in flesh exposed to the open air, nourished by the spirits of the forests and floods [rivers] in that ancient happy period [of the Ancient Britons], which history has recorded, cannot be like the sickly daubs of Titian or Rubens. Where will the copier of nature, as it now is, find a civilized man, who has been accustomed to go naked? Imagination can only furnish us with colouring appropriate . . . . As to modern Man, stripped from his load of clothing, he is like a dead corpse.   (*DC* 580-581)

There is an anecdote told in Parkman's *Oregon Trail* that comments obliquely,[6] but aptly on Blake's position:

> Savage figures, with quivers at their backs, and guns, lances, or tomahawks in their hands, sat on horseback motionless as statues. . . . Others again stood carelessly among the throng, with nothing to conceal the matchless symmetry of their forms. There was one in particular, a ferocious fellow, named The Mad Wolf, who, with the bow in his hand and the quiver at his back, might have seemed, but for his face, the Pythian Apollo himself. Such a figure rose before the imagination of [Benjamin] West, when on first

Illus. 2: *Vala, Jerusalem, and her Children* (J 32)

seeing the [Apollo] Belvedere in the Vatican, he exclaimed, "By God, a Mohawk!"[7]

Blake's "Mohawks" were the Celtic race of the Ancient Britons whom he describes in this way: "The Britons (say historians) were naked civilized men, learned, studious, abstruse in thought and contemplation; naked, simple, plain in their acts and manners; wiser than after-ages" (DC 577). Their physiques grace the pages of Jerusalem.

From childhood Blake was an enthusiastic admirer of Michelangelo, hence an additional source for his models can be assumed. While Michelangelo had the ample spaces of the Sistine Chapel to fill with his giants, Blake put equally heroic figures into the confines of a book—"on a smaller scale" (DC 565). When Blake's pictures are blown up to wall size, they do not become unglued and inflated, but rather move toward the titanic dimensions of "one hundred feet" in which some were first visualized (DC 566). Indeed, this challenging book conjures our imagination to provide such expansive projection.

"Without Contraries is no progression. Attraction and Repulsion, Reason and Energy, Love and Hate, are necessary to Human existence" (MHH 3). The organization of Jerusalem springs from the rhythms of such principles. Each of the four chapters harmonizes the terror of being a man with the wonder of being a man. The arrow of thought that unites the contraries is the question, "What is Man?" This ancient inquiry is the constant concern of the poem with vision and despair balancing on the trajectory of the search for an answer. A way of orienting oneself in Jerusalem is to notice the variations on "What is Man?" Characters reveal themselves by their response to this refrain.

When Jesus, as the Divine Vision, addresses Albion at the beginning of the poem, he enunciates an eternal truth about Man: "I am in you and you in me, mutual in love divine:/Fibres of love from man to man, thro' Albion's pleasant land.../Lo! we are one, forgiving all Evil" (J 4). However, Albion has a different perception of the nature of man: "We are not One: we are Many....Man [is] the enemy of man...Humanity shall be no more, but war & princedom & victory" (J 4). The education of Albion out of this destructive delusion is the process of the poem. Towards the end of the poem it appears to Gwendolen, a Daughter of Albion, that "Humanity, the Great Delusion, is chang'd to War & Sacrifice" (J 82). Albion's crazed goal of self-destruction has almost been reached when the Covering Cherub, a conglomerate of cruelty, marches against Jesus. In this precarious moment at the threshold of Eternity the question "What is Man?" is answered in a glorious vision towards which the poem has struggled to reach. Jesus explains to Albion, "If God dieth not for Man & giveth not himself/Eternally

354

Illus. 3: *Los Crosses the Threshold in the Quest to Save Albion (J 1)*

for Man, Man could not exist; for *Man is love/As God is love*" (*J* 86, emphasis mine). Albion discovers his humanity in self-sacrifice when he throws himself into the furnace of affliction to save his friend, Jesus. Subsequently, Albion is capable of commanding his original four-fold nature of wisdom, imagination, love, and instinct. His inherent powers to create space and time re-emerge when the error of vengeance is annihilated (*J* 96-99).

Another effective way of ascertaining what is basically happening in *Jerusalem* is to note the postures of the human forms that move through the book. Blake reveals his meanings in a relatively simple use of body language. The engraving known as *Glad Day*, made during his early thirties, serves as an exemplar for the awakened man (see p.174). In it Albion dances, arms spread wide, light emanating from his naked body. His eyes are wide open as he looks out from the picture. Such is Albion's condition when he is free. Any position that contracts from this openness, be it sitting, curled up, or lying down, indicates how far from full energy and expression the character is. Keeping that standard in mind, let us now tour the luminous precincts of *Jerusalem*.

On the cover of *Jerusalem* a pilgrim in a broad-brimmed hat has opened a door and is stepping into a dark space (illus. 3). The sandals on his feet show that he is prepared for some hard traveling. A beaming sun globe in his right hand illuminates his concerned face and lights the way into darkness. As bold as Odysseus on a harrowing journey, this is Los "entering the interiors of Albion's bosom in all the terrors of friendship" (*J* 31) and the reader/spectator follows him through the gothic doorway as the page is turned. Carl Jung describes the quest we are embarking on: It is "a descent into the dark world of the unconscious...the perilous adventure of a night journey, whose end and aim is the restoration of life, resurrection, and triumph over death."[8]

Once inside, Los finds Jerusalem in a swoon at the bottom of Plate 2 (illus. 1). She is a beautiful creature, "cover'd with Wings translucent, sometimes covering/And sometimes spread abroad, reveal[ing] flames of holiness" (*J* 86). The moon and stars are emblazoned on her flaming wings in golds and reds. Her winged body is exquisitely, openly sexual. Why is such a lovely creature so desolated? Albion has driven her, his own soul, from his heart. Because Jerusalem is exiled, "outcast...left to the trampling foot & the spurning heel...sold from street to street" (*J* 62), Albion fast approaches a suicidal death. He refuses to acknowledge his own interior light when he says "Jerusalem is not" (*J* 4).

Such is the situation at the beginning of the poem: soul and body split, man and woman split. The reconciliation of these polarities is the urge underlying the course of the poem. As Milton Percival remarks, "Sex is with

Blake, as with the Gnostics and the Cabbalists, a fundamental mystery. For that reason his system repeats the point of view of certain Gnostic systems which make the history of mankind the love story of sundered contraries."[9] The cure of Albion's "dread disease" (J 45), his return to wholeness, is contingent on reunion with the Emanation. Jung's concept of the anima clarifies Albion's harsh perplexity in accepting himself: "It costs...enormous difficulties to understand what the anima is. Men accept her easily enough when she appears in novels or as a film star, but she is not understood at all when it comes to seeing the role she plays in their own lives, because she sums up everything that a man can never get the better of and never finishes coping with. Therefore it remains in a perpetual state of emotionality which must not be touched."[10] Blake's epic poem is a heroic effort to articulate that dire confusion in Humanity—and to acknowledge the Emanation. The poem is itself a vast spell aimed at liberating Man and Woman for each other, and the means by which this will be done is Jerusalem's hallmark: forgiveness.

At the outset of the poem, however, Albion withers, stuck in an inferno, his fondest desire in chains of his own forging. The debilitating effect of self-torment is shown on Plate 9 where Albion first appears flat on his back, his toes higher than his head. Mantegna-like foreshortening intensifies the disjointed disposition of the body.[11] At the bottom of Plate 14 Albion, colored in a leprous grey, reclines in self-pitying torpor. Dark chaotic waters lap about him, yet this picture contains both vision and despair, since the colorful presence of Jerusalem hovers over his frowning head. A rainbow of hope, sparkled with gold, arches across the page. Night-lights of moons, stars, and planets shine for him to see if he would only open his eyes.

Chains, webs, entangling roots, and serpents bind human figures on various pages. The nadir of these horizontal prisoners is the Stonehenge victim that is chained to the bottom of Plate 67. He lies in a narrow space, oppressed by the weight of the text divulging tortures inflicted by Tirzah:

These nostrils that expanded with delight in morning skies
I have bent downward with lead melted from my roaring furnaces
Of affliction, of love, of sweet despair, of torment unendurable . . .
Fetch the girdle of strong brass, heat it red-hot,
Press it around the loins of this ever expanding cruelty.
Shriek not so my only love. I refuse thy joys.   (J 67)

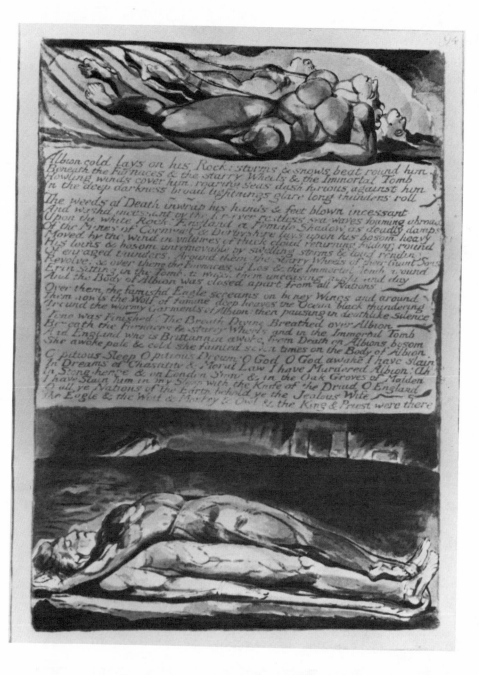

Illus 4 : *Albion Before His Reawakening (J 94)*

His feet are manacled to the right border, his hands to the left. The page is a procrustean bed upon which he is being stretched apart, or so a little fancy feels.

Amidst the catastrophes depicted in *Jerusalem*, Los is sometimes seen at his forge making both the sun and the moon for the sustenance of the Sons and Daughters of Albion and for Albion himself. The sun is associated with the divine energies of Eden, the moon with the restorative powers of Beulah. Albert Roe remarks that the eclipses and clouds obscuring the sun in much of *Jerusalem* are the effects of Ulro-darkened awareness:[12] but Los, with Vulcanic strength, continues to man furnaces whose fires are positively igneous (*J* 6). In active postures he wields his hammer, tongs, and bellows to create the lights of imagination. The moon that Los builds echoes in the many moon-arcs that float across the pages of the poem, bringing a measure of reflected, secondary light to the gloomy darkness in Albion's soul. On Plate 73 Los is shown pounding the sun-ball into shape with a mighty stroke of his heavy hammer: "The blow of his Hammer is Justice, the swing of his Hammer Mercy, The Force of Los's Hammer is eternal Forgiveness" (*J* 88). Suns in *Jerusalem* are usually highlighted with gold leaf, a materialization of light. Los refines the philosopher's gold which transmutes the leaden sorrows of Albion's children into the bright joys of Eden.

The emergence of Albion out of his death-stupor, the shift from horizontal to vertical, takes place as the sun rises. The dawn-motif is emphasized both in the text and the pictures from plates 94 to 100. Albion is clay-cold dead at the bottom of Plate 94 (illus. 4). The first lights of early dawn beam over the hill in sepia daybreak colors. Erdman notes that textually this sunshine is the "Breath Divine" breathing over Albion.[13] A touch of gold indicates the rim of the rising sun. On the next plate Albion is already rising (*J* 95, illus. 5). His eyes are open and he looks up. His arm reaches out, extending the limits of the page. His right leg is flexed for movement and his left leg stretches out behind. The posture looks like the exercise of a gymnosophist or martial arts adept. His old skin, a grey shadow at his feet, has been shed, as he raises himself up bathed in incandescent flames. Man is the phoenix.[14] A shiny worm makes a border along the bottom of the page, underlining the magnitude of Albion's recovery.

The resurrection is continued in Plate 97 (illus. 6). The transition from dormant to kinetic energy is shown graphically as Albion bounds along the green earth at "the very threshold of Eternal Life"—a precipice (*J* 93). It is Blake's version of the Tarot card, "the Fool." Infrequently does the central figure of a painting have his face turned completely away from the viewer, but he is looking inwards, "into the Worlds of Thought, into Eternity" (*J* 5). His right arm is raised in lookout as he surveys "new expanses" (*J* 98). His body is suffused with strength, his left arm muscled and veined like the arm

Her voice piercd Albions clay cold ear, he moved upon the Rock.
The Breath Divine went forth upon the morning hills Albion mov'd
Upon the Rock, he opend his eyelids in pain; in pain he moved
His stony members, he saw England. Ah! shall the Dead live again

The Breath Divine went forth over the morning hills Albion rose
In anger: the wrath of God breaking bright flaming on all sides around
His awful limbs: into the Heavens he walked clothed in flames
Loud thundring, with broad flashes of flaming lightning & pillars
Of fire, speaking the Words of Eternity in Human Forms, in direful
Revolutions of Action & Passion. thro the Four Elements on all sides
Surrounding his awful Members.Thou seest the Sun in heavy clouds
Struggling to rise above the Mountains. in his burning hand
He takes his Bow, then chooses out his arrows of flaming gold
Murmuring the Bowstring breathes with ardor! clouds roll round the
Horns of the wide Bow, loud sounding winds sport on the mountain brows
Compelling Urizen to his Furrow: & Tharmas to his Sheepfold;
And Luvah to his Loom: Urthona he beheld mighty labouring at
His Anvil, in the Great Spectre Los unwearied labouring & weeping
Therefore the Sons of Eden praise Urthonas Spectre in songs
Because he kept the Divine Vision in time of trouble .
As the Sun & Moon lead forward the Visions of Heaven & Earth
England who is Brittannia enterd Albions bosom rejoicing.
Rejoicing in his indignation! adoring his wrathful rebuke .
She who adores not your frowns will only loathe your smiles

Illus. 6 : *Albion/Los Surveying New Expanses* (J 97)

361

of Michelangelo's Moses. The torque of his turning and the stretch of his stride reveal a man unencumbered by the iron and mental chains of earlier times. He is "going forward, forward irresistable from Eternity to Eternity" (*J* 98). In his left hand is a sun-globe shining in reds, yellows, and gold. "Dim chaos brighten[s] beneath, above, around" (*J* 98), as the radiant colors penetrate the darkness. By the way, an earth-gnome's face peeps out from the hillside in the right corner, as the whole universe becomes recognizably human.

While this plate depicts Albion's recovery, it simultaneously pictures Los on his long night watch. As W.J.T. Mitchell says, there is a "multiplicative rather than additive relationship between visual and verbal form."[15] Here Los is looking for the "Signal of the Morning" (*J* 93): "Los walks upon his ancient Mountains in the deadly darkness,...watchful/Looking to the East.../[The workers in Golgonooza] view the red Globe of fire in Los' hand" (*J* 85). The "Signal of the Morning" is the first hint of dawn, which Los is actually bringing with him. The pivot motion of his body indicates that the moment of knowledge has occurred: "The Night of Death is past and Eternal Day/Appears on our Hills" (*J* 97).

Los can see auspicious signs in the sky. The morning star, say Venus, is conjunct to the moon. Venus and the moon together attend a time of harmony.[16] This configuration of the sun and waning moon happens only in the very last phase of the moon. On the day before the new moon, the waning crescent moon can be seen in the East just before dawn. Chapter 1 of *Jerusalem* begins with a new crescent moon in the night sky, which is seen just after sunset (*J* 4). In the first two chapters waxing moons predominate. In the middle of the book on Plate 50 there is a full moon, as Erdman has noted,[17] and the waning lunar cycle nears completion in Plate 97. Originally Blake conceived of *Jerusalem* as being composed of twenty-eight chapters, which indicates he felt the whole poem as a completed lunar cycle, within one epoch-long night.

While Blake was leery of astrology, he was not ignorant of the movements of the heavenly bodies, and he was deeply read in alchemy, which uses astrological notation.[18] The active attitute of Albion/Los, the morning star, and the waning moon all look toward the time of birth, which takes place at the new moon. As the poem draws to a close, the new moon is approaching, which is coincident with the conjunction of the sun and moon. This conjunction is syntactically literal as well. In a grammatical pun Blake effects the conjunction: "The Sun & Moon lead forward the Visions of Heaven & Earth" (*J* 95 and 96—the line is repeated). The ampersand is the conjunction that forges the link. "Sun & Moon...Heaven & Earth" join in a marriage of contraries. Jung notes that "the alchemist's endeavours to unite the opposites culminate in the 'chymical marriage,' the supreme act of

362

Illus. 7: *Reunion of Albion and Jerusalem (J 99)*

union in which the work reaches its consummation...the last and most formidable opposition...the alchemist expressed very aptly as the relationship between male and female."[19]

The consummation-conjunction itself is represented on Plate 99 (illus. 7). Multi-colored flames engulf the page. These fires have been seen earlier, burning in Los' forge (*J* 6). A white-robed and bearded Albion holds a dark-hued and naked Jerusalem to himself amidst fires that do not consume. Jerusalem's gold-flecked hair sweeps up like flames. She is being held, arms outstretched in acceptance, and together they float up. Gravity has been overcome in their reunion and union. Age and youth, cold and heat, heaven and earth bend to one another.

Erdman writes that "these two persons [on Plate 99] must now symbolize all the divided persons in the now whole Song: he all the flayed, chained, decapitated, deluded, accusing and divided men in the poem, now united in One: she all the separated and separating women, now ready for trust and love."[20] The ecstasy of the pair does not pre-empt understanding; in fact, profound care is reflected on the faces in awareness of the weight of all that has come before in this poem of human history, and of all that is being forgiven. Irene Chayes has described the feeling and gestures in the picture: "Pity and forgiveness bring together the Universal Man and his Emanation, as they bring together man and God and Albion and his 'children'....The upraised arms now express reception rather than yearning, and the gesture is offered to the heavens, toward which Jerusalem is rising in the embrace of a repentant Jehovah-like Albion whose arms are lowered. Pity and forgiveness may also come from below."[21]

Forgiveness is the elixir that revives both Man and Emanation and pictured is the consequent reunion. In Isaiah (52: 1-2) the Lord calls to Jerusalem: "Awake, awake, put on thy beautiful garments, O Jerusalem, the holy city....Loose thyself from the bands of thy neck, O captive daughter of Zion." Jerusalem's ultimate faithfulness, despite periods of despair, through "a long season & a hard journey & a howling wilderness" (*J* 62) is justified at the finale of the poem when Albion cries, "Awake, Awake, Jerusalem! O lovely Emanation of Albion....Awake, and come away!" (*J* 97). In Plate 99 we see her "Awakening into his Bosom in the Life of Immortality."

The embracing figures of Albion and Jerusalem amidst the fires of Los' furnace are the visual equivalent of Blake's daring boast that "Heaven, Hell & Earth henceforth shall live in harmony" (*J* 3). The poet has made good on the effort to integrate the seemingly irreconcilable. This creative fusion releases worlds of energy. On the final plate of the book the sun is risen. The once-rebellious side of Los, the Spectre, "labour[s] obedient" now, holding the sun aloft on his workingman's shoulders (*J* 8).[22] Enitharmon weaves the arc-moon and starry night sky. Los, as Urthona, stands between them with

364

hammer and compass-like tongs in hand. The Druid temple behind him has been restored, with wings added. Even that former vehicle of torture has been re-made into a temple for the imagination. Urthona moves forward—one step done, another begun. The energies of Eden always lead us further as Whitman well knew: "From each fruition of success, no matter what, shall come forth something to make greater struggle necessary."[23] In *Jerusalem*, as in the *Four Zoas* and *Milton*, an apocalyptic ending is really the revelation of the "new expanses" surrounding us. (*J* 98). The entrance to these worlds is approached with energy, love-released by forgiveness dared. "Thunder of Thought, & flames of fierce desire" result (*J* 3).

In alchemy the final step is not the conjunction of the sun and moon. "Rebirth and transformation...follow the conjunction [and] take place in the hereafter," Jung observes.[24] Blake desired to catalyze a reaction in the "dear reader" (*J* 3), and the "hereafter" can be understood in the sense of the enduring effect of the book after it has been written by Blake and closed by the spectator. The poem is a continuation of the divine work of redemption, a stage of which is "to open the immortal eye/Of Man inwards" (*J* 5). Like the alchemists, Blake has "staked his whole soul for the transcendental purpose of producing a unity, a work of reconciliation between apparently incompatible opposites."[25] He has fused poetry and painting, matter and spirit, learning and inspiration in a Herculean effort to increase our awareness of just how much "Eternity is in love with the productions of time" (*MHH* 7).

*   *   *   *   *   *

In Great Eternity, every particular Form gives forth or Emanates
Its own peculiar Light; & the form is the Divine Vision
And the Light is his Garment. This is Jerusalem in every Man,
A Tent & Tabernacle of Mutual Forgiveness, Male & Female Clothings.
And Jerusalem is called Liberty among the Children of Albion.

(*J* 54).

Notes

[1]William Blake, *Blake: Complete Writings*, ed. Geoffrey Keynes (Oxford: Oxford Univ. Press, 1966), p. 611. Subsequent references to Blake's writings will be made in the text. Page numbers will be used when plate numbers are lacking. The following abbreviations will be used:

MHH—*The Marriage of Heaven and Hell*
DC—*A Descriptive Catalogue*
VLJ—*A Vision of the Last Judgement*
J—*Jerusalem*

Lao—*The Laocoön*

OHV—*On Homer's Poetry and on Virgil*

The illuminated copy of *Jerusalem* is owned by Mr. Paul Mellon. There is a beautiful facsimile edition from the Trianon Press (1953) that was limited to 526 copies.

[2]Quoted in Henry Crabb Robinson, "Reminiscences" (1852), in *Blake Records*, ed. G. E. Bentley, Jr., (Oxford: Oxford Univ. Pres, 1969), p. 229.

[3]"The Structures of *Jerusalem*," in *Blake's Sublime Allegory*, ed. Stuart Curran and Joseph Anthony Wittreich, Jr., (Madison: Univ. of Wisconsin Press, 1973), p. 341.

[4]"The Recluse," 11. 714-15.

[5]*The Illuminated Blake* (Garden City: Anchor, 1974), p. 321. Hereafter cited as *Illuminated*.

[6]For an even more oblique reading of Blake, see the story by David Ohle in this volume.

[7]Ed. E. N. Feltskog (Madison: Univ. of Wisconsin Press, 1969), pp. 164-165.

[8]C. G. Jung, *Psychology and Alchemy* (Princeton: Princeton Univ. Press, 1968), p. 329. Hereafter cited as *Alchemy*.

[9]*William Blake's Circle of Destiny* (1938; rpt. New York: Octagon Books, 1970), p. 107.

[10]C. G. Jung, *Archetypes of the Collective Unconscious*, pt. 1 (Princeton: Princeton Univ. Press, 1959), p. 271.

[11] The foreshortening of Albion in Plate 9 is perhaps an ironic pictorial allusion to Mantegna's "Dead Christ." The perspective is reversed, however, in that we see Albion from the head but Christ from the feet. Albion's collapse is a result of self-torment, rather than self-sacrifice.

[12]Albert S. Roe, *Blake's Illustrations to the Divine Comedy*. (Princeton: Princeton Univ. Press, 1953), p. 141. See "Blake's Symbolism" by Albert Roe in this volume.

[13]*Illuminated*, p. 373.

[14]*Illuminated*, p. 374.

[15]*Blake's Composite Art: A Study of the Illuminated Poetry* (Princeton: Princeton Univ. Press, 1978), p. 33.

[16]Frances Sakoian and Louis S. Acker, *The Astrologer's Handbook* (New York: Harper & Row, 1973), p. 285.

[17]*Illuminated*, p. 329.

[18]Blake refers to both Jacob Boehme and Paracelsus in the *Marriage of Heaven and Hell* (21-22). He also read Hermes, Agrippa, Thomas Vaughn, Robert Fludd and others.

[19]C. G. Jung, *Mysterium Coniunctionis* (Princeton: Princeton Univ. Press, 1963), p. 89. Herafter cited as *Mysterium*.

[20]*Illuminated*, p. 378.

[21] "The Presence of Cupid and Psyche," in *Blake's Visionary Forms Dramatic*, ed. David V. Erdman and John E. Grant (Princeton: Princeton Univ. Press, 1970), p. 243n.

[22]*Illuminated*, p. 379.

[23]"Song of the Open Road," in *Leaves of Grass*, stanza 14.

[24]*Alchemy*, p. 479.

[25]*Mysterium*, p. 554.

Aethelred Eldridge

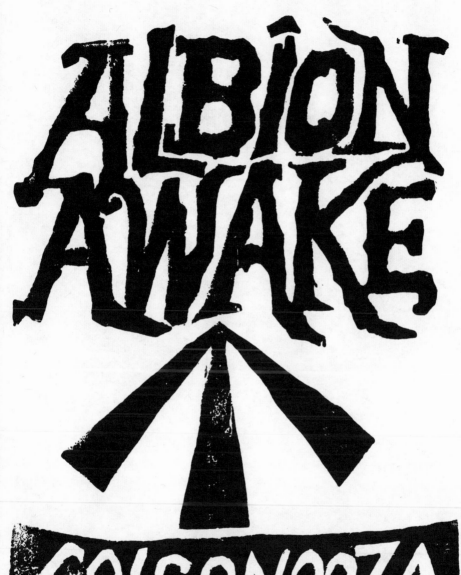

Jared Carter

The Man Who Taught Blake Painting in His Dreams

Is still around somewhere . . . survived the smoke
And fires, the footsteps melting into stone,
The city dark within its haze of time;
Endured, somehow, that face both epicene
And bold with innocence, though now withdrawn,
Diminished, paled like some further star
To sit behind a stall near London Bridge;
Yet lasted, since for painting lessons Blake
In turn taught him to sing, and in those dreams
They labored over angels, burning tigers,
Bade their host prophetic spears cast down
And joyously to praise the Lamb—
                      and found
Themselves, still dreaming, charmed outside their dream.
Blake sailed away, for on each cobblestone
Or casement glimmered visions of that realm,
And madly through the streets he danced and sang;
The man who taught him painting in his dreams
Was left alone.
                Around him coiled the smoke
He watches through today, from park bench, pub,
Or moving 'bus: listening for that strain
Alone empowered to dream him back again.

Great & Marvellous are thy Works
Lord God Almighty

Just & True are thy Ways
O thou King of Saints

So the Lord blessed the latter end of Job
more than the beginning

After this Job lived
an hundred & forty years
& saw his Sons & his
Sons Sons

even four Generations
So Job died
being old
& full of days

In burnt Offerings for Sin
thou hast had no Pleasure

W Blake inv & sculp

London Published as the Act directs March 8 1825 by William Blake Fountain Court Strand

Roger Keyes

Seeing from Within: Sharing Blake's Vision

We can know a person like Blake from the outside or from the inside. From the outside we can establish the chronology of his work, the patterns of his life, identify the things that interested him, and reflect on all of this from our own experience. When we do this, however, we are far from knowing Blake as he knew himself. We are far from understanding the necessity of each of his works and from understanding why we are moved by his work; we are far from appreciating his true greatness. This article is an attempt to bridge these gaps in our understanding, and make it possible for us to enter into the imaginative world of Blake and other great artists more easily.

When our attention is focused, we automatically enter into a state of awareness in which we lose the ordinary sense of separation we feel between ourselves and the rest of the world. Since we have only one mind and one body, we begin, when we enter this identifying state, to experience thoughts, feelings, and sensations as our own, that actually belong to other people. Unless we are aware that these identifying states are not only possible but common and normal, we are apt to be confused by many of our changes of thought and moods. And even as we become aware that we identify with other people, it is often difficult at first to distinguish between their thoughts and our own. Increased consciousness of this overlap can make it easier for us to make these crucial distinctions.

In the identifying state there is a release or transfer of energy. Since we normally enter the state briefly, we commonly experience this phenomenon as a short-lived excitement. But if we can maintain a focused contact with the object and stabilize our attention, a variety of mental events ranging from information-transfer to mystical experiences will spontaneously arise in this state of mind. To illustrate what I mean by these broad statements, I would like to describe a few of my own experiences with a single engraving by William Blake: "And so the Lord blessed the latter end of Job more than the beginning."

This is the last picture in a series of *Illustrations of the Book of Job* that Blake engraved between 1823 and 1825; he was in his late sixties then. The engravings were based on a series of watercolors that Blake made for his young friend John Linnell in 1821; these, in turn, were copies of another set of twenty watercolors Blake painted for his patron Thomas Butts sometime earlier. The dating of this first set is still a matter of some controversy.

When I looked at an impression of this engraving recently, I experienced a great feeling of excitement which I was not able to explain satisfactorily. The particular impression I looked at was very fine, and my eye was certainly attracted to the brilliant contrast of the black ink and the white paper, but when I looked at the picture closely, I found that I was dissatisfied. Compared with engravers I admire, like Dürer and Goltzius, Blake did not draw very well, nor did he approach their mastery of the technique of engraving; I did not find the design of the plate particularly beautiful or striking. And yet, momentarily, the picture had seemed alive, and in spite of my reservations, I was still attracted to the print.

I looked more closely at the picture and began to notice the variety of different textures that Blake had created with his burin. As I became absorbed in these patterns of lines and dots, I forgot my previous criticism of Blake's technique; but before long I began to feel a new and uncomfortable sense of effort and confinement. This surprised me, because I had never felt these sensations when I looked at engravings by other artists, and I wondered if this might be a reflection of Blake's experience. Several weeks later I found some confirmation of this in a letter wherein Blake spoke of his struggles: "I curse & bless Engraving alternately because it takes so much time & is so untractable, tho' capable of such beauty & perfection." Still, my initial excitement and my continued attraction to the print remained unexplained.

So I returned to the engraving. This time my attention was drawn to the figures of Job, his wife and daughter at the center of the print. As I became absorbed in looking at the figures I once again forgot my earlier criticism of Blake's figure drawing, and noticed instead a calm radiance that seemed to shine through the figures, almost as though there were a light behind the print. Wondering if this, too, might reflect some personal quality of Blake, I turned to his biography and learned that during this period, at the end of his life, Blake was indeed calm, and even radiant. I was interested to read, however, that in his early fifties Blake had shown a completely different temperament: vain, irritable, righteous, angry and indignant. He was also ambitious, and in 1809 mounted an exhibition of his watercolor paintings in a desperate effort to force the public to recognize his greatness. The exhibition was a total failure, and in 1810 Blake withdrew from public life until the late 1810s when John Linnell met him and began to introduce him to his friends.

As I read, I thought about Blake's longing for public recognition and success, and the bitter disappointment he must have felt when his exhibition failed. How like Job Blake was, I thought, misunderstood and suffering; and

I suddenly wondered if Blake began to identify himself with Job after the failure of the exhibition, as he had apparently identified himself with the poet Milton until then. And if Blake had done this, had begun to heal and transform himself through a meditation on the Book of Job after the failure of the exhibition, could he have painted the first set of watercolors in 1810?

Most recent scholars date the Job watercolors before the exhibition, because some are signed with a monogram that Blake largely abandoned around 1806. But one painting with the same monogram is dated 1810, and there is a record that Thomas Butts paid Blake £21 for unspecified work in 1810. Butts owned the first set of Job watercolors; he usually paid Blake 21 shillings per painting; and as there were twenty watercolors in the Job set, it seems quite likely that Blake did paint them in 1810.

I have described two experiences in which sensations received in a state of focused attention led to information about Blake that I had not and could not have known previously, and which I was able to confirm from Blake's biography and writings. The second experience led to a chain of inquiry in which I learned something about the importance of the earliest Job set to Blake, and was able to suggest a plausible date for the first watercolor set. I would now like to describe two experiences of focused attention in which information appeared which cannot be confirmed with written documents, but which led in each case to plausible insights.

The first occurred after I had read about the failure of Blake's exhibition and wondered how he may have actually felt at that time. When I reached a state of focused attention, the image of the engraving disappeared and in my mind's eye I saw Blake standing before an angel who had a sword in hand. The angel approached Blake, lowered its sword, and pierced him. In great anguish, his soul separated from his body and drifted among large, frightening creatures through darkness until it reached a cliff overlooking a barren red plain with a ruined city, and the vision ended. I was an observer and a companion through all this, but I also felt desolation, pain, and grief. The strongest feeling, however, was the pain of separation. This is not a feeling that I experience myself, but I could see it operating like a leitmotif throughout the whole of Blake's life: the lonely child who saw angels; the lonely, unacknowledged genius visited by spiritual companions. Pride was the antidote to the pain of separation: the belief of being better than the rest, that increased the separation. In his drawings, all the figures are separate, even when they touch or overlap, each bounded by a distinct outline. Blake even wrote of the importance of the separating outline in the catalogue for his exhibition. Although he felt the pain of separation, he clung to it. He yearned for union, but refused to relinquish his precious consciousness of self. What kind of union was possible for a person so committed to separation?

In the experiences recounted already my attention was focused on the surface of the print. On one occasion, however, while my eyes rested on the surface of the picture, I withdrew my attention to a point within my head. As I did this, I immediately felt a strong physical sensation almost like flooding in the lower part of my torso which grew stronger as I kept my attention focused and let my eyes continue to rest upon the print. As the sensation grew stronger, I began to feel physically uncomfortable until suddenly a wave seemed to leap up from my torso and turn into excited thoughts inside my head. One of these thoughts was that Blake finally realized that he was in a state of constant communion with all people and objects around him, as he was with artists of the past through their work; that he suffered, as we all do, from an illusion of separation. And that the basis for the communion was the energetic exchange that occurs in the state of focused attention. These are my words, of course, because my experience of Blake and my expression of it is necessarily refracted through the lens of my own vision and experiences.

Another thought was that Blake's contemporaries disliked his work precisely because they felt this energetic presence, whether they were consciously aware of it or not. It made them uncomfortable, and they explained their discomfort, as I had earlier, by criticizing Blake's skill as a draftsman and engraver. We value the enormous energy in Blake's work, but we are just as apt to refer it to the surface and credit Blake with being a better engraver, draftsman or poet than he actually was. Another thought was that in one sense the surface of a picture is simply a magnet to attract our attention and a focusing device to put us in relation to the absent maker of the work. When we realize how much more deeply we are affected by the unseen maker than by the surface, I think we will need to change our sense of what is beautiful in works of art.

When we are absorbed in the rich surfaces of works of art, information, insight, and other increments of awareness spontaneously flow between ourselves and another. I believe that this merging is a common, everyday experience, particularly in personal relationships and in professional life among scholars and creative artists. Most of us are not usually aware of this identifying state, however. The simple reason is that in the identifying state we experience the thoughts, feelings, and even the essential energetic quality of the other person as our own. I know from my own experience that it is often difficult to distinguish our thoughts, emotions, associations, imagination and projections from those of others. But I also know that with practice and attention it is possible.

Blake wrote of a marriage between heaven and hell. When we are able to celebrate the marriage of intuition and intellect we will witness the birth of a new, larger, and clearer understanding of the human spirit. Artists and writers of all nationalities have a particular contribution to make to this new understanding. Each of us can assist at this birth by speaking out with courage, discrimination and insight from the fullness of our own experience.

CODA: Ortega y Gasset, the Spanish philosopher, wrote that the Renaissance was a period of great simplification; that intellectual life had become so complex that most subjects were beyond the reach of even intelligent people, so more and more prople turned to the actual world around them and the things they could experience directly with their senses; that physical science was born out of the delighted play of the intellect with the direct experience of the senses.

But nothing was settled, and now life seems just as incomprehensible as ever, and even more complicated. So once again, people are beginning to turn back again, and ask what do we really know from our own experience; what sense can we make of all this?

But the "all this" now includes the entire range of our emotional, mental and spiritual life, as well as our physical experience; the exploration of the inner as well as the outer world; and the discovery that the two are not entirely separate.

And what exuberance and excitement begins to fill the air now as we find satisfaction, depth and insight in our own experience; as we see that anything we learn is useful to others; as we watch the old traditions come to life again.

A vision of the whole truth is beyond any one of us singly, but I really believe that each of us holds an aspect of the truth, like a facet of a crystal, and that groups of us can form, sustain, and share a common vision.

I see groups gathering now, and discovering their common purpose like streams gathering into rivers. I see people of very different walks of life serving one another: poets and scientists, farmers, prisoners, and businessmen. I see bonds formed that transcend time and physical distance, like links between generations.

I see us all converging on a new public understanding that will make it easier to cherish ourselves, and respect one another, and preserve the continuity of human life on this planet.

Rouze up O Young man of the New Age! set your foreheads against the ignorant Hirelings! For We have Hirelings in the Camp, the Court & the University: who would if they could, for ever depress Mental & Prolong Corporeal War.

From Milton: A Poem

William Blake dreams of Job in Prosperity while guarded by the spirit of his dead brother Robert.

S. Foster Damon

Blake's Tarot Deck

The correspondence of the Job engravings to the Tarot Cards is too striking to be ignored. Court de Gebelin in 1781 (*Monde Primitif*, viii.) had announced that these cards, introduced into Europe centuries before by the gypsies, and used everywhere for games and fortune-telling, were really a book written by the ancient Egyptians to explain through symbols 'the entire universe and various states to which the life of man is subject' (p. 367). This book, he asserted, was highly systematized, being based on the sacred number 7. But Gebelin's explanations of the individual cards were superficial, and his system involved considerable rearrangement; Etteilla, a later student of the cards in the eighteenth century, also missed the system in the normal order. Since their day, and Blake's, a vast literature has grown up around the Tarot, a thorough knowledge of which is considered essential to any understanding of Kabalistic philosophy. Its origin is no longer thought to be Egyptian but Hebraic, for its relations to the Hebrew alphabet and the *Sepher Yetzirah* are obvious.

In these few pages it would be impossible to explain the system of the Tarot, a subject which already has filled volumes. We can only give Blake's interpretation of the cards, trusting Tarot students to see for themselves where Blake has penetrated the traditional meanings, and where he has abandoned it in favour of his own system. His order, however, is the normal order. For the general reader it should be sufficient to state that, as usual, Blake accepted only as much as he saw fit, and often inverted meanings in his paradoxical way, calling some things bad which seem good, and *vice versa*.

0. *The Fool*, in both systems, represents the descent of the Uncreated.

1. *The Magician* is the hero at the beginning of the great story.

2. *The High Priestess* ('la Papesse'), holding the book of the Torah (law), represents to Blake the evil of moral law in the spiritual world. The prominence of the books in Job's heaven are the key to this plate.

3. *The Empress* signifies the descent of moral law from the spiritual to the material plane; Blake shows us the result of this in the destruction of Job's children.

4. *The Emperor* symbolizes Job, the tyrant on the material plane.

5. *The Hierophant* ('le Pape') symbolizes Job's God, the tyrant on the spiritual plane.

6. *The Lovers* is almost unchanged in Blake's plate, except that he substitutes Satan with his arrows for the armed Cupid. (An archangel replaces Cupid in Mr. Waite's modernized version of the Tarot.)

7. *The Chariot* drawn by the sphinxes of Good and Evil is represented by the arrival of Job's friends.

8. *Strength* (in the old cards) is symbolized by a woman who opens a lion's mouth. 'After this opened Job his mouth and cursed his day.'

9. *The Hermit* wandering at night in the snow is paralleled by Eliphaz in the Forest of Error.

10. *The Wheel of Fortune* is demonstrated by the mockery of Job's friends.

11. *Justice:* Job beholds the God of Justice.

12. *The Hanged Man* (the 'Crucifixion Upside Down') is surely what Job sees, as his eyes are now being opened.

13. *Death* is represented by Blake as the mystical whirlwind, which is the Death of the Selfhood. The thirteenth plate of *The Gates of Paradise* is also a mystical vision connected with Death.

14. *Temperance* in the Tarot appears as an angel transferring the contents of a cup in the left hand to a cup in the right hand: the symbolic significance is Transmutation. Blake interprets it as the New Birth in the vision of the Morning Stars.

15. *The Devil,* according to Tarot doctrine, is the apparent evil of generation. Blake's plate represents the Creator explaining the material world.

16. *The Tower* is almost exactly Blake's Last Judgment—the casting out of error.

17. *The Star* pours out its influences: Job sits in mystical contemplation.

18. *The Moon* draws lower animals upward; so Job is drawn upward by prayer.

19. *The Sun* is apparently not paralleled at all, unless we say that Job is now basking in the rays of his neighbours' love.

20. *Judgment* (really the Resurrection) is according to Blake a contrast with 16, which was a casting out of Error: this is a second Judgment, being the appraisal of the True by means of art. Job's three daughters are revived; the Tarot trump (in the old cards) shows the resurrection of three people.

21. *The World* (or rather, the Universe) represents in both series the final, complete attainment.

Thus it was that Blake revised according to his own doctrines the 'Book of Thoth,' in his day considered the oldest book in existence. His ingenuity in following the Tarot, card by card, yet not swerving from his own system of the Seven Eyes of God, is astonishing. The Tarot has been called a mirror for each mind; we may wait long before another interpretation equally admirable is given to the world.

from *William Blake: His Philosophy and Symbols* (1924)

George Quasha

Parapoetic Seeds Shaken From The Blake Tree

(for Jim Bogan & Fred Goss)

The order of statements eludes the speaker.
He tells in order to read.
Ideas of order appear in quarreling pairs, zeugmaic.

•

What is this, is it a picture, is it a poem, is it the mind stretched out
across the world?
Questions beneath the surface of every page.

•

In my reverie he connected with me: William wanted a window,
and the window gave way to the thought:
Any way out is a way to wake
on the other side of want.
Wh wh, the wind with the glass.

•

Neither organic nor inevitable.
Infamously interchangeable, the parts con-
fuse. Anything is anywhere.
That whatever it is it appears
where it is is the mystery of manifestation.
Something, when I hadn't asked.
Nothing, when I wanted something.

•

Why is there something instead of

•

I demolish the sense in order to change.
Such is the nature of the materia in which I grave.

•

The future edits.
Deletion [in] [of]
orders[s]
[to] bring[s] forth.
Reading is probable.

•

His sentences do not parse easily.
It joy'd: [*America* 2:4]

•

There is a high probability that the poet is indifferent to the kinds of order
that make his poem intelligible to you.

•

Where is the where it leaves me?
Putting pen to paper he found himself in Greechie Space
where no points obtain.

•

August augury authors
augmented augury.
Reader is auxete.

•

As Bromion rends Oothoon and Orc, Enitharmon,
Blake rent art. It joy'd.

Reader pierces and pieces
herself together.

•

The time of the poem is not irreversible.
The future is written and the past is open
to revision.

Making it, breaking it, embodying
inside it, and taking the lid off
in any order
and at once.

Reading happens in the Moment in each Day   [*Milton* 35:42]
that Satan cannot find.

Two souls in one breast, two dark nights
for any soul, two Night VIIs
for one poem: I cannot make it cohere.
No blame. Not merely tragic.
It is more than I can handle, favoring the right hand,
right writing, righteous pursuit of the code
with only one mind. It co-
heres in-
comprehensibly.

His person changes
hands.

Read and be duped.
Reflex the book back to its author de-
structed one & all, once & for all, one in all, wall-
less: what page was it I was trying to read?
The words are not on paper.
Look in the Rough Basement, between house & [en-]
grave, store of the interconscious.
The rules of the game change
tongues with the person.

The Circumference is Within   [*Jerusalem* 71:7]
and the form of the poem is internal
to the choices it makes probable.
The Reader journeys in to reach out along the edges
carrying the sun in his hand. Bright book.

He wrote himself out across a plate.
Thought sought its density in copper and
languageness.

Interpreting a poetic datum is like roping a wild horse,
every catch disperses the herd.

Every reading a new periphery.
Circumtextuality: walk through and the language forms round.

●

The poem alters
in your hands.

●

The fibers of speech are interconscious with the world.
Wordscape.

When the word escapes back
into the world there is unconsciousness.

●

Change is laborious (copper resists)
[brackets the text] to a fault
in the circumtext.
                    The fall
is not
but happens only.

●

Wor[l]d
              [The Editor]
●

Bios blisters, breaks, bleeds, blends back
into mind.

Weaving, unweaving, Penelope,
the text unwrites its facts
at the instant of becoming precedent.

●

Every thought is (ex-tension)
mind-degradable.

●

Vortext
(the before-word rises from the torsion of the text)

●

Nothing is back there.

•

Try and follow
the narrative
subverts

•

You	It	You
fall	only	catch
through	seems	your
the	to catch	self
text.	you.	or not.

•

Where do all these voices speak and to what purpose?
Between. To learn the will of reflexive reading.
Intertaxis. Converse aboard the ship DiaLogos.
Life in the interverse. Writing interverse. Zeugma.
That we can speak of it at all is paraversal.
When all the selves inside the self are heard
composing in paraverse
lifestory skips a beat &
it joys

Stanley Lombardo

Distant Funeral

I

Twelve floors up the wind hummed
Against the dark panes of the Mariott.
A great-grandfather's death
Was just lighting the sky's rim.

At breakfast the moon was setting
Near the hotel, preternaturally large
Even in the early blueing sky.

Walking back a jingle began

> Pop is dead
> His sculpted head
> And great hands rest
> In Greenwood now

And subsided as the sun rose in wind.

II

Zazen in the hotel room for a funeral:

Black cushion on the black mat
One bow, body into an iron wall
With breath beating against it

> And against the miles of coal he stoked
> On the railroads that ran through my imagination
> The huge goblets of cold wine on Sundays
> The gravel of his voice, stories
> Like cannons under southern flowers
> His dog Mike, the wagon he named Red Devil
> And the pillar of his shoulder

On sleepy rides back from the country
Along the river road

One clap, then in a low voice
The Dharani of Great Compassion
To Avalokiteshvara, to the Blue-necked One,
And the Heart Sutra, until

No old age and death
And also no extinction of them

    And Pop with the blue veins
    On his ironwrought hands
    And the black rosary around his neck
    Breathing hard against the hospital gown

Gone, gone
Gone beyond
Gone completely beyond

Chanted in the half-light that now filled the room.

III

He was the giant in the house
His tools in the dark shed had forged the world
And it was his hand which in our childhood dreams
Saved us from the grinding jaws of the machine.

The small altar in the bedroom removed,
The house will disappear now into the facade of the street.
His voice would crack with indignation a moment
But we need only remember

When he tamped the earth it trembled,
When he silvered the spikes on the iron fence
And the lion-head on the gate
We gleamed with pride.

John Nelson

A Pilgrimage

In mid-November of 1978, I left Hokkaido, Japan, en route for the United States, where numerous obligations had grown during the two and a half years I'd been away teaching. Japan had given an incredible wealth of experiences, all of which deepened my engagement to learning what Forces I'm a part of. Years earlier, Blake had pointed the way, and though his cosmology often overwhelmed me I'd trusted the clarity of his Vision as one of my guides. It was only right, then, that I should "happen" to have him in my pack when I walked through the Annapurna region of the Himalayas—a journey to visit the mythological birthplace of the Hindu god Vishnu and to witness cultures and mountains unlike anywhere else on earth. The ordering of my entire trip (west from Japan), its possibilities, even of my expectations for discovery had been set down nearly a century and a half ago by the owl-eyed man himself, and reminds us all of where it is we *truly* are:

> Thus is the Earth a Vortex not yet passed
> By the traveller through Eternity.

1-28
AWAKE, AWAKE!   Jump from dreams back to Pokhara, Nepal
                 & answer strong psychic summons from immense

PRESENCES
              of *this* world   (O, the rain clouds are gone!
Machapuchere seen first, then entire north horizon line,
                            jagged at 22,000'

     Gods
              Annapurna, Lamjung, Dauligiri, Machapuchare
     compel
           jet stream to break
                            here

the white clouds rolling,

first golden rays

on ancient, snowy peaks

*

Walk to the opposite shore of Lake Phewa for a better view & there find recently graduated priests from an Osaka Zendo staying in a high-class inn —heads freshly shaved for the trip they tell me. All bow slow when saying "good morning," all snap a thousand pictures of the spectacle northward— one older priest rubs his chilly pate while standing transfixed, says over and over "sugoiiii/increeedible!" They'll go no closer than this.

> (Jo-josha, upon being overwhelmed by Rinzai's understanding & receiving two blows because of it, stood silent, unmoving, until another monk said, "Why don't you *bow*, Jo-josha?" He did, and reached sudden enlightenment.)

1-30

Four and a half hours on the mainline, Pokhare to Muktinath, has led to a small stone room at a ridgetop inn; its gifts include an impeccable view of the entire Annapurna Himal, the terraced slopes of the valley I walked today, & a wildly blooming apricot tree as well! I need only cross the village's single street to see the other side of the ridge, back to the Lake, & with imagination to the very table I had dinner on last night. But between here & there, how many centuries have I walked through today? How many are woven into the stones & twists of this old silk route to Tibet & deeper China? How many pilgrims' feet have taken them this way to Vishnu's shrine at Muktinath? An old clock strikes six but that's not the answer—it's somewhere among the Tibetan refugee settlements, among the 87 levels of stone-wall terraces like steps up a mountain, among the tea stalls and mud-wattle huts of Nepali Hindus sitting quietly in brilliant sun, minds intent on some small task (breaking rocks, sewing, picking nits, gambling) not distorted by hurry or obligations. I wanted to squat down beside them but was obsessed with reaching Naudanda by this eve & couldn't do as my aching limbs wanted; instead, leaned up very steep slopes for over an hour, wondering if I *really* needed the lump of cheese, the jar of honey, the little Blake book of V.S. Avinash's favorite quotes, bought in Varanassi expressly for this climb. At first I questioned whether some old professor emeritus knew what to include, but upon cracking the frayed cover I heard numerous Songs, saw the rocky shores of *Visions*, and felt the universe-rumblings of *Milton, Zoas*, and *Jerusalem*. Somehow I'd been led past the sleeping cattle, funeral pyres, curio/pharmacy/hardware stores to find this dusty copy

(1941) waiting for me in a used-book store . . . a gift, wrapped in the colors of the Hindu's holy city on the Ganges, for me to lug up mountains in hopes Blake's clarity might increase my own. Mostly though, I wonder about beyond the beyond—the 58 miles to go. "This time does not come again," so may I truly *see* it, please?

*

Namaste. Do you have a room? "Yes, you have a room."
Well, may I see it please? "Okay. I may see it, please."

*

Night piss necessary, leave warm sleeping bag
& suddenly galaxies on my head, their roar
echoing up from a dark river far below.

*

1-31
Wake to far-off bells of donkey trains as they come up the valley side, bells strangely resonant with the reverberations of Japan temples calling the neighborhood to prayers. Thru screened window I see Machapuchare's pre-dawn grey & am warmed enough by the view to go outside & bow: this the way to start each morning. Sun climbs higher, upper realms of Annapurna glow pink, even clearer the sharp rocks and icy folds of distant ice falls. I wonder what those Osaka priests are doing right now? Saying sutras? Meditating? Will any of them sneak away from the group & give an irreverent bow to these mountains? Would the Buddha really mind that much?

*

Immediately outside Naudanda the mountains vanish as trail stays on the south side of the ridge. They don't reappear until 4 hours later, at Chandarkot on cliff-edge, where a sharp twist in the trail suddenly imposes their energy again. Much closer now, my vision stripped of the slumber of distance; I remember reading last night of the sky being "an immortal tent." How perfect, then, these mountains as the support "poles."

2-1
Goodbye January: month of revelations, of Thailand, of Burma's Sri Dagon pagoda & Mandalay markets, of India's suffering & enlightenment & illness

389

& rebirth—goodbye main trail (for a couple days) as I go towards Annapurna sanctuary base camp to reach Ghandrung village. The day clouds over & wind picks up, casting a gauzy veil over the surrounding peaks. This lets me focus on the village itself—an exhausting effort to even imagine the decades of carrying, shaping, heaving, placing stones into houses (some two-story), walls, pathways, fences, terraces. Boys play soccer in a small front yard, women wash clothes in freezing water from upper mountain runoff, black cattle wander narrow lanes, the men conspicuously absent during the afternoon (drinking tea at the local shop)—and above the village, on a long bamboo pole swaying slightly in the wind, the head of a bear.

(The people used to live in harmony with the Yeti, who would help with stone lifting & wood gathering—but they were ridiculed once by some drunken men & went up into the mountains & deep folds of valleys, never to return, except to kill livestock & terrify villages. But the older, original demons have always been a problem.)

After a fine dinner of curry, rice & cornbread (ah, that honey!) the owner of the lodge comes and asks questions in a painful, slow English about China/U.S. relations, Russia, about who "leads the world now." He says elections are outlawed in Nepal with the King in total control—also, a murder & robbery in Naudanda a few months back still bother him, "first thing like this to ever happen."
Then he hauls out a recent Time magazine, picked out of the trash in Pokhara, and asks about a color photo of a huge volcano on Mars. After much explaining he says, "Yes, I understand. It is not on earth but not a star either—it is between lands." His wife, a small young woman with a string of red coral (found in Himalayan stream!) round her neck, also wants to know about the picture but he shoos her away. "Even if I tell her, she absolutely *not* believe it."

2-3

Thanti Deorali, over & over a song in my head this name of the 9500' pass I spent seven hours *approaching*. Up one ridge & down its backside, over & over, thru moss-cloaked alder forests, across slippery stream rock crossings, once scared shitless by a band of langurs—only later did I appreciate their black faces surrounded by lovely silver/grey manes—so glad they weren't the bears I expected. Came upon one broken-down shack just before entering snow (wondering what hermit made this his home) then followed a little stream until it froze over. I'd heard from the owner of the inn at Ghandrung there was a frozen waterfall on this trail ("with my own eyes seen five summer ago!") believed haunted by Sherpa porters. They refused to go this way no matter how much expeditions begged or bribed them. A good story I thought at the time, but the little frozen stream put me in mind of the possibility again. When I eventually rounded that sudden, magic corner and found the falls deep in mid-day shadow, I was still dumbfounded in spite of my expectations. Perhaps 20' high and a pale pale blue, the trail led to its base then vanished, leaving no choice but to clamber up a rock wall out of the shadows and silent chill. Once on top, gasping, I realized I'd held my breath for the longest time, trying to eavesdrop on the secret shared by the objects in this place. Writing this now near the warmth of a fire, surrounded by several German fellows & a Nepali official, it seems too easy to say there was a mystery, but I *did* feel watched & because of that, walked away fast. Who can tell what this world is capable of?

2-5

2,000' of stone face before me; behind, a waterfall flanked by tall green pines—mist slips thru the air, vanishes on greywhite granite above Ghasa-town. I forget the two hours of walking time still available, disregard an old map saying "don't stay here," and settle for the delights in a musical rock basin: cow & donkey bells, the distant song of the Kali Gandaki river, this waterfall the soprano full of spattering harmonics. Near by, in a little cave built under the roots of an oak (or, more likely, the tree has grown its 200 years on top) is a shrine with three stones, three ochre circles painted on each one. It's not difficult to recognize this homage to the god possibly living in this place—a local manifestation of those Powers behind the stars. If crops are to grow, wives to bear children & demons to be subdued, you've got to take care of those spirits wandering about & guide them your way. It's no different whether Japan, Thailand, Burma or Taiwan—pure Belief is what makes these shrines. This one seems Hindu since I know Vishnu's color is the same shade as on the stones—still, I wonder if it is strictly so—perhaps a forgotten holy place of older beliefs instead? At least I know this much: to walk once around & bow . . . glasses speckled with fine mist.

*

Evening balcony views:
    Spotted cow drags bad leg home,
                udder brushing the ground,
    What happens in that head
              besides meat?

*

Chickens fight over, then

gobble up
                    my balcony spit.
        Oh Asia! Don't you love me?

                            *

To move black yaks from Muktinath to Pokhara
get yourself a strong bamboo staff,
& with authority learn to shout . . . . . "Oi!!!"

                            *

With this rock basin as echo walls, kids here yell
a lot, relishing the sound of it coming back. A 4 year
old makes blood-curdling jungle howls to his friend
in a field, early evening. Keep those demons at bay . . .

                            *

Several pack trains of tough donkeys come through, a tall shaggy plume on
the leader's harness with a round mirror in its center. The plumes I can
figure out but that mirror is a mystery (as they all are), recalling the mirror
at the center of Shinto altars—reflecting the heavens wherein the gods
dwell? But they're here too, in the tired & lined face of the Tibetan
packmaster, in the little shrine by the waterfall, in the forests & frozen
crevices of the upper Himal where I'll be in a few days (if they allow). The
sentence ends with the last donkey lumbering by, headed, no doubt, for the
outskirts of town; a place to make camp, heat up the black-bottomed pans
for cooking tsampa mush, tell companions what's been in mind all day.
Something strikes me as being "wild west" about those hitching-post
campsites I've seen here & in earlier villages—the sound of a harmonica,
smell of strong coffee or cigarettes wouldn't surprise me at all.
        "Howdy, partner! And an 'Om Mani Padme Hum'
        to you too! Headed Muktinath way?"

2-6
Leaving this morning down a steep trail, I was suddenly shocked by lower
Ghasa village (a different caste perhaps?)—charred ceiling beams, broken
stone walls, a bad & mysterious fire a week earlier I'm told. Though Blake
says "pity divides the human soul," I felt it deeply for these folks who've lost
so much: homes, wood piles, icons, food supplies. Men swing sledges
against black rocks, cattle stand where kitchens used to be, not a single child
anywhere. One look from an old woman says it all—"life pours down in

cataracts." At the edge of this sad Ulro a green sign welcomes me to the kingdom of Mustang; painted flowers round its edges.

*

Tea time above a gorge, seven miles this morning. There must have been some kind of bad magic still lingering in the burned-out village because my mind fragmented on the trail soon after. Old spectres of U.S. cities, decadence, pleasures, DISTRACTIONS rise up and beckon me to walk over their cliffs. Then it's old AM radio songs, women, Japan travels, the retarded child in Ghandrung, a hot plate of tempura & rice all pushing & shoving like a bunch of ruffians. I said "Enough! Or too much!" & dug out Blake so as to memorize a poem, thus staving off madness. Found "The Fly" immediately & used its cadence to pace myself, one beat for each step ("...Am not I / a fly like thee? / Or art thou not / a man like me?") drawing closer to Tibet. But really—what would these mountains have visioned him to write? What would the great shrines of Izumo or Daisen, the coasts of Hokkaido, or the jungles of Thailand have done in place of London & Lambeth? Is't conceivable?

*

Presto! A field of blooming mustard flowers beside a waterfall! Too precious to walk by—off the pack & into a grassy spot for refreshment. In the moony vales of Har there must surely be a corner just like this.

*

Cross the bridge by falls, round a corner & come face to face with one of the steepest climbs yet—almost straight up a rockwall via millions of switch-backs. It's the river that caused it, tumbling with a great roar through this canyon's narow straits. I recall now the shopkeeper in Ghasa telling me the trail ahead is "for men"—though his pretty wife stood beside him with a basket full of wood on her back.

I dredge up the image of that woman to comfort me while climbing & perhaps because of her am suddenly surprised on a tight corner by a stumbling donkey train. Somehow I ended up on the outside rim, praying all the animals stay precisely in line—another two feet & it'd be India before they ever found me—the river is Kali's, Goddess of Death, and its rapids eat all sound. The water comes so fast through here & with such volume the very walls themselves seem to be vibrating, alive, sheer rock turned to soundboard. No place for a body to hide.

2-6

Who understands this? Cross a thin-cable bridge & go up 10 or 12 switch-backs to find, suddenly, a great river plain stretching far away from the eye. It's the most space seen since leaving India's flatlands & it wants to swallow me . . .

A few huts stood beside this mile wide rock lake, doors locked, windows boarded over, not even a turd in their corrals. Farther along was a shabby tea stall in a pine-bark hut; behind it the forest climbed high on rockwalls, jumped up to ledges to deposit a few pines, eventually reached snow. These shelters and a piercing grey wind made the last hour of trekking quite eerie — perfect places for bandits and soul starved demons to attack hapless pilgrims. One long stretch into Larjung was the worst: while picking a path through loose round stones & sand drifts, ankles straining not to yield, sharp blasts of wind came sweeping across the valley. My only protection was to hold prayer shawl to face & double over when they hit — Asian relatives of Kansas dust devils. If I was a native I'd fear for my spirit when these things approach — truly, there was a low moan.

And the backdrop for this dust-blown drama? A giant mass of looming stone: 23,000' Dauligiri/veiled Sun on its rim.

*

I had hopes for Larjung (maybe some tea & a place to stay) but it too turned ghostly, run-down, the people hiding somewhere. But I did see a major difference: a two-tier temple sat on a high spot in the middle of the village, gold sphere on top it all where Buddha's land begins!

I didn't stop to investigate — kept walking on the trail which now ran *under* houses — yet still felt considerable power in this place shadowed by such an immense mountain, Tibetan culture starting here. Did Nepali & Indian influences "end" at the rock straits above Ghasa? Did all the garbage in my head also have to emerge & be cast off into the river before entering this upper stage of the journey? If so, then say a quick prayer to a trusty scoopshovel "Om", the mantra of locomotion through the dung heaps of my life.

2-7

Marpha reached today in mid-afternoon just as a low ceiling of clouds descends. When I climbed the slope behind the village (whose main street so charmed me with its whitewashed walls, tight alleys, & aqueducts) I found crumbling ruins of a much older settlement; an excellent vantage to peer into the courtyard of a red-walled gompa just below. Not much happening — only white prayer flags, spouting from every rooftop, fluttered madly in the wind.

394

Within an hour the snowstorm I saw moving sheet-like down
the valley
                falls
                                democratically
            upon every house's wood pile,
            every farmer's rocky field,
                      upon
            three little pups,
                      heads stove in,
    back alley garbage

                              *

My dinner of curry & rice digesting, sit back a few moments when a steady
stream of visitors begin coming to the hearth fire; eleven men in all, each
face's lines & furrows illuminated by fire glow. There is an old Tibetan with
high turban (finishes his rakushi/wine & splits, belching), a silent young
man of very intense eyes, a loudmouth with little rat moustache, a cowherd
missing his entire lower lip, and ganja-man, who sits huffing & puffing on a
chillum the whole time—everyone arguing, drinking, telling stories about
the snow, discussing the minute particulars of their worlds at day's end. The
volume of voices almost conceals a distant conch-shell call, followed a few
minutes later by drums from the village gompa announcing a break in the
clouds & the rise of the full moon. No one lifts an eyebrow or cocks an ear to
the summons except me—out to the rooftop in a flash. Still a few minutes of
very cold shadow until a faint halo begins rising from the far valley ridge &
snowy Nilgiri-Himal turns into smooth glowing porcelain.

                              *

Would that the man in my book were with me now...("The head of an
Angel! O wondrous knowing Light!")...or that any of my distant friends
could share in this beauty. Instead, I let it stream in, absorbing as much of
these rare moments as my small mind allows, praising utter whitestone
ascending slow into starry sky.

2-8
Start slowly while there's light to see the page—legs warm in sleeping bag
under blankets the color of rainbows, upstairs in the Red House Inn,
Kagbeni, place out of dreams. That I walked the 15 miles here from Marpha
through ankle-deep snow (later mud), cursing the river rocks' unnegotiable
paths, fighting the canyon wind I've learned must be avoided at all costs—
all this serves to instruct in lessons of distance & hard-earned pleasures. This

is as far north as a foreigner can go—from Kagbeni onward a region of tension with the Chinese, although the locals move around freely. These land disputes are nothing new I'm sure, because the town itself is built like a fortress—high mud walls rise 30 feet straight up with only two entrances to the inner village's maze of streets. To the dark brown faces of the inhabitants, this is Home. But to this Traveller thro' Eternity it is utterly wondrous and ancient, again posing the question: how many centuries have I traveled in one day? Certain items help bridge the chasms between my sources and theirs—the transistor radio of a Nepali guard, a magnifying glass an old woman uses to sew, plastic buckets to haul water—but most of what I see is continuous with the traditions of a thousand years of Tibetan culture. Alive, alive-o.

*

The prayer flags here are all fairly new, likewise the temple in better shape than ones further down valley. I'm told the Red House used to be monastery living quarters but the monks eventually went to other temples. This the reason for the wall paintings of this dark & gloomy sleeping room; a smiling Buddha and some Chinese-type sages all riding silver clouds. Touch this mud wall & leave your time.

When I go out to the rooftop, after watching a young girl dance & sing in a high falsetto (cheered on by two drunk yak herders so gentle in their ways), the clouds are gone, Orion beams forth, & I hear Blake whispering how a man takes his heavens with him when he moves. Final blessings of the day go to a smoky alcohol-wick flame by which I discover that old Avinash included the very quote alive tonight in this place. Let me bring it in.

> Standing on his own roof, or in his garden on a mount
> Of twenty-five cubits in height, such space is his universe;
> And on its verge the sun rises & sets; the clouds bow
> To meet the flat earth & the sea in such an ordered space.
> The starry heavens reach no further, but here bend & set
> On all sides, & the two poles turn on their valves of gold,
> And if he move his dwelling-place, his heavens also move
> Where'er he goes, & all his neighbourhood bewail his loss.
> Such are the spaces called 'Earth', & such its dimension.

(Milton, Bk. 1)

Amen & Amen.

2-10

It's most important to be true to the moment—hands so stiff as to barely scrawl—just down from the cold mountain trail. Kagbeni again & lunch soon to come, this rooftop a carrot on a stick to help me keep moving through the drifts & rocks & voids, down, always down, knees whining the whole way. Two things:

*   Perfect Ghasa tangerine
                        surpasses, in earthly bliss,
          snow blowing silver
                       from an unnamed peak

*   To have been walking through the snow & space of the great Muktinath basin, somewhere the shrine of Vishnu ahead, all mountains over 17,000', and suddenly stop, choking off my gasps for air, was to be absorbed & enveloped by this incredible silence—deeper & more *intense* than any I've come upon. No matter which way I turned my head it still reached me; a distant, melodic ringing. I'd walk a few yards, stop, walk down a slope & stop again, but it embraced everything. And is this the music sustaining hermits and priests of the high temples in their fasts and meditations?

                        *

I fell into that expanse of silence again and again on the 9th, day of exceptional clarity & mountain panoramas while en route to Muktinath. Snow up to my knees most of the way, only one other set of footprints indicating the trail. There is a considerable difference between how far a place looks   and how long it actually takes to get there. Jarkot village, perched on a rise in upper glacier basin, does not gain size until I quit thinking about arriving (destination as obstacle—it's the journey that counts—*It* takes Me).

When I do stagger through the gates I find a weird place of crumbling walls and houses much older than Kagbeni. The highest structure in town is one decaying tower, formerly part of the main man's dwelling (where folks planned festivals, discussed grievances, had marriage feasts, maybe funerals too since no temple is here). Even though, practically speaking, this is Tibet, I'm beseiged with visions of Mohenjo Daro, Mesa Verde cliff-dwellers, Babylonian ruins, so resonant are the mud-walls with what I know.

My entertainment during lunch is a wild-haired old man repairing his boots, two women stretching a blanket they've just dyed, plus incredible clusters of peaks against a cobalt blue sky. I ask, "Muktinath?" and the old one shows with his fingers how far it is—a long inch. Even though I must use my "Om" snowplow to subdue the demons so anxious to arrive, the final two hours of the ascent is dazzling. After 62 miles of walking I wouldn't have it any other way—and could the mythological source of Vishnu's issuing into the world be any other way? "Eternity shines with its own internal light" I'm reminded—how else to hang words on a place of such rarified beauty?

>Snowy giants watch my effort,
>Brilliant sun fires me on.

*

Only one other set of footprints lead to the high temples, where all hums with the purity of altitude & atmosphere. For 2,000 years lowland Hindus have been making pilgrimages to stand where I now stand: before a two-story stupa flanked by four bathing pools. I follow the walkway, lay my seashell offering atop an old altar, bow and hear again the deep silence of holy places, ringing through all. A slow trickle of water flows through serpent head spouts into the bathing ghats, then begins a long fall to the Kali Gandaki where it falls further to the Ganges at Patna. I set my small heart adrift.

*

Flanking the Vishnu shrine are two Buddhist temples some 30 yards away—entrances guarded by a fantastic & grotesque array of saber-tooth demons, snakes, gargoyles, leering skulls. In the walls are numerous crannies, each with a blue prayer wheel, but the biggest damn prayer wheel I've ever seen is at one end of the entry. Seven circular layers of Om Mani Padme Hum on the cylinder, taller than I am (as all prayers must be)—I give it a spin and hear it groaning, rumbling on its axis, transmitting the Jewel in the Lotus to those in the world never able to even imagine the first facts of Buddhahood, the myriad souls seeing all things through "the narrow chinks of their caverns." May we all come back higher.

*

O, the not seen. The waiting chance. I knew the temples would be locked when I came here, but I returned a second time (after shouldering pack) and went round the corner *behind* the prayer wheel, finding there a stairway leading up to the roof.

Up four, turn left, then up seven to the sky—spin a small prayer wheel before exiting, quick glance & find that somehow, thru all the years, I must have done something right to win a skylight on the temple's roof—moment of greatest need. All I can see of the main altar are four lacquered Buddhas resting on white clouds, snakes and vajra-wands in their attendants' hands, a tiny spider walking its web from a snarling guardian to one single sun ray. The rest falls to darkness below.

*

To work so hard to see inside, peering from various corners, and then turn over and be flooded with range upon range of mountains (*this* high upon one planet, 12,500') is to be permanently altered, because from that instant onward the dimensions of my life must account for what was seen. I know it's my task to "live upon Earth until the time of my awakening," and would choose here, this temple shell, a tiny island in the Void, to integrate these Images with the Momentum they've yet to reveal.

*

Sing a song for this

short life,

an exception

among　　　　　　stars

*

My bed that night was two cushions in the dark house of a family of Tibetan farmers—took me in with big smiles as I gestured "sleep". Stayed too long at Muktinath & had to hurry through the shadows & drifts to find somewhere to stay, wondering the whole time what kind of demons the local folks believe come out at night. But I felt as if guided here, far end of the basin, by some beneficent magic—the Dali Lama would be treated no better. Already the events of today have set up homes in my head & heart, but so much more than simple images, fading with time. Permanence isn't the point (even though I'd like to keep this day always)—these are happenings which outgrow their planetary grids of here & now, resonating freely with future times & places & transforming *them*, inside out.

But already I'm being pulled downward, southward, east to Europe & America—distances inconceivable to my moon-faced hosts, all huddled around the cook-fire enjoying each move I make. I draw maps, pictures, show my charms and watch, then bow deep and full of gratitude before seeking out my sleeping bag. Little else remains to complete this cycle of wonder but to go outside at 5 a.m. and see a late moon above the gleaming white basin. Venus bright in the east sky soon swelling with dawn.

January 28 to February 13, 1979

Blake engraving pl. 14 of his set of engravings for the Book of Job, Catherine grinding paint. Their friend Samuel Palmer climbing the stairs and a chimney sweeper shouting "weep weep." 3 Fountain Court, 1827.

John Clarke

"New Light on Space & Time"

Osiris is not jealous of Horus his Avenger
hidden in the bush of Isis' distinguished
Contrary, the Negation of which has been
the norm since the Great Pan died, a total
failure of animus, thus consciousness (time
acting as a physical marker-off of space)
almost wholly non-existent now because
it takes so much 'death' even to maintain
in the face of the sleeping ego of People,
as Lily Tomlin said, "the trouble with the
rat race is that even if you win you're still
a rat," so all the talk of a new age coming
better allow for an inversion of psychological
values in those who will be at the stake of Bruno.

The True Vine

Jesus' radicalism was in his disconcern with high or low
levels of past performance as a yo-yo, his sword cut that
hanging judge situation, his point was to bring nothing more
than you to his transaction, to invest your pieces with
enough energy that you could feel the present level (baptism),
that only this wine of love could relieve you of your doom,
that it all depended upon your sacrifice of yourself for
another, your ability to give investiture as shirt
off your back, to clothe the naked (guy in the sheet),
literally nothing else mattered, no other way to the
Kingdom of Heaven in post-Mosaic situation, having seen
the Father (not just his backside), that he could create
you new, & that you could do the same for your own
kind, if they went to pieces & asked for your help.

402

From Creation to Knowledge

As Eve took a chance on a 'meaningful necessity'
taking those steps to cosmos the unredeemed space
of retarded eternity when the mind thought to negate
the contraries of Body & Soul (hear the way Trane
& McCoy play it) X-Quick she risked it all by
eating the fruit that would bear the twins (Popul Vuh)
that someday her breasts would in fact aegis the very
logos by tallying the Word composed in genetic
code of concrescence in guardianship of the Earth
existence she had physically felt from the beginning
to be actual exodus out of dilemma like the Red Sea
parting to allow thought again to flow into Canaan,
the promised land of the Middle Kingdom where Yuruga
gains his release from Egyptian bondage to the chronic.

Hecatoncheires

The Jackal emerging from Anthill blackened,
the sum of days, writing, verse & prose, golden
string of Ariadne leading to Jerusalem's Wall
as data-cluster story-limit of my perception
by image of the real United States of America
within the heterochrony of the Aeon (meaning
changes take place at any stage, St. Francis
falling out of competition), Vision of Quetzal
vs. Indo-European failure to step from sexual
to the final quarter of love as human possibility
limited to the isomorphic speech-times of the 50
States of the Unconscious Uncle who doesn't care
that his children think they are interchangeable,
like Ahab, he knows Moby Dick has already won.

403

Karleen Middleton Murphy

A Vortex

Sixty...sixty-five...seventy...
Hellbent for Sometown
Late when bang—
The swerve curves close to the margin.

Shaking I sit, frustration replaces fear.

The burly good Samaritan in the Mack
Finally stops with a smile, a spanner, and a jack.

"Nice day," he says, broad seamed face tilted to the sky.
        Blue greets blue.
"This kinda day, I wanna breathe in every moment."

I tap my toe impatient, explain the importance.

Intent, observant, he scrutinizes the lug nut in his palm,
        "'Juh ever notice the shape?
        Strange, how them little grooves
        Hold the world together."

I tap my Swiss-made gold circle.

"Close," he says, calculating glance catches a patch
        of blue at the edge.
He leaves my maimed car monstrously tilted on three wheels.
        "Look! Aint that purty?"
"You're breaking down my structures!" my mind screams,
        resisting the blue conspiracy.
"I have to...I must...ought..."

        Beneath a gold-crowned dandelion tuft
        A clump of misplaced scilla,

Abyss pendent, precipitious perch,
Shyly shows its vernal accolade—
Azure patch,
      Blue against blue.

Outside
     The blue triangle,
I offer; he grins refusal,
      "Breaks the monotony."
I insist; he taps his cap with the spanner,
Points it at me.
      "Yuhall take care now!"

Breathless, I arrive, almost late,
     for a seminar on eternity
     and those dark satanic wheels.

Randy L. Waln

Snake in the Roots

Anton Vogt

Environmental Ethics in Fourfold Time

These are the Sons of Los & these the Labourers of the Vintage.
Thou seest the gorgeous clothed [Butter]Flies that dance & sport
Upon the sunny brooks & meadows; every one the dance
Knows in its intricate mazes of delight artful to weave:
Each one to sound his instruments of music in the dance,
To touch each other & recede, to cross & change & return:
These are the Children of Los; thou seest the Trees on mountains,
The wind blows heavy, loud they thunder thro' the darksom sky,
Uttering prophecies & speaking instructive words to the sons
Of men: These are the Sons of Los: These the Visions of Eternity,
But we see only as it were the hem of their garments
When with our vegetable eyes we view these wondrous Visions.

Milton 26

A water ouzel bobs on a log beside Clearwater Falls in southern Oregon. I sit on the same log. It is summer, early morning. On a moss-backed stone opposite us waits a smaller, younger ouzel.

I watch the old feed the young, amazed at the coordination of dipping beaks. The little one is of course insatiable: for forty minutes I follow as the mature ouzel works her way downstream. She plunges into whitewater, glides beneath the surface, pops out of the current with a beakful of aquatic larvae, then flutters unhurriedly over to the younger dipper, repeating this process with variations until I realize that it has all the serious playfulness, the grace and intensity—even the symmetry—of...I want to say "dance", but dance is an artistic event cast apart from our lives, and what I am seeing —what I am coming to take part in—dissolves the present divisions between art, work and play; between energy, purpose, and desire. I feel growing in myself a delight—seeing, sheer delight; the search underwater, sudden birth into warm and turbulent air, return and contact:

How do you know but ev'ry Bird that cuts the airy way,
Is an immense world of delight, clos'd by your senses five?[1]

Active perception involves us in the co-creation of meaning and identity. There is a way of perceiving, not encouraged by our culture, that is grounded in the realization of relationship and the sharing of presence. The conventional limits of "human being" burst wide to include dippers, cedar trees, living water. Our culture offers us instead the shrunken identities of spectator, passive consumer, or alienated producer. The energy and responsibility of relationship become the ennui of Spectacle and Commodity: windshield landscape and postcard.[2]

When I am numb to my involvement in the co-creation of time/space with dipper, tree, and water—when I am not mindful of participation—my senses contract. I am lost to delight. I literally see, smell, hear, taste and feel less. Distracted, irritated, bored, I experience the world as Ulro. Events become things: dipper, woods, and water become props and sets for a drama featuring only myself. I lose the mutual identity of world and self in fullness of presence. Because integrated identity is created in the matrix of relationship and has the shape of Person, I become dehumanized as I retreat from relationship. When I am no longer present to the world, it is no longer present in me—as if I were asleep, not even dreaming.

The world as Ulro is composed of lifeless, manipulable matter. That such a view of the world was given scientific sanction in the eighteenth century is not surprising, for it is a worldview compatible with the needs of industrial capitalism, which was on the rise in the same century. But Ulro is ultimately too lifeless to contain the energy and imagination of the very scientific disciplines which first gave it form. Scientific speculation followed the prophetic insight of poets such as Blake in exploring the illusory boundaries of Ulro and discovering worlds beyond. By the twentieth century we have even begun to question the very basis of our knowledge of what is "natural". John Rodman writes:

> The only really revolutionary stance is that 'nature' is the greatest convention of all. . . . The distinction between Man and Beast is at bottom a political rather than a scientific distinction. It is ultimately an act of domination rather than of knowledge; or, rather, it is an act of knowledge-as-domination, the imposition upon the complexity of experience of a rigid dichotomy that authoritatively assigns roles but cannot be scientifically defended.[3]

Knowledge-as-domination has its cost. Another writer, George Leonard, tells us that the "illusions of separateness and alienation have been created only by enormous and exhausting efforts. The walls between us and our fellow beings are merely one aspect of the ruins of a dying culture."[4]

Illusions have a borrowed power: Blake challenged the scientific and philosophical views of reality that arose with industrial capitalism just as he prophesied against the Empire those views ultimately came to serve. Bacon, Locke, and Newton were the first of many who quite unwittingly gave metaphysical underpinning to that ethos of competition, isolated individualism, exploitation, and consumerism on which Empire still thrives in its myriad forms.[5] And just as Blake struggled to free his readers from the mind-forg'd manacles of his era, so there are those today engaged in similar acts of Mental Warfare.

In *The Transformation*, Leonard describes his meeting with an oak tree on Mt. Tamalpais: he enters "its double life of light and darkness, air and earth," and after a moment, falls back into habitual separateness. Mining the data of post-Newtonian physics which describes fundamental reality as "fields of energy" or "interpenetrating centers of vibrancy," Leonard fashions for himself another mode of perception to break beyond the cultural conviction "that we are solid and separate, forever walled off from our wives and lovers, brothers, fathers, friends and children":[6]

> Only a conspiracy of my genes makes the tree opaque to me. In the experience of living being from which I am descended, electromagnetic radiation within the narrow band we call visible has proved to be useful for guidance and survival in a particular terrestrial mode of existence. Through long evolution we have developed eyes sensitive only to the radiation vibrating between 10^4 and 10^{15} times a second. Therefore the tree appears impenetrable to my physical body, a handy correspondence. Its opacity, however, is operational, not ultimate. . . . Underlying everything, forming itself into what we now call electrons, protons, neutrons, and all the rest, obliterating basic distinctions between matter and energy, substance and spirit . . . there is the elemental vibrance. . . . All existence—whether mountain, sky, star, shaft of sunlight, thought, song, or self—is vibrancy. And the oak tree (if only I had eyes to see) is a particular arrangement of vibrant energy. The oak tree (if only I had ears to hear) is a consummation of its constituent vibrations, thus a perfectly harmonious strain of music. The oak tree (if only I had ways to learn) is available for me to enter and experience fully. . . . But I have been taught that it is a "thing", solid and separate from me. . . .[7]

As Leonard reveals, most of us still live within the confines of a mechanistic, crudely Newtonian worldview; our unexamined collective assumptions about physical reality are reinforced daily by an impoverished and fragmented social existence. How can we even begin to understand Blake's insistence that the universe is human without questioning these assumptions and this existence? Within the emerging paradigm of a new physics, Leonard works to form an intellectual/perceptual ground for the immediate experience of empathy and mutuality.

Gregory Bateson's work witnesses to an analogous struggle from the perspective of the life sciences. Definitions of what it means to be "human" have usually taken it for granted that consciousness is an exclusively, or at least uniquely, human attribute. But Bateson, maverick anthropologist and biologist, argues that "Mind is a necessary, and inevitable function of complexity wherever that complexity occurs."[8] Minimal characteristics of mind include the ability to operate with and upon differences; the flow of information along pathways; and the manifestation of self-correctiveness. Bateson suggests that these characteristics and the complexity they necessarily imply are found "in a great many other places besides the inside of my head and yours...a redwood forest or a coral reef with its aggregate of organisms has the necessary general structure. The energy for the responses of every organism is supplied from its metabolism, and the total system acts self-correctively in various ways."[9] Blake, whom Bateson refers to throughout his essays, put forth an analogous description of human activity: "Energy is the only life, and is from the Body; and Reason is the bound or outward circumference of Energy" (MHH, p. 149).

Bateson asserts that all complex biological organisms and systems "think"—information is not only processed, but has relevance and context to the organism or system. And "story is a little knot or complex of that species of connectedness we call relevance...thinking in terms of stories does not isolate human beings as something separate from the starfish and sea anemones, the coconut palm and the primroses...thinking in terms of stories must be shared by all mind or minds, whether ours of those of redwood forests and sea anemones."[10]

> Seest thou the little winged fly, smaller than a grain of sand?
> It has a heart like thee; a brain open to heaven and hell (M, p. 502)

Darwin proposed species or subspecies as the evolutionary unit of survival, but Bateson contends that "today it is quite obvious that this is not the unit of survival....The unit of survival is organism plus environment. The organism which destroys its environment destroys itself."[11] He continues:

> If, now, we correct the Darwinian unit of survival to include the environment and the interaction between organism and environment a very strange and surprising identity emerges: *the unit of evolutionary survival turns out to be identical with the unit of mind.*
>
> Formerly we thought of a hierarchy of taxa—individual, family line, subspecies, species, etc.—as units of survival. We now see a

different hierarchy of units—gene-in-organism, organism-in-environment, ecosystem, etc. Ecology, in the widest sense, turns out to be the study of the interaction and survival of ideas and programs (i.e. differences, complexes of differences, etc.) in circuits.

Let us now consider what happens when you make the epistemological error of choosing the wrong unit: you end up with the species versus the other species around it or versus the environment in which it operates. Man against nature. You end up in fact, with Kaneohe Bay polluted, Lake Erie a slimy green mess, and "Let's build bigger atom bombs to kill off the next-door neighbors." There is an ecology of bad ideas, just as there is an ecology of weeds, and it is characteristic of the system that basic error propagates itself. . . .When you narrow down your epistemology and act on the premise "What interests me is me, or my organization, or my species," you chop off consideration of other loops of the loop structure. You decide that you want to get rid of the by-products of human life and that Lake Erie will be a good place to put them. You forget that the eco-mental system called Lake Erie is part of *your* wider eco-mental system—and that if Lake Erie is driven insane, its insanity is incorporated in the larger system of *your* thought and experience. . . .[12]

Mind is not an abstract, ethereal quality: "When you separate mind from the structure in which it is immanent, such as human relationship, the human society, or the ecosystem, you thereby embark. . .on fundamental error."[13] Mind is embodied. Mind emerges in the "eco-mental system", in the relationship between bodies. A fourfold epistemology is neither anti-scientific nor only scientific: in Eternity, Newton and Shakespeare ride together. The perception of mind outside "my head and yours" is also a fourfold perception of bodies, bodies which are "that portion of Soul discern'd by the five senses" (*MHH*, p. 149). Listen to poet and farmer Wendell Berry:

Blake said that "Man has no Body distinct from his Soul. . . ." and thus acknowledged the convergence of health and holiness. In that, all the convergences and dependences of Creation are surely implied. Our bodies are also not distinct from the bodies of other people, on which they depend in a complexity of ways from biological to spiritual. They are not distinct from the bodies of plants and animals, with which we are involved in the cycles of feeding and in the intimate companionships of ecological systems and the spirit. They are not distinct from the earth, the sun and moon, and other heavenly bodies. . . .The body cannot be whole alone. Persons cannot be whole alone. . . .

411

Contempt for the body is invariably manifested in contempt for other bodies—the bodies of slaves, laborers, women, animals, plants, the earth itself. Relationships with all other creatures become competitive and exploitive rather than collaborative and convivial. The world is seen and dealt with, not as an ecological community, but as a stock exchange. . . . The body is degraded and saddened by being set in conflict against the Creation itself, of which all bodies are members, therefore members of each other. The body is sent to war against itself. . . .

By dividing the body and soul, we divide both from all else. We thus condemn ourselves to a loneliness for which the only compensation is violence. . . . For no matter the distinctions we draw between body and soul, body and earth, ourselves and others—the connections, the dependences, the identities remain.[14]

And so Albion, divided, degraded and saddened, searches for himself among "the connections, the dependences, the identities" of "the Creation itself, of which all bodies are members, therefore members of each other.":

Man looks out in tree and herb and fish and bird and beast
Collecting up the scatter'd portions of his immortal body
Into the Elemental forms of everything that grows. . . .
He touches the remotest pole, and in the center weeps
That Man should Labour and sorrow, and learn and forget. . . .
In pain he sighs, in pain he labours in his universe,
Screaming in birds over the deep, and howling in the wolf
Over the slain, and moaning in the cattle, and in the winds,
And in the cries of birth and in the groans of death his voice
Is heard throughout the Universe: wherever a grass grows
Or a leaf buds, The Eternal Man is seen, is heard, is felt,
And all his sorrows, till he reassumes his ancient Bliss. (FZ, p. 355-56)

Opposed to either "a religion of detached spirit" or "a worship of dehumanized material force,"[15] Blake struggled to awaken the perceiver to the creativity inherent in the act of perception and to recognize the common ground of perceiver and perceived: we are all members of the Body of Creation, which for Blake had a human shape, the shape of Person. The universe is continuous with ourselves. The Human Imagination itself shares identity with the creativity of the universe: we not only belong here, we continually co-create "here". But wearing the mind-forged manacles appropriate to a fallen life in the vast marketplace of Empire, we have forgotten both our identity and our mutuality with the universe. So as to deal with the world "not as ecological community, but as a stock exchange," Empire must

412

require its subjects to accept ideologies that not only diminish the value and richness of the perceived, but also isolate and numb the perceiver.[16]

Acceptance of Newton's system accentuates the rupture of relationship characteristic of life under Empire. The mutuality of life in the wider ecomental system is replaced with a perception of lifelessness which denies relationship. Human society is depicted as existing without a living context, in a universe devoid of human meaning, alone in a void.

As the universe is diminished so is the human. Since creativity is nurtured in the ebb and flow, the checks and balances of relationship, the creativity blocked by a Newtonian perception of the world assumes the distorted proportions of megalomania, succumbs to meaninglessness and nihilism, or disappears into the insecurity and anxiety of the isolated perceiver.[17]

The dehumanization of the universe in Blake's time has its counterpart in a worldview which posits a fallen human society against the divine immanence of nature. The possibility of struggle for true human community is abandoned: redemption comes only to the passively receptive individual. The connections and interdependencies which for Blake made urgent the need to proclaim redemption as a communal process are denied. When all value is localized ONLY in the perceiver or ONLY in the perceived, the common ground of both is eclipsed.

The champion in Blake's Mental Warfare against dehumanization is the person. Beyond all else, fourfold perception is the recognition of Person; anything less is abstract and by definition lacks presence. The golden thread that runs through and unifies all his discourses is the perception of, and the recovery of, Person: person, not isolated, but in community. It is not merely for the sake of literary convention that Blake discusses physics as well as politics and religion in terms of Person, or recognizes Person in the abstractions of psychology when he creates the Zoas. As M. C. Richards tells us in a profoundly Blakean meditation, life is absent when Person is eliminated. We are all called upon "to dwell in the world as in a Person." Life is not "transforming energy, but transforming person. Energy is the means. Being is not WHAT but WHOM." Spirit, "moving form, the living word, lifedeath, art-life, corpus, body, being, all persons."[18] THIS is our universe:

> All Human Forms identified, even Tree, Metal, Earth and Stone
> (J, p. 746-47).

Because we are human, it is through our Humanity that we recognize Person. Blake refused to separate the destinies of humanity and nature: the impoverishment of one reflects the impoverishment of the other, since both are united in the Human Imagination. Thus Blake castigated not nature, but those *concepts* of nature—religious, aesthetic, philosophical, or scientific— the acceptance of which threatened to retard active perception and marginalize

413

human energy and imagination.[19] Affirming the primary unity of perceiver and perceived, he asserted that with the coming of true human community we will realize our mutuality with the universe and the liberated Human Imagination will identify the Human Forms of "Tree, Metal, Earth and Stone." And to those who would justify the status quo of a fragmented and suffering Humanity by referring to an impersonal and abstract Nature (and its God), or stress the immanent divinity of such a nature, Blake proposed that nature is barren where humanity is absent.[20] Again, it is through our humanity that we recognize Person: an unredeemed, dehumanized or horrific nature reflects a fallen humanity, part of whose fallenness is the acceptance of this *view* of nature as a definitive and autonomous reality.

In this context we can look at the whole of Blake's work and see Blake's aphorism—"Where man is not, nature is barren" (*MHH*, p. 152)—as prophetic: "If you go on So, the result is So" (*AW*, p. 392). For if only humans are recognized as the ones who can perceive, value, and "think in terms of stories," then the result is a barren, i.e. "non-human," world. But if each grain of sand, each rock and hill, herb and tree, mountain, star, cloud, and meteor "Are Men Seen Afar" (*TB*, p. 805), if "ev'ry Bird that cuts the airy way Is an immense world of delight" and "the little winged fly . . . has a heart like thee; a brain open to heaven and hell," then "every thing that lives is Holy" (*MHH*, p. 160). Leonard's physics of delight and Bateson's "wider eco-mental system" are, in our age, one context for thinking about Person, for recognizing a world in which all partake in creativity and "every particle of dust breathes forth its joy" (*E*, p. 237).

Though the process of active perception in which Person is revealed involves an outward embracing, there is also a simultaneous inward journeying, an awakening of the Imagination which binds together the world within and the world without. One night in the desert I was overwhelmed by stars, sorrowing at their remoteness, unable to sleep, possessed by a beauty that seemed entirely alien. Suddenly the *location* of that beauty, that sorrow, became apparent. "All Things Exist in the Human Imagination" said Blake (*J*, p. 707). I relaxed into the delight of recognition: stars shone within me as well as without. Inwardly I touched stars, spoke to them, all of us shining. I saw beauty and felt it unfolding simultaneously within. Neither lost in myself nor overwhelmed by what once seemed an alien universe, I was at home.

In active perception we reawaken our numbed senses and the birthright of creative power Blake wished to restore to his readers. Yet Blake's emphasis on the Human Imagination inevitably raises questions about anthropomorphism—the projection of human attributes to the non-human. From the standpoint of the new physics and Bateson's theories of "mind," however, the concept of anthropomorphism is itself in need of revision. The dualisms it implies are currently under heavy criticism. As Bateson suggests, human attributes are themselves an expression of what can be seen in the natural world—that world out of which and with which, after all, we evolved.

The assumptions about subjectivity and objectivity implied in the concept of anthropomorphism are also being reformulated in a way congenial to Blake's insistence on the centrality of the Human Imagination. Scientist Russell Hanson and philosopher of science Marjorie Grene, among others, contend that all of our understandings of the world—including the scientific—are intellectual creations, human products rooted in social experience.[21] The development of early evolution theory illustrates just how deeply our understanding of reality unfolds through consciousness and so reflects not only our personal but also our social existence. Darwin, living in a society dominated by an ethic of intense competition, saw nature through that prism. His theory of evolution was consequently appropriated and misused by those in his society who felt they had to justify the incredible human cost of industrial capitalism: "nature, red in tooth and claw" was extended to include the social order, where "the survival of the fittest" became the ultimate slogan of social Darwinists. Conversely, Peter Kropotkin—geographer, biologist, and anarchist—grew up observing peasants in Russia living communally and cooperatively with little direction and less benefit from formal economic or governmental institutions. Not surprisingly, it was Kropotkin who discovered in his studies of Siberian wildlife that cooperation—"mutual aid"—was at least as important a factor in evolution as competition. In his critique of Darwinism, Kropotkin proposed that "the fittest" in a social species might just be the most cooperative.[22]

Thus scientists accept paradigms of reality within which they process sense data.[23] Hanson dramatizes this by asking us to consider two microbiologists, both looking at a prepared slide. One sees an artifact, a coagulum resulting from inadequate staining techniques. The other, with a different training and understanding, sees a cell organ, a "Golgi body" revealed by this same technique of fixing and staining. Both begin from the same data, are visually aware of the same object, but see different things: just as Kepler, who regarded the sun as fixed, and Brahe, who believed the earth was fixed and that celestial bodies moved around it, would experience the same sunrise quite differently.[24] As Marjorie Grene reminds us, perceptions of matter are human perceptions, not "the things themselves" as we often believe.

None of this would surprise Blake, who knew that one must see *through* the eyes, not merely with them: who wrote that "Nature has no outline, but Imagination has," (*Gh A*, p. 779), and "The tree which moves some to tears of joy is in the Eyes of others only a Green thing that stands in the way. . . . As a man is, So he sees. As the Eye is formed, such are its Powers" (*TDT*, p. 793).

A Blakean commitment to the primacy of the Human Imagination would, contrary to the implications contained in the idea of anthropomorphism, make one *more* responsible for one's perceptions and behavior, because one is aware that reality is co-created and not just passively received. Because the world is humanly significant, because one is aware that the way one views nature carries something of the state of one's own social existence, there would be less tendency, for example, to blindly project the sort of hatreds and fears that historically motivated the wanton slaughter of wolves and other predators.[25]

A Blakean ethic would respect otherness as part of a whole in which one participates: because all is united in the Human Imagination, otherness can be known. There is relationship and the possibility of creative and dynamic harmony (think of the Four Zoas in Eternity as a paradigm for living "in the world as in a Person"). In recognizing the humanity of the world we enter *perceptually* the relationship Marx prophesied would be made concrete in a post-revolutionary society: "the unity of being of man with nature...the naturalism of man and the humanism of nature both brought to fulfillment."[26] As William Leiss suggests, such a society would not "regard the essence of human technique as the ability to dominate nature. Rather...we should view it as the mastery of the relationship between nature and humanity," a mastery that would "do justice to the subtle interplay of internal and external nature...a kind of mastery no longer bound to repressive demands arising out of the structure of domination in society..." a mastery "in relation to human FREEDOM rather than...human power."[27]

Such a relationship between human society and nature neither mystifies nor devalues either of the participants. Wendell Berry points us in this direction when he writes: "We are working well when we use ourselves as the fellow creatures of the plants, animals, materials, and other people we are working with. Such work is unifying. It brings us home from pride and from despair, and places us responsibly within the human estate. It defines us as we are: not too good to work with our bodies, but too good to work poorly or joylessly or selfishly or alone."[28]

Granting Person-status to non-human beings would mean living among them not as conquerors but as fellow creatures.[29] It would mean allowing the wild to exist in its own right; yet if we do not live in a society which allows *human* persons to live without oppression or exploitation, what can we expect for the natural world? As long as profiteering, racism, and sexism persist, so will degradation of the natural world, mirroring the degradation of the human. It is because of this that Berry's egalitarian vision is subversive, for life and work as he advocates it—participatory and creative—cannot be realized by most of us in a society ruled by the marketplace and its current reductionistic "metaphysics of death."[30] The energies that we might use and replenish in a convivial mode are either repressed or mocked by a Satanic,

416

shadow creativity: the alienated productivity of factory and office, which carries over into school and home.[31]

> . . .the Chimney-sweeper's cry
> Every black'ning Church appalls;
> And the helpless Soldier's sigh
> Runs in blood down Palace walls (*SE*, p. 216).

Yet watching the ouzels at Clearwater Falls, I understand what Berry is talking about. That vision is available to us now. But, like Blake, we must go beyond vision, for in Eternity — which integrates all worlds, including the mundane — there is Mental Warfare and the constant joy and obligation of creation. Active perception co-creates relation, and so implies an ethic, a way of acting in the world. The intellectual's temptation in a society divided by class, sex, and race is to refuse to acknowledge or enter the conflict, to rest in the Beulah of momentary insight and intellectual resolution without translating these into concrete, political action. To compose environmental ethics in fourfold time requires not vision alone, but, in respect and love for Minute Particulars, the communal working out of that vision in everyday life.

"Not too good to work with our bodies, but too good to work poorly or joylessly or selfishly or alone," we are all summoned, like Theodore Roethke, to join Blake in the dance of Creation:

> What's greater, Pebble or Pond?
> What can be known? The Unknown.
> My true self runs toward a Hill
> More! O More! visible.
>
> Now I adore my life
> With the Bird, the abiding Leaf,
> With the Fish, the questing Snail,
> And the Eye altering all;
> And I dance with William Blake
> For love, for Love's sake;
>
> . . .dance on, dance on, dance on.[32]

NOTES

1. William Blake, *Blake: Complete Writings*, ed. Geoffrey Keynes (Oxford Univ. Press, 1966), p. 150. In subsequent references to Blake's writings, I will use the following abbreviations:

AW   —*Annotations to Watson*
E   —*Europe, a Prophecy*
FZ   —*Vala, or the Four Zoas*
GhA —*The Ghost of Abel*
J   —*Jerusalem*
M   —*Milton*
MHH—*The Marriage of Heaven and Hell*
SE   —*Songs of Experience*
TB   —*To Thomas Butts* 2 October 1800
TDT —*To Dr. Trusler* 23 August 1799

2. See Guy Debord, *Society of the Spectacle* (Black and Red, Detroit, 1972); see also John Berger, *Ways of Seeing* (Penguin and B.B.C., London, 1972).

3. John Rodman, "The Dolphin Papers," *The North American Review* (Spring 1974), p. 16.

4. George B. Leonard, *The Transformation* (Dell, N.Y., 1972), p. 11.

5. On Blake, Empire, and industrial capitalism, see: David V. Erdman, *Blake: Prophet Against Empire* (Princeton Univ. Press, 1977); J. Bronowski, *William Blake and the Age of Revolution* (Harper & Row, N.Y., 1965); G. R. Sabri-Tabrizi, *The 'Heaven' and 'Hell' of William Blake* (International Publishers, N.Y., 1973); and Eleanor Wilnor, *Gathering the Winds; Visionary Imagination and Radical Transformation of Self and Society* (Johns Hopkins Univ. Press, 1975). On modern Empire and the ideologies of capitalism, see Jeremy Rifkin and Ted Howard, *The Emerging Order: God in the Age of Scarcity* (Putnam, N.Y., 1979); William Appleman Williams, *Empire as a Way of Life: An Essay on the Causes and Character of America's Present Predicament, Along With a Few Thoughts about an Alternative* (Oxford Univ. Press, N.Y., 1980); Richard J. Barnet and Ronald E. Muller, *Global Reach: The Power of the Multinational Corporations* (Simon & Schuster, N.Y., 1974); and Herbert I. Schiller, *The Mind Managers; How the Master Puppeteers of Politics, Advertising, and Mass Communications Pull the Strings of Public Opinion* (Beacon Press, Boston, 1973). A good introductory text is Robert Lekachman and Borin Van Loon, *Capitalism for Beginners* (Random House, N.Y., 1981); also see Howard Zinn, *A People's History of the United States* (Harper & Row, N.Y., 1980).

6. Leonard, p. 11.

7. Ibid., p. 10-11. For more on the new physics, see also Fritjof Capra, *The Tao of Physics: An Exploration of the Parallels Between Modern Physics and Eastern Mysticism* (Shambhala, 1975).

8. Gregory Bateson, *Steps to an Ecology of Mind* (Ballantine, 1972), p. 482.

9. Ibid., p. 482.

10. Gregory Bateson, *Mind and Nature: A Necessary Unity* (Bantam, 1980), p. 14-15.

11. Bateson, *Steps to an Ecology of Mind*, p. 483.

12. Ibid., p. 483-484.

13. Ibid., p. 485.

14. Wendell Berry, *The Unsettling of America: Culture and Agriculture* (Avon, 1977), p. 103-106.

15. Wilner, p. 171.

16. See Murray Bookshin, "Beyond Neo-Marxism," *Telos* no. 36 (Summer 1978), p. 13-20.; Guy Debord, *Society of the Spectacle;* Jeremy Rifkin and Ted Howard, *The Emerging Order: God in the Age of Scarcity;* William Leiss, *The Domination of Nature* (Beacon Press, 1974); and William Leiss, *The Limits to Satisfaction: An Essay on the Problem of Needs and Commodities* (Univ. of Toronto Press, 1976). For the concrete, historical connections between ideologies and Empire in U.S. history, see

Richard Drinnon, *Facing West: The Metaphysics of Indian-Hating and Empire-Building* (New American Library, 1980).

17. On Newton, Blake, and active perception, see specifically the conclusion of Donald D. Ault, *Visionary Physics: Blake's Response to Newton* (Univ. of Chicago Press). See also Thomas W. Herzig, "Book I of Blake's *Milton:* Natural Religion as an Optical Fallacy," *Blake Studies*, vol. 6, no. 1 (Fall 1973).

18. Mary Caroline Richards, *Centering: in Pottery, Poetry, and the Person* (Wesleyan Univ. Press, 1964), p. 7.

19. The dialectics of Blake's attitude towards the natural sometimes carried him into a neo-Platonic idealism, but at his most insightful Blake attempted to overcome the dualism between materialism and idealism; see Stanley Diamond, *In Search of the Primitive* (Transaction Books, 1974), p. 194-197. Thomas Herzig reminds us that "Blake's argument for redeemed vision and redeemed experience does not entail the total rejection of the material world but only its delusive aspects, those and the Urizenic assumption that materiality is everything." Herzig, p. 29.

20. Blake never accepted that nature could be redeemed if humanity still suffered. Thus he was troubled by both the Deists and by Wordsworth's romantic poetry.

21. Norwood Russell Hanson, *Patterns of Discovery* (Cambridge Univ. Press, 1958); Marjorie Grene, *The Knower and the Known* (Univ. of California Press, 1974).

22. See Peter Kropotkin, *Mutual Aid: A Factor of Evolution* (New York Univ. Press, 1972).

23. See Thomas S. Kuhn, *Structure of Scientific Revolutions* (Univ. of Chicago Press, 1970).

24. Hanson, p. 1-12.

25. See Barry Holstun Lopez, *Of Wolves and Men* (Charles Scribner's Sons, N.Y., 1978).

26. Karl Marx, *Economic and Philosophic Manuscripts of 1844*, ed. Dick J. Struik, trans. Martin Milligan (Lawrence and Wishart Ltd., 1973), p. 43; cited in Wilner, p. 151.

27. Leiss, *The Domination of Nature*, p. 198 and p. 212.

28. Berry, p. 140.

29. Although perhaps Native American attitudes in this regard are not directly adaptable, they still offer instructive insights into this mode of relationship. See *Teachings from the American Earth: Indian Religion and Philosophy*, ed. Dennis Tedlock and Barbara Tedlock (Liveright, N.Y., 1975); and *Seeing With a Native Eye*, ed. Walter Holden Capps (Harper & Row, 1976).

30. The phrase and basic idea of a "metaphysics of death" is from William Barrett, "On Returning to Religion," *The Nation* (November 1976), p. 35.

31. See Richard Sennett and Jonathan Cobb, *The Hidden Injuries of Class* (Random House, 1972); Harry Braverman, *Labor and Monopoly Capital: The Degradation of Work in the Twentieth Century* (Monthly Review Press, N.Y., 1974); Eli Zaretsky, *Capitalism, the Family, and Personal Life* (Harper & Row, N.Y., 1976). For some alternatives, see Murray Bookchin, *Post-Scarcity Anarchism* (Ramparts, Berkeley, 1971); Michael Albert and Robin Hahnel, *Unorthodox Marxism* (South End Press, Boston, 1978); Ursula LeGuin, *The Dispossessed* (Avon, N.Y., 1974); the final chapters of Susan Griffin, *Woman and Nature: The Roaring Inside Her* (Harper & Row, N.Y., 1978); all of the works of Ivan Illich, particularly *Tools for Conviviality* (Harper & Row, 1973); and Andre Gorz, *Ecology as Politics* trans. Patsy Vigderman and Jonathan Cloud (South End Press, Boston, 1980).

32. Theodore Roethke, *The Collected Poems of Theodore Roethke* (Anchor Books, 1975), p. 243.

Paul Piech

Michael McClure

Dream: The Night of December 23rd

—AND HUGE LIKE GIANT FLIGHTLESS KIWIS TWICE THE SIZE OF OSTRICHES

they turned and walked away from us
and you were there Jane and you were twenty-two
but this was the nineteen-forties,
in Wichita, near the edge of town, in a field
surrounded by a copse of cottonwoods. It was
getting dark and the trees around the bridge
almost glowed like a scene by Palmer.
The two Giant Birds—Aepyorni—from Madagascar,
extincted A.D. one thousand, turned and walked
from us across the bridge. Even in the semi-darkness
the softness of their brown feathers made
curls pliant as a young mother's hair. There
was a sweet submission in the power of their enormous
legs (giant drumsticks). Their tiny heads
(in proportion to their bodies) were bent
utterly submerged in their business and sweeping
side to side like a salmon does—or like a wolf does—
but with a Pleistocene, self-involved gentleness
beyond our ken. My heart rose in my chest
(like the metaphysical poets say, with
purple wings of joy) to see them back
in life again. We both looked, holding hands,
and I felt your wide-eyed drinking-in

of things.

Then I turned and viewed across the darkening

field and there was a huge flightless hunting fowl
(the kind that ate mammals in the Pliocene).
He stood on one leg in the setting sun by the sparkling

stream that cut across the meadow to the bridge.
He had a hammer head and curled beak, and after my
initial surge of fear to see the field was dotted,
populated, by his brethren, each standing in the setting

sun, I saw their stately nobility

and again

the self-involvement.

We followed the Aepyorni
across the old wooden bridge made of huge
timbers. The bridge was dark from the shadows
of the poplars and the evergreens there.
The stream was dimpled with flashing moonlight

—and I think it had a little song.

Then

I found that on the bridge we were among
a herd of black Wildebeestes—Black Gnus.
One was two feet away—turned toward me—
looking me eye-into-eye. There was primal
wildness in the upstanding coarse (not
sleek as it really is in Africa) fur on
the nobby, powerful-like-buffalo shoulders
(remember this is a dream). I passed by him
both afraid and unafraid of wildness as I had passed
through the herd of zebras at the top of Ngorongoro Crater
in front of the lodge, where from the cliff we could see
a herd of elephants like ants, and the soda lake
looked pink because of flamingos there.
There is an essence in fear overcome
and I overcame fright in passing by those zebras

and this black wildebeeste.

Then we passed

over the heavy bridge and down a little trail

on the far side of the meadow walking back

in the direction we had been.

                              Soon we came

            to a cottage of white clap boards
        behind a big white clapboard house and knocked
          on the door; it was answered by a young man
      with long hair who was from the Incredible String Band.
          He took us inside and he played an instrument
            like a guitar and he danced as he played it.
        The lyre-guitar was covered with square plastic
            buttons in rows of given sizes and shapes.
        The instrument would make any sound, play
          any blues, make any creature sound, play
                any melody . . . I wanted it
          badly—it was a joy. My chest rose,
        I figured I'd have to, and would be glad to,
          give twenty or thirty thousand for it . . .

                Then the dream broke
          and I was standing somewhere with Joanna
        to the side of a crowd of people by a wall
        of masonry and I reached into my mouth
            and took from my jaw (all the other
      persons vanished and I was the center of everything)
              a piece which was eight teeth
              fused together. I stared at them
          wondering how they could all be one piece.
          They were white . . . It was some new fossil.
      Down on the bone there were indentations like rivulets
          like the flowing pattern of little rivers.

Poem by Amiri Baraka

	A man
	is what
Balang	he is and always
	must be. You see there is Death
AG	in the wings. The wings of Death hover
	over me. There's now now
AG	No Way—No Way to call it back
Boro	or re-create the dead hands to hold
	me or thee. We glow like the breeze
NAGH	on the pink or black skin. The win
	is too late to conquer the ease with
AH	which we enter the dark. The lark
TH	on the fences hangs there in CHILD
	HOOD like Robin and Little John and Maid
N-NN	Marian.

                    Call us back to the cities.
Call us back to the SLEAZE. Note
I am not you. This is not what you wrote.
The old men are young now on the street
below. They're kids with their bottles
planning a joke.
This is your stroke and not mine.
Wine turns them on. Young and tanned
with beards and big bellies like Odysseos
rising, trapped in vino, from Homer.
                                        Franz Kline
dead drunk and joyously talking at the Cedar.
                    It's all part of the great
             brush that we have with the law.
We gnaw ourselves sick with it.
But still we are here with dark on
                    our wings.

The lady calling her cat wakes me
at dawn. She's down facing the lawn
from her back porch. Making baby
calls to the puss. I know,
I know she's the universe's center.
                    Any point is
                    the center
                        of things.
                The starling squawking
            or the kids on boats
                starving in Asia.
            I listen to the voices
    of honored mass murderers on the old radio

        on the old radio

                    ****

Sleeping out under the stars on solstice night I dreamed I was typing a
poem by Baraka. Waking up, I was moved by the poem and quickly typed it
—remembering its shape.

Roger Easson

On Building a Blake Library

When the editors of *Sparks of Fire* asked me to compose a checklist of useful books for beginning students of William Blake, I found myself with an old question. Do I follow tradition and suggest those wonders of scholarship and critical insight that inform the academic path to William Blake or do I recommend those contemporary wonders of spiritual erudition and wisdom which shape the geography of soul Blake attempted to illuminate? I decided to review both. In the first part are the principal contributions to the academic tradition of four generations of Blake scholars. Part II suggests other Blakean directions in psychology, religion, and mythology.

I

We have made great strides in understanding William Blake's Art and Poetry since Damon wrote his *Dictionary*, Frye his *Fearful Symmetry* and Bronowski his *Blake and the Age of Revolution*, though these are well-heads from which we still draw great nurture. And for that student who desires to enter into this community of conversation these texts are important first steps.

It is important in undertaking the task of collecting a useful reference library of Blake materials to see the body of this material as representing three great efforts. The first great effort is the persistent melding of print and text that seems to have been with the Blake community since Gilchrist. Men such as Camden Hotten, Pearson and Muir undertook facsimiles of the illuminated books. Yeats and Ellis, in their great edition of 1893, attempted a text meshed with a facsimile. The popular Dent facsimiles of the last 30 years speak to the continued recognition that these graphic elements must not be neglected in the search for an understanding of Blake's career. Secondly, we must confront the very real problem of his text. Even today, as I write, a new edition is about to be released by the University of California Press which promises to replace the long definitive Erdman/ Doubleday text. And still the debate rages whether a reader's text or a scholar's text is the necessary avenue to reading Blake. Shall we regularize Blake's highly idiosyncratic spelling and punctuation? Or, shall we preserve these departures from modern conventions to the degree that modern typography permits? Thirdly, we must applaud the extraordinary efforts of literary scholars to study Blake's iconography, to learn to "read" his graphic designs, and to confront the impact they have on his texts. We are learning to see Blake's art as a synthesis of these two traditions, the graphic and the verbal, and it has been no easy task.

THE TEXTS

As it is Blake's poetry and prose that most often brings the general reader into a desire to build a reference library it is fitting we should consider what assortment of texts might be most useful.

1. Keynes, Geoffrey, ed. *Blake: Complete Writings With Variant Readings.* London: Oxford University Press, 1976.

   If we owe any scholar a deep vote of gratitude, Sir Geoffrey Keynes deserves it first. His Blake texts have been the traditional way by which students for sixty years have read Blake's poetry and prose. His is, however, a "reader's" text, not a scholarly text. It attempts to fix Blake's highly original etched text, and present it so the expectations of the modern reader will not be wildly disrupted. This is the old stand-by which has seen many, many editions of which the 1976 is only the most recent.

2. Stevenson, W. H., ed. *The Poems of William Blake.* London: Longman Group Limited, 1971.

   Here, with the cooperation of F. W. Bateson and D. V. Erdman, Stevenson has also fixed Blake's eccentricities of "spelling, punctuation, and the use of initial capitals regarding them as undesirable to the modern reader." The notes...Ah! such notes. These notes are a magnificent addition to the young reader's library inasmuch as they inform and explain where otherwise confusion would reign.

3. Johnson, Mary Lynn, and John E. Grant, eds. *Blake's Poetry and Designs: Authoritative Texts, Illuminations in Color and Monochrome, Related Prose, Criticism.* New York: W. W. Norton & Company, 1979.

   The Norton Critical Editions are a peculiar blend of a text and selected criticism in the great tradition of the casebook classroom text. Here Blake is again presented in his regularized general reader dress. Major works are presented in fragments, but the notes are superb. The 32 additional illustrations (some in color) are well chosen. A very handy text indeed.

4. Erdman, David V., ed. *The Poetry and Prose of William Blake.* Garden City, New York: Doubleday & Company, Inc., 1965.

427

Erdman's text is the scholar's edition which attempts to reproduce Blake's manuscript and etched text faithfully. Harold Bloom's notes are interesting as a historical statement of the critical position of the 60s. As a scholar's edition this is probably the only text a serious student cannot do without. Erdman's forthcoming California University Press edition will, however, replace it.

4. Ostriker, Alicia, ed. *William Blake: The Complete Poems*. Harmondsworth, Eng.: Penguin Books Ltd. 1977.

Based upon David V. Erdman's edition, this somewhat diverges from Erdman's choice of punctuation, but for the most part is an inexpensive scholar's text. This is a portable text designed for a serious reader, one it would be good to own.

FACSIMILE EDITIONS

Obviously if we read Blake's illuminated books correctly, and yet do not abuse the museum collections—it is said the Victoria and Albert Museum (London) has had to retire its copies of Blake's illuminated books because heavy use has seriously damaged the prints, for example—it is essential to know about the fine facsimile editions now available to the general reader. The awesome Trianon Press facsimilies published by the late Arnold Fawcus are often available in University Rare Book Rooms, but are usually beyond the reach of the average reader's pocket. It cannot be doubted that these are the closest most of us will ever come to actually owning or having continued access to Blake's illuminated books. However, there are now available a series of useful and inexpensive Blake reproductions.

5. Erdman, David V. *The Illuminated Blake: All of William Blake's Illuminated Works with Plate-by-plate Commentary*. Garden City, New York: Anchor Press/Doubleday, 1974.

If you may only acquire a single text, this would have to be it. Even though it contains only black-and-white reproductions of the plates— and that sometimes means very muddy reproductions when transforming colored plates into black and white—it is certainly the most affordable collection. In addition, the plates are accompanied with notes containing some of the most astute and imaginative guesswork as to what Blake's designs mean.

6. Keynes, Geoffrey, ed. *Songs of Innocence and of Experience with an Introduction and Commentary*. London: Oxford University Press, 1970.

First printed by Rupert Hart Davis, this volume has been reprinted many times. Alas, however, this is a photographic reproduction of the great Trianon Press facsimile of the Library of Congress copy. It is thus a facsimile of a facsimile and as a result the details are blurred and fuzzed. It is, anyway, a fine piece of eight-color lithography, and an impressive look at this important copy.

7. Thorpe, James. *William Blake: Songs of Innocence and of Experience: Selected Plates Reproduced in Facsimile from Originals in the Huntington Library.* San Marino, California: The Huntington Library and Art Gallery, n.d.

   A beautiful and inexpensive little booklet, available at a very reasonable price—$1.00 at last purchase from the HEH Museum Bookshop. It is an elegant little volume which reproduces the plates somewhat larger than the original from the very beautiful copy in the Huntington Library. This is a nice place to start—I give them away to friends regularly when I want to infect them with the Blake crazies.

8. Hofmann, Werner, trans. *William Blake: Leider Der Unshuld und Erfharung.* Berlin: Insel Verlad, 1975.

   This German facsimile is the product of the recent excitement created in Germany by the traveling Tate Gallery show that lately played there with such success. It is an important reproduction of the British Museum copy of *Songs* which contains one of the most interesting versions of Blake's *Tyger* plate. And then every collection needs a little oddment to keep the interest high. But when we read what German does to Blake's "The Sick Rose": *O Rose, du krankst! / Der Tuckische Wurm, / der fliegt in der nacht, / in heulenden sturm*, etc., we must be grateful Blake stayed in the rough basement of English rather than digging into the well of German.

9. Keynes, Geoffrey, ed. *The Marriage of Heaven and Hell.* London: Oxford University Press, 1975.

   A brilliant facsimile of the wonderful copy in the Fitzwilliam museum in Cambridge, England. This is not flawed in the same way the OUP *Songs* is, because they have worked here from the original and not from the Trianon Press facsimile. Keynes has given us magnified views of the interlinear designs which are very helpful in seeing the complexity of these illuminated plates.

10. Easson, Kay Parkhurst, and Roger R. Easson, eds. *William Blake: Milton, A Poem.* Boulder, Colorado, and New York: Shambhala and Random House, 1978.

    A full-color reproduction of the Huntington copy of Blake's penultimate illuminated book—45 plates in full color for less than $10.00! The text is a reader's text and the commentary is, well modesty does not permit an honest evaluation. But we may say that it attempts to discover in *Milton* Blake's travel guide for mental travelers.

11. Easson, Kay Parkhurst, and Roger R. Easson, eds. *William Blake: The Book of Urizen*. Boulder, Colorado, and New York: Shambhala and Random House, 1978.
A full-color reproduction of Blake's most important short illuminated book, 28 plates. The unusual clarity of these reproductions and the unusual quality of the text make it possible to read Blake nearly as he wished to be read. The commentary sees the work as Blake's attack on the print medium and the rationalist/orthodox world view it inspires.

12. Bindman, David. *The Complete Graphic Works of William Blake*. London: Thames & Hudson, 1978.
765 black-and-white illustrations of Blake's printed works is nothing to dismiss lightly. But as the title seems to suggest, there will be found here no reproductions of paintings and drawings. An important resource.

13. Butlin, Martin. *The Paintings and Drawings of William Blake*. New Haven, Connecticut: Yale University Press, 1981. 2 vols.
Although this is an expensive book, no student of Blake will ever again be able to acquire more important material for an equal amount of money. These 1,193 plates present a view of Blake's artistic career unparalleled in any other published work. Butlin has completed here the great Keynes and Todd catalogue begun in the 1940s and after many years of patience and persistence Butlin has produced a masterwork of the Art Historian's craft.

14. Todd, Ruthven. *William Blake: The Artist*. New York: E. P. Dutton, 1971.
A nice little volume: a sort of artistic biography which broke the ground for the recent flood of such books.

15. Essick, Robert N. *William Blake: Printmaker*. Princeton, New Jersey: Princeton University Press, 1980.
From the unusual vantage point of scholar and eminent collector, Essick has investigated Blake's printmaking career with unusual insight and energy. This is a major step forward in understanding Blake's unique engraving method. It is the definitive study of Blake the engraver.

16. Mitchell, W.J.T. *Blake's Composite Art: A Study of the Illuminated Poetry*. Princeton, New Jersey: Princeton University Press, 1978.
One of the most important attempts to examine Blake's artistic intent in the combination of poetry and graphics. This is a necessary, if not essential study of the connection between the art and the poetry.

CRITICISM

By far the most interesting characteristic of recent criticism is the trend towards volumed of collected essays which focus on a particular problem in Blake criticism, or on a particular work or works. And on the other hand there has been a parallel trend towards fewer major career embracing book-length studies. It is as if a subtle recognition of scholars has taken place, a recognition that Blake's career is simply too massive to admit the possibility of a systematic and comprehensive examination. Those that do appear are seldom the work of recognized scholars; they tend to be written by the younger scholars who still dare such monuments of critical energy. Nevertheless there are several major works we cannot pass by in this brief suggested library.

17. Frye, Northrop. *Fearful Symmetry: A Study of William Blake*. Princeton, New Jersey: Princeton University Press, 1947.
    Perhaps the most often reprinted critical work on Blake, *Fearful Symmetry* has achieved a kind of legendary status among Blakeans. This is probably the single work which has launched more Blake scholars into the work of interpreting Blake's poetry and art. Standing as it does at a kind of headwaters it makes a major attempt to understand Blake's mythic imagination, and sets the tone of several generations of Blake criticism.

18. Erdman, David V. *Prophet Against Empire: A Poet's Interpretation of the History of his Own Times*. Rev. ed., Princeton, New Jersey: Princeton University Press, 1969.
    Erdman's political history of Blake's career is probably the single most important critical biography yet written about Blake. In fact, it is the best modern biography yet written, though Michael Davis's *William Blake: A New Kind of Man* (Berkeley, California: The University of California Press, 1977) is better for the beginning student, Erdman's careful handling of historical materials makes this the book Blake students finally must gravitate toward.

20. Rosenfeld, Alvin H., ed. *William Blake: Essays for S. Foster Damon*. Providence, Rhode Island: Brown University Press, 1969.

21. Erdman, David V. and John E. Grant, eds. *Blake's Visionary Forms Dramatic*. Princeton, New Jersey: Princeton University Press, 1970.

22. Curran, Stuart, and Joseph Anthony Wittreich, Jr., eds. *Blake's Sublime Allegory: Essays on the Four Zoas, Milton, Jerusalem*. Madison, Wisconsin: The University of Wisconsin Press, 1973.

23. Paley, Morton D. and Michael Phillips, ed. *William Blake: Essays In Honor of Sir Geoffrey Keynes*. Oxford: Oxford University Press, 1973.

24. Essick, Robert N. and Donald Pearce, eds. *Blake in His Time*. Bloomington, Indiana: The University of Indiana Press, 1978.

25. Michael Phillips, ed. *Interpreting Blake*. Cambridge: Cambridge University Press, 1978.

These six books contain some of the most powerful and most provocative insights into Blake's work available outside periodicals. The general reader could not find a more open and productive and informative introduction to the critical debates than may be found here. Here is no system building, and no lengthy argument as will be found in most book-length studies. And here the reader will be able to find many essays that will whet his or her appetite for more.

OTHER USEFUL BOOKS

26. Erdman, David V., ed. *A Concordance to the Writings of William Blake*. Ithaca, New York: Cornell University Press, 1967. 2 vols.
Once the passion for Blake has set in, and serious conversation begins, few of us can continue without the Concordance. There will always be that moment when you remember a phrase but cannot remember where you read it. In such frustrating times, there is always the need for this important tool.

27. Bentley, G. E., Jr. *Blake Books: Annotated Catalogues of William Blake's Writings in Illuminated Printing, in Conventional Typography and in Manuscript, and Reprints Thereof, Reproductions of His Designs, Books with His Engravings, Catalogues, Books He Owned, and Scholarly and Critical Works About Him*. Oxford: The Clarendon Press, 1977.
One of the most important books yet printed in Blake studies, this is the definitive bibliography of the primary works, the secondary works, and any additional related works you might wish catalogued. Absolutely exhaustive, and invaluable.

28. Bentley, G. E., Jr. *Blake Records*. Oxford: The Clarendon Press, 1969.
Patterned on *Milton Records*, Bentley's book is not really a biography. It is rather notes toward one. It is simply the most exhaustive compilation of everything we know about Blake's life. One of the most useful tools a Blakean can own.

29. Gilchrist, Alexander. *Life of William Blake*. New York: Phaeton Press, 1969.

Originally published in 1863, this is the reprint of the second edition of 1880. Probably no other book is so responsible for Blake's modern reputation, and I still think it is the best biography ever written. In this Phaeton Press edition the reprint house has done us a great service, once again, by making available an important, and now rare, book to the general reader.

30. Damon, S. Foster. *A Blake Dictionary: The Ideas and Symbols of William Blake.* Boulder, Colorado: Shambhala, 1979.
Originally printed in 1965, this book revolutionized Blake scholarship. It is based upon the idea that within Blake's poetry is a system of symbols which like a great jigsaw puzzle can be fitted together if we will only assemble the pieces correctly. Unfortunately, this is not the case, but it makes an interesting tool as it assembles many parallel themes, characters, and events from the prophetic books. Too often, however, the general reader finds it easy to use this book as a crutch rather than a tool, so use it wisely.

31. Easson, Roger R. and Kay Parkhurst Easson, eds. *Blake Studies: A Semi-annual Journal of Scholarship and Criticism.* Published independently at Memphis State University by the editors and The Center for the Study of William Blake.
Initiated in 1968, this privately funded scholarly journal continues to publish major articles of criticism and scholarship. It is heavily illustrated and remains the central journal of Blake criticism.

32. Paley, Morton D. and Morris Eaves. *The Blake Newsletter/Blake: An Illustrated Quarterly.* Published by the Department of English, The University of New Mexico, Albuquerque.
This is one of the most useful publications for Blake scholars as it houses a forum for notes, discussion and debates, reviews books, publishes annual bibliographies, and contains many useful announcements about goings-on in the Blake community.

BLAKEAN NOVELS

Four novels of great interest to Blakeans have been published which it would not be fitting to exclude from such a list as this. They are in many ways important indexes of Blake's continuing fascination to modern authors.

Cary, Joyce. *The Horse's Mouth,* Andrew Wright, ed. George Rainbird in association with Michael Joseph, 1957. Contains Cary's own illustrations for his work.

Wilson, Colin. *The Glass Cage: An Unconventional Tale of Mystery.* New York: Random House, 1966.

Duffy, Maureen. *All Heaven in a Rage*. New York: Alfred A. Knopf, 1973.
Nelson, R. F. *Blake's Progress*. New York: Lasar Books, 1975.

II

A NOTE ON SOME OTHER BOOKS OF INTEREST FOR THE STUDENT OF THE TRANSFORMATIVE CONSCIOUSNESS: A VIEW FROM THE 1980s.

As a student of the poetry and art of William Blake, I have discovered that there is something about Blake that draws me into all sorts of interesting explorations and readings. These readings have nothing to do specifically with Blake; indeed, I am quite sure the more conservative readers will see nothing at all relevant in this list. However, I have always been interested in the Psychology of Religious Experience, and the fundamental human events evoked by Religion. Blakes's *All Religions Are One* embodies that idea which he may have picked up from the Syncretic Mythologers who swarmed Basire's shop while he was an apprentice there. It seems appropriate for a Blakean to follow that idea in the 1980s' style.

For us that means an investigation of Myth Studies, Jungian Psychology, Buddhism, Taoism, Judaism, Sufism, Gnosticism, Hinduism, Mysticism, Transpersonal Psychology, the History of Religion, and the History of Science. I can hardly touch all these fields in a short list, and what I do list reflects no particular method of encounter, but rather a kind of casual list of the best I have found during the last 15 years of active reading. My study of these fields can hardly be called conclusive, or even professional; it has been a kind of intellectual hobby, and I would appreciate hearing from the readers of *Sparks of Fire* about their own favorite titles in such a like enterprise.

1. Tart, Charles T., ed. *Transpersonal Psychologies*. New York: Harper & Row, 1975.

    Transpersonal Psychology is the title given to an emerging study of those *ultimate* human capacities and potentialities that have no systematic place in positive behavioristic theory ("first force"), classical psychoanalytic theory ("second force"), or humanistic psychology ("third force"). The emerging Transpersonal Psychology ("fourth force") is concerned with the *empirical*, scientific study of such human events usually named by such terms as "becoming," "unitive consciousness," "peak experiences," "ecstasy," "mystical experience," "awe," "transcendence," and so forth. There is an interesting journal devoted to it, and one might say that Transpersonal Psychology is what has happened to the Psychology of Religion after the LSD research of the 1960s.

At any rate, I have been fascinated by the attempt to create a dialogue between the scientist and the religious teacher, which is what Transpersonal Psychology undertakes. I am often quite put off by the systematic charting they do, but then I am just as fascinated by the kinds of materials they evoke in their studies. In this book there are 11 essays which cover a range of subjects from Zen, Yoga, Gurdjieff, Arica Training, Christian Mysticism, to Western Magic. But I am most interested in Tart's essay, "Some Assumptions of Orthodox Western Psychology" which is a brilliant examination of the embedded ideas in contemporary Western scientific world views. These, without our knowing it, often prevent our understanding Blake's poetry and art. It makes, I think, a very valuable corrective to our current intellectual context.

2. Ornstein, Robert. *The Psychology of Consciousness.* New York: Viking, 1974; 2nd ed., 1979.

A general introduction to some of the major innovations in brain research and its implications for better understanding of human consciousness. This is a major book which deals with such important subjects as split brain research, hemisphericity and mystical tradition.

3. Lilly, John C., M.D. *Simulations of God: The Science of Belief.* New York: Simon and Schuster, 1975.

Lilly was one of the first voices to speak in this investigation of the relationship between brain structure and consciousness. He has authored such books as *Programming and Metaprogramming and the Human Bio-computer, The Center of the Cyclone* (an autobiography) and *The Deep Self* (about sensory deprivation tank work). This particular book investigates the kinds of "software" inherent in the various kinds of belief systems, and the impact upon the nature of consciousness that results from them. A fascinating book, but it needs to be read in context with his computer metaphor/typology of the human brain.

4. Pearce, Joseph Chilton. *The Crack in the Cosmic Egg.* New York: Julian Press, 1971; see also his *Exploring the Crack in the Cosmic Egg.* New York: Julian Press, 1974.

I confess to be drawn to this book because of Blake's own cosmic egg design in his poem *Milton* (1805), and I was delighted to encounter Pearce's conversation about "metanoia." Metanoia is one of the basic elements in religious experience as well as in scientific discovery, and I was pleased to see Science and Religion so clearly yoked at this psychological level.

5. Staal, Fritz. *Exploring Mysticism: A Methodological Essay*. Berkeley, California: The University of California Press, 1975.

   A brilliant study which focuses on ways to approach mysticism both theoretically and experientially. Surely, any reader interested in mysticism can use such a guide.

6. Weil, Andrew, M.D. *The Natural Mind*. Boston: Houghton Mifflin Co., 1972; See also his recent *The Marriage of the Sun and Moon: A Quest for Unity in Consciousness*. Boston: Houghton Mifflin Co., 1980.

   Andrew Weil is one of the foremost American researchers into psychedelics and was one of the first to do real medical research on cannabis. He writes here in a rapidly growing field of medical anthropology which examines the impact drug use has had on consciousness as well as culture. I do not include this because I think Blake was involved with the use of specific psychedelics, but it is a subject I always have to deal with sooner or later when teaching Blake. It pleases me to think there is a larger (?) phenomenon behind Blake's visions, but students often come to Blake's work because of their own experience with psychedelics. Consequently, I find it useful to be conversant with the literature of psychedelics.

7. Shah, Idris. *The Sufis*. Garden City, New York: Doubleday, 1964.

   Sufism is an interesting form of Islamic mysticism, and I find its curious tales deeply Blakean in a way I can not very well explain. I was introduced to Sufism by Ornstein's book, above, and have continued to read Shah's dozen or so wonderful anthologies of Sufi tales as they are released.

8. Bly, Robert, trans. *The Kabir Book: Forty-Four of the Ecstatic Poems of Kabir*. Boston: Beacon Press, 1977.

   Kabir was a fifteenth-century Indian poet whose writings were deeply influenced by Sufi poets and the ideas of the Hindus. Bly's versions of these poems are re-workings of an earlier edition by Tagore and Evelyn Underhill and are part of Bly's attempt to put the poet back into scholarly translations. This is a magic book for me; one I find that captivates most of the Blakeans I have introduced to it.

9. _____. *News of the Universe: Poems of Twofold Consciousness*. San Francisco: Sierra Club Books, 1980.

   If you were to look for Blake's tradition in modern poetry, this book is the place to start. This is an anthology of poems that demonstrates the evolution of the intuition and the ecstatic in poetry. A fantastic read!

10. Watts, Alan. *The Book*. New York: Pantheon, 1966; rpt., New York: Vintage Books, 1972. See also his *Beyond Theology: The Art of Godsmanship*. New York: Pantheon, 1964.

Watts was one of those men whose joy it was to try and say what it was impossible to say. As a result, his writings take us deeply into Christian tradition as well as into Zen traditions as he explores the whole notion of the religious experience. However, I find the most exciting Watts material is not in print but in audiocassette form (available only from MEA, Box 303, Sausalito, CA 94965). A second set of tapes is available from The Electronic University, Box 361, Mill Valley, CA 94941. These tapes are perhaps the most amazing lectures I have heard as they are Watts at his best and most eloquent.

11. Huxley, Aldous. *The Doors of Perception.* rpt., New York: Harper & Row, 1970. See also his *Heaven and Hell.* rpt., New York: Harper & Row, 1971.

    Aldous Huxley was one of the great popularizers of Blake and these two books are among those writings that spoke most to the 60s (they were published originally in 1954 & 1955, respectively) about the nature of the visionary experience, and whether true religious experience could be had from drugs. Huxley and Alan Watts both said yes. (Watts's statement on this subject will be found in his book *The Joyous Cosmology,* and in a masterful tape called *The Alchemy of LSD.*) As a result, Watts and Huxley are often seen as having been either the cause of great mischief, or the cause of a great spiritual revolution, depending upon whether one believes the general availability of religious experience to be a good thing.

12. Ram Dass. *The Only Dance There Is.* Garden City, New York: Doubleday, 1974.

    Ram Dass is Richard Alpert who, with Timothy Leary, led much of the earliest University-sanctioned experimentation with LSD at Harvard. After he was fired he went on a pilgrimage to seek a holy man who might explain what was happening in LSD experiences. This book is a record of that expedition and his findings. Originally published in *The Journal of Transpersonal Psychology,* this is a record of an amazing transformation I have found continually useful.

13 Popenoe, Cris. *Inner Development: The Yes! Bookstore Guide.* Washington, D.C.: Yes! Inc. 1975. (Distributed by Random House)

    The Yes! Bookstore specializes in religious books of a very eclectic nature, and this is a catalogue of its stock. Because much of it is now out of print, this catalogue is a valuable source of books often thought unobtainable. It is 654 pages of sheer bibliographic delight and has 65 different sections ranging from A: "African Philosophy" to W: "Women and Men." As good a place to end such a list as this, I have not found. If your appetite for more is to be sated, then probably the *Yes! Guide* is the place. The books all can be ordered directly from the store by using a handy order blank found in the back of the text.

shaman psalm

by
James Broughton

Listen Brothers Listen
The alarms are on fire
The oracles are strangled
Hear the pious vultures
condemning your existence
Hear the greedy warheads
calling for your death
Quick while there's time
Take heed   Take heart
Claim your innocence
Proclaim your fellowship
Reach to each other
Connect one another
and hold

Rescue your lifeline
Defy the destroyers
Defy the fat vandals
They cry for a nation
of castrated bigots
They promise a reward
of disaster and shame
Defy them   Deny them
Quick while there's hope
Renovate man
Insist on your brotherhood
Insist on humanity
Love one another
and live

Release your mind from
the handcuffs of guilt
Take off your blinders
Focus your insight
Take off the bandages
that infect your fears
See your wounds heal when
you know your birthright
Men are not foes
Men are born loving
welcome being tingled by
the touch of devotion
Honor one another
or lose

Come   Brothers   Waken
Uproot hostility
Root out the hypocrites
Warm up your phoenix
to arouse a new era
Disarm the cutthroats
Sever the loggerheads
Offset the history
of torment and curse
Man is the species
endangered by man
Quick while there's time
Abandon your rivalries
or mourn

Deflate pugnacity
Magnify friendliness
Off with your mask
Off with your face
Dump the false guides
who travel the warpaths
Uncover your loving
Discover surrender
Rise in your essence to
the tender occasion
Unwrap your radiance
and brighten your crew
Value one another
or fall

Come forth unabashed
Come out unbuttoned
Bury belligerence
Resurrect frolic
Only through body can
you clasp the divine
Only through body can
you dance with the god
In every man's hand
the gift of compassion
In every man's hand
The beloved connection
Trust one another
or drown

Banish animosity
Summon endearment
You are kindred to
each one you greet
each one you deal with
crossing the world
Salute the love ability
in all those you meet
Elicit the beauty that
hides in all flesh
Let freedom of feeling
liberate mankind
Love one another
at last

Hold nothing back
Hold nothing in
Romp and commingle
out in the open
Parade your peculiar
Shine your monkey
Rout the sourpuss
Outrage the prig
Quick while there's room
Revel in foolhardy
Keep fancies tickled
Grow fond of caress
Go forthright together
or fail

Affirm your affection
Be laughing in wisdom
You are a miracle
considered a moron
You are a godbody
avoiding holiness
Claim your dimension
Insist on redemption
Love between men will
anachronize war
bring joy into office
and erogenate peace
Accept one another
and win

Relish new comrades
Freshen new dreams
Speak from the heart
Sing from the phallus
Keep holy bounce in
your intimate ballgames
Sexual fervor can
leap over galaxy
outburst the sun
football the moon
Give way to love
Give love its way
Ripen one another
or rot

Extend your vision
Stretch your exuberance
Offer your body to
the risks of delight
where soul can run naked
spirit jump high
Taste the divine on
the lips of lover
Savor the divine on
the thigh of friend
Treasure the divinity
that ignites the orgasm
Surprise the eagles
and soar

Let the weapons rust
Let the powers crumble
Open your fists
into embraces
Open your armslength
into loving circles
Be champions of hug
Be warriors of kiss
Prove in beatitude
a new breed of man
Prove that comradeship
is the crown of the gods
Cherish one another
and thrive

Listen Brothers Listen
The alarms are too late
This is the hour for
amorous revolt
Dare to take hold
Dare to take over
Be heroes of harmony
in bedfellow bliss
Man must love man
or war is forever
Outnumber the hawks
Outdistance the angels
Love one another
or die

This manuscript of *Shaman Psalm*
was written out by wm·stewart

cover drawing:
Raven

TO CREATE A LITTLE FLOWER IS THE LABOUR OF AGES

Notes on the Contributors

HELEN ADAM—Born in Scotland 1909. Writes ballads and short story poems, and for years has done readings of them on both coasts of America and in Europe. Books: *Ballads*—Arcadia Press; *Selected Poems and Ballads*—Helicon Press; *Turn Again to Me*—Kulture Foundation; *Gone Sailing*—Toothpaste Press; *Ghosts and Grinning Shadows*, a book of short stories of the supernatural—Hanging Loose Press.

STEPHEN ADDISS, after seventeen years performing traditional and modern music of the world in thirty-five countries, now teaches Asian art history and music at the University of Kansas. He is particularly interested in the Oriental literati tradition, in which painting, poetry, calligraphy and music are joined in the work of artists who expressed their personalities and visions for their friends, rather than as a profession. Publications by Dr. Addiss include *Obaku: Zen Painting and Calligraphy* (Spencer Museum, 1978) and *A Japanese Eccentric: The Three Arts of Murase Taiitsu* (New Orleans Museum of Art, 1979).

F. ADIELE—Poet who has won awards from the Poetry Society of America and others. Currently being published in several anthologies. "In regard to *The Fountain*, its creation was an odd one. Being bed-ridden with a burned leg, several art books and a bottle of pain killers led to the digestion of philosophical and biographical work on Blake and his art. When all emerged weeks later, the work was almost complete, though not the plot. When I compared it to some pieces of the Master's poetry that I had never read, I found direct parallels in concepts and even sentences. Felt I might actually have been on B's wavelength for a time—but would anyone else?"

AETHELRED, THE UNREADY—"I elected Albion for my Glory. From the leaning of my Presence Death is fat in His Reactor. Little Flock, I come: Albion Rises! Aethelred, the Unready in Golgonooza."

KENNETH ALLEN has worked a wide variety of jobs, ranging from taxi driver to teacher, to be able to continue writing on a daily basis.

JEFFERY BEAM lives in Chapel Hill, North Carolina. He has published two books—*The Golden Legend* and *Two Preludes For the Beautiful*. He has also published widely in *Gay Sunshine*, *Blue Buildings*, *Hard Pressed*, *Thunder Mountain Review* and others.

JOHN BRANDI lives in a canyon at the edge of the high desert in the Jemez watershed of New Mexico. He wanders out from there, paints, writes, and travels back in.

JAMES BROUGHTON is a San Francisco poet and teacher, an author of many books and plays, and a widely known pioneer in the realm of avant-garde cinema and poetry. He remains, in fact, the only established American poet consistently engaged in filmmaking. His *Seeing the Light* is a poetics of cinema.

STEVE BUNCH lives in Lawrence, Kansas, where he edits *Tellus* magazine.

447

JARED CARTER is an Indianapolis-dwelling poet, editor, book designer and journalist. He has published several books of poetry and non-fiction. *Work, For The Night Is Coming*, published in 1981 by Macmillan is the latest. He was awarded the Walt Whitman Award of the Academy of American Poets for this book. His poetry has appeared in *The New Yorker, Poetry, Nation, College English* and *Prairie Schooner*.

MICHAEL CASTRO often sings his poems, accompanied by jazz musicians. His work is published in *Bright Moments: A Collection of Jazz Poetry* (Abraxas Press, 1980), *Voices Within the Ark: The Modern Jewish Poets* (Avon Books, 1980), and in the volume *Cracks* (The Cauldron Press, 1977).

ERIC CHAET's works include *Old Buzzard of No-Man's Land* (poetry), 1974; *Unraveling Smoke* (fiction), 1975; and *Solid and Sound* (album of songs), 1977.

KENT CLAIR CHAMBERLAIN—Born January 22, 1943, Abilene, Dickinson County Seat, Kansas. Since 1945, Ashland, Oregon. January, 1961, started Poeting it. Since 1962, Slant-Line, Sight-Patterning them. ASHLANDONIAN, not prosaic Ashlander, but, one with whom the Muse "hath an appointment." Editor, *Lithian Ashlandonian* (1980). Founding Parnassian, *Of Parnassus, Poets* (November 22, 1976). 1980-81 President, *United Amateur Press Association of America*.

MICHAEL CHRISMAN—Vocational counselor with proud but beleaguered CETA, Greenfield, Massachusetts. Residence in sinewy, feminine hills of Heath. Favorite quote from Cocteau: "Since these mysteries are beyond me, let's pretend we're organizing them."

JOHN CLARKE—poet/Blake scholar—teaches at SUNY Buffalo—book of poems: *The End of This Side*

JOHN CURL—Born 1940, New York City; ethnic background: English Protestant-Irish Catholic-Roumanian Jew; education: NYC Public Schools, CCNY (graduated 1965); Part of a family of 3 (the third being an 11-year-old daughter); by trade a cabinetmaker; politically a collectivist. Author of several chapbooks of poems, including *Ride the Wind* and *Insurrection/Resurrection*. His most recent book is a flight into prose: *History of Work Cooperation in America*.

S. FOSTER DAMON's *William Blake: His Philosophy and Symbols*, published in 1924, was a pioneer work in Blake criticism.

DIANE DI PRIMA's *Collected Poems* were published by North Atlantic Press.

W. S. DOXEY is a professor at West Georgia College, author of three published novels and one chapbook of poetry.

ROBERT DUNCAN lives in San Francisco. His *Truth and Life of Myth* is especially pertinent to those who have an interest in Blake.

ROGER EASSON is a bhikku who impersonates a bibliomaniacalanalretentive Professor who has interesting dreams about word processors and white river canoeing (which are very nearly the same thing). He avers a certain inclination to hyperbole and hot-and-sour soup. He is currently co-editor of *Blake Studies*, co-director of The Center for the Study of William Blake at Memphis State University, and is co-warring on Blake's Polypus on the banks of the Mississippi.

MORRIS EAVES (University of New Mexico) is co-editor of *Blake/An Illustrated Quarterly* and author of *William Blake's Artistic Theory*, to be published in 1982 by Princeton University Press.

ALEXANDRA ELDRIDGE is co-keeper of Golgonooza: The Church of William Blake, an English Church in the Wilderness of Ohio.

GAYLE EMMEL lives in a cave at the foot of the Cerne Giant in the Valley of the Frome.

THEODORE ENSLIN—poet, homeopathist—has written many books of poetry including *Synthesis*, *With Light Reflected* and *Ranger*.

CLAYTON ESHLEMAN's most recent collection of poetry is *Hades in Manganese* (Black Sparrow Press, 1981); he is currently translating the complete poetry of Aimé Césaire and editing *Sulfur*, "A Literary Tri-Quarterly of the Whole Art."

Middleaging Oregon native VIC FLACH draws, paints, photographs, writes poems and essays (exhibiting and publishing some), makes multiwalled murals in public buildings, structural and graphic designs, and experimental films, edits lit and art journal *In/Sert*, teaches painting, design, visual structures-and-metaphor, and iconography at the University of Wyoming, and claims it's not dabbling, but *ordering his experience, which returns growth and joy* rather than wealth or fame.

MARGARET FLANAGAN has had more than seventy poems published by magazines and anthologies, two in Canada. She has had several short stories published, one in an Australian science fiction/fantasy anthology.

MITCH, a.k.a. MICHAEL TAYLOR, FLYNN, was born and makes his daily bread along the shores of Lake Erie, in Buffalo, as a free-lance writer. First met Blake in 1969.

GARY GACH—Born 30.XI.47; Los Angeles, California. Typesetter. Golden Gate swimmer. Recently embarked with C. H. Kwock on high adventure of translating Chinese poetry, tz'u, linked verse, shamanka trance, etc.

BARRY GIFFORD is the author of two novels, *Landscape with Traveler* and *Port Tropique*; *Jack's Book: An Oral Biography of Jack Kerouac*; *The Neighborhood of Baseball*; and *Beautiful Phantoms: Selected Poems 1968-1980*.

ALLEN GINSBERG has been guided by Blake's genius through most of his career. Books include *Planet News*, *Kaddish*, *The Fall of America*, and more recently, *Mind Breaths*.

ARTFUL GOODTIMES—Son of a bombadier and onetime candidate for ordination in the popish rites, he chases the lyric valuables from Land's End to the Ophir Needles playing his earth flute.

CATHERINE GOSS lives on a farm in the Missouri Ozarks with her husband and daughter. She raises chickens, grows organic vegetables, rides horses and reads books.

JONATHAN GREENE is the author of ten books, most recently *Trickster Tales* Toothpaste Press, 1981), *Quiet Goods* (Larkspur Press, 1980), *Once a Kingdom*

Again (Sand Dollar, 1979), and *Peripatetics* (Truck Press, 1978). He lives at the end of a road to nowhere which makes sitting naked with spouse in the garden possible.

RICHARD GROSSINGER's most recent book, *The Night Sky*, is published by Sierra Club Books.

JACK HIRSCHMAN has published some 40 books, including translations from 5 languages. He is a member of the Union of Left Writers (ULW) and the Roque Dalton Cultural Brigade.

MICHAEL HOROVITZ is an editor-publisher (*New Departures*) and troubadour based in the UK (*Bisley, Stroud, Glostershire*), but happy to travel anywhere for poetry, money, love. Now completing enlarged sequel to Penguin anthology of *Children of Albion*, and continuing with the internationalist *Poetry Olympics* project.

WILLIAM HUNTER is a graduate assistant in English at the University of Missouri. He thinks that Blake's thought fills immensity, because it seems to.

PAUL JOHNSON, who has beaten Urizen at chess, is preparing his *Delusions of Grammar* for publication.

LINTON KWESI JOHNSON was born in Jamaica and has lived in Britain since 1963. He is an active spokesman for the Black community in London. His reggae music-poetry is distributed worldwide.

DR. JO-MO—"Earliest known incarnation as Marcel Govichi, Italian army officer early 1600s. Then reborn in Ireland as Scott Eric McCree early 1800s where I was a whiskey seller. Next known incarnation: Mobile, Alabama, 1941. Founded the Nail Press in 1968 and self-published *Ecuadernos*—poems of Ecuador. Read poetry in Bay Area. Dr. Jo-Mo's *Handy Holy Home Remedy Remedial Reader* (Nail Press, 1973). First book of poetry published in 1963 *The Four Mirrors*—a visionary evocation, Colonail Press. Also published in *Beyond Baroque, Ecsay, Soltide* and others. His life's work: the *Dictionary of the Nail* remains unpublished. Been working on an autobiographical science-fiction cartoon-novel for past 10 years. I AM an artist and sculptor by trade. I AM also both a student and teacher of metaphysics in the School of Metaphysics. "Dr. Jo-Mo" is both a pen-name (For FRED MARCHMAN) and a character in my cartoons/novels."

ROBERT
work-smith, teacher, voyager,
sees Rembrandt tulips, silver roadways, wild geese flying,
hears Bach inventions in starry night,
rose scent in dawn,
feels green grass growing,
tastes life,
JONES.

ROBERT KELLY—Latest book: *Spiritual Exercises* (1981) from Black Sparrow. Working on next collection *Under Words*. *The Book of Water* continues. Deeply involved with the inter-arts M.F.A. program of the New Avery Graduate School of the Arts (of Bard College), an intense and innovative experiment.

ROGER KEYES is an art historian who lives in Woodacre, California. He has written many books and articles on Japanese woodblock prints.

MARTHA KING's collection of poems, *Weather*, was published in 1978 by New Rivers Press; her poetry and fiction have appeared in *Mulch, The Falcon, #, Niagara*, and, by the time this book appears, *Sun, Chelsea*, and others.

LAWRENCE LAZZARINI was born in San Francisco in 1937. A former school teacher, he is now retired and gainfully unemployed in making poetry.

BO OSSIAN LINDBERG—Born in Abo, Finland, in 1937. Since 1974 has worked at the University of Lund, Sweden. He specializes in the materials and technique of painting, and the care and preservation of works of art. "I wrote my dissertation on Blake, but at that time (c. 1970) I was still very ignorant of the things I am beginning to understand now."

STANLEY LOMBARDO was born and educated in New Orleans. He now teaches Classics at the University of Kansas in Lawrence, where he lives in bliss with his wife and son.

DENISE LOW edits *Cottonwood Review* in Lawrence, Kansas, where she teaches writing and watches the stars.

MICHAEL McCLURE lives in San Francisco with poet Joanna McClure. The title piece of his recent *Antechamber* is a visionary nature poem. McClure's *Josephine: The Mouse Singer* received the *Obie Award* for Best Play.

HOWARD McCORD recently preached Blake to the Juneau Ice Field and Revillagigedo Island, asking "What is so far as the Near Island?" See his newly re-issued *Arctic Desert* and discover.

SUSAN MERNIT has published 2 books of poetry, *The Angelic Alphabet* and *Tree Climbing*, and is at work on a novel about popular music and musicians. She edits *Hand Book*, a journal.

KARLEEN MIDDLETON MURPHY of Anglo-Irish parentage was born and schooled in Jamaica. Went to Montreal, Canada—B.A., Sir George Williams University; M.A., McGill—nearly died from psychic shock at the climatic difference. Moved to Toledo—Ph.D., University of Toledo—where she now resided in a house by the Ottawa River with four children, one hairy mutt, and a beautiful garden. "I am contemplating going into plumbing (about which I know nothing), or politics (where it wouldn't matter), but at present am teaching at Bowling Green State University."

DAVE MORICE—Creator of *Poetry Comics* in Iowa City. Christmas book out: *A Visit from St. Alphabet*. Coming soon: Blake's *Songs of Innocence and Experience* as a feature-length animated cartoon (wishful thinking).

E. B. MURRAY has published a book on Ann Radcliffe, articles and reviews on Blake and Shelley, and is currently preparing an edition of Shelley's prose for Oxford University Press.

JOE NAPORA—Ohio poet. Most recent book: *Poetry in the Middle: notes on land and language*. Most recent child: Erek Steven *not* Ezra William.

JOHN NELSON, born in Kansas in 1953, currently makes his home in northern California after spending the years 1976-79 in Japan and elsewhere in Asia.

TOM NICHOLS is a wandering minstrel who teaches English at the University of Missouri and draws visions in cement.

451

DAVID OHLE's novel *Motorman* was published by Knopf. He is also an editor, along with Spider Martin, of the *City Moon*.

THOMAS PALADINO lives somewhere in New Jersey.

MICHAEL PALMER has lived in San Francisco since 1969. Recent publications include *Alogon* (Tuumba Press), *Transparency of the Mirror* (Little Dinosaur) and *Notes for Echo Lake* (North Point). He is currently preparing a new collaborative work with the Margaret Jenkins Dance Company.

JEAN E. PEARSON is a writer and translator who teaches German at Moravian College, Bethlehem, Pennsylvania. She spent 1980 in Sweden and got in touch with Blake through Bo Lindberg's paintings.

PETER PAUL PIECH is the proprietor of the Taurus Press in England. He illustrates the works of Jesus, Gandhi, Martin Luther King among others.

GEORGE QUASHA is the author of several books of poetry including *Somapoetics*, *Word-Yum*, *Giving the Lily Back Her Hands*, and *Traveling in the Castle*. He has edited *America a Prophecy: A New Reading of American Poetry from Pre-Columbian Times to the Present*, *Open Poetry*, *An Active Anthology*, and the magazine *Stony Brook*. His critical writings have appeared in *Blake's Visionary Forms Dramatic*, *New Literary History*, and elsewhere, and will be published in a collection by Treacle Press. He is publisher of Station Hill Press and Director of Open Studio in Barrytown, New York.

DAVID REISMAN is 22 years old and is currently a graduate student in painting at the University of Illinois. Coming from an educated and upper middle class background, he entered the field of art under the well-advised protests of his family.

ALBERT S. ROE teaches at Cornell University. His beautiful edition of *Blake's Illustrations to the Divine Comedy* was published by Princeton University Press.

HOWARD SCHWARTZ was born in St. Louis, Missouri in 1945. He attended Washington University, and presently teaches courses in creative writing and Jewish literature at the University of Missouri, St. Louis. In addition to *The Captive Soul of the Messiah*, he is the author of three books of fiction, *A Blessing Over Ashes*, *Lilith's Cave*, and *Midrashim: Collected Jewish Parables*, and *Rooms of the Soul*; two books of poetry, *Vessels* and *Gathering the Sparks*; and a book-length selection of his dreams, *Dream Journal*. He has also edited *Imperial Messages: One Hundred Modern Parables* and co-edited (with Anthony Rudolf) *Voices Within the Ark: The Modern Jewish Poets*, both for Avon Books. He is currently editing *Gates to the New City: A Treasury of The Four Who Entered Paradise*. *Elijah's Violin: A Treasury of Jewish Fairy Tales* is forthcoming from Harper & Row.

GARY SNYDER—Poet, scholar, Pulitzer Prize winner, counselor of governors does the real work from his home in the Sierras. His books include *Myths and Texts*, *Earth Household*, *Regarding Wave* and *Turtle Island*.

JOAN STONE—"Perhaps gesture is a more accurate name for what I do than dance.

I work in a studio overlooking a Kansas wheatfield, combining gestures with words for video."

ALGERNON CHARLES SWINBURNE wore a cork suit before he was reformed by Theodore Watts-Dunton, a literary critic.

ARTHUR SZE—30 years old, Chinese, and lives in Santa Fe, New Mexico. Two books of poems have appeared: *The Willow Wind* and *Two Ravens*. A new collection, *Dazzled*, will be published in 1982 by Floating Island Publications. Currently doing a writing workshop with women inmates at the New Mexico State Penitentiary.

SHAWN THOMPSON lives in Canada and has written a Ph.D. thesis on Blake.

EVAN TONSING—composer, cellist, teacher, toy pianist, retired rock-n-roller keyboardist, part-time hermit, nearing forty-two, living with three dogs and a grand piano in a country bungalow with a forest, lake, and quiet. Complete performance scores of *A Transformation of the Book of Thel* (8½ × 11 inches, $5.00 each, two needed for performance), large (2 × 3 feet, $11.00 with mailing tube) and small (1 × 1½ feet, $5.00 with mailing tube) poster scores of Part I (movements 1 through 7), and cassette recordings of the complete opus 64 and other works with toy piano (*Crystallization* opus 62, *The Fable of the Worker and the Nightingale* opus 59, Incidental music for *A Midsummer Night's Dream*, and *Rag in memory of Bob West*, $4.00, 45 minutes) are available from the composer, Evan Tonsing, Route 1, Box 21, Glencoe, Oklahoma, 74032, (405) 669-2613.

SHLOMO VINNER is a mathematician-violinist-poet who lives in Jerusalem.

ANTON VOGT was last seen headed for the Cascade wilderness, leaving behind him a trail of knee-capped billboards.

RANDY L. WALN was born in Wyoming in 1952 to two strong individuals and was raised to Be. He found Minds at the University of Wyoming that nurture Being and with his prints hopes to make new Beings.

JANET WARNER is an Associate Professor of English at Glendon College, York University, Toronto. She does not usually write poems.

NORMAN WEINSTEIN is a poet and critic, author of a study of Gertrude Stein's writings and of two chapbooks of poetry. Working with Senior Citizens in Creative Writing Project supported by Idaho Arts Commission. Blake speaks to him—constantly. Sometimes he listens.

CAROLYN WHITE—Folklorist and author of two books published in Ireland: *A History of Irish Fairies* (Mercier Press, Cork) and *Kerry Tales* (Hawthorn Press, Dingle). Travels frequently to Europe, gathering and telling stories. (And dangling modifiers.)

FRED WHITEHEAD—Worked four years as a Son of Los in Kansas (industrial welder and poet), and publishes *Quindaro*, a magazine of midwestern radical literary culture.

KIT WIENERT—born June 12, 1951. B.A., Bard College, where Blake and Kelly combined as lodestar of my birth into poetry. Author, *The Everywhere Province;* editor-publisher, White Dot Press. Lives in Baltimore.

ROGER ZELAZNY—Originally from Ohio and now resides in New Mexico. Professional writer since 1962 with four story collections, one book of poetry, and 23 novels, including *Lord of Light.*

DANIEL ZIMMERMAN studied at Buffalo, teaches Rough Basement at Middlesex County College, Edison, NJ. Edited *The Western Gate* and *Britannia* (1970). His most recent book is *At That.*

Credits *continued*

JOHN BRANDI: "Homegoing, After Joaquin's Birth" used by permission of Great Raven Press. Poem © 1978 John Brandi. "Poem for the New Year," "Poem Reflecting World Events," "Poem to You O Goddess" used by permission of John Brandi. Poems © 1982 John Brandi.

JAMES BROUGHTON: "To the Fire-Bearers of Sagittarius," "Proverbs of Heaven," "The Golden Positions," "Prayer to the Body" used by permission of James Broughton. Poems © 1982 James Broughton. "Two Photos" from *The Golden Positions* by James Broughton, 1970. Graphic © James Broughton.
"Shaman Psalm used by permission of James Broughton. Poem © 1982 James Broughton.

STEVE BUNCH: "Yeats, Thoreau, Dr. Williams, Jim Morrison, and Mr. Blake" used by permission of Steve Bunch. Prose © 1982 Steve Bunch.

JARED CARTER: "The Man Who Taught Blake Painting in His Dreams" used by permission of Jared Carter. Poem © 1982 Jared Carter.

MICHAEL CASTRO: "Auguries from Experience" used by permission of Michael Castro. Poem © 1982 Michael Castro.

ERIC CHAET: "Report to Blake" used by permission of Eric Chaet. Poem © 1982 Eric Chaet.

KENT CLAIR CHAMBERLAIN: "Unsymbolic Digresion" used by permission of Kent Clair Chamberlain. Poem © 1982 Kent Clair Chamberlain.

JOHN CLARKE: "Four Poems" from *The End of This Side* by John Clarke, Black Book, 1979. Poems © John Clarke.

MICHAEL CHRISMAN: "Coming into the Cabal, Unawares" used by permission of Michael Chrisman. Poem © 1982 Michael Chrisman.

ROBERT CREELEY: "On Seeing Blake's Name on Drain Hole Cover in Bathroom of Shippensberg State College Dormitory," "Blakean Haiku" used by permission of Robert Creeley. Poems © 1982 Robert Creeley.

sensible topographies" used by permission of Daniel Zimmerman. "on, you huskies," "spirit level," and "salt for lotos" are from *At That*, Western Gate Press, 1978. "on, you huskies" also appeared in *Perspective*, Institute of Further Studies, 1974. Prose and poems © Daniel Zimmerman.

We would also like to thank the following libraries, museums, and collectors for permission to reproduce Blake illustrations:

The British Museum for *Visions of the Daughters of Albion*, plates 2 and 7.
The Huntington Library for William Blake: *Visions of the Daughters of Albion*, frontispiece, and *Milton*, title page.
Sir Geoffrey Keynes for *The Bowman and the Spirit of Inspiration*.
The Paul Mellon Collection for *Jerusalem*, plates 1, 2, 25, 32, 67, 96, 97, 99.
The Rosenwald Collection for *Milton*, plate 32 and *Book of Urizen*, plate 20.
The Tate Gallery for "Portrait of Catherine Blake" and "The Man Who Taught Blake Painting."
The Whitworth Art Gallery for "The Ancient of Days."

****

"Where are the Blakes?" I asked the young woman at the information
desk of the Yale Center for British Art.
"Well, there's only one on display — very disappointing —
small and muddy — on the top floor opposite the rest rooms."
I had to go through rooms of paintings by Reynolds and Gainsborough
and their followers to get to the Blake.
A small dark painting but full of meaning.
A madonna and child, the gestures of the child's hands reflected
in the mother's hands and finally in the stars.

                                                    Joan Stone

Enough,

or

too much!

ODDMENTS AND 'SPARE PARTS'

A Partner in Paradise

Diamond in the Daisy
Gold in the buttercup
Devil's on the downbeat
God's on the up and up

reverberates off the stars.

Angels

Deadline is February 15, 1981.

having knees & elbows that are not simply glued together

pa, Chögyam. *Cutting Through Spiritual Materialism.* Boulder, Colorado: Shambhala Publications, 1973. See also his *The Myth of Freedom.* Boulder, Colorado: Shambhala Publications, 1976.

When Gary Snyder came to Memphis State University to read in 1977 we talked a great deal about Blake, and he introduced me to the writings of Trungpa saying, "They touch the depths of Blakean experience." So I followed his lead, and found him mostly right. The first in particular is important because it speaks to the idea of spiritual travel which I personally think central to Blake's position.

limit of Opacity
visible

Palatino 14/23:

Sparks of Fire

GALLEY UUU

Imaginary Picture

lines as desired]

The world of imagination is the world of eternity. For, as Billy says, "There exist in that eternal world the permanet realities of everything which we see reflected in this vegetable glass of Nature." And, I thought, in the works of Gulley Jimson. Such as red Eves and green Adams, blue whales and spotted giraffes, twenty-three feet high. Lions, tigers, and all the dreams of prophets whose imagination sustains the creation, and recalls it from the grave of memory.

—Gulley Jimson

FRED GOSS: I met Blake amidst the usual gang of Romantics, found truth in his vision, and worked with and from him ever since. His urgency led me beyond the academic to this book and to a devotion to human wholeness in my writing, teaching, living, and loving. Other guides and inspirers include Melville, Charles Olson, John Coltrane, Miles Davis, and daughter Erin.

JAMES BOGAN: Born near the shores of Lake Michigan, I grew up in a willow tree and was educated in Chicagoland, Rome, Kansas, and the Ozarks. William Blake has led me to delightful friends and worlds within. In addition to Blake studies, my abiding research and teaching interests include Missouri artist Tom Benton, American Film from Keaton to Broughton, art-admiration in general. *Ozark Meandering*, a book of maximal poems and the tall river-tales, nears completion.

The editors are currently fantasizing the compilation of Messenger of Eternity: A Visionary Biography of William Blake. *Readers of* Sparks of Fire *are invited to submit ideas, prose/poems, graphics, scholarship, open forms of a specifically biographical nature to: BLAKE, Art Department, University of Missouri-Rolla, Rolla, MO 65401. SASE, please and thank you.*